In 1984 the Press celebrated four hundred years of continuous printing and publishing. This history, now published for the first time as a paperback, provides a readable introduction to that unique period, with a new foreword by Gordon Johnson who comments on the continuing achievement of the Press at the turn of the millennium.

This is the story of the development of the printing and publishing arm of the University of Cambridge, from the medieval system of resident stationers who dealt in manuscripts to the modern international printing and publishing house of today. The narrative is given its proper setting in the development of the University, which inevitably has determined the history of the Press itself; in the history of the book trade as a whole; and in the intellectual and political history of England which has at times affected the fortunes of the Press. Unique elements of the story include a royal charter on which the University's right to print and publish was founded, a commitment to Bible printing from the beginning, and the development of an equal commitment to learned printing and publishing.

'This is a most handsome, well-written and well-researched account...a distinguished and on the whole soberer one than the curiously disjointed history of its ancient rival.'                                               *Church Times*

'Cambridge University Press has a history of which it is justly proud, and in Mr Black has found a historian who has done full justice to this remarkable story.'                                                                  *The Library*

'Black has written a landmark study of a unique British institution. The scholarly publishing community is richer for this study of its origins.'
                                                                    *Educational Studies*

'This is an altogether admirable book, hugely enjoyable and informative... Black's prose is lucid and frequently witty, while the work is far less self-serving than most volumes of a similar kind.'                        *Nature*

MICHAEL BLACK is an Emeritus Fellow of Clare Hall, Cambridge, and formerly University Publisher

# CAMBRIDGE UNIVERSITY PRESS

## 1584–1984

M. H. BLACK

CAMBRIDGE
UNIVERSITY PRESS

PUBLISHED BY THE PRESS SYNDICATE OF THE UNIVERSITY OF CAMBRIDGE
The Pitt Building, Trumpington Street, Cambridge, United Kingdom

CAMBRIDGE UNIVERSITY PRESS
The Edinburgh Building, Cambridge CB2 2RU, UK    www.cup.cam.ac.uk
40 West 20th Street, New York, NY 10011–4211, USA    www.cup.org
10 Stamford Road, Oakleigh, Melbourne 3166, Australia
Ruiz de Alarcón 13, 28014 Madrid, España

First published 1984
Reprinted 1984
First paperback edition 2000

Printed in the United Kingdom at the University Press, Cambridge

*Typeface* Bell MT 12/13.5 pt.

*British Library Cataloguing in Publication data*
Black, M. H.
Cambridge University Press 1584–1984.
1. Cambridge University Press—History
I. Title
338.7′61′07050942659    Z232.C17

ISBN 0 521 26473 1 hardback
ISBN 0 521 66497 7 paperback

# CONTENTS

List of illustration                                    *page* vii

*Preface (1984)*                                              ix

*Acknowledgements*                                          xiii

*Foreword (1999) by Gordon Johnson,*
*    Chairman of the Press Syndicate*                         xv

1  Introduction                                               1

2  Precursors: The Stationers and Siberch                     6

3  The Letters Patent of 1534: The Stationers' Company       22

4  The Foundation of the Press: Thomas Thomas                35

5  Early Printers: John Legate, Cantrell Legge,
   Buck and Daniel                                            50

6  The Commonwealth and Restoration                          68

7  Bentley's 'Public Press'                                  87

8  The Eighteenth Century                                   104

9  The Nineteenth Century – I                               124

10 The Nineteenth Century – II: Charles John Clay           151
   and the Partnership

11 R. T. Wright and the Secretaryship                       172

12 Waller and Roberts as Secretaries: Lewis as Printer      194

13 From 1945 to 1972                                        224

14 Recovery: 1972–4                                         246

15 Charitable Status Recognised                             265

16   From 1974 to 1984                                              284

17   Conclusion                                                     306

*Appendix I The Letters Patent of 1534*                             316

*Appendix II Statute J of the University: The University
   Press*                                                          318

*Appendix III University Printers 1583–1984*                        320

*Index*                                                             321

# ILLUSTRATIONS

1    Part of Hammond's map of Cambridge, 1592    *page* 17
2    Henry VIII's Letters Patent of 1534    25
3    Two of Thomas Thomas's first publications, 1584    42, 43
4    The first Cambridge Bible, 1591    51
5    The Cambridge emblem, 1600    57
6    Buck and Daniel, the Bible of 1638    63
7    Buck's printing house    65
8    Milton's 'Lycidas', from *Obsequies*, 1638    70
9    The first edition of Herbert's *The Temple*, 1633    72
10    Richard Bentley    89
11    The new printing house, 1697    92
12    The second edition of Newton's *Principia*, 1713    97
13    Baskerville's Bible, 1763    113
14    The Cambridge Stereotype Bible, New Testament, 1805    127
15    The Pitt Building    131
16    An early volume in the Pitt Press series    159
17    R. T. Wright    173
18    Lord Acton and F. W. Maitland    181
19    S. C. Roberts    199
20    Bentley House Library    207
21    Walter Lewis    212
22    Stanley Morison    214
23    The Pitt Building from the river    221
24    The University Printing House, 1963    232
25    The Edinburgh Building    291
26    The Edinburgh Building: the opening ceremony    295

# PREFACE (1984)

THIS HISTORY is published in 1984 to celebrate four hundred years of continuous activity by Cambridge University Press as printer and publisher, and the four hundred and fiftieth anniversary of its charter, the Letters Patent granted by Henry VIII in July 1534. It is the work not of a historian or archivist, but of one of the Press's officers working full-time at his normal duties, and so helping day by day to make that current and rather urgent sector of the Press's history which leaves little leisure for its writing. Writing it against time, I have often been reminded of the words of a very early colleague, that fine University Printer, Thomas Thomas, for whom across four hundred years I have come to have a fellow-feeling. He signed the address to the reader in his Latin dictionary:

> From our offices at Cambridge, in moments snatched from the hum of work
>
> (Cantebrigiae ex nostris aedibus, carptim inter operarum susurros)

This book has been written in the same conditions, but with pleasure and as a labour of love.

And indeed it would have been wrong to let 1984 pass by with no attempt to mark its significance for the Press. This account is written first of all for the interest and I hope the pleasure of my present colleagues, the Press's now quite large staff who in the recent years of severe trade depression have with cheerfulness and loyalty continued to foster the remarkable expansion of the Press's activities which has characterised the same period. That spirit is partly born of the consciousness of working for a unique British institution in which it is proper to feel great pride. On its four hundredth anniversary these hard-working people may justifiably raise their heads from the immediate task, draw breath, and reflect on the point which the Press has reached, and the long distance it has travelled. It seemed also that the Press's many authors, editors and advisers, and colleagues in printing, bookselling and allied activities might take a friendly interest in the record of what is certainly the oldest printing and publishing house in the United Kingdom – and, so far as can be ascertained, in the world.

And finally, because the Press has played that long role in the English book trades and in the history of scholarship itself, and because it is important and unique (for Oxford University Press, though a sister organisation and of almost equal venerability, has a distinct character of its own and a history which is interestingly different at important points), it was felt that the record might be published more generally, if its limitations are made plain – the most important being that much of it is based on printed sources which will be familiar to the scholar.

No history of the Press has been published since 1921, the year of S. C. Roberts's *The Cambridge University Press 1521–1921*. That book was written in very similar circumstances, to mark the quatercentenary year of Siberch's first Cambridge press. Siberch is not now claimed as a direct ancestor of the University Press proper; but his brief activity in the city of Cambridge has its interest and importance, and it is not surprising that in 1921 he was celebrated as more than the precursor that he really is. Roberts's book was written under much the same conditions as this one, and he has left this characteristic account of its genesis, which has made me associate him and Thomas in my mind as spirits which would look kindly on my own labour:

Charles Sayle, meeting me one day on King's Parade, inquired: 'What are you going to do about 1921?' I was puzzled.

'Cambridge printing began in 1521', he said, 'and someone ought to write a history of the 400 years.' I reported the conversation to Waller [then Secretary of the Syndicate]. 'I've no time for that sort of thing', he said, 'I must leave it to you.'

I went home and thought about it. I had, in fact, written an article on the Press for Ogden's *Cambridge Magazine* in 1912, based largely on Robert Bowes's *Notes on the Cambridge Printers* (1886). In those *Notes* there was frequent reference to Registry MSS relating to the Press. The Registry was then in the tower of the Pitt Press, and, after dipping into the documents, I decided to make the attempt. I had had no training in 'research' and many of the handwritings were formidable, but, fortunately, I had a quite definite time-limit. The book had to be published not later than 1 October 1921 or not at all. If I had undertaken it just as a leisurely parergon, I might well have spent years upon it. In fact, *A History of the Cambridge University Press 1521–1921* duly appeared at the beginning of the Michaelmas term.

Roberts, Adventures with Authors, 47

If a publisher cannot meet a publisher's deadline, he can hardly expect others to. I have, like Roberts, met my deadline, and that must be the reason, if not the excuse, for the relative brevity and the derivative nature of what follows. Though sixty years have passed since he wrote, his is not only the sole continuous history of the Press, but the only published source for certain periods, and I have depended on him for the outline of the whole. Fortunately both he and others have written on particular topics and periods, most notably John Morris on Thomas Thomas, and D. F. McKenzie in his massive study of the Bentley revival: *The Cambridge University Press 1696–1712*. Roberts was brief about the period most recent when he wrote; but in his retirement wrote more in his Sandars Lectures, *The Evolution of Cambridge Publishing* (1956), and his memoirs, *Adventures with Authors* (1966). Much more is now known about Siberch himself, and there are articles and chapters in books on other aspects of the Press's history. Much has also been published since 1921 about the history of the University, and I have drawn on this, envisaging readers who are not familiar with it or will enjoy being reminded of it, and who would welcome some links with that setting and with the wider history of printing, publishing and bookselling.

It has been brought home to me, however, how badly whole tracts of the Press's history need first-hand research in the archive, and if this book were to prompt that work, it would serve a useful purpose beyond the celebrations of 1984. In particular the period from the beginning of the nineteenth century, or at least from the time of the Royal Commission, cries out for more detailed treatment. It is the most important part of the whole story, after the laying of the constitutional foundations in the sixteenth and seventeenth centuries. The history of British printing and publishing naturally began with a concern – even an obsession – with origins. But the real growth of modern publishing took place in the nineteenth and early twentieth centuries. It is during this period that the modern history of the Press begins – surprisingly recently, as it turns out. Something more is said about this in the relevant pages below, but I am aware that it is not enough.

This account is written from direct personal knowledge of the years from 1951 onwards, and conversations with some now retired colleagues whose memories go back to the 1930s. Although there are the usual difficulties about writing about recent times (which account for Roberts's reticence) it is very desirable to say what one can, since the great advantage of the chronicler or anecdotalist is that he was there and knew what it felt like. Nor is it merely parochial to say that the period since 1945 has seen by far and away the most rapid development in the whole story, accelerating to the present day; and that the last twelve years are marked by crucial analyses and decisions which make the Press today a body much more conscious of its nature and function. These provide the standpoint from which this history is written. They make sense of the history as the history makes sense of them.

In writing the final chapters, I have had the great advantage of access to the records and notes made during the 1970s by Geoffrey Cass as events unfolded, and also of his own recollections. I have not hesitated to make the fullest use of this first-hand material, and I am most grateful for his assistance, which has helped me to give an adequate record of important events.

For all these reasons, it is hoped that the future historian of the Press with leisure to carry out the task with the care that is so much needed may occasionally find himself quoting these pages. They are dedicated to the three Secretaries of the Press Syndicate whom it has been my good fortune to work for: R. J. L. Kingsford, R. W. David, Geoffrey Cass.

CAMBRIDGE                                                                    MHB
*Autumn 1983*

# ACKNOWLEDGEMENTS

A number of colleagues and friends have read this book as it was being written; I am grateful to Richard David, David McKitterick, Anthony Parker and John Trevitt for helpful suggestions and corrections. Dorothy Owen and Elisabeth Leedham-Green and the staff of the Manuscript Room at the University Library made consultation of the University Archives pleasant and easy. Ann Parr, Pat Gifford and Pat Cobb typed chapters with willingness and accuracy, as fast as they were written.

The portrait of Bentley is reproduced by kind permission of the Master and Fellows of Trinity College, and those of Lord Acton and F. W. Maitland by permission of the Trustees of the National Portrait Gallery. The British and Foreign Bible Society gave permission to reproduce number 4. Nan Youngman lent her copy of Gwen Raverat's wood-engraving of number 23. Numbers 1, 2, 3, 6, 7, 8, 9, 12, 13, and 15 are from photographs supplied by the University Library, Cambridge, and are reproduced by permission of the Syndics of Cambridge University Library.

# FOREWORD (1999)

Frederick York Powell, a great polymath, Regius Professor of Modern History at Oxford from 1894 until his death in 1904, and especially noted for his work on Scandinavian and Icelandic literatures, once said that a University consisted of a library and a press. By this he meant that the modern University was not primarily, or even mainly, a place where students were taught, but rather a place where fundamental research and new scholarship were pursued and the results of that work were widely disseminated. This was not a particularly popular point of view in the Oxford of the later nineteenth century where the main thrust of academic reform had been to promote better and more careful teaching designed to civilise and bring out qualities of public leadership in generations of young men. In fact, Powell disliked teaching undergraduates (and in truth was not very good at it) and he believed that scholars at a serious University needed only the freedom to work untutored in a library or laboratory to follow their vocation and to be able usefully and creatively to add to the world's store of knowledge. What they discovered in the library had then to be made known so that knowledge was advanced to the benefit of everyone. A printing and publishing house was, therefore, an essential part of a fully-fledged University.

Powell's own scholarly reputation rested on editions and commentaries on the northern sagas, a task which he undertook in collaboration with Gudbrandr Vigfusson (who had come to Oxford in 1866 to edit the *Icelandic–English Dictionary* for the Oxford Press), and he took a leading share in founding the *English Historical Review.* But he also believed (perhaps driven by fierce socialist and atheist convictions) that the scholar was obliged to reach the widest possible readership. He contributed a volume on Early England to Longman's series *Epochs of English History*, edited by Mandell Creighton, he wrote a school textbook, *England from the Earliest Times to the Death of Henry VII* (which was remarkable for its use of chronicles, ballads, and romances), he established a series of books, *English History from Contemporary Writers*, and he was a regular contributor to newspapers and popular periodicals. For nearly twenty years he was a Delegate of the Clarendon Press, constantly urging his colleagues to publish scholarly work which would not make money and, on one occasion, delighting in their acceptance of 'an improper book', namely Thomson's *Human Anatomy for Art Students*.

Powell's view of the proper purpose of a University, and the way he implemented it in his life, brings home to us a fundamental truth about the role played by scholarship in safeguarding and preserving for transmission to future generations that which is noble and good in a civilisation, and it reminds us that scholarship has also the task of seeking out new knowledge, pursuing new ideas, and making the results freely available. This is a heavy responsibility, and it is not always easy and agreeable work; for knowledge is often as unsettling and subversive as it is exciting and pleasurable, and we have known since the fall from Paradise that its discovery, possession, and use often raise hard ethical questions we would rather not be asked. The huge tapestry version of R. B. Kitaj's 'If not, not' hangs in the entrance of the British Library, a stunning visual image of the terror and beauty which knowledge holds.

Cambridge is a serious University because it has both a library and a press and they are among the oldest institutions it possesses. Without manuscripts and books there could be no place of learning; and by virtue of royal letters patent, the University has had the right to print and sell books throughout the kingdom since 1534. In fact, work has been published at Cambridge under the authority of the University every year since 1584. Initially, that authority was exercised by the Chancellor or his deputy and three doctors, but from 1698 the

University set up a committee for the Press. The first meeting of a recognisable Press Syndicate was held on 23 August of that year and got straight down to business by deciding that the London bookseller, Jacob Tonson, should be given leave to print editions of Virgil, Horace, Terence, Catullus, Tibullus, and Propertius in quarto with the double pica letter, paying 12 shillings per sheet for an impression of 500 copies, 14 shillings for 750; that a Cambridge bookseller, Edmund Jefferies, print an edition of Tully in duodecimo with brevier letter at £1 10s 0d a sheet per 1,000 copies; and that Cornelius Crownfield be sent to Rotterdam to buy 300 lb weight of new types.

As both printer and publisher the Press has a long, complex and varied history. Sometimes it has been successful and prosperous; at others its fortunes have touched a low ebb and its affairs have been dogged by controversy. For much of its history, the Press has been primarily a printer, wrestling with changing technologies, cantankerous craftsmen, failing machinery, crises about supply of fonts and paper, temperamental authors, and how to sell the finished book. For part of the history, printing and publishing the Bible and the Book of Common Prayer have dominated its operations. On the printing side, this was a major operation, but the sales side was not without problems: even the Bible could be difficult to distribute and sell. At times the largest institutional customers – the Bible societies – would gang together to drive down prices and play Cambridge off against Oxford and the Royal Printer, leaving the Press as vulnerable economically in the market-place as a farmer growing only sugar and tobacco. Sometimes textbooks, especially schoolbooks, have provided much of the work. But though the printing shop was glad of it, too often the profits of the sales went to other publishers or booksellers, like Deighton or Macmillan.

Since the early part of this century, the Press has been genuinely owned and managed as a University institution, though one which has its own quite distinctive characteristics – most notably the authority to control its own affairs and the lack of any financial investment in its activity by the University itself; but in earlier years it was not unusual for the Syndicate to work in partnerships, both explicit and implicit, with other bodies and as part of the wider book trade; and the Syndicate, composed of academics, has always depended very heavily on the quality of the professional management it has employed, in both printing and publishing.

For much of the first part of the twentieth century, the Press thrived because it maintained a strong backlist – a stock of books that sold out over a number of decades. The initial investment might have been quite high, but the steady return over the years, when there was little inflation, the demand was there, and there was no need to take serious account of the costs of storage, insurance, and other overheads, meant that the Syndicate could meet in a gentlemanly way on a Friday afternoon to approve new books much as it fancied. The inflation of the 1970s, and a drop in the sales from the backlist section of the catalogue that occurred at the same time, put paid to that. Survival required a shift of emphasis to publishing more new books and journals and keeping the prices of those already in stock up to date in real terms. Funding for the expansion of higher education, which in retrospect seems to have flowed generously in earlier decades, now became more restricted. What there was had to be made to go further, and while there was now a greater demand from the massively increased number of those working in higher education for more to be published, greater selectivity came to be exercised over what was bought, and priority tended to be given to that which had greatest currency. Moreover, almost imperceptibly, in the twentieth century the publishing side of the business had overtaken printing in the scale of the Press's operations, and as the century ended not only did printing face new waves of technological developments, the most revolutionary since the invention of type itself, but scholarly publishing also had to face the prospect of competing in a global market-place: the right to sell throughout the realm had become a challenge to sell throughout the world.

Such a long history, and such a rich one: so it is somewhat surprising that Michael Black's *Cambridge University Press 1584–1984*, published to celebrate four hundred years of printing and publishing at Cambridge, was the first comprehensive history of a remarkable University institution. There had been other accounts of individual printers, or bibliographical studies of parts of the Press's output, but never had there been a coherent history of the Press as part of the University, nor an attempt to see how it had evolved over the years. The book broke new ground in that, within modest compass, it brought together a previously disconnected history. It is elegantly written and lucidly argued, and has a strong claim on the general reader wishing to understand the nature of an important and long-lived university institution.

But more than this: it was written with a purpose and with some passion. The late 1960s and early 1970s were an appalling time for the Press. Structures and strategies which had served it well over a number of decades buckled under the impact of economic and industrial turmoil and the pressures brought to bear by new technologies and the unprecedented growth of higher education throughout the world. These were, perhaps, the most difficult years the Press had ever faced professionally and financially, and there was a real risk that the University would lose its printing and publishing arm. Had this happened, Cambridge's position as a major University would have been seriously damaged. The later chapters of this book analyse what was done, under the leadership of Geoffrey Cass and his colleagues, to put the Press on a clear trajectory. An important part of their strategy was to think afresh about the special requirements of scholarly printing and publishing – how they differed from other types of printing and publishing – and then to devise means of providing for them. This involved adopting a positive approach to problems and a determination to use creatively past experience and privileges. The objectives of the Press were made explicit; they were shown to have a long and respectable history; and they were put at the centre of the plans for its future viability. Circumstances may change, but fundamental purposes do not: if they hold, means will be found to achieve them. Michael Black's account of four hundred years of the Cambridge Press, written by one of the participants in the changes of the 1970s, and with a certain polemical edge to it, helps us to understand the special nature and requirements of scholarly publishing: in fact, it sets out for our time the ideological justification and intellectual arguments in support of a University Press, and it describes some of the requirements for its successful management.

The University Press is a part of the University. It has a particular objective which is to print and to publish, as Statute J now has it, 'in the furtherance of the acquisition, advancement, conservation, and dissemination of knowledge in all subjects; to the advancement of education, religion, learning, and research; and to the advancement of literature and good letters'. In order to do this effectively, the Press's position within the University has evolved over the years and it has been enshrined in charters, statutes, and ordinances. It is more than three centuries since the University established a Syndicate to be responsible for its printing and publishing. The Syndics, appointed by the University, are a body of trustees with considerable independent powers to manage the affairs generally of the Press, to control all its capital and income, and to apply those at their sole discretion for the purposes of the Press – namely, scholarly printing and publishing. This is recognised not only by University Statute but by external authorities such as the Inland Revenue and foreign governments which exempt the Press, as a charitable trust, from the payment of certain taxes. The Syndicate employs persons to work for it and it possesses its own University Seal for use in Press business. Moreover, nothing is published without the Syndicate's explicit authority. This is what was recognised at the end of the seventeenth century when the University ceased to be a passive licensing body for a printer and first took positive responsibility for an academic publishing programme. All fields of knowledge are appropriate for consideration by the Press, and authors may come from all over the world. The Syndicate gives positive support to accepted learning while encouraging originality. It has to balance traditional learning with the new, and in so doing makes judgments about what will appear under the University's imprint. But the Syndicate's role is not to censor (although it derives its position from a time when the privilege to print was, in part at least, an attempt to control what was published), nor to give special credit or credibility to what is published. In deciding what to take on the aim is to spread knowledge so that others, the readers, left free to roam the library shelves, can determine its value and importance.

Cambridge University Press operates within some self-imposed restraints. Its special obligation is to the educational and scholarly world. It is not a general publisher and has no business in publishing simply as a commercial concern. It looks to maintaining the highest possible standards, seeking to publish that which is excellent of its kind in the most appropriate way. This may be done in the form of a monograph or journal article, containing new work and new ideas aimed at readers who are already well versed in the subject; a textbook will present a synthesis of known work in a whole field, reaching out explicitly to students with little or no previous knowledge. The skill to write that sort of book is quite different from that displayed in the learned monograph or journal article, although many scholars, as the example of Frederick York Powell shows, have combined these qualities and have felt a keen responsibility to inform as many readers as possible about what they have discovered. The presentation of information for reference, or for children, or for those learning English as a foreign language, all call for distinctive approaches. The publisher's task is to recognise this and to see that widely different types of publication are treated appropriately to find the desired readership.

Similarly, the physical presentation of information varies according to category and, as Michael Black's history reveals so well, the owners of books and journals have always been concerned with the quality of paper, lay-out, type-face, binding, and design. Concern with the highest standards of both form and content marks out the University Press from many commercial publishers, who have to respond primarily to the need to move stock quickly and to pay dividends to shareholders. Such considerations also prevent many publishers from taking on work which may have a lengthy and costly gestation period and which, once published, needs to be kept in print for long periods of time. There is considerable investment in a 'Cambridge History', which may take ten or twenty years to complete, or in something like the Cambridge School Mathematics Project, or a new reading scheme for schoolchildren, or the development of English-language courses: an author does not simply deliver a typescript which is then printed and published. Many people with many skills are called upon to contribute to the finished product, and the investment may not be recovered for several years.

This leads inevitably to the special economic and managerial considerations the Syndicate takes into account in discharging its responsibility for the Press. If it is to function properly, the Press must have financial autonomy. A powerful theme running through the whole of Michael Black's account is that scholarly publishing cannot be secure unless the Press is financially self-supporting and self-determining. The costs of academic publishing are high; the markets are small or fickle: almost by definition, something taken on by a university press is too specialised for a publisher in the general commercial market-place. A scholarly press has to be able to look to long-term interests, to support heavy advance investment and to keep in print studies which, by normal accounting rules, would not be economically justifiable. This is a difficult business strategy to deploy with nerve and consistency. Simple subsidy has never proved to be a satisfactory solution to the problem; and anyway, a modern university would not be able to find funds on the necessary scale from its regular budgets for teaching and research. Hence the wisdom of establishing the Press as a distinct institution with responsibility to order its own affairs. Cash has to be generated from the activity of printing and publishing itself, and funds have to be held to be spent at the right moment to meet the needs of the Press itself. From the late 1690s Dr Bentley was a great fund-raiser for particular projects (his edition of Horace required advance investment of around £800, a huge sum in the early eighteenth century), but even his invigorated Cambridge Press lived from book to book and never accumulated sufficient working capital to avoid recurrent financial crises. The present century also has shown how quickly an apparently strong financial position can be overturned by changes in the economy or by a need for new investment to keep abreast of changes within the printing and publishing industries worldwide. Thus it is right and proper that a press dedicated to the spread of learning and contributing to the culture of nations, without bringing profits to private interests or to individuals, should claim the privileges associated with the charity of learning. But recognition of this in no way diminishes the obligation to apply strict business disciplines and to encourage and reward entrepreneurship at every level within the institution. The Press has to work with academics and also has to deal, survive, and thrive in the highly competitive world of business and industry. The Syndicate has to ensure that the business of the Press is efficient and that its resources are deployed in the most economical way; and this sometimes requires the academic world to be more realistic about things than it might wish. But the Syndicate has also to ensure that those whom it employs understand and are in sympathy with the purpose for which the Press exists: those charged with the actual discharge of the business side of the Press must also, as they secure its revenues, understand its history, its traditions, and the purposes it exists to promote.

Finally, a university press, and particularly Cambridge University Press, works with the international academic community in mind. This has always been the case — Bentley, for instance, called on colleagues in Germany and Holland to print and publish with Cambridge three hundred years ago — but it is even more true today with over 23,000 authors on the Cambridge list (9550 from the UK, nearly 8500 from the USA, over 1400 from Australia and more than 500 from each of Canada, France, and Germany) and with North America the largest market for Cambridge books and journals. The University Press is not a vanity publishing house for Cambridge departments, but draws upon and seeks to reach higher education across the globe. For many people, in many countries, Cambridge University Press belongs as much to them as it does to those who live and work in Cambridge itself; that they choose to publish with Cambridge University Press brings credit to the University itself.

The growing international dimension of the Press's work means publishing for a number of different educational markets so as to further the whole enterprise. Particular attention is paid to the spread of English as an international language, much as Latin was the language of learning in the seventeenth century. English-language courses are in great demand and have given the Press business opportunities in Asia and Latin America. In Brazil, where the courses are particularly highly regarded, an awareness of the Cambridge name has led to an interest in the rest of the publishing list, working in partnership with Martins Fontes, a Press bookshop has been opened in São Paulo which has tempted and begun to satisfy a growing Brazilian appetite for Cambridge monographs, textbooks, and Bibles.

When the Syndicate meets, fortnightly in term and monthly out of term, with agenda papers rarely running to less than 1000 pages a meeting, the professional editors present well-prepared proposals in line with carefully conceived publishing strategies on which decisions are made. The Press does not have the resources to publish everything, so the Syndicate has to make choices. It seeks to build on strengths in the list (though these may change with time); it attempts to balance the list, mixing in the right measure monograph and journal and text-book and reference work. In making decisions, the Syndicate aims to serve the University and the whole world of learning. It will not satisfy everyone, because not everyone will agree with how the Syndicate strikes the balance. But, as this book shows, Cambridge can look back over the years and take some pleasure from its publishing achievements – Bentley's list, the Baskerville Bible, the 'Cambridge Histories' or those textbooks written earlier this century by leading scholars and scientists which have remained in print for over fifty years. The Press has enlivened the studies of the schoolchild and its current English Language Teaching programme is as attractive and innovative as any in the market.

Since this book was first written, the Press has grown consid-erably. It would have been tempting to ask the author to add a chapter to bring the story up to the year 2000. But in the end it seemed wisest to leave the original text much as it was, for it stands in its own right as a remarkable history of a remarkable institution written from a particular perspective at a crucial moment in the Press's development. Of the many changes since 1984 one might note in passing that the Press's own bookshop now occupies the premises on the corner of Trinity Street and the Market Square, then tenanted by Bowes and Bowes; the list of publications currently in print has gone from 7000 to more than three times that number; various 'Cambridge Series' have now passed their half-century and *Cambridge Studies in Medieval Life and Thought* has its sixth grouping of academic editors. The North American and Australian Branches have celebrated their fiftieth and thirtieth anniversaries respectively, and have been joined by Branches in Spain and South Africa, with others in prospect. When on 20 July 1534 King Henry VIII gave of his 'special grace' to his 'beloved in Christ the Chancellor, Masters, and Scholars of our University of Cambridge' the right to license printing and 'to exhibit for sale, as well in the same University as elsewhere in our realm, wherever they please' all manner of books, it was a privilege he conferred 'for ever'. How that benefit has been used for the good can be judged by the readers of this excellent book; and those charged with the responsibility of maintaining the privilege in perpetuity can draw inspiration, and some comfort, from its pages.

GORDON JOHNSON
*Chairman of the Press Syndicate*
*9 August 1999*

# 1

## INTRODUCTION

A VISITOR to a modern university city will expect to find in it a number of institutions, agencies and businesses concerned with books: several libraries of course; and one or more bookshops, which will stock both textbooks for students, standard reference works, and the advanced monographs which teachers need in order to keep abreast of research in their subject. An important bookshop will also sell foreign books, and will probably have a second-hand or antiquarian department. These bookshops, if they are old-established, may be part of a family of businesses, and may also still call themselves 'printers, publishers, booksellers, bookbinders and stationers' or some combination of those terms. The bookbinding most often done nowadays is of typescript dissertations submitted for higher degrees; though the university library will probably have a bookbinding department, in which old books are repaired and new books rebound in a standard style. Not far out of town, near a suitable river, there may be a papermaking business, though these small mills are now very few indeed. Smaller shops in the town, also calling themselves stationers, will sell file-paper for students' notes, and the pens, inks, special papers and other instruments needed for specialised forms of draughts-manship, mapmaking, illustration and so on. What you buy in stationers' shops is obviously called 'stationery'; but many people reverse the thought-process, and assume that stationers are so called because they sell 'stationery'. That is to put things the wrong way round: the term 'stationer' derives from the Latin *stationarius* and it means a shopkeeper, one who does business from a fixed address. The name became attached to sellers of books and related materials. Thomas Fuller, the historian of Cambridge and much else, explained that stationers were those 'publicly avouching the sale of staple-books in standing shops (whence they have their names) as opposite to such circumforaneous peddlers (ancestors to our modern mercuries and hawkers) which secretly vend prohibited books'. Those words 'secretly' and 'prohibited' remind us that the press was not always free (could not be); and that the University of Cambridge in particular was a licensing authority before it became a publishing centre, and it became the second because it had long been the first.

Similarly the old formula 'printers, publishers, booksellers, bookbinders and stationers', still met with in English towns and especially the university towns, harks back to a time before all the trades concerned with books had separated out into single specialisms – as they mostly now are – each capable of being pursued by different business organisations on a large scale. That rationalisation is still not complete – perhaps it never will be, since the materials and processes concerned with the making, selling and conservation of books are obviously very closely related. But, by and large, one can say that papermaking, printing, binding, publishing, bookselling, and the retail trade in stationery have become separate identifiable trades and industries; and it is now much more rare than it used to be to find a single business combining more than two of them. It is also clear that the whole function of librarianship from quite early times became a highly professionalised and quite separate expertise, though there are great libraries which run a small printing unit for their own purposes, or publish for themselves, or run a bookstall within their own premises.

To return to our imagined university city, it is quite likely, if the university is large and of international standing, to have attracted publishers to it, and especially scholarly publishers, since the scholars and scientists on the university staff will write books and journal articles as a natural product of their research and their teaching. One of the local publishers may indeed be the university press, and this title implies a special status – namely that the university itself has decided that it is a natural part of its function as a centre of 'education, religion, learning, and research' (the Cambridge formula, which will be met again below) to make available to the rest of the learned world those books which its own members entrust to its press, and the other books which it decides to publish from among those submitted to it by authors living elsewhere, attracted to it by its eminence, or its special skills and interests.

There are now many university presses throughout the world, but the institution is for all practical purposes a British invention, since the ancient presses of the universities of Cambridge and Oxford are the only two scholarly presses from the early period of printing which have a continuous record of activity under the same ownership and authority to the present day, and which are actually governed by the universities themselves; and it is these two which have essentially provided the pattern on which other university presses have usually modelled themselves. The pages which follow give a concise account of the history of the Press of Cambridge University, which received its royal charter in 1534 and has been printing and publishing continuously since 1584. These dates make it the older of the two by one year, since Oxford University began its continuous activity in 1585, and had no charter until 1632. Cambridge can therefore claim to be the oldest printing and publishing house in the English-speaking world – and so far as we know in the entire world, judged by the criterion of continuous activity under unchanging authority, name and ownership: that of the University of Cambridge itself.

The record is one of long evolution, sometimes slow, sometimes rapid, during which the Press has passed from being the small local printing house in which a licensed master-printer, working partly on his own account, also worked on specified terms for the University, receiving the title 'Printer to the University', to become what it now is: a large international publishing and printing house, staffed by professional officers, but still governed by the University. The evolution has been continuous, and at times has involved phases of self-transformation. At any given moment, the historian can expect to find only the constitution, the technology, the industrial structure and the trading practices which belong to the era concerned. Most obviously, if the evolution is pursued backwards in time the historian reaches the very early days of printing, and its invention marks a decisive point after which all the book trades changed profoundly, if not immediately. Similarly in the early nineteenth century the introduction of steam-driven iron presses drastically increased the speed and quantity of production; in the later nineteenth century universal education and a national examination system immensely broadened the reading public and the educated public; and this called for a new kind of publishing. In our own century two technological changes – first mechanical typesetting and then the more radical change from old-style hot-metal printing types to computer-aided photocomposition – have revolutionised printing so that it is technically quite unlike the process that Gutenberg invented in Germany in the 1450s, except that ink is still transferred to paper in letter forms that earlier centuries would recognise.

Alongside these technological and social changes, evolutionary changes in the organisation of the book trades have led to the kind of specialisation touched on in the first paragraphs above. But part of the interest of this sort of history is the characteristic British mixture of continuity with change. We still have some stationers and booksellers who also publish; and the history of Cambridge University Press begins with stationers who were bookbinders and booksellers, who became printers, and in course of time were recognised as what we now call publishers.

The argument from continuous evolution produces a natural difficulty: where do you start? There would be very good grounds for saying that Cambridge University Press in its exact present form 'really started' only a few years ago, with the formal recognition of its charitable status in 1976; or in 1981 when the University decided that the activities of the Press required a new Statute which enshrined its status and re-defined the rules for its government. But both these crucial events were simply organic stages in a continuous development, and depended on the analysis of a historical record and an existing consciously pursued set of activities of long standing. At the other end of the process, it is possible to point out that the University has in one way or another controlled certain of the trading activities to do with books since the very earliest days of its existence before Gutenberg invented printing, so the long history of the Press is part of something even longer. But before the invention of printing there could be no printed books, so that the beginning of the sixteenth century is a natural turning-point. The political and religious turbulence of the early sixteenth century made the organisation and control of the recently introduced craft of printing in England, and the import of possibly heretical printed books from Europe, literally a burning issue, and it is in this period that the historian will naturally look for a plausible beginning. The first crucial date in this history is 1534, the date of the royal Letters Patent which Henry VIII granted to the University of Cambridge, the charter on which all subsequent University printing and publishing activity is founded. If we need to look before that date it is in order to recognise the precursors – the early stationers and the first printer in Cambridge – who provide the natural link backwards with the history of the book trades in the University during its medieval period, and indeed back to the time of its foundation in the thirteenth century.

# 2

## PRECURSORS: THE STATIONERS
## AND SIBERCH

THE UNIVERSITY ITSELF was founded at the beginning of the thirteenth century and from the beginning had the nature of a body of scholars wanting to form themselves into a new corporation, and fighting quite fiercely to acquire and maintain certain rights. Their opponents were two: that other corporation, the older borough, with which it struggled for centuries to establish which was to have jurisdiction over essential matters of policing and supply; and the ecclesiastical authority, the Bishop of Ely, who would normally expect to have jurisdiction in spiritual matters. The Bishop was soon content to accept that the University was its own authority, but the conflict with the town went on until the late nineteenth century.

An essential part of this struggle centred on the status of certain of the University's suppliers. Before the invention of printing, Cambridge like all other medieval universities needed to make formal provision for the supply of manuscripts of the books which were read and lectured on to students in 'the Schools'. The trade was organised by stationers, and those of them who were licensed to reside and trade within the University were recognised as having a kind of membership and so enjoying its protection as well as coming under its discipline.

Indeed the earliest surviving mention of the book trade in Cambridge is in a judgement by the Bishop of Ely in 1276, declaring that 'the writers, illuminators and stationers who serve the scholars only' were not under his jurisdiction but under that of the University. So the right was established very early. It was confirmed naturally by the decree of Convocation in 1408, which dealt with the aftermath of the Wyclifite heresy.

Wyclif had been a university teacher in Oxford, and his doctrines had threatened to shake the Church and the State as well as the University, since in those days theological matters were inseparable from political ones. The fact that the trouble had arisen in one of the universities did not lead the central government to dismantle the authority of those universities, but rather to strengthen it. The provision which concerns us here was that Wyclifite writings were not to be used in the universities' Schools, but only books which had been examined and approved by the Church or by the universities. These were to be passed 'in the name and by the authority of the University to the stationers to be copied; and, a faithful collation being made, the original should be deposited in the chest of either university, there to remain for ever'.

Licensing and censorship are two sides of the same coin, naturally enough: it is more of a surprise to realise that those apparently authoritarian concerns were linked to the scholar's concern for accuracy of the text (for a sealed copy, kept in the university chest, can be used as an exemplar to copy from, and acts as a check on that copy when made); for preservation of a body of texts (so the chest can become a library); and ultimately as the source of the concept of copyright. All the present concerns of scholarship prove to have been once related to those of Church and State.

The relationship with the borough was, in this matter, resolved in 1502. After a dispute it was agreed that

all Bedells of the said Universitie, and all Mancipills, Cooks, Butlers, & Launders of everye Colledge, Hostell, & of other places ordeyned for Scolers, Students, & places of religion in the said Universitie, & all appotycares, Stacioners, Lymners, Schryveners, Parchment-makers, Bokebynders, Phisitions, Surgeons, & Barbers in the sayd Universitie, brought up principallye in the learninge in everye of the said Occupacions, or at his or their first dwellinge in the said Towne set up any of the said occupacyons, shall be reputed & taken as Common Ministers & Servants of the said Universitie, as long as they shall use eny such occupacion, & shall have & enjoye like privilege as a Scolers Servant of the same Universitie shall have & enjoie...& all such Persones as be above rehersed, & none other, shal be from the tyme of the sayd award accepted & taken as Scolers & Scolers Servants, & Common Ministers of the said Universitie.

Cooper, *Annals* I, 262

[ 7 ]

Among the signatories is one Garreitt Stacioner, who adds his name (probably as the representative of a group) among those of The Launder of the King's College, Belle the Mason of the University, Bowen Surgeon, Norton Brewer, The Barber of Peterhouse, and several manciples.

The issues being resolved here were numerous, but in particular who was entitled to impose discipline or keep the peace, who received dues and taxes, and who saw that fair rates were charged for services. The University was assuming this role, as it had already assumed the other role of ensuring that what was written, read and taught was conformable to the doctrine of the national Church.

In particular the stationer had to derive his status both from the trade guild of which he was a member, and from the corporation, the University in this case, in which he lived and worked. Trade association and University jointly fulfilled other functions: they regulated trade, so that prices should be fair; they organised entry into the trade, and training, conditions of labour and progress within the profession; and they were ultimately responsible to the State for good order, godly life, and the peace of the realm. Just as the supervision of licensing and censorship prefigured other modern concepts, so the trade organisation prefigured our legislation for employment and unionism.

The covenant with the town made in 1502 can also be given a modern gloss. The University was in effect saying to the town that its 'assistant staff' as we should say nowadays, as well as its main suppliers of scholarly material, had a status as corporate members of the learned body itself. The word 'stationers' is followed by a number of terms which indicate that the book trades, then as now, included specialisms: 'limners' we should now call draughtsmen or illustrators; 'scriveners' wrote out documents in fair copy or in legal form.

The first recorded member of any specific book trade in Cambridge is one William Pergamentarius (i.e. parchment-maker) who is noted as resident in 1314–15. William de Nessfylde is recorded simply as a 'stationer' in 1309–10, and John Hardy is in 1350 described as a 'stationer of the University'.

Such stationers had from very early times a specific university function distinct from but related to that of their knowledge of the book trade. As dealers in books, they were best placed to value them. Books were, before printing and for a long time after, very valuable properties: buying a book then was like undertaking now a major item of consumer-durable expenditure. It was Chaucer's clerk's dream that he might own as many as twenty books, and a well-endowed college library might by bequest and other means have acquired two or three hundred by the sixteenth century. Because of their value, books were used as pledges. Students had to deposit with the University a 'caution', either by way of pledging a fee or as a guarantee that they would duly reside in Cambridge and take their examinations, a regulation which survived into the twentieth century. Poor students fulfilling this requirement, or wanting to secure a loan, would often offer a book instead of the money which they could not find. The books were valued by the stationer, placed in a college or university chest, and eventually redeemed by payment. If not redeemed, the books were sold or placed in a library. So among his other functions the stationer had a part in this transaction, which placed him near the financial and disciplinary centre of the University. No doubt he also valued the books of dead scholars for probate, as we say today. He wore a special gown as a mark of his status, and received standard fees from the University for performing his functions: usually half a mark (six shillings and eightpence, a third of a pound) or a mark. It is to be assumed, though, that his main income came from selling or lending books, or from the use of a skill such as parchment-making, ink-making, bookbinding, and so on. He might also be a middleman, organising the skills and selling the products of such specialists in the form of manuscript books produced to his order; and in that respect he would be the forerunner of later booksellers and publishers.

The period from the time of the founding of the University to that of the invention of printing, the renaissance of learning and the Reformation seems to us in retrospect relatively quiet intellectually. The students in the Schools followed a traditional curriculum which changed only slowly. It was an educational system which was much more 'oral' than that of today. Lectures are a survival from that period: but the lectures of the Middle Ages were much more like readings. Those who did not know or did not possess the books listened to them being read by a scholar who could also pause to say what they meant. At the end of the course the student did not sit a written examination; he had to maintain a more or less skilful debate, in Latin, in public, against contemporary scholars of similar ability: appropriately, these performances were called 'acts' and 'opponencies', and the system survived until late in the eighteenth century, when the examination took place in the Senate House.

Though the staple of education was the spoken word, it had to be based on the written word; and books were the ultimate authority. The books which the University stationers supplied were the standard texts in moral and natural philosophy, grammar, logic, medicine, history, theology and canon and civil law. These were not grandly illuminated manuscripts in beautiful scripts, but mostly simple copies produced as cheaply as possible; and indeed poor but devoted students would often borrow a book or hire it from a stationer in order to copy it out themselves.

One of the most important aspects of the invention of printing, from the English point of view, was that it took place elsewhere, and a long way away. The new skill, developed in Germany round about 1450, spread to Italy, France and the Low Countries. By the time it reached England in 1476, the relatively much more developed skill in the main printing and trade centres in Europe was already beginning to be associated with new intellectual movements which were also initiated in Europe. This meant that for many years the technological skill could be acquired only abroad, so that Caxton, the first English printer, Theodoric Rood, the first printer in Oxford, and John Siberch, the first printer in Cambridge, all learned the skill in Cologne. The trade in important scholarly printed books was an import trade, just as the skilled practitioners of the new technology were also by definition foreigners; and so were the craftsmen – punch-cutters and typefounders to give the most obvious examples – who supplied them.

Just as the new learning had its eventual effect on university studies, so did the new technology have its effect on the stationers. The part of Europe nearest to Cambridge is the Low Countries, whose great trading ports and financial and trade centres provided the channel through which passed all trade and influence to and from – but mostly from – Germany and central Europe. England, as an island, had always had its continental trade, including intellectual trade; manuscript books had reached it before the time of printing, and there were among the foreign traders with rights of residence as 'denizens' in London and elsewhere many who dealt in books. But the advent of printing initially changed the relationship to one of almost total dependence, in many classes of publication. It was a great advantage to both parties that the language of learning was Latin, since books printed in Latin in Germany, Switzerland, France and Holland would have an international sale, while books printed in the vernacular had only a national – indeed a local – sale.

At the end of the fifteenth and the beginning of the sixteenth centuries, therefore, one would expect to find in England a number of stationers of foreign origin, and in Cambridge they would be likely to be Flemish, Dutch, German or French. They would be useful to scholars because they would be in touch with the developed centres of scholarly printing: through Antwerp in particular there would have come down the great riverways of Holland and Germany the products of scholar-printers in the European heartland. Ships would sail direct to the Wash, and up-river to Cambridge, which was a port in those days.

These books were on the whole unlikely to have arrived in England already bound: it seems that the most economical way of transporting early books was in unbound sheets, rolled up in a bale or enclosed in a barrel. Binding would take place to individual order at or near the place of eventual purchase; and given the expense of books, and the hard use they would get from generations of readers (for instance in college libraries) binding was designed to give the precious product as many years of life as possible: the 'boards' were originally of wood and the outer covering of leather. The earliest Cambridge bookbinders are identified only by the ornaments they applied by roll or stamp to the leather, but three of them are known by name. They were all foreigners resident in Cambridge, and it should be explained that their names have come down to us in several variant spellings, of which one has been chosen here. Garret Godfrey (the 'Garreitt Stacioner' whom we met above) and Nycholas Spierinck or Sperynge were Dutchmen, who were denizens of Cambridge for many years. Another such bookbinder, Johann van Laer or Lair of Siegburg near Cologne in Germany, happened also to be a printer, and brought his equipment and his skill with him, to become the first printer in Cambridge, where his name was anglicised to John Siberch.

Godfrey and Sperynge came to England before Siberch, and remained longer. Indeed they must have become what we should now call naturalised. Godfrey's bindings have been dated from 1499, and he is mentioned as a stationer in several records. He was named as churchwarden of Great St Mary's Church in 1516 and 1521, and was buried there in 1539, so he may have worked and traded nearby. A tradesman of forty years' standing is likely to have been successful and well-known. More than two hundred examples of his work have survived, so he probably employed other workmen.

Sperynge may have been slightly younger: he is first recorded in 1505/6, was also churchwarden of Great St Mary's, and was buried there in 1545/6. Both men have a tiny place in European intellectual history, because they were compatriots of the great humanist scholar Erasmus, knew him, and may have played some part in attracting him to Cambridge. Godfrey at any rate seems to have acted as Erasmus's host during the period 1511–14 when he was not residing in Queens' College: Erasmus refers to him cordially in letters of 1516 and 1525.

The other stationer of that early period whose name has come down to us is Segar Nycolson, also a Dutchman. He was younger than Godfrey: it seems even possible that he was a second-generation denizen. He was actually a student at Cambridge, being a pensioner of Gonville Hall in the 1520s. That was the time of the beginnings of the Reformation: Luther had nailed his theses to the door of the church in Wittenberg in

1517, and his New Testament was to appear in 1522. Gonville Hall had a reputation for heresy: 'Ther is', said Bishop Nix of Norwich, 'a college in Cambridge called gunwell haule of the foundacion of a Bishoppe of Norwich. I here of no clerk that hathe come aught lately of that collage but saverith of the friainge panne though he speke never so holily.' Nycolson was to savour of the frying pan all his life, and saw first his books and then his friend in the actual fire. He became known as having reforming sympathies, and was actually imprisoned in 1529 for owning Lutheran books, was harshly treated, according to Foxe, and forced to abjure. The second twenty years of the century were a heroic and a dangerous time in Cambridge. If you go into the tiny church of St Edward, just off Peas Hill, you will see in that beautiful interior the very elegant oak pulpit in which Latimer preached stirring sermons. On the present site of the new building of St Catharine's and King's on King's Parade there stood until 1823 an inn called the White Horse. It could be approached discreetly from the back by an alley called Flute's Lane, and up this muddy path slipped the Cambridge Lutherans to talk together, till the place got the nickname 'Germany'. Bilney, later martyred, was the centre of the group. Coverdale and Frith, Tyndale's assistant, were members; Tyndale himself was in Cambridge at the time, and may have attended. Nycolson was a minor member of this group; and a man of Dutch origin in the book trade could have had an essential role as supplier of dangerous books – quite soon, forbidden books.

In 1520 Luther was excommunicated, and his books were condemned to ceremonial burning. There was a bonfire before the west door of Great St Mary's, and perhaps those church-wardens who were also stationers watched with mixed feelings as the books were burnt. Two shillings were granted in the proctor's accounts to the Deputy Vice-Chancellor 'for drink and other expenses about the burning of the works of Martin Luther'. Not all copies were burnt, evidently, and Segar Nycolson might, as bookseller, have been conscious of a rise in the rarity value of his undeclared property, as well as of an uncomfortable sensation of warmth. On 12 May 1521 there was a similar ceremonial burning in London, at Paul's Cross, and the ceremony was marked by a speech in the House of Lords by Cardinal Fisher, who was also Chancellor of the University. Here too there is scope for irony, but more for sadness. Fisher, who for the moment was proclaiming the ascendancy of the old Church and its alliance with the State, was himself to suffer martyrdom for refusing to acknowledge the supremacy of Henry VIII. He was executed on Tower Hill in 1535, the first of five Tudor Chancellors of the University to die in that manner. Yet the speech which he gave in 1521, translated into Latin, was one of the first books to be printed in Cambridge; and the printer, John Siberch, was a German who knew Erasmus, and was himself likely to have advanced views.

A good deal is now known about Johann Lair of Siegburg, more usually referred to as John Siberch. Siegburg is a small town south-east of Cologne. The son of a substantial wool-weaver, property-owner and town councillor of Siegburg, Johann Lair was admitted to the University of Cologne in 1492 at the age of sixteen. He was probably intended for holy orders from the very beginning, and became a tonsured clerk in minor orders, but as such was still free to marry. His marriage into a family of printers and publishers diverted him into another career. He had become brother-in-law of the Cologne printers Arnold and Franz Birkmann, the Antwerp printer Johannes Grapheus, and the Louvain printer Servaes van Sassen. So he was introduced to a trade network which linked Cologne to England through Antwerp, for Birkmann had an outlet in St Paul's Churchyard, then and later the metropolitan book-selling centre of England. Johann Lair seems to have become a travelling representative of the family firms, moving as far afield as Leipzig, the site of the main European book-fair. As bookseller, and representing one of the most important trade dynasties, he met important authors, and in Leipzig met Richard Croke, the Cambridge humanist. Croke had met Erasmus in Paris in 1511, taught Greek in Cologne, Louvain, Leipzig and Dresden; returned to Cambridge as Fellow of King's and Reader in Greek in 1518, and in 1522 became Public Orator. He wrote an elementary Greek primer in order to have a textbook for his pupils, and a second impression of this was financed by Siberch and printed in Cologne in 1520. Siberch probably brought it with him in sheets when he came to Cambridge, and would have expected to sell copies to Croke's students and listeners in Cambridge, as well as to booksellers in London. All in all, therefore, it is likely that Siberch's arrival was a personal initiative by Croke, and had nothing to do with the University.

Croke can be presumed to have had the intention of furthering the new learning in Cambridge. Erasmus in his visits and his residence had provided prestige and the first impetus: it was now for his friends and supporters, the Cambridge humanists, to carry on the enterprise. There were others beside Croke who shared Erasmus's friendship, notably Henry Bullock, Fellow of Queens', Robert Aldrich and John Bryan of King's, and Thomas Lupset who had been Erasmus's assistant. But there was quite a substantial group with humanist interests and leanings, whom Erasmus mentioned or sent greetings to in his letters. From their knowledge of the European centres of learning, they would have become aware of the part that printing played in its dissemination, and some of them must have thought that Cambridge could never be as important unless it also had its printers. Obviously none of the great established scholar-printers was going to move out of Basel, Cologne, Antwerp, Louvain or Paris; and though they would have wanted to sell their books in England there was no reason why they should set up a subsidiary printing house there. But Croke's printer Siberch, it seems, had the right connections and was available; and at the age of forty-five, presumably with his wife and children, with some stock of books, and with material for a press and the necessary types (not available, of course, in Cambridge) he came to England and set up his business some time in 1520.

Siberch's status once he had set up in Cambridge is obscure and therefore debatable. Erasmus in a letter of 1525 referred to him among others, all booksellers (*bibliopolas*). In very general terms Siberch would have been thought of as a stationer, and it seems conceivable that he could have been a University stationer the somewhat loose sense which prevailed before 1534. Indeed he even had a loan from the University. There are entries in the Grace Book and the Audit Book for the time which show that the University lent him £20 (a very considerable sum, in those days), and senior members of the University stood surety for him both when the loan was first made, and when it was renewed – though by then the names had changed.

The Latin entry which specifies that Doctor Manfeld has taken the place of Magister Norres as guarantor of the loan, describes Siberch as 'Johannes bibliopola', John the bookseller, and this strengthens the view that Siberch had status in that known role rather than in the totally unprecedented one of printer. And the fact that the University lent him money also makes his status ambiguous; for a loan implies a form of countenancing or support which falls short of total acceptance.

It is known where Siberch traded (and most tradesmen lived over the shop). He worked in the tenement called the King's Arms, in a lane of houses long since demolished to make the Trinity Street range of the Tree Court of Caius College. This is within a hundred yards of Great St Mary's Church where Godfrey and Sperynge were churchwardens, and indicates that then as now the bookselling area of Cambridge was in and around what was then the High Street and is now Trinity Street. The name of the tenement has sometimes been given as a reason for Siberch's use of the royal arms as a printer's device on some of his books; but it is unlikely that this would have been taken as a sufficient reason for so bold a claim; and the fact that he also used the phrase *cum gratia et privilegio* may mean that he had secured some form of protection from London as well as some sort of sponsorship in Cambridge. Printing outside the capital city was extremely rare, then and later, for the good reason that the London stationers always hated provincial competition, and the government at all times preferred to see printing centralised in London where it could be more easily controlled. Siberch was experienced in the book trade and would know that it was quite impossible to sell whole editions in such a small town as Cambridge. He had to be able to sell in

London, and he had both to establish his status and to protect his copyrights. How much bluff there was in his title-pages we may now never know, but it is inherently unlikely either that his venture was totally unsecured, or that his status was absolutely clear.

Part of Hammond's map of Cambridge, 1592. Siberch had his house and shop on or near the old High Street (now Trinity Street) on the present site of Tree Court of Gonville and Caius College. Thomas Thomas later worked nearby, opposite Great St Mary's. In the seventeenth century Buck started printing in the market, between Sherer's Lane and Shoemaker's Lane, before removing to the old Austin Friars' building, at the very edge of the illustration, opposite Corpus Christi College. The Old White Horse Inn, nicknamed 'Germany', was near the junction of High Street and Plott and Nuts Lane.

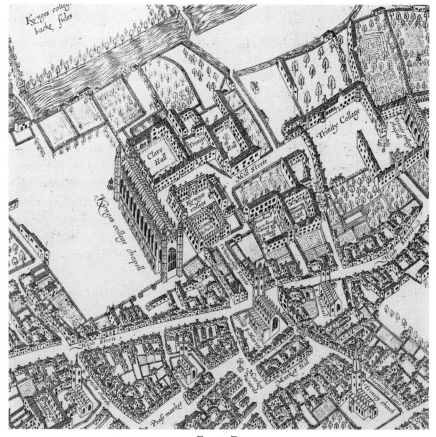

The loan, at any rate, was never repaid until the University Press thought it would be amusing to close the account in 1971: the £20 was duly repaid, without interest, and without allowance for inflation. It had been carried in the University's books until 1553, and Siberch was twice referred to in the records of the later years as an 'alien priest'. Indeed by this time he had long since returned to Germany; he left Cambridge late in 1523 or early in 1524, his wife having died in England. He is known to have taken part in family lawsuits in Siegburg in 1526, took orders, lived in Siegburg, and died in 1554, aged seventy-eight. One possible reason why the record of the loan from the University is not repeated in the accounts is that Siberch was now beyond reach. Bullock had died in 1526, and others of the original sponsors were either dead or dispersed, and it might have been thought hard to call in the loan from those others who had agreed to stand surety in their stead.

Siberch's printing and publishing has been analysed by E. P. Goldschmidt, who sees in it a kind of editorial policy (as we should now say). His total output cannot have been large: he only worked in Cambridge for a couple of years; he probably had only one printing press. He would have had to bring his workmen with him since it is improbable that anyone then in Cambridge had the skill, and he could hardly have brought many. Indeed, a new regulation of 1523 prohibited alien printers from having any but English apprentices, and from employing more than two foreign journeymen, and it is not inconceivable that that pressure, among others, caused Siberch to leave England. The University could not, in 1523, protect him against that legislation, since it had not as yet established the right to have its own printers.

At any rate, he is known to have printed ten books in roman type, and two books and some broadside printing jobs in black-letter (the old 'gothic' type also known as 'English'). The books in roman could be said to constitute a humanist programme of a kind found in other universities at the time, where a consciously forward-looking group, favouring the new learning, and probably opposed by a conservative majority in the same university, invited a printer to set up shop and work in their interest. At the other places, too, the result was a brief burst of activity followed by a collapse probably caused by economic and political pressures. In Cambridge in particular, remote from the trade centres, and facing the commercial hostility of London tradesmen, the chances of success were slight from the start.

Siberch's publishing was not without its commercial shrewdness: for instance he printed the first edition of Erasmus's little book on letter writing – *De conscribendis epistolis*. Erasmus had a European reputation, and was the first best-selling author in history, so the chances of a rapid and wide sale were good. It was an unauthorised edition, and Erasmus himself was irritated by the liberty Siberch had taken: which argues that Siberch's commercial sense overrode his sensibility. Siberch also printed Lily's and Erasmus's little grammar textbook *De octo orationis partium constructione* (on the eight parts of speech) which became the standard schoolbook of the time. These two books would have had good commercial prospects and constituted a 'selling line'. The first publication of all, Henry Bullock's *Oratio* – the text of a speech given before Wolsey on his visit to Cambridge – was an elegant oration showing Bullock's potential skill as scholar-diplomat. Bullock probably paid for this to be printed, so that he could present copies to possible patrons or other influential people, and Siberch probably lost nothing by it and gained the reputation of being associated with a leading humanist. Bullock's other publication was a Latin translation of Lucian's *Dipsades*, a rhetorical exercise likely to appeal to renaissance taste. It sets the two words of the Greek title in actual Greek types, and the few lines of Greek text quoted by Bullock are also typeset, so that this was the first use of Greek moveable types in England, and justified Siberch's claim (in another book) to be *primus utriusque linguae in Anglia impressor* – the first printer of both languages in England (the two languages being of course Latin, the speech of the educated, and Greek, the language of the forward-looking).

Two of Siberch's books had real substance as publications. He printed the first edition of Linacre's translation into Latin of Galen's *De temperamentis*, a fundamental source in the medicine of the time. He also printed an interesting original composition, the *Hermathena* of Papyrius Geminus Eliates, a pseudonym now thought to conceal the identity of Sir Thomas Elyot. This too has some quotations in Greek.

The ten books in Latin were of course in roman type; 'of course' because humanists felt that the new letter-form was appropriate to the new learning and the purified Latin in which it should be expressed for a cultivated audience throughout Europe. Siberch's publications in English: indulgences, prognostications of the new deluge, and secular poetry, were for another, more popular audience, and were in blackletter. They were far more likely to have been bought, read, passed from hand to hand and read to pieces; and that is why they have survived only in fragmentary form (to be found, for instance, pasted into contemporary bindings as waste-paper which could be used for humble purposes) – why also we can say only that Siberch *may* have printed more such popular, or 'jobbing' items, which probably did more than the learned printing to keep his business going. But the learned printing was his pride, and his *raison d'être*, and it was on these books that he made the most of printing 'in praeclara cantabrigiensi academia', or 'in alma Cantabrigia', or 'apud praeclaram Cantabrigiam', as he proclaimed on his title-pages. The historian may think also that the publication which most clearly showed which way things were about to go was the speech of Cardinal John Fisher, Bishop of Rochester and Chancellor of that same 'praeclara Cantabrigiensis academia', 'on the day on which the writings of Martin Luther with public ceremony were cast into the fire'. It was the beginning of the period in which first the old generation of English Catholics, such as Fisher himself, were to suffer for disputing the royal supremacy; then the Protestants under Mary; and finally the extremes, whether Catholic recusant or puritan Protestant, under Elizabeth. Fisher was executed in 1535; in the 1540s and 1550s it was the turn of the Protestants. Between 1531 and 1558 twenty-five members of the University died as martyrs; and in Mary's reign some ninety known Cambridge men, mostly Fellows of Colleges, went into exile in Protestant Europe. There was one burning in Cambridge itself, not just of books, but also of John Hullier of King's, executed on Maundy Thursday 1556 on Jesus Green. Harry Porter relates his end, quoting Foxe's *Book of Martyrs*:

But his end was not short, for it was a blustery Cambridge day, the fire was badly set, and the flames blew to his back. His friends caused the sergeants to turn it and 'fire it to that place where the wind might blow it to his face'. One of them gave him bags of gunpowder to hang round his neck, but this errand of mercy failed too, for the powder did not catch fire until after Hullier was dead. Splendidly, in the sickening horrors of his last hour, he found consolation in the Book of Common Prayer: 'there was a company of books which were cast into the fire; and by chance a communion book fell between his hands, who received it joyfully, opened it, and read so long till the force of the flame and smoke caused him that he could see no more'.

> Porter, *Reformation and Reaction*
> *in Tudor Cambridge*, 72–3

Cooper's extract from Foxe's *Book* shows that the person who 'gave him certain gunpowder' was 'Seagar', and one can only suppose that this was Segar Nycolson, seeing with grief and horror the last act of the drama which had opened with the burning of Luther's books. Nycolson's former colleague John Siberch, leaving England because of the death of his wife, the failure to prosper (we suspect) of his printing enterprise, the impossibility of employing foreign apprentices, and the inability of the University to do anything to help him, since he had no official status as printer, may also have thought that the troubles about to divide Europe might as well be lived through in his own country. He died in bed in the town of his birth.

# 3

## THE LETTERS PATENT OF 1534:
## THE STATIONERS' COMPANY

HISTORIANS OF THE PRESS over-eager to claim Siberch as its
true founder have not faced the logical consequence of the fact
that between 1522 and 1584 there was no printing in Cambridge;
so that the 'start' was immediately followed by a long 'stop',
and then the real start after sixty years. In short, 1584 is the
only true starting date. Before that time we are in the period
of the University stationers. If Siberch is taken as one of their
number – a licensed alien like Godfrey, Nycolson and Sperynge
– his distinction is that he was the only stationer who also had
the skill of printing, and he briefly exercised it under the
patronage of a group of influential resident Cambridge humanists, notably Croke and Bullock. Neither his arrival nor his
departure fundamentally changed the system by which the
University maintained a general right to supervise the trading
activities of those suppliers whose trade most closely affected
its interests. They were recognised, if not formally licensed;
they wore a gown as a sign of their status; they received fees
for particular duties; but mostly they traded on their own
account, and in some matters would have felt as much obligation
to their guild as to the University.

The guild, representing the corporate interest of all its members, could procure legislation in its favour. In particular the
number of foreigners allowed to trade in England either as
aliens or as denizens had always been kept under supervision.
There was an Act of 1484 which allowed complete freedom to
foreigners trading as printers, binders and scriveners; this for the
good reason that until 1513 there *were* no English printers except
Caxton, Thomas Hunt of Oxford, and possibly an anonymous

printer at St Albans. But a trade dominated by aliens is not ultimately acceptable; hence the regulation of 1523 which prohibited foreign apprentices and limited the number of foreign journeymen. An English printing trade had to be fostered.

In 1529 a new Act prohibited the setting-up of any new press by an alien, though those already resident could continue to trade. In the same year the University of Cambridge petitioned Wolsey, then Lord Chancellor, for the formal right to license three stationers. 1529 was the year in which Nycolson was charged with the unlawful possession of Luther's books; it was four years after the printing of Tyndale's New Testament in Germany; and the import of this and other forbidden books through the Low Countries, and the consequent searches, seizures and prosecutions, were well under way. It was no doubt with this political and religious situation in mind, as well as the practical trade considerations, that the University suggested

that for the suppression of error, there should be three booksellers allowed in Cambridge by the King, who should be sworn not to bring in or sell any book which had not first been approved of by the censors of books in the University, that such booksellers should be men of reputation and gravity, and foreigners (so it should be best for the prizing of books,) and that they might have the privilege to buy books of foreign merchants.

Cooper, *Annals* I, 329

Almost certainly, the University had in mind that the existing situation be recognised and institutionalised. There were such men trading in Cambridge, and they were foreigners. Two of them were men of reputation and gravity, even if the other had heretical leanings. The University obviously felt able to deal with the Protestants in its midst, since it had the authority to do so; and it was now appealing through Wolsey to the King to recognise its ancient right to act as a licensing authority and to confirm it in the new context.

The appeal was successful, if not immediately, and the terms of the grant were wider than the appeal. 1534 was the year of the Act declaring the Royal Supremacy, so that Fisher's refusal to accept it became high treason and brought about his death. It was also the year of an Act regulating printing, which repealed the Act of 1484 on the ground that whereas before, 'there were but few books, and few printers, within this realm at that time...at this day there be within this Realme a greatt number cunning and expert in the said craft of printing, as able to exercise the said craft in all points as any stranger'. From now on, aliens could only sell their wares wholesale to an English-born printer or stationer, and no bound books were to be imported at all. So the retail trade passed into the hands of English stationers, and binding became an exclusively English trade.

In the characteristic way in which a corporation, such as the University, might be granted a specific right which exempted it from general legislation, Letters Patent of Henry VIII on 20 July 1534 gave licence to the Chancellor, Masters, and Scholars to appoint printers as well as stationers. The text in the original Latin is given as Appendix I. The English translation is as follows:

Henry VIII, by the grace of God King of England and France, Defender of the Faith, and Lord of Ireland, To all to whom these present letters may come, greeting. Know ye that we of our special grace, and by our certain knowledge and mere motion, have granted and given licence, and by these presents grant and give licence, for ourselves and our heirs, to our beloved in Christ the Chancellor, Masters, and Scholars of our University of Cambridge, That they and their successors for ever may, by their writings under the seal of the Chancellor of the said University, from time to time assign, appoint and in perpetuity have among them, and perpetually remaining and dwelling within our aforesaid University, Three Stationers and Printers or Sellers of Books, both aliens born outside our obedience and natives born within our obedience, having and holding houses both leased [?] and owned. These Stationers or Bookprinters, assigned in the aforesaid manner, and any of them, shall have lawful and incontestable power to print there all manner of books approved, or hereafter to be approved, by the aforesaid Chancellor or his deputy and three doctors there; and also to exhibit for sale, as well in the same University as elsewhere in our realm, wherever they please, all such books and all other books wherever printed, both within and outside our realm, approved or to be approved (as aforesaid) by the said Chancellor or his deputy and three doctors there. And that the same Stationers or Printers born (as is aforesaid) outside our obedience, and every of them, for as long as they dwell in the aforesaid University and occupy themselves in the aforesaid business, shall in all things and by everyone be reputed, taken and treated as our faithful subjects and lieges, and each of them shall be so reputed, taken and treated. And they shall be entitled to enjoy and use all and singular liberties, customs, laws and privileges, and each of them shall be so entitled, freely and quietly, such as any faithful subject and liege in any manner can use and enjoy. And they shall pay and render Lot and Scot, taxes, tallages, and all other customs and impositions none otherwise and in no other manner than our own faithful subjects and lieges pay and render to us; any statute, act, ordinance or provision made, published or provided to the contrary notwithstanding. Provided always, that the said Stationers or Printers so born (as is premised) outside our obedience shall pay to us all and all manner of customs, subsidies and other monies owing to us from time to time for their goods and merchandise to be exported from or imported into our realm, in such wise as aliens pay us and not otherwise. In testimony of which matter we have caused these our letters to be made patent. Witness myself, at Westminster, the 20th day of July, in the 26th year of our reign [1534].

This is the royal charter of the University's printing and publishing, appealed to as the legal basis of its activity in these

Henry VIII's Letters Patent of 1534. Although it was written on vellum, which is very durable, the document, now in the University Archives, has been carelessly treated at times over 450 years; but the fine initial, with the King's portrait inside it, and the large first line of script are still clearly discernible.

trades in all the years that followed, and especially in the disputes that arose with printers and publishers in London, from 1583 to 1963.

It is inevitable that a legal document addressed to a certain situation and giving certain powers will, unless it is amended or repealed, subsist into a different situation, and so provoke questions about its scope and power. The Letters Patent were at first clearly addressed to the Cambridge of 1534 and earlier. The immediate consequence was that the University appointed Godfrey, Sperynge and Nycolson as the 'three stationers and printers or sellers of books residing in the university' – and this despite the known fact that Nycolson had been in trouble with the authorities for owning books which the Chancellor or his deputy and three doctors could not officially approve, since they were forbidden by another Statute. However, it would not have been hard to find in the University more than three doctors who did approve of them secretly: Nycolson merely represented that constant Protestant, and later puritan, faction in the University which was always powerful, and in the 1580s and thereafter tended to be the Cambridge orthodoxy. Meanwhile the University had not merely institutionalised an existing situation by giving a privileged status to its principal resident stationers: it had also had confirmed its old right to be a licensing authority, and so not subject to the jurisdiction of the metropolitan authorities (Star Chamber, the Bishop of London, the Archbishop of Canterbury) or of the local authority, the Bishop of Ely.

This was a benefit of a quite practical kind. Censorship or the control of publication was regularly reasserted by legislation in the sixteenth and seventeenth centuries. The licensing authorities, who were in principle supposed to inspect everything that was published, obviously could not exercise the role as the volume of publications increased, and London printers found themselves either waiting months for a licence, or taking the risk of severe punishment if they published an unlicensed book which proved to be objectionable. Once again, restriction and protection were two sides of one coin. In Cambridge, the printers who eventually appeared were licensed under a system which was subject to far less pressure and then offered the possibility of protection in all parts of the realm (though this had to be argued). Their authority under the Letters Patent therefore offered a form of copyright protection: or in the circumstances of the time, it offered one form of protection which could be asserted against the other forms which coexisted, or could be claimed in opposition.

Though the Letters Patent specifically envisaged stationers who might also be printers, as Siberch had been, no successor to Siberch seems to have appeared for fifty years after 1534. 'Seems' is the right word because the records are few, obscure and sometimes unreliable, and fifty years is a long time. As an example of how little we know, and how hard it often is to say what that little means, there is the case of Remigius Guidon. Thomas Fuller mentions one Remigius (the Latin form of the French name Rémy) as a papermaker who had been brought back to Cambridge by Thomas Thirlby, Bishop of Ely, after a visit to the court of Charles V. Remigius worked a papermill which was then leased to Corpus Christi College in 1559 and probably converted into a cornmill. It was in the Fen Ditton area, and it is a pleasant fancy that it was on or near the site of the beautiful old house still called Papermills which stands unoccupied and neglected on the Newmarket Road. Remigius suddenly acquires a surname, another activity, and some interest for this history, in the record of the visit to England of Christoph Froschauer the younger (1532–85), who came to England and visited London, Oxford and Cambridge in 1550–1. He spent three days in Cambridge, and met Remigius Guidon from Lorraine, who was 'a skilled craftsman at papermaking and printing. From his own mouth I heard how at the court of King Edward VI he with other great lords standing by had made paper and also carried out printing before their eyes, so that they could see and understand how things went in actual papermills and printing houses, and was thereupon made regius typographus Cantabrigiae.' It is unlikely that Guidon printed in Cambridge; though one might ask why he was making paper a good week's journey by ox-drawn cart from the printers of London. Guidon's rather impulsively bestowed title may cast some retrospective light on Siberch's claim to print *cum gratia et privilegio*; but it is unlikely that the London printers would have been pleased with the possibility of yet more competition from foreigners, and the Cambridge authorities and their stationers could have felt their rights were also infringed. And indeed, the story, evidently set down in good faith, may be a misunderstanding of what Guidon said; or Guidon may even have been a great romancer.

This period is obscure partly for well-understood religious and political reasons. Christoph Froschauer's uncle, the great scholar-printer of Zürich, had printed an edition of Coverdale's English Bible in 1550; and an English issue appeared in the same year using imported sheets prefaced by London-printed preliminary pages. The younger Froschauer may have been in England about his uncle's business. But the accession of Mary to the English throne in 1553 put an immediate stop to the stream of Bibles printed in England, and started the fires of Smithfield. Like many Englishmen in Cambridge (a few of whom lodged in Zürich with Froschauer), Remigius Guidon may have taken that as good cause to leave England, as Siberch may have done thirty years before.

At the moment when Mary's reign was followed by that of Elizabeth in 1557–8, there took place another crucial event. On 4 May 1557 Mary promulgated a charter incorporating the Stationers' Company of London, and Elizabeth confirmed its rights in further legislation of 1559. It became a liveried company of the City of London in 1560. The Monarch, as head of both Church and State, had an interest in the regulation of printing so that neither heresy nor treason should be disseminated. The chosen method was to give legal status to a corporation of printers and booksellers with monopoly rights, to confine its activities to a restricted number of printers all working in London, and to require it to police itself or to suffer penalties which might include loss of rights. It was a system which worked fairly well, since it made the tradesmen concerned act conformably out of economic interest; and the corporation as a whole had a natural tendency to curb those of its members who either infringed the interests of other members out of greed, or brought risks on themselves and others out of idealism.

The new Company was very like the old guild. It was a hierarchy consisting of a Master, two wardens, liverymen and freemen. The number was controlled at about a hundred members. The trade could only be entered through the time-honoured method of seven years' apprenticeship, and only a freeman could have an apprentice (a liveryman could have two). In fact some who traded as stationers and booksellers had been and still were members of other companies (one noted trouble-maker was a member of the Fishmongers, and some who traded in books among other commodities had been Grocers and Mercers in the past), but the tendency was toward trade monopoly policed by the single corporation. Within the Company it soon began to be increasingly clear that those booksellers who acted as entrepreneurs, and either alone or in partnership with others financed the printing of books which they then sold through the trade in London and the provinces, had increasing wealth and power. The printers who merely waited to be offered these printing jobs were forced more and more into economic dependency on those others, who were in effect acting as what we should now call publishers, though they went on being called booksellers until the eighteenth century.

The Company also provided the machinery by which the central government's standing preoccupation with control of heresy and treason could be administered. The licensing authorities remained those of Church and State; but the Company now provided a register in which every new publication was supposed to be entered, and the keepers of the register were meant to see that each was approved by an appropriate authority. The usual double purpose was achieved: the submission to control also gave the person in whose name the entry was made the sole right to print that book (always provided that nobody else claimed a competing right). We get our modern term 'copyright' from this procedure: theoretically, the registrant took along the actual copy from which he proposed to print, undertaking to add or subtract nothing. This copy was inspected, so that the imprimatur of the licensing authority could be verified, as applied to that copy. The bookseller or printer paid his six-pence registration fee, the 'copy' was 'entered', and the right was established: the book was thenceforward that person's 'copy'.

Of course, the system was quickly bypassed, for various reasons, including speed. An unlicensed copy might be provisionally entered, on the understanding that if it was found to' be objectionable the printer would withdraw the publication from sale, or suffer other consequences. Many books were simply not entered, either because they were innocuous or because they were not. But by and large the system was worked fairly conscientiously because of the advantages it brought to the members of the Company.

There were difficulties and conflicts, however, which sprang from the Tudor practice of giving specific rights to certain individuals which cut across general rights or jurisdictions, or specific rights given to other individuals. It is already clear, for instance, that the right given to the University of Cambridge in 1534 was an antecedent right given to the University and its licensed stationers, so exempting them from any general right claimed by the Stationers' Company and its London members. That right was based partly on the University's claim, as corporation, to control the activities of its principal suppliers; partly on its ancient role as teaching centre which had since 1408 made it a licensing authority in matters of publication. But there were also specific rights given by royal authority to individual persons who had been loyal, helpful or accommo-dating, and who were rewarded at little cost to the Crown by being given certain trading rights; and these could cut across the rights claimed by rank-and-file members of the Stationers' Company, especially those poor printers who found themselves looking round for a safe selling line in order to make a little money on their own account, and whose eyes naturally, indeed inevitably, fell on the best-selling kinds of books. These were Bibles, prayer books, catechisms, psalters, almanacs, ABCs, and best-sellers like Lily's Grammar (which Siberch had printed). If any private person or group of persons acquired a monopoly of any of these best-selling categories, then the ordinary unprivileged printer was *ipso facto* cut off from the most lucrative areas of the whole market. When it happened, there would be an outcry; the orderly would go to law, and the disorderly would simply try to print and sell a pirate edition or two under the noses of the monopolists.

These monopolists had by the end of the sixteenth century become quite numerous. Lovers of Tudor church music today may not feel indignant that William Byrd and Thomas Tallis, for their virtues perhaps, or their talents, held a monopoly of music printing and ruled music paper. John Day, perhaps the best-known printer of his time, had the sole right during his life to print Cuningham's *Cosmographical Glasse*: to us that looks like a normal copyright, and causes no offence; in the language of the time, other printers would recognise it as 'his copy'. They would have been more uneasy at the thought that William Seres had a patent for the printing of primers and the catechism; that John Day also had a licence for the Psalms in metre and the little catechism; that Richard Tottell had the exclusive right to print 'all manner of books of the common law'; that Thomas Marshe and Thomas Vautrollier held a patent for certain very popular schoolbooks; Henry Bynneman for chronicles and dictionaries; Richard Watkins for almanacs and prognostications. These were among the lines which sold best; and to be cut off from them severely limited the commercial prospects of a printer or bookseller with no monopoly of his own.

Another kind of privilege was held by those who were appointed Royal Printer. This was an office established quite early in the history of English printing, with the aim of securing the printing of official decrees: Anthony Marler was the first Royal Printer, appointed in 1541/2. John Cawood, appointed Queen's Printer by Mary in 1553, was given 'the office of our printer of all and singular our statute books, acts, proclamations, injunctions, and other volumes and things, under what name or title soever, either already, or hereafter to be published in the English language'. Cawood and Richard Jugge became joint Royal Printers under Elizabeth. Now Jugge also had the right to print the Bishops' Bible in quarto and the New Testament in that translation in 16mo, by an arrangement with the other printers which left them free to print in other formats. That, at any rate, was the situation in 1575, the date of the death of Archbishop Parker, who kept a very close watch on the Stationers and had been determined not to let the alternative English version of the Bible, the more popular and more radical or puritan Geneva version, be printed in England. That explains why John Bodley, who actually had the right to print the Geneva version, never exercised it; why after 1575 the Geneva version started to be printed in England; and why in 1575 the other printers moved in to share the Bishops' Bible, though they were willing to use Jugge's printing facilities for the purpose. The situation was a characteristically complex network of accommodations and compromises with a religious and political background, but in essence the office of Royal Printer at that moment conferred no *ex officio* monopoly of Bible printing as a whole.

When Jugge died in 1577 his patent as Royal Printer was secured by the very enterprising Christopher Barker. Barker himself was protected by the powerful Sir Francis Walsingham and had already engaged in Bible printing. Another friend at court was the diplomatist Sir Thomas Wilkes, who somehow secured the Royal Patent for himself before transferring it to Barker – no doubt for a considerable payment (Barker referred in 1582 to 'the great somme I paid to Master Wilkes'). Wilkes managed to have conferred on Barker a new patent which gave him, or seemed to give him, a complete monopoly of Bible printing – to the consternation, no doubt, of other members of the Stationers' Company, who were, under the accommodation reached in 1575, setting up a joint venture which later led to the creation of the Company's 'Bible Stock', where a number of printers jointly paid for the printing, and then shared the sale. Barker did some Bible printing on his own behalf; and in 1589 secured a fresh patent for his own lifetime and that of his son Robert. He died in 1599 – rich, no doubt. His position was such that he could either choose to insist that all Bibles printed in England be printed by himself; or (more realistically and no less lucratively) that he should have some part in the printing of all Bibles in England – if only that he was paid for his consent, so that the printers and publishers could call themselves his deputies and assigns.

Barker's patent, translated and summarised by A. W. Pollard, is to the effect that

the Queen, in consideration of the skill shown by Christopher Barker in the art of printing, grants to him, for herself, her heirs and successors, the office of royal printer for all statutes, books, bills, acts of parliament, proclamations, injunctions, Bibles and New Testaments, in the English tongue of any translation, with or without notes, whether previously in print or to be subsequently printed by her command. Also of all service-books ordered to be used in churches, and all other volumes, however called, ordered to be printed by the Queen or Parliament, whether in English or in English and some other language (save only Latin grammars) and makes Christopher Barker her printer, to exercise the office personally, or by a sufficient deputy or deputies for his natural life. Wherefore she forbids all and sundry her subjects in or out of her dominions to print any book etc. of which the printing is hereby given to the said Christopher Barker, or to cause any book of the said Christopher Barker's printing to be printed abroad or at home...And she gives to Christopher Barker and his assigns the right of seizing and arresting without let or stay. Moreover she gives the right of impressing skilled workmen when needed for his service.

Pollard, *Records of the English Bible*, 323

If therefore the University of Cambridge were, under its charter of 1534, to appoint a stationer who was also a printer, the Stationers' Company would at once sense competition. It was theoretically envisaged that printing could take place outside London only in Cambridge, which had its Letters Patent; in Oxford, which had no such instrument but had in its Vice-Chancellor and doctors a competent licensing authority; and in York, the seat of the other metropolitan. But no such activity took place until 1583, when the University of Cambridge took active steps to set up a press. If the University, having in general terms decided to implement its charter of 1534, then licensed the printing of a title which was the 'copy', or a kind of book which was the monopoly, of a London printer, there was obvious occasion for a lawsuit by that printer, backed by the London printers as a whole. The stage was therefore set for a conflict, in which the University would have to assert and defend its right, as against the Company or individual London stationers asserting *their* rights. The unprivileged London printer would be especially outraged if he saw a Cambridge outsider able with impunity to infringe a monopoly which he would dearly like to infringe himself but dared not; so that if monopolies were a cause of conflict between London stationers, the action of an outsider would have the effect of healing these divisions and uniting the pack against the outsider.

Like all other liveried companies, and like the guilds before them, the Stationers' Company accepted also the role of benevolent society. It aimed so far as it could to protect loyal members in sickness and misfortune, and their widows and orphans. An extension of this concern was born of the tension between the bookseller-entrepreneurs and the ordinary printers, and the monopolists and those who coveted their monopolies. The Company set up the Stocks already mentioned, rather like funds which could be used to finance collaborative publishing and printing ventures in which risks and profits, and the printing work itself, were shared around the Company's members, and some residue left for charitable purposes. This helped the monopolists to 'farm' their privileges, while redistributing some of the proceeds. As time went by the English Stock (mainly dealing with popular titles like schoolbooks) and later the Bible Stock became powerful cartels; and meant that outsiders like Oxford and Cambridge were facing not just a single outraged monopolist only half-supported by other jealous stationers. They antagonised a substantial section of the trade which had acquired an interest in the privileges.

The Stationers' Company had been given an inquisitorial right of search in London; it had a kind of posse going around the printing houses, checking to see that no unlicensed printing was going on; and it destroyed any such unlicensed books and took proceedings against the printers. Given this sort of power in its own domain, it would quite naturally attempt to take the same measures in the provinces, if need arose; and in the early 1580s it found that need had arisen in Cambridge.

# 4

## THE FOUNDATION OF THE PRESS: THOMAS THOMAS

Archbishop Matthew Parker, who had prevented the Geneva Bible being printed in England during his lifetime, and had for doctrinal reasons strengthened the power of the Stationers' Company in London, was a Cambridge man. He had been Fellow and Master of Corpus (then called Bene't College), and had spent some time and energy on the sharp little disputes which blew up in the Colleges, and usually involved a puritan faction which self-righteously thought that less doctrinaire colleagues were the 'dregs of popery' and that the wearing of a surplice was the nearest road to Hell. An underlying note in all these disputes was the University's insistence that it had the right to discipline its own members (or not) and that its prerogatives should not be infringed by outsiders – as against the central government's insistence that it was going to have uniformity, or at any rate the uniformity of the moment, and that fractious subjects must be subdued. The powerful men appealed to by the University in these disputes as patrons or arbiters might be the Archbishop of Canterbury, supreme authority in the Church; or a great statesman, such as William Cecil, who became Lord Burghley; or the Chancellor of the University, who was now chosen precisely because he was a great churchman or a great statesman and was likely to take the University's part. Each would be able to pour oil if he had been a Cambridge man (Parker and Burghley both were: indeed Burghley was at once Lord High Treasurer and Chief Minister of the realm and Chancellor of the University) and each could express his affection for the *Alma Mater* while repressing the strife of her children.

The true beginning of Cambridge University Press can be

seen as part of this history. In Siberch's time Cambridge was a centre of the movement for early Protestant reform, and the young radicals of the time revolted against the old Church. In the 1580s this radical tradition had hardened into a puritan orthodoxy which was dissatisfied with the achieved reform, the Anglican *via media*. Cambridge puritan activists of the 1560s and 1570s had adumbrated a kind of presbyterianism; the theory being contained in a Latin treatise of 1574 by Walter Travers. When in 1583 the University appointed a printer, the catalysing element which at least twice enabled the Stationers' Company to intervene and to prevent the printing or to seize and burn the books was the theological nature of the offence: one of the books so treated was an abridged version of Travers's treatise, and the Stationers must have been delighted to have so good a reason for protecting their interests.

Certain documents enable us to establish a sketchy background to the conflict. A Grace of 8 February 1576/7 approved by the Cambridge Senate appointed a printer, John Kingston. He was specifically called 'impressor' not 'stationarius' in the Grace, and he was well known in the London trade, having printed a Chaucer in 1561. In July of 1577 Burghley wrote to the Vice-Chancellor saying that he disapproved of any attempt to infringe the monopolies of the London printers. He specifically mentioned psalters, Books of Common Prayer and the privileges of Seres, Jugge and Day; but said he would not object if the University printed for its own domestic purposes. It looks therefore as if the shrewd Kingston had seen in the Cambridge Letters Patent a protection against the Letters Patent granted to his London rivals; and he may have sought appointment as University Printer in order to set up a provincial opposition. The University for its part, or perhaps a puritan faction in it, may have seen a way of escaping London censorship. Nothing seems to have come of this initiative, but it served to indicate a possibility to some and a risk to others; and it would have drawn the attention of the Stationers, as it did that of Burghley.

Things began to move in 1583. The first surviving record is a letter of 18 March 1582/3 from Burghley to the current

Vice-Chancellor. It seems that Burghley was replying to earlier letters sent to him by the University, and carried by one Thomas Thomas, who was also the bearer of Burghley's reply. The letter states that Thomas is

one of that universitie and desirous to put in ure the art of printing there under the priviledg of the universitie graunted by Charter. Wherein besydes myne own opinion I thought good also to use the advice of the Mr of the Rolles. Who hath considered lykewise of your charter whereof I sent him the Copie. And finding it in his opinion concurring with myne a graunt of good validitie, I do assent to that which yow shall think fitt for the appinting of Mr Thomas to print by vertue thereof, having regard that he be sene to be furnished with all thinges fitt and requisite for that purpose, and that his letters [i.e. his type] and paper be answerable with any of the foreyn printes and the prices lykewise agreable. Of which thinges or any others to be thought of and considered in this matter if yow shall conceve some instru-ment by waie of articles or decre, I will be redie to give myne assent and furtheraunce as shall be requisite....

[Postscript] I thynk it good that the partyes that shall be licensed or authorized to print, may have their authorite with Condition, or otherwise bound to stand to the order of the Chancellor and the heades [of houses], in case of any cause of mis-lykyng of the use of the sayd authoritie.

Thomas Thomas was an M.A. of the University, and a Fellow of King's. He was born in 1553, had been educated at Eton, had gone up to King's as a scholar, and became Fellow in 1574. He was theologically trained, and a Cambridge puritan. He married Anne Sheres, widow of a bookbinder, and like his stationer-predecessors, including Siberch, entered the other book trades – in this case printing and bookselling – from the vantage-point of a quite prosperous bookbinding business.

The University was clearly minded to exercise its privilege, and equally clearly was going about it in a methodical way, securing its ground in advance. The support of Burghley being assured, on 3 May 1583 a Grace was passed appointing Thomas as printer. The Grace is much longer and more formal than its laconic predecessors; and it is natural to think that here too the Univer-sity was well aware that there was going to be trouble and was being quite careful to stake out the ground of any legal dispute:

Conceditur 3° Maii vt magister Thomas sit vnus ex tribus vestris librorum impressoribus cum omnibus privilegiis eiisdem impressoribus assignatis et super hac vestra concessione literas vestras habeat sigillatas sigillo vestro communi ea tamen conditione vt antequam hoc vestro privilegio gaudeat obligetur ad illas conditiones articulos et leges que prenobilis noster Cancellarius vicecancellarius et maior pars prefectorum collegiorum in scriptis indentatis assignabunt.

*Grace-Book* Δ, ed. Venn, 370

It was agreed on 3 May that Magister Thomas [i.e. Thomas was an M.A. of the University] should be one of your three printers of books with all the privileges assigned to those printers and on this your agreement he should have your Letters [Patent] sealed with your common seal on condition however that before he enjoys this your privilege he shall be sworn to those conditions, articles and laws which our noble Chancellor, Vice-Chancellor and the greater part of the Heads of Houses will set out in indentured articles.

The references to 'one of your three printers of books' and 'your privilege' clearly refer to the charter of 1534, which was to be the foundation of any case about the University's rights. This Grace of 1583 is a landmark in the history of the University, for it heralded the physical birth in 1584 of Cambridge University printing and publishing – for which the constitutional and legal foundation had been laid in 1534 by the Letters Patent of Henry VIII.

The Stationers' Company acted at once, seizing Thomas's press and types before they could be sent from London. This brought into the dispute yet another authority, John Aylmer, Bishop of London, who was the licensing authority whom the Stationers recognised. Aylmer, as they may have hoped, felt that his own prerogative was infringed and wrote a long letter to Burghley, enclosing a petition from the Stationers. The substance of the letter was that he, Aylmer, was responsible for seeing that printing was supervised, since it was all supposed to take place in London and he was the ecclesiastical authority there. Apart from the danger of heresy and sedition, there should not be too many printers because there was not enough work for them all. He had been backing the Stationers in their inquisitorial searches 'in secrete corners and Darke cellers'. 'There was alsoe found', he went on, 'one presse and furniture which is saide to belonge to one THOMAS a man (as I heare) vtterlie ignoraunte in printinge, and pretendinge that he entendeth to be the printer for the vniuersitie of Cambrige. This was stayed

amonge the rest till order taken. Herevppon master Doctor
BELL vicechauncellor of the vniuersitie hath written to me
requiring the same to be releassed....'

Bell had promptly sent Aylmer a copy of Burghley's letter
and the charter, being prepared for the emergency. Aylmer referred politely to these documents, saying that it was not his
wish to infringe the University's rights, but he wanted assur-
ance that they were not going to be used seditiously, or to the
prejudice of those who had rights of their own. These, of course,
were the Stationers, and Aylmer enclosed their long and plausible petition to him. This was a fairly lick-spittle document,
though some of the superfluous spittle could be observed to
lubricate the grinding of an axe. Printers outside London (it
said) would fear neither the Bishop nor the Company, would
teach apprentices badly, print seditious works, infringe copyrights, be unable to secure their own copyrights, and be generally troublesome. The Stationers gave a pretty clear hint that a
trade war was likely, and that they could both pirate Thomas's
books and deny him access to the London market. If one privilege was to be set against another, theirs was the stronger. If
Thomas would back down, the Stationers would compensate
him, and on the whole they thought that if they could persuade
him to do so 'we doe the said scholler a greate good turne, and
are a meane that he doe not vndoe himself'.

Neither the University nor Thomas felt like bowing to this
mixture of threat and blandishment. The Vice-Chancellor and
Heads of Houses (the University's 'cabinet', so to speak) wrote
to Burghley as follows:

To the right honourable the Lord Treasurer of England and most lovinge
Chauncelor of the universitie of Cambridge, 14 June 1583.

Our humble duties to your honour remembered. Whereas we vnderstande
by your honours lettres, that certaine of the company of the Stationers in
London haue sought to hinder therectinge of a print within this vniuersity
of Cambridge and to impugne the auntient privilege graunted and confirmed by divers Princes for that purpose to the great benefitt of the
vniuersitie and advauncement of Learning. Theise are in most humble
manner to desire your honour not so much in respect of Master Thomas
(who hath alredy receaved great iniury and damage at theire handes) as in
behalf of the vniuersity (which findeth yt self very much agreved with the

wrongfull detayninge of those goodes wherewithall as we are persuaded in right and equity they ought not to meddle) to continue our honorable patron, and to direct your favourable warrant to the wardeynes of the Stationers that he may haue his presse delivered with speede, lest that by their meanes as he hath bene dissappoynted of Master Whittakers his book, so by theire delayes he be prevented of other bookes made within the vniversity, and now redy for the presse. As for the dowbtes which they [the Stationers] rase (rather in respect of theire private gaine and commodity, and to bring the universitys more auncient priuiledges in this behalf then theirs vnder theire jurisdicion at London, then for any other good consideracon, the decidinge or perill whereof also partaineth not to them) we dare vndertake in the behalf of Master Thomas whome we know to be a very godly and honest man that the presse shall not be abused eyther in publishinge thinges prohibited, or otherwise inconvenient for the Churche and state of this realme. And this we promisse the rather for that his grace (whereof we haue sent a coppy to your honour by him self) was graunted vnto him vpon condicion that he shoulde stand bounde from tyme to tyme to such articles as your honour and the greatest part of the heades of Colledges should tye him vnto. And for the conference wherevnto your honour moveth us, yf yt shalbe your honour's pleasure we as desirous of peace and concorde (the premisses considered) shalbe ready to shewe our willingnes therevnto, yf yt shall please the company of the Stationers in London to sende hither some certaine menne from them with sufficient aucthority for that purpose. Thus most humbly desiringe that his presse may no longer be stayde, and hopinge that your honour will furder our desire hearein, we do in our dayly prayers commend your lordshippe to the blessed tuicon of the almighty. From Cambridge, this 14. of June.

your Lordships most bounde

|  |  |
|---|---|
|  | Jhon Bell Vicechancellor |
| Robert Norgate | Andrew Pern |
| Edmund Hownds | William Fulke |
| Thomas Nevile | John Still |
|  | Tho Legge |
|  | Edmund Barwell |

It was a well-considered letter, and led to the first and briefest of many truces. The press and furniture were released, and Thomas printed at least six books with them in 1584. But the books themselves caused further trouble. The one by Whitaker, mentioned in the appeal to Burghley, was an indication of the kind of thing Thomas and his friends and sponsors wanted to publish. William Whitaker was a noted Calvinist controversialist, Regius Professor of Divinity, Master of St John's, the

centre of a good deal of strife and by no means an uncontro-
versial first choice. In June 1584 Thomas played into the hands
of his watching enemies by printing a book by Walter Travers.
It was a translation of the original Latin treatise of 1574 on
Church government, edited by Thomas Cartwright, Fellow of
Trinity and Lady Margaret's Professor of Divinity, and another
stormy petrel of puritanism, who had like Whitaker made a
reputation as a trouble-maker in the previous generation.

And now yet another authority entered the dispute. The
current Archbishop of Canterbury was John Whitgift, who had
been Lady Margaret's Professor, Regius Professor, Master of
Pembroke, Master of Trinity, and twice Vice-Chancellor. He
can be taken to have retained a love of the University, but he
had a greater love of order and was a sharp reprover of young
activists. He wrote to Burghley about the new developments in
a depressive vein:

Ever sens I hard that they had a printer in Chambridge I dyd greatlie fear
that this and such like inconveniences wold followe, nether do I thingk that
yt wyll so stay, for allthowgh Mr Vicechancellor that now ys, be a verie
careful man and in all respectes greatlie to be commended, yet yf yt may
fawle owt hereafter, that some such as shal succeade hym wyll not be so well
affected, nor have such care for the publike peace of the Church, and of the
state, but whatsoever your Lordship shall thingk good to be done in this
matter, or wyll have me to signifie to Mr Vicechancellor ether in your name
or in my owne yf yt shall please you to signifye the same to Mr Dene of
Westminster or otherwise I wyll performe yt accordinglie. I thingk yt verie
convenient that the bokes shold be burned, being veri factius and full of
untruthes: and that (yf printing do styll there continew) sufficient bonds
with suerties shold be taken of the printer not to print anie bokes, unlesse
they be first allowed by lawfull authoritie, for yf restrante be made here, and
libertie graunted there, what good can be done. The boke ys the same which
Travers ys supposed to have sett forth in Laten, without anie addition or
retraction.

Thomas lost two battles: the book by Whitaker seems not to
have been printed at all, and the book by Travers was so effectively suppressed that no copy survives. But he won the campaign as a whole because the University was determined to back
him. His position was constitutionally secured. He was reappointed University Printer by a Grace of 11 February 1585/6,

# FABVLARVM

## OVIDII INTERPRE-
TATIO, ETHICA, PHYSICA, ET
Hiftorica, tradita in Academia Regiomontana à
GEORGIO SABINO, & in vnum collecta &
edita ftudio & induftria T. T.

*Acceffit etiam ex Natalis Comitis Mythologys
de fabularum vtilitate, varietate, partibus &
fcriptoribus, deق́ apologorum, fabularum, æno-
rumق́ differentia, tractatio.*

Cum Indice verborum & rerum præcipuarum in
Ouidio & Sabino comprehenfarum.

CANTABRIGIÆ,
Ex officina Thomæ Thomæ celeberrimæ Aca-
demiæ Cantabrigienfis Typographi.
1 5 8 4.

Two of Thomas Thomas's publications of 1584. The interpretation
of Ovid is edited by Thomas himself (the T.T. of the title-page).

# TWO TREATISES
## OF THE LORD HIS
### HOLIE SVPPER:

## THE ONE INSTRVCTING THE
### SERVANTS OF GOD HOW THEY
ſhould be prepared when they come to the
holy Supper of our onely Sauiour
Ieſus Chriſt:

*Whereunto is annexed a Dialogue conteining the principall
points neceſſarie to be knowne and vnderſtood of all them
that are to be partakers of the holy Supper:*

The other ſetting forth Dialoguewiſe the whole vſe of
the Supper: Whereunto alſo is adioyned a briefe
and learned treatiſe of the true Sacrifice and true
Prieſt.

*Written in the French tongue by Yues Rouſſeau and Iohn de
l'Eſpine Miniſters of the word of God, and latelie tranſla-
ted into Engliſh.*

I. CORINTH. II. 28.  Let a man examine himſelfe, and ſo let
him eate of this bread, and drinke of this cup.

IOHN 6. 58.  This is the bread which came downe from
heauen: not as your fathers haue eaten Manna, and are dead.
He that eateth of this bread, ſhall liue for euer.

PSAL. 51. 16.  Thou deſireſt no ſacrifice, though we would
giue it: thou deliteſt not in burnt offering. The ſacrifices of
God are a contrite ſpirit: a contrite and broken heart, O God,
thou wilt not deſpiſe.

Imprinted by Thomas Thomas Printer to the
Vniuerſitie of Cambridge.
1584.

and on the same day entered into a bond with the University to the effect that his materials should be good, his prices fair, his books not seditious, that the University authorities should license his publications, and that he would give a copy of everything he printed to the University Library. There was a further Grace to the effect that, because the Stationers were pirating, or threatening to pirate, the books printed at Cambridge and Oxford, only the original printings were to be sold in the University. For in 1585 the University of Oxford too began to issue books from its printing house; and this may have helped to bring about the Star Chamber ordinance of 1586 which limited the number of master-printers and of apprentices nationally, and specified that no book was to be printed without the approval of the Archbishop or the Bishop of London – obviously an attempt to retain a central control by censorship. It was also decreed in the same ordinance that the two universities should employ only one apprentice each – an effective way of limiting output.

In 1586, Thomas was in theological trouble again. Whitgift wrote to the Vice-Chancellor of Cambridge late in the year:

To my very loving friend the vicechancellor, &c.

Salutem in Christo. I doo understand that there is nowe in printinge by the Printer of that Universitie a certen book called Harmonia Confessionum fidei in English, translated out of Latin; which book for some speciall causes was here reiected, and not allowed to bee printed. Theis are therefore to requyre you, that presently upon receipt hereof you cause the sayd book, to be stayed from printing any furder; and that nothing bee done more therein, untill you shall receave furder direction from mee. And whereas there is order taken of late by the Lordes of the Councile that from hensefourth no book shall bee imprinted either in London, or in any of the Vniversitees, unlesse the same shall bee allowed and authorized by the Bishopp of London or myself, I doo lykewise requyre you to take speciall care that hereafter nothing bee imprinted in that Vniversitee of Cambridge, but what shall bee authorized accordingly. And so not doubting of your diligent circumspection herein, I committ you to the tuition of almighty god. From my House at Croyden, the VIIIth of August, 1586.

Your loving Frende in Christe
Jo: Cantuar.

There was no response to this. The book was published in the same year, so it was presumably found unobjectionable in

Cambridge. But in any case the University had clearly been given in 1534 its own power to approve the books it licensed for publication; and would be inclined to assert its own right against Star Chamber. Moreover all these centralising efforts at control broke down on practical grounds. By the 1580s books were being published in England at such a rate that no central licensing authority could possibly have kept up: it is reckoned that well over four thousand titles were published in the period 1580–1603. The only practical course, therefore, despite Whitgift's gloomy reservations, was to trust to the University's own sense of responsibility in matters of religion and politics. That, however, would not solve the other problem – the monopolising tendencies of the London Stationers, and their specific claims to certain titles or categories, which were in evident conflict with the University's claim that it had the right to print 'all manner of books' provided only that they were approved by the University itself. That conflict was not going to be quickly resolved, and more must be said about it below, since the struggle between the University and the Stationers is the main constitutional element in the first century of the history of the young University Press, and it was on that anvil that the nature of the University's aspirations and obligations as a publisher began to be hammered out. It started as an assertion of one prerogative against another: Cambridge's Letters Patent, enabling it to print 'all manner of books', against the charter of the Stationers' Company, empowering it to restrict printing and publishing to its members in London; together with the specific monopolies enjoyed by certain of those members. It turned into something much more principled as the University reflected on its position: there was first a somewhat angry and perhaps *ex parte* economic argument – that the University must see that its members, who *had* to buy books, were not overcharged by monopolists. There followed a more mature and disinterested ambition: the University had to be free to disseminate certain works (of education, religion, learning, and research, in the modern phrase) as a natural part of its primary function as a place where knowledge was pursued for its own sake. That all had to become clear through the clouds of a long-continued dispute set off by the generous or politic grants made to different persons in the past by monarchs who were concerned only with the single issue of the then present moment.

Meanwhile the person at the centre of the struggle was Thomas Thomas who, with one press, perhaps two or three journeymen-printers and an apprentice, worked in his shop in the Regent Walk, a long-demolished row of houses immediately opposite the west door of Great St Mary's. He died young – he was only thirty-five – and was buried, like his stationer predecessors, in Great St Mary's churchyard in 1588. In the five years or so in which he worked for the University he printed some twenty books. They included the controversial puritan writings of Whitaker and the *Harmony of Confessions*; an edition of Ovid's *Fables* edited by Thomas himself; an important textbook, Peter Ramus's *Dialecticae*; and of course Thomas's own Latin Dictionary.

We can discern here, as in Siberch's publications, the outline of an editorial policy. Whitaker catered for the serious intellectual interest of the age, which was at once religious and political. Ovid and Ramus were texts, with the chance of a fair local sale to Cambridge students. The Dictionary, a standard work of reference, was Thomas's own work. Like all lexicographers, he built on the work of others: Starnes and Allan Stevenson have shown that he used Guillaume Morel's Latin-French dictionary as adapted into English by Henry Bynneman – the holder of the patent for dictionaries. But Thomas introduced his own adaptation, using another dictionary by Cooper to produce a third distinct identity, which included aids to pronunciation. The effect was to produce the most serviceable and widely used beginners' Latin dictionary of the time. It was much reprinted by Thomas's successors as University Printers, and constituted one of the staple sellers, the good 'backlist' titles, which all publishers need to have in quantity. In the eleventh Cambridge edition of 1619 John Legate paid this tribute to the compiler:

He was about 30 years ago a famous Printer among your Cantabrigians; yes something more than a Printer such as we now are, who understand the Latin that we print no more than Bellerophon the letters he carried, and who sell in our shops nothing of our own except the paper *black with the press's sweat*. But he, a companion of the Stephenses [the Estiennes, the great dynasty of scholar-printers in Paris and Geneva] and of the other, very few, printers of the true kind and best omen, was of opinion that it was men of learning, thoroughly imbued with academic studies, who should give themselves to cultivating and rightly employing that illustrious benefit sent down from heaven and given to aid mankind and perpetuate the arts. Accordingly what more fit than that when he had wrought what was worthy of type, he should himself, needing aid of none, act as midwife to his own progeny.

Words and thoughts like that go to the making of a tradition. Yet to descend to the reality of the market-place of the time, Thomas's Dictionary was an obvious infringement of Bynneman's monopoly, and the Stationers pointed out that it should have been given to him to print and publish. The University, realising that it had engaged in a long struggle in which it could not afford to relax its vigilance, despatched a letter to Burghley which is worth quoting at length because of the terms in which the University's case is made:

Oure humble duety to youre Honour remembred, &c. Wheras ther hath bene an ancyent privilege, graunted to this Vniuersitie for the mysterie of printinge, and the same by her most excellent Maiestie in oure Charter most gratiously confirmed, and of late yeares by your honours favourable approbation put in practyse: May it please your Honour to vnderstand, that the case standing as yt dothe, we finde yt a verie hard matter, eyther for oure Vniuersitie to maynteine this royall privilege, or for oure Printer to doe anie good by his trade, by reason of the Companie of Stationers and Prynters in London: who as they have heretofore taken divers of his Copies and printed them againe, to his greate losse and hinderance, so doe they still threaten to attempt the lyke hereafter: namely and specially, with a Dictionarie of his owne compiling, and lately set oute by him: and this they challenge as their owne right and proper Copie, by vertue of a generall Clawse, graunted to them from her Maiestie *To prynte all Dictionaries whatsoever*: which generall Clawse, eyther for Dictionaries or anie other bookes, if vnder your Honours correction we may interprete, in our judgment extendeth to suche bookes and Dictionaries only, as were then extant, when this graunt was made, and not to any that should afterward come forthe. For elles might yt be verie preiudiciall, and hinder the setting forth of manie good and profitable bookes, if learned men might not make choyse of their printer, eyther to reape the frute of their laboures themselves, or otherwise bestowe them on whome they thought good: but must all come to the printers in London only, and have their workes publisht by them.

Whiche practyse of their supposed privilege, hath already greatly discouraged and almost utterly disabled our Printer to goe forward in his trade: in so muche as we perceave, yf it be not looked unto in tyme, yt will tourne to the vtter overthrowe of printing in our Vniversitie for ever. Thes reasons thus moving vs, we are bold to become humble suters to your honoure, that you would be so good patrone, as to oure wholle Vniversitie at all tymes, so to oure pore Printer at this tyme, as to become a meanes to her highnes in this behalf, that as of her gratious goodnes heretofore she hathe confirmed our Charter for the mysterie of Printing, so nowe also it may please her Maiestie of her prerogative royall to graunt a speciall lycence for to privilege to our Printer, as well the forsayde Dictionarie of late by him set forthe, as also hereafter from tyme to tyme anie suche booke or bookes, as he shall lawfully and according to order appointed in that behalf, print, or cawse to be printed: So as both we may mainteyne a print in oure Vniversitie with credyt, according to her Maiesties intent and the tenore of our Charter, and also oure Printer may followe his trade with some profyt, and not be molested, as heretofore, to his great hinderance and impayring of his pore stock. Thus hoping that as you are wont, so still your honour will be readie to procure her Maiestie to shewe this, and all other gratious favour, nedefull for the maintenance of good learning, to her pore Vniversitie, we cease for this tyme to trouble your Honour any further: beseching the Almightie to blesse you and all yours, with long continuance and greate increase of true honour to the good of this his Churche and common wealthe. Cambridge the first of maye, 1588

Youre honours most humble to commaunde,

Thomas Legge, Procan'

| Thomas Preston | Umphry Tyndall | Andrew Pern |
| Lawrence Chaderton | John Copcot: | John Still |
| | Guil. Whitaker | Roger Goade |

The University had, in 1585, taken a more positive step by passing a Grace prohibiting Cambridge booksellers from buying any book printed in London or elsewhere which had been or should have been printed at Cambridge or Oxford, thus displaying solidarity with the sister university which had begun the same struggle very shortly after Cambridge. It was a retaliation of a sort; but of course the major market was in London itself, and that market was needed by the University Printers of Cambridge and Oxford who could nct survive without it. In that sense the London Stationers always had an advantage, and they had another in that they could always undercut the prices of the university presses, especially in the market for popular books, such as schoolbooks. It is a tribute to the ingenuity and persistence of the universities in maintaining their right against superior opposition that they survived and eventually prospered. They did so, I suggest, because it was finally recognised that a university press fulfilled a special function and was not merely a commercial competitor.

# 5

## EARLY PRINTERS:
## JOHN LEGATE, CANTRELL LEGGE,
## BUCK AND DANIEL

THOMAS'S SUCCESSOR as Printer, John Legate, was appointed
by Grace of 2 November 1588, was active in Cambridge until
1601 and died in 1620. He was a freeman of the Stationers'
Company, which might have slightly softened the Company's
attitude towards him, but he quickly found himself embroiled
in the same disputes as Thomas: his books were pirated by the
Company, which complained for its part that he was infringing
its rights. In particular he printed a New Testament in (?)1590
and a whole Bible in 1591. This was the Geneva version, then
the most popular of the English versions and appealing particularly to the puritan wing of the English Church. Legate's
edition was an octavo, in roman type of a small size, and had
all the features which gave the Geneva Bible in that format its
powerful commercial lead over the Bishops' Bible: handy size,
modern type-face (the Bishops' Bible was printed in black-
letter), copious if tendentious notes, and some supplementary
aids.

This was a most important precedent. Bibles could of course
be printed in Scotland, which was still in those days another
kingdom. But until now in England only one book of Scripture
had been printed outside London – a New Testament printed
at Worcester by John Oswen in 1551, an isolated occurrence
which predated Mary's reign, the incorporation of the Stationers'
Company, and the Royal Printer's Patent given to Barker. Since
1577 it had been accepted that the Bible was not just a London
monopoly, but the special privilege of the Royal Printer. Legate's
initiative was very much a test case. If the University could

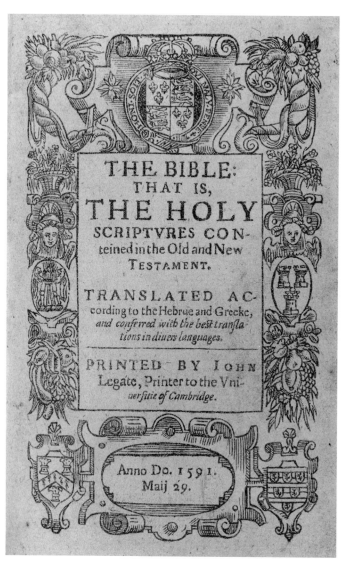

THE BIBLE:
THAT IS,
THE HOLY
SCRIPTVRES CON-
teined in the Old and New
TESTAMENT.

TRANSLATED AC-
cording to the Hebrue and Greeke,
and conferred with the best translations in diuers languages.

PRINTED BY IOHN
Legate, Printer to the Vniuerſitie of Cambridge.

Anno Do. 1591.
Maij 29.

The first Cambridge Bible. John Legate's octavo gives the text of the Geneva version, which was the preferred version, especially among more puritan readers, until 1611.

prove that its charter was not limited by Barker's monopoly, the Bible would give any University Printer at Cambridge an assured market, for there was no other book which sold in such quantities or was assured of perpetual sale.

The dispute between the University and the Stationers therefore moved to a new ground, in which the most powerful interests of all were affected. Once again, the University was quick to back its Printer. Knowing that Barker was involved and would seek to prevent the sale of the Bible in London, the Vice-Chancellor and Heads wrote to Burghley in June 1591 seeking his protection. Another letter followed in July, reaching a forceful peroration:

Right honourable, and our singular good lord,

Such is the importunity of our adversaries, in devising against us new complaints, as we are forced eftsoons to renew our just defence, ever while they charge us as doing wrong to Mr. Barker, in printing a Bible of the lesser volume. Now they accuse us as offering like injury to Mr. Day, in publishing therewith the Psalms in metre. They seek, in dividing the persons, to make us seem guilty of many crimes. Whereas, in very truth, our printer having for his copy one only volume, wherein both those books are joined together, could not conveniently set forth the one without the other, seeing both do jointly and usually serve for the public celebration of divine service. The suit which they have made unto your lordship for the stay of our printer until the next term, is so prejudicial to the poor man, as if they should prevail therein, it could not but tend to his utter undoing; especially Sturbridge-fair now drawing near; being the chiefest time wherein he hopeth to reap greatest fruit of this his travail.

We are the rather therefore right humbly to crave of your good lordship, that if they cannot be pacified otherwise your lordship would be pleased to require the opinions of the master of the rolls, the lord chief Justice of the common pleas and Justice Peryam; who all or some of them, as we hear, either already are, or shortly will be there in London. Ourselves have conferred with divers of good skill of the laws of the land, who, not drawn to favour us in respect of our fee, but uttering freely their resolute judgment, find no just reason whereon the adverse party may safely rely. For the chief ground they seem to lay, viz. that the prince by virtue only of prerogative, may, by a later grant, either take away or abridge a former, being no ways hurtful to the state, is not only against the rule of natural equity, but also dangerous to all degrees, opening a way to the overthrow of all patents and privileges, as well of inferior trades, as of offices, lands and livings whatsoever.

We have not sought to call in question the validity of their monopolies and engrossments, whereby such effects do daily ensue, as poor scholars are either driven to be destitute of most needful books, or to buy them, to their singular hinderance, at excessive prizes. We shall account ourselves well appaid, if our poor printer may, with their good patience, now and then deal with some few of the most saleable copies for his necessary maintenance in honest art; if your honourable persuasion (whereunto it might well beseem him, in a case of such equity, to give better ear to) cannot induce them to yield to this, rather than our dutiful regard should seem to be wanting in the necessary defence of this our charter, so equitable in itself, so commodious to the students of the University, so beneficial to many other subjects of the realm, granted by her majesty's most noble father, ratified by the gracious bounty of herself, established by act of Parliament so many years past, may not be thought sufficient against their grant so late obtained, we know not upon what privilege we may hereafter repose our trust.

Wherefore once again most humbly beseeching your good lordship to continue your honourable favour toward the university, in preserving the ancient and lawful charters of the same. From Cambridge, the 16th of July, 1591.

| | |
|---|---|
| Robert Some, vice-chancellor, | Lawrence Chaderton, |
| William Whitaker, | Roger Goad, |
| Tho. Byng, | Umphrey Tyndal, |
| Tho. Legg, | Jo. Duport, |
| Tho. Preston, | |

Cooper, *Annals* II, 491–2

For a time there seems to have been a truce: there is no record of actual dispute between the University and the Stationers until 1620, when hostilities began again. It may partly be due to the fact that Legate very effectively healed the personal breach pantomime-fashion, by marrying the daughter of Christopher Barker and becoming Master of the Stationers' Company in 1604. He left Cambridge in 1601, but retained the title of Printer to the University until his death in 1620. He inaugurated the recurrent practice of seeking a working accommodation with the Stationers as an alternative to hostilities.

Legate's printing and publishing has a certain interest. He regularly reprinted Thomas's Dictionary. He also printed in 1603, the year of the new King's accession, a translation of James I's *A Prince's Looking Glasse*, which no doubt pleased the royal author. Printed by Legate's successor in 1616 (and re-printed in 1619) there followed James's *A Remonstrance for the Right of Kings*, which opens an important constitutional topic. James was more moderate on this matter than his son, who ultimately died for just this cause. James was so far from being a total autocrat that he (somewhat autocratically) had a Cambridge book suppressed in 1610. It was called *The Interpreter* (1607), and the author was John Cowell, Master of Trinity Hall, a distinguished lawyer, who here strayed into dangerous territory. He held the view that 'The King is above the law by his absolute power', and James either thought this was not true or did not want it said: or, to his credit, both.

Another sign of the same storm brewing was David Owen's *Herod and Pilate Reconciled* (also 1610). Ralph Brownrigg, Fellow of Pembroke, read it, invited Owen to his rooms and questioned him as to whether a king breaking fundamental laws might be opposed. Owen himself was nervous or offended, but the Vice-Chancellor trumped Brownrigg's suit by reminding him that he, the Vice-Chancellor, with three doctors had approved the book for printing, so that Brownrigg was out of order for questioning his authority. What is more, he had propounded seditious views to Owen. On both grounds he was therefore deprived of his degrees in the Vice-Chancellor's court. Brownrigg recanted and was reinstated. As so often in these academic teacup-storms, no harm seems to have been done, so long as there was a climb-down; Brownrigg eventually became Bishop of Exeter.

In 1603 Legate printed two volumes of celebratory verse, one called *Threno-thriambeuticon Academiae Cantabrigiensis ob damnum lucrosum & infoelicitatem foelicissimam, luctuosus triumphus*; the other, more or less translating the first: *Sorrowes Joy or a Lamentation for our late deceased Soveraigne Elizabeth with a triumph for the prosperous Succession of our gracious King James.* These collections, usually of Latin verse, were issued throughout the century (indeed they went on well into the eighteenth century) to mark royal births, marriages and deaths. In the last case, the occasion called for what Shakespeare called 'one auspicious and one dropping eye': the university poets were required to maintain with aplomb that they were prostrate with grief and, at once and no less, transported with joy, both requiring elegant expression. The volumes taken together provide a roll-call of Cambridge poets, statesmen and divines: in these two collections Phineas Fletcher; John Boys, who was to be one of the chief translators and editors of the Bible of 1611; Matthew Wren, later Bishop of Ely; Albert Morton, later Secretary of State; Stephen Perse, the great benefactor of Cambridge; John Williams, later Archbishop of York; and Andrew Downes, later Regius Professor of Greek. One point to remember about these volumes was that in assuring the Monarch of the loyalty of his University of Cambridge, they also reminded him that it had a Press: and he might be asked to maintain the rights of both. For similar reasons, whenever a royal person visited Cambridge in later years (and from James's reign onwards the Stuarts liked to go to Newmarket, often stayed at Royston, and several times visited the University en route) he or she was always presented with a Bible. We can be sure that it was printed in Cambridge, and that its superior elegance and accuracy were pointed out.

Legate's principal author, his best-seller, was the 'learned, pious and painful' William Perkins, formerly Fellow of Christ's, and a great puritan preacher in the 1580s and 1590s. Porter writes of Perkins:

Between 1590 and 1618 John Legate and Cantrill Legge printed nearly 210 books at Cambridge: of these, over fifty were works by Perkins. Before Perkins's death in 1602, Legate had printed over twenty of his works, beginning with *Armilla Aurea* in 1590; and some of them had run into three editions. A one-volume collected edition of Perkins's works appeared in 1600. After his death the flow continued: until there came from the Cambridge Press in 1616 to 1618 a revised three-volume edition, containing nearly forty separate titles. Some of these were translations of Latin treatises: 'A Golden Chain' (the English version of *Armilla Aurea*) by Robert Hill, Fellow of St John's; *The Art of Prophesying*, translated by Thomas Tuke; the treatise on predestination (to which Arminius wrote a reply), by Tuke and Francis Cacot; *Christian Economy*, by Thomas Pickering...a Fellow of Emmanuel, who edited Perkins's three books of *Cases of Conscience*, first published in 1606. Perkins's other posthumous editors were Thomas Taylor, Fellow of Christ's, one of his 'ordinary hearers in Cambridge', who saw through the press the *Sermons of Jude* in 1608; William Crashaw, Robert Hill, Ralph Cudworth, and Thomas Pierson.... Crashaw also edited the *Exhortation to Repentance*...which appeared in 1605. In the preface to this work, Crashaw took occasion to 'humbly praise the Lord of heaven, who gave me my time in the university, in those happy days, wherein (besides many worthy men of God, whereof some are fallen asleep and some remain alive unto this day) this holy man did spend himself like a candle, to give light unto others'.

Porter, Reformation and Reaction, 264–5

As a young man Perkins had got himself into trouble as a precisian: he had once in a sermon in the chapel of Christ's condemned the practice of kneeling when receiving the sacrament, and turning the face to the East. Called before the Vice-Chancellor, he was understood to have explained himself more fully. He was certainly less fierce than the H. Gray who on 8 January 1586/7 (i.e. just after the Christmas festival) had preached in Great St Mary's a sermon 'wherein he asserted that the Church of England maintained Jewish music, and that to play at dice or cards was to crucify Christ; inveighed against dumb dogs in the Church and mercenary ministers; insinuated that some in the University sent news to Rome and Rheims [i.e. to the English Catholic exiles]; and asserted that the people celebrated the nativity as ethnicks, atheists and epicures'. Gray too was called on to explain himself, and obviously had more to explain. Perkins was less violent and more spiritual, but had a vein of pious gallery-playing, as Fuller observed:

He would pronounce the word Damne with such an emphasis as left a doleful Echo in his auditours ears a good while after. And when catechist of Christ-Colledge, in expounding the Commandments, applied them so home, able almost to make his hearers hearts fall down, and hairs to stand upright.

The lasting and wide-ranging importance of Perkins, as Porter points out, was that the early settlers of New England included a hundred Cambridge men, six of whom had been Fellows of Colleges, and four of whom became Heads of Harvard College. They took with them the books which had formed their faith, and the sermons preached to Cambridge congregations by Perkins in the 1580s and 1590s, published in book form and carried across the Atlantic, moulded the piety of a whole nation as one of 'the most quoted, most respected, and most influential of contemporary authors in the writings and sermons of early Massachusetts' (Perry Miller, quoted by Porter).

Legate's successors as University Printers were Cantrell Legge, appointed in 1606; Leonard Greene, appointed in 1622; and

The first use of the Cambridge emblem, on the title-page of Legate's edition of Perkins's *A Golden Chaine*, 1600.

Thomas Buck, who was appointed in 1625, became founder of a dynasty of Cambridge printers, and either alone or in partnership appears and reappears until 1668.

Cantrell Legge had been John Legate's apprentice in London in 1589. This might at first have implied good relationships with the Stationers, but in 1620 hostilities broke out again: Legge had printed Lily's Grammar, the best-selling schoolbook, and the Company prosecuted him. This caused the University to look to its defences, and dignified Latin letters were sent to the Archbishop of Canterbury and to the Lord Chancellor, Lord Verulam (Francis Bacon, a Trinity man). The essence of the University's complaint was that the London Stationers charged high prices, and resented being undercut by the University Printer; and that the University must at least protect its own students from exploitation.

In 1621 the King passed through Royston, and the University seized the opportunity to present its case to the Crown as supreme tribunal. Legge accompanied a small deputation which

rode out to Royston, and delivered a petition. It is worth repro-
ducing in full:

To the Kings most Excellent Majestie<br>
The humble Petition of the Vice Chancellour & Heads of the Universitie<br>
of Cambridge

Most humblie sheweth

That whereas King Henry the VIII[th] by his Charter graunted to the
Chauncellour, Masters and Scholars of the Universitie of Cambridge the
XXVI[th] of his reigne authorised them to nominate & choose 3 stationers &
printers & gave them power to print all manner of bookes allowed & to be
allowed by the Vice-Chancellour, & 3 Doctors there, which charter is also
confirmed by Act of Parliamen XIII° Eliz & is since ratified by yr Majestie
II° of your Highness Raigne. Since which graunt one Mr Norton and
other Stationers Printers of London have procured from Your Majestie
divers Letters Patents by virtue of which they challenge to themselves the
sole printing and sale of the cheife vendible books in this lande. And have
also by colour of a Charter graunted to the Compnie of Stationers & strength
of other decrees and orders (which they have procured or made amongst
themselves) combined together that none of their Companie shall retayle any
bookes but those which are of their own coppies, or which they have
ingrossed from a poore Printer after 8 or 9s the Reame, that they may
retayle them after 20s to the great hinderance of learning & grievance of all
your Majesties subjects who are forced by their practises to pay vis–viiid in
xxs nay some 2 parts in 3 dearer for those books they have thus in Patent or
have ingrossed them otherwise they would and might be sold for.

By which their unconscionable dealing yr Petitioners perceiving their
cheif ayme was to overthrowe all Printers but their own Companie, and that
they abused the whole Common-wealth in the excessive prices of their
bookes bad paper and false printing. They licensed their Printer to imprint
Lilly's grammar which he (having printed amended & corrected of many
grosse faults) offered to sell the same a 3rd part cheaper than they did.
Whereupon Mr Norton who had (as he sayth) procured the sole printing
thereof to himselfe and yet farmed out the same for 300l fine and 300l rent
per annum, procured from your Majestie an order to restraine your Petitioners Printer from the sale of his books and also seized upon others of
them to the utter undoeing of the poore Printer.

Now for that the benefitt intended to the Vniversitie by their Charter is
utterly taken away, and all your Majesties subjects are abused by the said
Stationers printers May it therefore please your most excellent Majestie to
take us and this cause into your gratious protection, and either to sett down
such order therein as in your Princely care and favour to your universitie
you shall think fittest for the restoring of so great a benefit granted to so
fitt a place for the advancement of learning, reliefe of their poore Printer &

the generall good of the whole kingdom or to appoint Committes to heare, examine and finally determine these wronges & grievances which are moved & complayned of. And your Petitioners shall &c.

The King took the second course suggested to him: he asked the Archbishop, the Bishop of Lincoln, Lord Maundeville and the Lord Chief Justice to look into the matter. These great men 'having not tyme to discuss the Rights & Interests of the University and the Stationers at this praesent by reason of other severall and distracted imployments' gave an interim ruling that 'the Poore printer of the University' might sell the grammars in question without prejudice to the general claim of the Stationers.

However, the Stationers had their usual advantage: nobody could force them as booksellers to buy and retail the University's product, and they simply refused to do so, and (it is thought) 'leaned on' other booksellers who might be disposed to do so. The University in retaliation did what it could: it passed a Grace in June 1622 forbidding booksellers in Cambridge to buy from or sell to Bill, Norton, Barrett and Knight of London, or any partners of theirs; stipulating that the copyright in any book printed by a University Printer should pass after his death to other holders of the position; and that any graduate of the University who wrote a book should offer it to the University, and if he were a teacher should make his pupils use only Cambridge-printed books.

That showed spirit, but was hardly enforceable. The Privy Council, having deliberated on the dispute, offered a compromise ruling in 1623 which cannot have been to the University's liking: the University was not to print Bibles, grammars, psalms, psalters, primers or books of common law, and should print no almanacs 'but such whereof the first copy should be brought to them'. By another order, the University was not to print Books of Common Prayer; but was to have the right to print any other book of which the first copy was brought to it. Furthermore, it was to have only one press.

There must have been rejoicing among the members of the Stationers' Company. But to lose one battle is not the end; the University was engaged in a long and mostly well-conducted campaign. The end of a reign, for instance, produced another Monarch, who might be approached. Charles I came to the throne in 1625, and was duly presented with a volume called *Cantabrigiensium Dolor & Solamen: seu Decessio Beatissimi Regis Jacobi Pacifici et successio Augustissimi Regis Caroli Magnae Britanniae Galliae & Hiberniae Monarchae.* In 1626 the University elected the Duke of Buckingham as its Chancellor at the express wish of the King. It was a contested election, which caused a stir, all the more so because Buckingham was being impeached by the House of Commons. So the University had the Monarch's good will, at the price of that of the Commons. In the course of the heated discussion which was caused by the election, the King told the Commons

That the University of Cambridge and all Corporations derive their Right and Privelege from him; and that he hath Reason to esteem the Universities above any other, and is resolved to defend them against any, which either wilfully or by chance shall go about to infringe their liberties.

That must have fallen very pleasantly on Cambridge ears. Buckingham visited the University in 1626/7, and was 'wonderfull courteous to all Schollers of any condition both in the Regent House where every one that came in had his Grace's Congie & in the Towne as he walked if a man did but stir his Hatt he should not loose his labour'. The University must have made use of this affability: and perhaps it is no surprise that on 6 February 1627/8 the King gave it a new charter:

After reciting the grant to the University of the 26th Henry VIII., respecting Printers, the general parliamentary confirmation of the University Charters, the charters of the Company of Stationers of London, a decree made in the Star Chamber, in the 28th Eliz., a proclamation for the observance of that decree, 25 September, 21 Jac. I., and that doubts had arisen whether the University Printers could print and sell any of the books specified in the grants to the Company of Stationers: in order to abolish all such ambiguities, to put an end to all controversies, and for the encouragement of learning, the King ratified the grant made to the University by Henry VIII., and declared that the University by their Stationers and Printers might print and expose to sale within the University or elsewhere within his dominions, all books which he or Queen Elizabeth, or King James the first, had licensed any person or persons, bodies politic or corporate whatsoever, to sell, and also all other books whatsoever printed or to be printed, or which had been or should be by the Chancellor, &c., allowed as fit to be put to sale, any letters patent, or any prohibition, restraint, clause, or article, in any letters patent whatsoever, notwithstanding.

Cooper, *Annals* III, 199

It can be seen that, in general terms, this charter repeated the grant of Henry VIII in 1534. The University must have been pleased; but since the whole struggle with the Stationers turned on how conflicting charters were to be implemented, the situation was not made clearer. Another test case seems to have been instigated by the Stationers in 1629, and once again the University's right was upheld: the Lord Chief Justices stated that they had conferred with the Lord Chief Baron and other judges, and all had agreed that the three stationers and printers of books in the University of Cambridge, chosen and appointed by the Chancellor, Masters, and Scholars under the University Seal, might by law print there all manner of books approved by the Chancellor or Vice-Chancellor and Doctors of the University notwithstanding any patents for sole printing.

Very shortly after, in April 1629, the Privy Council made an order that the University might print any number of English Bibles in quarto and medium folio formats, with the liturgy in the same volume, and the singing psalms at the end, but not these alone without the Bibles (Legge had produced such an edition in 1623). The University might also print three thousand copies of Lily's Grammar every year. This measure offered a working compromise, and so gave the embattled parties a *modus vivendi*. In fact the arrangement favoured the Stationers, since the most popular format for the Bible with the psalter was the cheaper octavo, and the market for grammars far exceeded three thousand copies. But the University was being offered an agreed share; and it was better to have agreement than continual litigation. It was reasonable to take the ruling as confirming, rather than limiting, Cambridge's rights.

Thomas and John Buck did in 1629 print the first Cambridge edition of the now overwhelmingly popular new Bible which had been proposed at the Hampton Court Conference of 1604, when the puritan John Reynolds moved that there should be a fresh translation of the Bible. James I had accepted the pro-

posal and made himself in some sense the patron of the enterprise: so that although the Bible published in 1611 was never
formally authorised by Church and Parliament, and the English
name 'Authorized Version' is not strictly accurate, the American name 'King James Bible' is appropriate. The new version
was produced with exemplary speed, largely because the translators set themselves the task not of producing a completely
new version but of crowning the English tradition of Biblical
translation, which went back through the Bishops' Bible of
1568, the Geneva version of 1560, and the Great Bible of 1539
to the pioneers Tyndale and Coverdale. As the preface to the
King James Bible put it:

wee never thought from the beginning, that we should neede to make a new
Translation, nor yet to make of a bad one a good one, . . . but to make a good
one better, or out of many good ones, one principall good one, not justly to
be excepted against; that hath bene our indeavour, that our mark.

The work was done by 'companies' of translators, from the
universities of Cambridge and Oxford, and in Westminster.
Most notable among the Cambridge scholars were Lancelot
Andrewes, then Dean of Westminster, later Bishop of Chiches-
ter, formerly Master of Pembroke; his brother Roger, later
Master of Jesus; Lawrence Chaderton, Master of Emmanuel;
and John Boys, Fellow of Clare and later Dean of Canterbury.
As everyone knows, the Bible was published in 1611: but it is
not so generally known that what we should now call the subediting or copy-preparation of the text was defective, and the
printing, by Barker, was necessarily hasty, and in many ways
unsatisfactory. The rapid reprints which followed and were
quickly exhausted did not improve the text: rather they tended
to corrupt it further. Everyone has also heard of the so-called
'wicked Bible' of 1631 for which Robert Barker and Martin
Lucas were fined £200 and £100 for having left out the word
'not' in the seventh commandment. Ten years or so before,

Dr Usher, Bishop of Armath, being to preach at Paule's Crosse, and
passing hastily by one of the Stationers, call'd for a Bible, and had a little
one of the London edition given him out; but when he came to looke for his
text, that very verse was omitted in the print; which gave the first occasion
of complaints to the King of the insufferable negligence and insufficiencie of

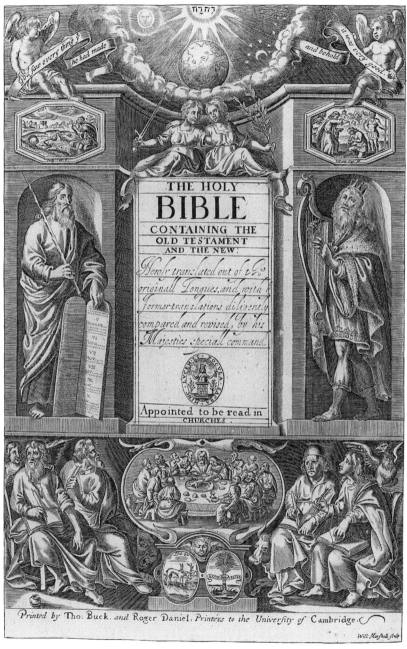

Thomas Buck and Roger Daniel: the folio Bible of 1638. The engraved general title-page.

the London printers and presse, and bredde that great contest that followed betwixt the University of Cambridge and London Stationers about printing of the Bibles.

Thoms's Anecdotes, cit. Cooper, *Annals* III, 142, n.

By the time the brothers Buck printed their first folio Bible, there had been nearly twenty years of such reprinting dictated by commercial considerations. But there were still available to a conscientious printer the surviving members of the original companies of translators, and there is evidence that Buck and Daniel were able to secure at least two of the Cambridge translators as editors. Their folio Bible of 1638 was notably accurate by the standards of the time: the nineteenth-century Biblical scholar F. H. Scrivener could find only three misprints in it. Though the story that Buck and Daniel in their pride put a notice on Great St Mary's door offering a free Bible to anyone who could find an error is probably apocryphal, Cambridge still had cause for pride, for it had inaugurated the tradition of care for the text which only the two universities maintained, and which was to be always the strongest argument for their exemption from the monopoly conferred by the Royal Printer's Patent.

Thomas Buck was appointed Printer in 1625. He was a substantial figure in Cambridge life; he was a Fellow of St Catharine's and Esquire Bedell; was a churchwarden; and to this day there is a country lane in Little Eversden leading to an old country house, and called Buck's Lane. His black marble funeral slab is to be seen in St Edward's Church, right in front of the altar, and seeming to assert in death a right to a prominent position. Legge, like Legate, seems to have printed in the house in Regent Walk used by Thomas. But Buck moved the printing house first to the north side of Market Hill, where Rose Crescent now joins it, and then to the site of the former refectory of the old Augustinian Friary, which had been dissolved in Henry VIII's time. These buildings had passed into secular use, and Buck bought them from Stephen Perse in 1636. The street is currently called Free School Lane because the Perse School was originally sited there, and the shop at the corner is still called Friar's House.

Buck's printing house, purchased by him in 1636: the refectory of the old monastery of the Augustine Friars, dissolved by Henry VIII in the previous century, and turned over to secular use. The pen and watercolour drawing was made in 1770, when the building had become the house of the Curator of the old Botanic Garden, which lay behind it.

The University, having the right to appoint three Printers, was usually careful to exercise its right, so that it should not lapse. This meant that at any given time in the seventeenth century (and still in the eighteenth), there might well be three persons with the title; but one or two of them might be booksellers acting as agents, or sleeping partners or sinecurists. Buck himself had a succession of partners, with whom he fell out. The first, Leonard Greene, was an experienced London Stationer, who was to supply trade knowledge and trade connection ('Mr Bucke being unexperienced, haveing lead a students life'). Greene also had certain rights acknowledged by the Stationers, so that Buck as his partner could join in the printing and publishing without litigation – or so it was hoped. Greene felt he was treated brusquely and disingenuously by Buck, and complained to the University. Greene died in 1630, and Buck, who was already in partnership with his brother John, secured the third vacancy for his brother Francis, having briefly contemplated bringing in the current Barker, inheritor of the King's Printer's Patent, who if he was not to be a friend and partner was likely to be the chief adversary. Francis Buck was a sleeping partner for two years and Roger Daniel took his place in 1632, becoming the effective Printer while Buck pursued his other interests as Esquire Bedell and man' of property. Daniel became tenant and occupier of the printing house, paying Buck a rent of £190, and receiving a third of the profits of the enterprise. Apart from the printing which the partners did for the University and its members, this meant, effectively, contracting to supply the London Stationer Edmund Weaver with Cambridge-printed schoolbooks, Weaver supplying the paper and paying London rates. In the three years 1631–4 Buck supplied:

| | |
|---|---|
| Aessop's Fables | 12,000 |
| Virgills | 3000 |
| Mantuans | 6000 |
| Castalians Dialogues | 4250 |
| Apthonius | 2000 |
| Pueriles Sententiae | 18,000 |
| ,,  Confabulationes | 6000 |
| Ludovic vir. Dialog. Epitome Colloquiorum | 3000 |
| Ovid, Epistles | 3000 |
| Stuvenius Epist. | 3000 |
| Ovid, Tristia | 3000 |
| Corderius | 3000 |
| Almanacks | 1560 |

Roberts, *Cambridge University Press*, 51

An obvious drawback was that Buck could not supply the other stationers in Cambridge, who had to buy from London at London prices. Daniel, too, becoming dissatisfied, appealed to the Vice-Chancellor in 1635, touching the always sensitive nerve:

it will appear that the University Presse is servant to the said Stationers and the University and Commonwealth deprived of that benefit which is intended by our Priviledge.

He also pointed out that personal relationships had reached a low point:

> He [Buck] is continually defaming chyding and brawling with your petitioner, often fighting with, beating, threatning and vexing your petitioners servants, so your petitioner and they are weary of their lives.

Weary or not, Buck and Daniel produced in 1638 their second important Bible, another folio. This was the summit of their achievement in Bible printing, and it may have been a specially bound copy of this edition which was presented to the King on a visit to Cambridge in March 1641/2, when 'The Vice Chan. met his majesty & with a long speech presented him with a very fair Bible'. Only two days before, the Prince of Wales had been presented with another copy by Dr Collins, Provost of King's. Two points were being made in these visits. First, the King was cementing a special relationship with the University. When Buckingham, his previous candidate for Chancellor, had been assassinated in 1628, he had immediately proposed as successor Henry, Earl of Holland, 'whose hearty affection to advance religion and learninge generally in our Kingdom, and especially in the fountaynes [sc. the universities] cannot be doubted of. Not that we shall cease to be your Chancellor in effect according to our promise...'. Second, the University for its part was seeking powerful patrons who would uphold all its privileges; and among these was the still contentious right to print in the University. The Star Chamber ordinances of 1586 had been intended to restrict printing severely, and to concentrate it in London; but had conceded a right to the two universities (a chartered right, in the case of Cambridge). A further Star Chamber decree of 11 July 1637 largely confirmed the old ordinances, but added other clauses. Again the right of the two universities to maintain a press was conceded, and the Vice-Chancellors were recognised as licensing authorities. There was also the beginning of another kind of copyright legislation: a copy of each book printed was supposed to go to the Bodleian Library in Oxford.

# 6

## THE COMMONWEALTH AND RESTORATION

THE PRINTERS TO THE UNIVERSITY, and notably Buck and his partners, were moving from the stage of confrontation, seizure and litigation to tentative accommodations with the Stationers in which the interests of both sides might be procured; but there was a heritage of bad blood and frustrated endeavour, and the conflict was by no means over. It was first to be blown to one side by the national crisis already impending in the 1640s. It had been no great surprise that Buckingham's candidature as the King's nominee for the Chancellorship was displeasing to Parliament; and the natural puritan tendency in Cambridge was sympathetic to Parliament. Buckingham was elected by only 108 votes to 102, and there were doubts about the honesty of the counting. East Anglia was a natural puritan homeland. The Cromwells were local gentry, and Oliver Cromwell, the MP for the town, had been at Sidney Sussex. By 1642 the King was asking the Colleges to send him money and plate, while Colonel Cromwell was sending arms to townsmen and training them in their use, and himself scouring the countryside to intercept some of the valuables sent to the King in Nottingham.

Certain of the publications of the time strike an appropriate note: John Cruso's *Militarie Instructions for the Cavallerie* (1632); *Directions for Musters* (1638); Cruso's translation of Du Praissac's *Military Discourses* and *Arte of Warre* (1639); his translation of de Rohan's *The Complete Captain* (1640). In 1642 the Press printed *His Majesty's Declaration to all his loving subjects*, and *His Majesty's Answer to the Declaration of Parliament of July 1*, a *Petition of the Commons of Kent*, a *Petition of Lords and Commons, and his Majestie's Answer*, a *Proclamation Forbidding all Levies of Forces*, and another *That no Popish Recusant shall Serve*. . . . On 23 August 1642 the House of Commons ordered 'that Roger Daniel, Printer to the University of Cambridge, be forthwith summoned to attend the House, concerning printing the Book set forth in Defence of the Commission of Array'; and on 3 September 'Ordered, that Mr Daniel. . .be injoined by this House, not to print anything concerning the Proceedings of Parliament, without the consent or order of one or both Houses of Parliament: And that he be discharged of further Attendance'. In May 1643 Parliament arrested the Vice-Chancellor, Dr Richard Holdsworth, and censured him for having licensed the reprinting at the Press of the King's Declarations, first printed at York. It would seem that Daniel had explained the constitutional arrangements at Cambridge, so that the licensing authority, the Vice-Chancellor himself, came into jeopardy.

All this danger and contention had led the University and its Press a long way from that period in the 1620s and 1630s when Cambridge was a nursery of poets. They included puritan poets, of course – the most notable being Milton. The Press published in 1638 the mourning verses for the young and talented Edward King who had drowned in a shipwreck on his way to Ireland. A volume of Latin and a volume of English verses were printed. In the latter was the first printing of Milton's *Lycidas*: the University Library copy has corrections in Milton's hand (including a line omitted in the printing). In 1633 Buck and Daniel printed the first edition of George Herbert's *The Temple*. Before retiring to his country parish at Bemerton, Herbert had been one of the rising stars of the University, elegant and distinguished as Public Orator. The book was several times reprinted. Richard Crashaw's *Epigrammatum Sacrorum Liber* was published in 1634 (Crashaw illustrating the opposite tendency: no less spiritual, he became a Catholic). There was a posthumous volume of Donne's sermons, also in 1634; a number of books by Giles and Phineas Fletcher, and in 1639 Fuller's *The Historie of the Holie Warre*.

If we take account also of Buck and Daniel's Bible printing, and the programme of printing for the Stationers, which provided a steady flow of bread-and-butter work assured of a London sale and paid for at London rates, it can be said that the partnership

*Sunk though he be beneath the watry floore:*
*So sinks the day-starre in the Ocean bed,*
*And yet anon repairs his drooping head,*
*And tricks his beams, and with new spangled ore*
*Flames in the forehead of the morning skie:*
*So Lycidas sunk low, but mounted high*
*Through the dear might of him that walk'd the waves;*
*Where other groves, and other streams along,*
*With Nectar pure his oozie locks he laves,*
*And heares the unexpressive nuptiall song;*
*There entertain him all the Saints above*
*In solemn troups and sweet societies,*
*That sing, and singing in their glory move,*
*And wipe the tears for ever from his eyes.*
*Now, Lycidas, the shepherds weep no more;*
*Henceforth thou art the Genius of the shore*
*In thy large recompense, and shalt be good*
*To all that wander in that perillous floud.*

*Thus sang the uncouth swain to th' oaks and rills,*
*While the still morn went out with sandals gray;*
*He touch'd the tender stops of various quills,*
*With eager thought warbling his Dorick lay:*
*And now the sunne had stretch'd out all the hills,*
*And now was dropt into the western bay;*
*At last he rose, and twitch'd his mantle blew,*
*To morrow to fresh woods and pastures new.*

*oosie*
*in the blest kingdoms*
*meeke of joy and Lob*

J. Milton.

Milton's 'Lycidas', first printed in the volume of verse *Obsequies* in
memory of Edward King in 1638. The copy in the University
Library is corrected in Milton's hand: a line had dropped out.

was a success both by 'business' and by literary and intellectual standards. The University Printers had balanced their accounts by entering into a prudent accommodation with their opponents: but in the long run that kind of arrangement could be seen to compromise the University's rights. The most frequent arrangements were either that the University Printer acted as sub-contractor to the London Stationers, who commissioned work, paid for it and sold it, mostly in London; or that there was a limited agreement to the effect that the University Printer would print only so many copies of a particular title in a given time for sale on his own account, so that the competition offered to London was known and limited; or that there was a 'covenant of for-bearance', as in 1639, under which the Stationers simply offered the University an attractive annual sum (£200) not to exercise its right in respect of titles which the Company saw as the strong-selling lines of its chief members, or only to do so at the order of the Company – and notably the partners in the English Stock. Other variants were that the University Printer might become a Stationer (Legate) or a London Stationer might be appointed (as a partner) under the University's Letters Patent, and so have a stake in Cambridge, or actually become Printer to the University, so becoming virtually an agent of the Company.

The titles mostly involved, other than Bibles and prayer books, were schoolbooks (and we have seen how Buck printed these for London sale) and almanacs. The best-known almanac in existence today is the celebrated *Old Moore's Almanac* which is still sold by colporteurs in the streets. Its predecessors combined the functions of a diary for the year (noting saints' days, markets and fairs, phases of the moon, and much astrological information) and the horoscope pages in newspapers and women's weeklies – except that the prognostications were not personal, but national and even universal. Thousands who would buy no other printed material would have an almanac, and the total sales in the seventeenth century and later must have been astronomical. They were essentially disposable – each year you needed another. There were many variants, according to the locality and the ingenuity of the compiler, and in 1627, for instance, Cambridge produced the Dove, the Frost, the Lakes, the Rivers, the Strof,

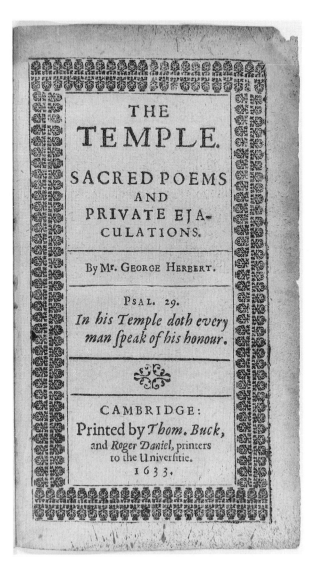

The first edition of Herbert's *The Temple*.

and the Waters; in 1629 the Clarke, the Pond, and the Rivers; in 1631 the Kidman. There are years however when no almanacs were printed; and it is to be supposed that in those years Cambridge had been bought off, or threatened.

The Bible offered the other immense and steady sale – though under peculiarly onerous conditions. Setting a Bible would need more type than a printer would possess or could afford; and it could be done only by the then usual process of setting a sheet, or perhaps two sheets, at a time, printing the sheet, and then releasing the type for the next one. In fact all books had to be reset every time they were printed because type for even a short book could not be kept standing. The Bible is one of the longest of books, and setting it again and again was the only way of supplying the market until in the eighteenth century the Canstein Society in Germany, as a charity, kept the necessary type standing, and in the nineteenth century stereotyping was perfected, and first put to use in Cambridge for Bible printing.

The constant resetting debased the text, especially where the printer was in too much of a hurry to read the proofs – the master-printer was usually his own corrector, usually too busy to do the job well, and too conscious of cost to employ another qualified person. For that reason Buck and Daniel's edition of 1638, which seems to have used an editor and a corrector, was an important event. But Cambridge's incursion into the Bible market had another effect. A pamphlet appeared in London in 1641 called: 'Scintilla, or a light broken into darke *warehouses*. With observations upon the monopolists of Seaven severall patents, and two *charters*. Practised and performed By a Mistery of some Printers, Sleeping *Stationers*, and Combining *Booksellers*. Anatomised and laid open in a *Breviat*, in which is only a touch of their *forestalling* and *ingrossing* of Books in *Pattents*, and Raysing them to excessive *prises*'. The author Michael Sparke (*Scintilla*, in Latin) was a puritan bookseller who was fined and pilloried for publishing the works of William Prynne. Here he turned his attention to the Bible market – telling for instance how when the brothers Buck produced their first Bible in 1629 at ten shillings, much lower than London prices, the 'Kings Printers set six Printing-Houses at work, and on an instant Printed one Folio Bible in the same manner...at 5s a Book, to overthrow the Cambridge Printing, and so to keep all in their own hands. It were well if they would always sell at this price.' Sparke also observed 'See the errors corrected in the *Cambridge* Bibles, which were printed in the London', but lamented that the Cambridge Bibles were now sold in London at London prices, 'And the Monopolists have compounded with them that they shall print no more Bibles, but for the monopolists.'

Sparke's point was that the patent system 'picks the Subjects pockets, that eats brown bread to fill the sleeping Stationers belly with Venison and Sacke', and he appealed to Parliament as the authority which must reform the situation. In due course, but not as a result of his intervention, the overthrow of the monarchy produced important changes in the regulation of the book trade: and Cambridge itself was profoundly affected.

Charles I was taken captive in 1647, and passed through Trumpington on his way to imprisonment, trial and death; taking with him to Carisbrooke Castle in the Isle of Wight his copy of the 1638 folio Book of Common Prayer printed by Buck and Daniel. The Parliamentary army spent June in the neighbourhood of Cambridge, refusing Parliament's invitation through Fairfax to disband itself. There were printed at Cambridge in 1647 an unusual number of politically interesting documents:

> Animadversions upon proceedings against the XI members
> Declaration from Sir Thomas Fairfax and his Councelle of Warre
> Five propositions to the Kings Majesty (by H. Hammond)
> Heads of a charge delivered in the name of the Armie
> Heads presented by the Army to the King
> Letter from the Court at Oatelands
> Manifesto from Sir T. Fairfax
> Proclamation by his Excellency Sir Thomas Fairfax
> Representation from Sir Tho Fairfax
> The Kings majesties declaration and profession
> Two petitions of the Counties of Buckingham and Hertford

Charles's Chancellor, Henry, Earl of Holland, was beheaded in March 1648/9, and Edward, Earl of Manchester, was elected in his place. His function was to reform the University politically and theologically, and the King's supporters and high churchmen were ejected from masterships, professorships and fellowships.

Roger Daniel's appointment as Printer was cancelled for neglect in 1650, and may have been part of the same process.

Daniel's immediate successor was John Legate, son of the earlier Legate, a freeman of the Stationers' Company and to all intents its agent. Appointed in 1650, he had his appointment terminated in 1655; again for neglect. But his business arrangements cannot have been to the taste of the University, except for the ever-influential Buck who remained in the background. There was a complicated agreement between him and Legate which shows that Buck had a vestigial right, which he was paid not to exercise; and of course the Stationers formed a third party:

> The said Mr Buck shall surcease to print in Cambridge, and soe long as he shall forbeare to exercise his printing place there, that the said Companie of Stationers...shall pay unto the said Mr Buck the summe of twenty pounds per Annum....
>
> Neither the said Thomas Buck nor his brother John Buck shall resyne their...Patents for the Printers place, without the consent of the aforesaid John Legate...soe as the said Mr Legate may enjoy the sole exercise of Printing in the University of Cambridge....
>
> In regard Mr Buck hath many Bookes which he hath lately printed in Cambridge now lieing upon his hand (some whereof he hath lately printed whilst he freed Mr Legate from takeing the share of the Presse in Cambridge whereunto he had otherwise been obliged) the said Companie of Stationers shall really, and bona fide, use the utmost of their best indeavours to sell all the said bookes....
>
> For all the letter in the Printinge house of Cambridge (mentioned in founders' Bills and bought since Mr Legate was first chosen to be a Printer in Cambridge, as also the long Primmer and Pica-greeke...) the Companie of Stationers shall pay unto the said Thomas Buck two full third parts of the several prices they cost....
>
> The said John Legate shall oblige himself soe to exercise the Priviledge of Printing in the University of Cambridge as may be most for the honor, and reputation of the said University, soe as the said Mr Thomas and John Buck may noe wayes be injured in their reputation, but may safely forbeare the exercise of their severall printinge Places in the said University.
>
> Roberts, Cambridge University Press, 62–3

It is noticeable that in Legate's term of office little was printed in Cambridge; and nothing that would seem to compete with the Stationers. A tribute was paid to Cromwell, who had become Lord Protector in 1653; the Press produced one of its collections of verse to celebrate the conclusion of peace with Holland: *Oliva*

*Pacis ad illustrissimum celsissimumque Oliverum Reipub. Angliae Scotiae & Hiberniae Dominum Protectorem...*

At this time the Stationers' Company was in a very uncertain situation and would have been vulnerable to competition. Star Chamber had been abolished in 1641, and so its supervision lapsed and its ordinances about printing became themselves questionable, though Parliament repeated some of the old provisions in 1649, notably the restriction of printing to London, York, and the two universities, though Finsbury was now added. With no Monarch, there could be no King's Printer, and for a time the Stationers invaded the Bible monopoly, and founded their Bible Stock. But by an order of 1656 Cromwell conferred the Bible monopoly on the partners Henry Hills and John Field. Field styled himself 'one of his Highness's Printers' and 'Printer to the Parliament' – so he became the equivalent of King's Printer. What is more, he also became in October 1655 Printer to the University, so he was becoming a monopolist on a grand scale.

During his term of office the University Press increased its output, printing Bibles, schoolbooks, psalters and almanacs – a clear sign of amity with the Stationers. It also printed some works of learning, including Isaac Barrow's Euclid, some of the useful as well as the elegant productions of James Duport, and Ray's *Catalogus plantarum circa Cantabrigiam nascentium*. Duport was Dean of Peterborough and Master of Magdalene, and sometime Regius Professor of Greek; Bishop Monk said of his Latin verse that 'we discover a sincere, candid and good humoured disposition, somewhat too prone to learned trifling'. It is as if the eighteenth century is being announced. Ray's catalogue, on the other hand, inaugurated the great tradition of taxonomic botany, founded initially on the study of the local flora, which still flourishes at the Press.

One of the extraordinary things about John Field is that he survived the Restoration. Roberts quotes *The London Printers Lamentacon, or, the Press opprest, and overprest* (?1660):

Who printed the pretended Act of the Commons of England for the setting up an High Court of Justice, for the tryall of his Martyred Majesty in 1648? Or, the Acts for abolishing King-ship, and renouncing the Royall

Line and Title of the Stuarts? Or, for the Declaring what Offences should be adjudged Treason?...or, the Proclamation of 13. of September 1652 after the fight at Worcester, offering, One Thousand pound to any person, to bring in his Majesties person? but only John Feild Printer to the Parliament of England (and since by Cromwell was and is continued Printer to the University of Cambridge!).... Have they not invaded and still do intrude upon His Maiesties Royall Priviledge, Praerogative and Praeeminence.... Have they not obtained, (and now keep in their actuall possession) the Manuscript Copy of the last Translation of the holy Bible in English (attested with the hands of the Venerable and learned Translators in King James his time) ever since 6 March 1655?

Roberts, Cambridge University Press, 64

Yet the death of Cromwell was marked, it would seem automatically, by the publication of *Musarum Cantabrigiensium Luctus ac Gratulatio* (1658), while the Restoration of Charles II was marked by *Academiae Cantabrigiensis* ΣΩΣΤΡΑ (1660). The printer of both was Field, who in his capacity to serve Protector and King, Stationers' Company and University, seems to have shown a happy flexibility which would have been admired by the Vicar of Bray.

This harmony lasted until 1662. This was the year of the first Licensing Act, which ignored the Stationers' Company, and set up a new licensing authority, the Surveyor of the Imprimery and Printing Presses. The Act reduced the notional number of master-printers. Otherwise it reinforced the provisions of 1637. It continued to recognise the two universities as licensing authorities, but did not permit them to license books which were the monopoly of others without the consent of the monopolist. Copies of every book printed were to go to the King's Library and both university libraries.

Under these circumstances the University entered a new dispute with the Stationers under a slight disadvantage. The University petitioned Clarendon, the Lord High Chancellor, while the King's Printer petitioned Archbishop Sancroft, formerly Master of Emmanuel. The situation seems to have been resolved by returning to previous agreements between the two conflicting parties. An important comment to the Vice-Chancellor by a sympathetic onlooker, signing himself W.D. (probably William Dillingham, the current Master of Emmanuel) places the whole long – and the reader may by now feel, tedious – dispute in an entirely new light:

The University'es priviledge is looked upon as a trust for the publick good, & theire [sc. the University's] printing of these bookes will force the Londoners to printe something tolerably true...who otherwise looking meerly at gaine will not care how Corruptly they print, witnes the 200 blasphemy's wch Mr B[uck] found in their bibles; & the millions of faults in theire school bookes, increasing in every edition, so long as Mr B's composition with the stationers held...whence it was that often errors were drunk in grammer schooles scarcely after to be corrected at the University, unlesse schoolmrs were so carefull as to correct bookes by hand before they lett theire boys have them. It being therfore the Universityes interest to have youths well & truly grounded in school bookes & the interest of the whole nation to have true bibles, I cannot but think the University trustees in both respects, & fear they would afterwards rew the betraying of so great a trust if they should sell it by farming.

McKenzie, *Cambridge University Press*, I, 5

W.D.'s remarks may be taken as a comment on the current situation. Field was in 'composition' with the Company, in as much as he had agreements of certain sorts. But 'farming' implied something even more radical – namely that the University might virtually rent its rights to the Stationers for an annual fee. It was unfortunately the case that Field's Bibles were far more erroneous than Buck's; there had been complaints about his editions of 1653, 1655 and 1656. If his limited competition with the Company had been replaced by total submission, there was reason to think that the quality would be even worse. In any case W.D.'s thoughts about public trust were capable of wider extension: the public might expect accuracy as one basic requirement; but a trust could be exercised in other ways which were even more important – such as the whole spirit and tendency of the enterprise – and it is interesting to see that the thought was beginning to occur, and important to note that it was the seesaw of dangerous conflict and somewhat shameful accommodation with the Stationers that was leading thoughtful members of the University to look for something better.

An important feature of Field's time as Printer is that in 1655 he moved the site of the printing house to Queens' Lane. He had a dwelling-house on the corner of Queens' Lane and

Silver Street; running back behind it, on the site of the present Master's Lodge of St Catharine's, he built a long building which housed the Press itself. With one brief intermission, Printers to the University were to remain on this site until 1827.

Field died in 1668; and for a time it appears that Thomas and John Buck, who still held appointments as Printers, exercised their interest. There was an interim appointment of Matthew Whinn, the University Registrary in 1669, so that all three posts should be held; and then in the same year the University appointed John Hayes, on condition that there should be no further treaty with the Stationers. He was to pay the University £100 a year for the privilege 'of receiving the issues and profitts thereof to his own use, and was to execute the saide printers place solely by himselfe'. Hayes had a long and active term of office; until he died in 1705 he was in some sense Printer. But during that term five other men held nominal office as Printer: the University can be taken once more to have deliberately exercised its right to have three Printers, so that the custom should not lapse. It was during Hayes's time too that the new Press set up by Bentley started to operate. That is the topic of the next chapter. The fact that it could coexist with Hayes's operation as an old-style Printer to the University suggests that the notion of public service, or service to scholarship, was at first seen as something quite distinct from a day-to-day printing business serving mostly commercial needs.

Meanwhile Hayes was active and productive. He printed Bibles, almanacs, psalters, and schoolbooks. Among the authors and editors who appeared were Marvell and Newton; Dryden was among the authors of the congratulatory verses which continued to appear on state occasions. Theology and Biblical scholarship remained a scholarly preoccupation; but the spectator begins to feel that, as 1688 came and went, the relationship between Church and State moved more into the background. The new concern of the experimentally minded academic was – or should have been – philosophical and scientific, and classical scholarship was focusing on the texts. In 1672 Ramus was still being printed; but Varenius's *Geographia Generalis* was edited by Newton, and there was an edition of Pufendorf's *Elements of*

*Jurisprudence*; in 1682 there was another work of Pufendorf, and J. Schuler's *Exercitationes ad principiorum Descartes primam partem*. In 1684 a volume of the University Statutes was printed. English history was represented by J. Barnes's *History of Edward III*; and classical scholarship by Barnes's folio edition of Euripides, which was thought to rank with the productions of the European scholarly printers.

Hayes's activity, and the suspicious absence of conflict with the Stationers, implies that he had broken his undertaking. In 1670 he had obtained a guarantee of work at agreed rates, and there was another agreement of a scandalous kind. George Sawbridge, a London Stationer, Field's executor, and one of the Managers of the English Stock, bought the lease and the equipment of Hayes's printing house, and took a share of the profits. Since the work was being supplied to the London Stationers, Sawbridge was profiting on both sides of the account; moreover he actually defalcated by disposing of some of the Cambridge-printed stock on his own account, without passing it through the books of the English Stock that he was supposed to be managing. This was Sawbridge's misappropriation, not Hayes's; but it showed how secret deals could by an easy transition become embezzlements. In 1679 Sawbridge was found out by the Company, but not prosecuted – and the relationship with Hayes went on, such that Hayes was really only a manager of the Press on Sawbridge's behalf, in return for an annual payment and a rent-free house. When Sawbridge and his son died, Hayes made a similar agreement with the Company, who were therefore virtually, if secretly, in control of Cambridge printing. It was a nadir; and it was perhaps because things had reached this pass that in 1696 a serious attempt at a new start was made.

At the end of just over a century of activity, the University Press had reached a curious situation, which mixed the elements of victory and defeat. Victory, because it had survived in a period of sustained ecclesiastical and constitutional conflict, including a civil war which had touched the University and the town very closely; it had also survived more than a hundred years of intermittent trade-warfare with the Stationers' Company, which would have been very happy, in 1584, to have seen the Press abolished as soon as it was founded. But at the end of the long conflict the Stationers, who always had the economic advantage, had effectively limited competition from Cambridge by exercising a covert control over it; and that was the Press's defeat.

It may be useful here to summarise the issues which were involved. The principal issue was the right of the University itself – or rather a number of related rights. Two of them go back to the Middle Ages. The first was the right of the University, as a teaching authority, to pronounce on matters of doctrine to its pupils, half of whom until the late nineteenth century regularly took holy orders, becoming teaching and preaching members of the Church. Convocation of 1408, wanting to suppress Wyclifite heresy, laid on the two universities the responsibility for seeing that orthodox doctrine was being taught, and unorthodox suppressed; and this had to be done through the written word as well as the spoken. From that time at least, the two universities were seen as independent licensing authorities comparable with central government, with the Archbishop in each province, and the Bishop in each diocese; and that status was regularly recognised in legislation about printing when the time came. The Vice-Chancellors and doctors acting officially were competent persons to license books.

The right to censor or to license is related to but not identical with the right to publish; and this was the extension which the two universities had to claim and to justify. It was based first on the medieval university's sense of itself as a corporation in conflict with others. In the Middle Ages, the university first exempted itself from the authority of the Bishop, and then asserted its pre-eminence over the town. This led to endless disputes, which may seem ridiculous to the modern reader, but which were waged in deadly earnest at the time, since the standing and power of the two corporations were involved. The right to license vintners was one such: there was a bitter conflict, including some physical violence, between the University and the agents of Sir Walter Raleigh which parodied the conflict with the Stationers over Bible printing, and started at virtually the same time. Raleigh had a monopoly – of licensing vintners throughout the kingdom – which resembled the King's Printer's monopoly of Bibles. But from time immemorial the University had licensed vintners in Cambridge, and it was not going to recognise any apparent right of subsequent patent-holders from outside. The patient Burghley had to hear about this too, in long letters from the Vice-Chancellor complaining that the University's officers, pulling down the sign of the offending vintner, Raleigh's licensee, were 'purposely resisted with such provision as they little looked for, as namely with skalding water mingled with lyme and aishes, and with stones and brickbattes...as is yet to be seen'. The Vice-Chancellor for his part had haughty letters from Raleigh (beginning 'I cannot a little marvaile at your peremptory and proud manner of dealing'...and ending 'Your Frind as you shall give cause. W. Ralegh'). The University's privilege was upheld; Raleigh had to get his fees from other towns. Fortunately perhaps, the Crown, which could cause such trouble by giving patents, could also solve problems by removing heads; and for that very effective reason Raleigh finally gave no more trouble to anyone. The University went on licensing vintners until after 1894.

This insistence by the University that it regulated essential matters of its own supply, licensed some tradesmen and gave privileged status as members of its own body to others, had been importantly connected with the operations of stationers precisely because they also affected its role as a licensing or censoring body: two functions absolutely crucial to publication. Cambridge University had, as Oxford had not, formalised this matter by its own petition in 1529, answered by the Letters Patent of 1534, which coincided (it is surely no accident) with the legislation of 1534: the Act for the Printers and Binders of Books. In other words, the custom of the University had acquired the force of statute; this was put to the test and validated both in 1584 and in the second charter of 1628, and was recognised in all legislation about the book trade, which after 1586 recognised the ancient right of the two universities to license books, and also Cambridge's recent right to print them.

For the Stationers, the struggle with the two universities in the seventeenth century was a defeat because they had recurrently to recognise the universities' rights, which were regularly confirmed by the central authorities. They were able, however, to vindicate their own right to certain monopolies, so that the universities' infringements were as regularly limited to a specific format, or a specific number. In effect the central authorities were trying to vindicate both rights concurrently, and to get the parties to reach an accommodation.

This they did, but any accommodation reached by the University with its stronger adversary was likely to be a demeaning compromise. At this distance in time especially, an observer still engaged in the business of publishing can feel a practical sympathy with both parties, based on a shared sense of the economic pressures which constrained them. Both the Stationers and the University Printers were for the most part decent tradesmen, who had survival as their first objective, and the condition of all others. They had to win a living, and if possible prosperity, in a small, almost entirely English market, in which there was little effective protection offered by an agreed law of copyright. The substitute, entry in the Stationers' Register, did not apply to the books which were held as the peculiar right of monopolists; and these were usually the books which any active publisher needed if he were to have steady backlist sales to keep his press occupied, and his wages and rent paid. Conflict was therefore inevitable, and between the Stationers and the universities it was a principled conflict, based on an appeal to valid charters on both sides. It was conducted mostly by recourse to law or appeal to the administrative officers of the Crown, and it produced equally responsible attempts to reach a *modus vivendi*. Given the final economic strength of the Stationers, who controlled the London outlets, the University was not ever likely to win more than a tolerated but limited activity; and was always in danger of becoming a kind of colonial outpost of the Company, either openly farmed or secretly controlled by the Company's nominee. When this happened the Stationers would recognise the University's rights by making a substantial annual payment. It was not in itself shameful to take this money; but it is at this point that the sense of holding a trust should have been crystallised. In applying the funds to its own ordinary uses, the University as a charitable corporation was not doing wrong. If it had, however, held the money in trust, created a fund, and applied it specifically to the purposes of scholarly publishing, then it would have been doing what conscientious University Printers might eventually have done if they had continued to exercise their right of printing the more sellable kind of book in order to subsidise the publication of works of learning. The arguments for printing almanacs are simpler than those for printing Bibles and prayer books, where questions of accuracy in a period of inaccurate printing, and of doctrine in the period before and after the Act of Uniformity of 1662, made their correct content and wide availability a legitimate concern of the University in its traditional role of fount of orthodox teaching on behalf of the national Church. But the issues here were clouded by the fact that Bibles were also the most sellable books of all, and therefore a highly commercial matter. To a university press, however, the ability to fulfil a religious obligation (to supply the Authorized Version), a scholarly function (to maintain the purity of the text, and to advance Biblical scholarship) and simultaneously to derive a substantial revenue from it, would mean that the revenue could both pay the overheads of the business and supply a surplus which could be used to finance capital-intensive and slow-selling works of scholarship.

That is, in effect, the first outline of a classical theory of scholarly publishing. But it is not surprising that these things became clear very slowly. The far-sighted W.D. had a glimpse of it in 1662. Archbishop Laud had reached a somewhat similar conclusion in his thoughts and activities in Oxford, and so had his successor Bishop Fell, who carried the thinking further just before Bentley. It was the great Blackstone, thinking about both university presses in 1759, who crystallised these perceptions, prompted by an admirably sensible judgement from the Court of King's Bench, and Mr Justice Foster in particular (see below, p. 109).

Meanwhile there was virtually no possibility of such far-sightedness, or much self-consciousness at all, from a Press which essentially consisted of a single master-printer, a few journeymen, and an apprentice or two in Cambridge. It was a little printing house like any other, except that the master-printer had entered into an agreement with the University which had become a traditional arrangement of some authority, and so no longer thought about. He had been appointed, and his appointment confirmed by Grace of the University's Senate; he had entered into recognizances not to print heretical or treasonous matter and had undertaken to pay the University an annual sum for his office. He had to recover this sum – a kind of rent – from his printing and bookselling, as well as paying the rent of his printing house, buying and replacing his equipment, and paying his men. The University owned neither the shop nor the presses and types. But he knew that if he were in trouble with the Stationers the University would back him; and to make sure that in any lawsuit the terms of the charter had been implemented, he might keep a book of imprimaturs, in which a copy of the title-page of each book he published was signed by the Vice-Chancellor and three doctors. For the University itself it was understood that he would print combination papers, Tripos verses, other notices, assizes of bread and other commodities, and volumes of celebratory verse when royal persons ascended the throne, married, had children, won battles or signed treaties. (Combination papers were lists of university preachers. Tripos verses were Latin verses specially composed for the opening of the tripos examination and handed out at the ceremony. The assize of bread (or ale) sprang from the University's ancient right to control the weights and values of essential supplies. The deputy Vice-Chancellor decreed that the penny white loaf should weigh six ounces, five drachms, and so on. Other notices might include a proclamation that a tradesman in the town had been 'discommuned', i.e. that no member of the University should buy from him: this brought unruly tradesmen to their knees by economic pressure.) If a sermon in Great St Mary's caused a stir, the author might bring it to be printed. The dons themselves were a constituency of potential authors, editors and advisers. As well as selling books to them, he might publish for them, or commission work from them, or be advised by them what to publish if he was a venturesome person. He would print his edition – usually 500 or 750 copies of a learned work; 1500 and upwards for a schoolbook, almanac or Bible – and then had to sell it. His shop and the other local shops in Cambridge would take only a few. The great fair on Stourbridge Common near Barnwell every year was one of the great trade fairs of England – of Europe even – and it had a booksellers' lane until nearly 1750. A Cambridge printer-bookseller might well dispose of copies there, especially to country booksellers. But in the end he had to send the bulk of his edition to the London booksellers in St Paul's Churchyard for sale or exchange. That required good-will between the two parties; in its absence, it was a standing temptation to take the easier course – to print for one of the big London booksellers, to take his money and not have the trouble, cost and delay of selling the product against competition or opposition. These men were already well on the way to becoming what we now call publishers: those who commanded the labour of the mere printer. The first great publisher in the English book trade, Jacob Tonson, ended his apprenticeship in 1678. McKenzie points out that he more or less defined the market for literature in the 1680s and 1690s; and he naturally became interested in the newly revived Press in Cambridge of which the well-known Richard Bentley was the real driving force.

# 7

## BENTLEY'S 'PUBLIC PRESS'

I N 1696 Richard Bentley was Chaplain to the King and Keeper of the Royal Library at St James's. He was later to become Regius Professor of Divinity and Master of Trinity: the greatest classical scholar of his time and one of the most active controversialists, quick in a personal quarrel as well as in intellectual debate, immensely self-willed, active, capable, at times insufferable, but always able to frustrate any opponent. It was characteristic of him that he later referred to the new 'Publick Press' at Cambridge as having been 'projected and founded solely by myself, and purchased and endowed solely by my friends'. (The word 'public' at this time in Cambridge meant 'not belonging to any College'. We should now use the word 'University'.)

In fact the idea was presented to the Senate in a letter by the Chancellor, Charles Seymour, sixth Duke of Somerset, in June 1696. He wrote:

As I have ye honour to be a servant to you all, soe am I ever thinking of wt may bee most for yr interest, & for ye support of that reputation, & great Character wch ye University have soe worthily deserved in ye opinion of all good, & of all learned men: & in my poore thoughtes, noe way more effectuall, then the recovering ye fame of yr own printing those great, & excellent writinges, yt are soe frequently published from ye Members of yr own body; wch tho' very learned, sometimes have been much prejudiced by ye unskillfull handes of uncorrect printers. Therefore it is, yt I doe at this time presume to lay before you all, a short, & imperfect scheame (here enclosed) of some thoughtes of mine, by way of a foundation, for you to finishe, & to make more perfect; wch tho' never soe defective at present, yett they have mett with aprobation among some publick spirited Men (much deserving ye Name of friends to us) whoe have freely contributed eight hundred poundes towardes ye Carying on this good, & most beneficiall Worke.

Now, Gentlemen, their is nothing wanting of my part, to endeavour the procuring the like su͞me againe from others, but yr aprobation, & consent, to have a Presse once more erected at Cambridge: & when yt whall be resolved on, then to give a finishing hand (like great Masters as you are) to my unfinished thoughtes, yt I may bee proude in having done some thing, yt you think will bee for your service; wch I doe hope wilɪ bee a meanes to procure mee a generall pardonn from you all, for laying this Matter before you, having noe other ambition, then to bee thought yr most obedient & most faithful humble servant.

McKenzie, Cambridge University Press I, 6

This sounds like the attractive modesty which often goes with ability and originality. The Duke was in many respects of the same mettle as Bentley. He had been at Trinity, and had married a great and noble heiress, Elizabeth Percy, daughter of the last Earl of Northumberland (a family immortalised in Shakespeare's *Henry IV*). Somerset was out of favour in James II's reign for being actively and objectionably Protestant; but after 1688, while he set about rebuilding Petworth, the seat of the Percys, he also entered upon a political career of some influence. He became Chancellor of the University in 1689. He was obsessed with his lineage; he insisted that his children should stand in his presence, and he cut a daughter out of his will when he woke from a nap to find her seated. He habitually went down to breakfast in court dress and wearing the blue ribbon of the Garter, and treated all his country neighbours with such insolence that he was never visited, and dined in solitary state. If we return to his letter, it would seem that his remarks about 'being a servant to you all', his 'poore thoughtes' and his 'short, & imperfect scheame' are to be taken as the classical rhetorical device known as *diminutio*, where a man abundantly confident of his superiority pretends to be modest. Coming from Somerset it may have caused a knowing eyebrow or two to rise in 1696; and the recipients would have noticed that this very rich man was not himself bearing very much of the proposed expense (though it must be said that he had given money generously to St Catharine's and Trinity).

The Chancellor was probably giving his name to a scheme which had been proposed and developed by his advisers, notably Bentley and perhaps James Talbot, also formerly of Trinity, now

BENTLEY

Richardus Bentleius. Æt: 48 vo.

Richard Bentley, from the portrait in Trinity College.

the Duke's secretary and chaplain, tutor to his son, and soon to
be one of the Curators of the Press. Others who had been consulted were John Eachard, Master of St Catharine's and Vice-
Chancellor in 1696, and Henry James, Fellow of Queens' and
Vice-Chancellor after Eachard. These were senior scholars;
Bentley was only thirty-four, but he had in 1692 given his celebrated Boyle lectures, which took Newton's theories as the basis

of a belief in an intelligent Creator of a systematic universe, and in the *Epistola ad Io. Millium* had embarked on his career as a critical scholar. The *Dissertation upon the Epistles of Phalaris* followed in 1699. He was a Fellow of the Royal Society; friend of Newton, Christopher Wren, John Evelyn, and Locke; and quite evidently the critical and classical star in that remarkable constellation. At this moment England was the intellectual centre of Europe. These were the men who were producing the important work of the time; Oxford and Cambridge were linked by the Royal Society, and the early years of what was in effect a national academy of a special kind certainly led to thoughts about the need for a learned press. Indeed the first edition of Newton's *Principia* (1687) had been sponsored by the Royal Society, so that Halley, the Secretary, was editor and production manager – and responsible for paying the printer.

It was Bentley therefore who was given the University's authority to purchase types for the new Press by Grace of 10 July 1696, two weeks after the receipt of Somerset's letter, and the Grace itself gave him power of attorney to act on behalf of the University. In effect Somerset's initiative had prompted the University to move from the position of merely being a controlling authority, which appointed a tradesman to carry on University printing, into being the owner of a building, of presses and type. This capital equipment was to be bought with the money lent by Somerset and subscribed by his supporters, and Bentley was to supervise its use. Bentley himself did not go off to Holland to buy the types. He sent Cornelius Cronefelt or Groenevelt, later known as Crownfield, an able, active and skilled Dutch printer, whom he had in mind as the manager (or, as he was to be first called, Inspector) of the new Press.

This raises the question of the now ageing John Hayes, appointed Printer in 1669, and firmly established in his own new printing house as the manager, mostly on behalf of the Stationers' Company, which was paying the University a considerable annual sum for its rights. Negotiations had to take place with the Company, which was assured that the University was set on providing a 'public press' for the learned works of its own members, that this was scholarly publishing in its purest form, and not intended as competition: '...they had no intencon to print anything in prejudice to the Company in any wise but only to print some Classick Authors, and such books of learning as they shall find to be wanted, and that their desire was to Rent the Companys Printing-house...'. This was all quite safe, the Stationers must have felt: they had no cause to be alarmed at anything so quixotic.

At first the new Press was housed in a new building – or rather a conversion to the new use of a little theatre a few yards further up Queens' Lane from Hayes's own printing house. This had been meant at first for Hayes, but Hayes refused to move, so the University took it instead. It is odd that a theatre should have been used: perhaps the Sheldonian Theatre at Oxford was the example, though that fine building was totally unsuited to the use and could not have been more inconvenient to the printers themselves. At any rate the little Cambridge theatre was converted in late 1697, and was used for a few years. It was returned to the University in 1716 and used as a demonstration room in chemistry and as an anatomy theatre (it is illustrated in one of Ackermann's prints), and was demolished in the 1840s: the only survival today is possibly one of the pedimented doors in the wall of St Catharine's Fellows' car-park.

Hayes meanwhile had persuaded the University to let him remain in his house for the rest of his life (he died in 1705). An incentive to permit this was the fact that he paid a rent to Queens' (of which Henry James was President) and that he also paid the University £150 a year for his post as Printer – or rather the Stationers paid it through him. When he died, the Stationers raised their payment to £210, on the understanding that the University itself would not print a hundred and more titles which the Stationers wanted a free hand with, and that the Company would not print in Cambridge. So here was an important truce, which got the Stationers out of Cambridge, but tied the University's publishing arm behind its back by removing any profitable printing from its ambit.

Under these conditions, the little theatre printing house would have been large enough, but in the middle of 1707 Crownfield, who had at first been called the Inspector of the Press, and had become University Printer in 1705, moved his equipment into

The new printing house converted in 1697 from an old theatre. Just outside the picture in the foreground to the right, on the corner of Queens' Lane and Silver Street, was John Hayes's house and printing house, built in 1655. Crownfield moved into this building in 1707, and the 'new' printing house was returned to the University.

Hayes's much larger and more convenient printing house. He had somehow to make Somerset's and Bentley's venture pay its way. He failed in the end to do so, but not for lack of energy or skill. With the advantage of hindsight, the historian can say that the experiment had to be made; it was the first of the University's attempts to discover what particular organisational structure and what form of activity would produce a successful formula for the effective owning and running of first a printing house and ultimately a publishing business.

This first experiment by the University took the form of using capital to build and equip a printing house of its own, appointing a manager (Crownfield as Inspector) and having the intention of making this scholarly press available to high-minded entrepreneurs who were interested in the publication of scholarly books only. This was one important initiative: the University has ever since that time owned the buildings and the equipment of its Press. Crownfield was an employee – but as Inspector and later as Printer he was paid only a small salary, and it is clear that he had to supplement this by acting as one of the entrepreneurs mentioned above, and publishing on his own account; by bookselling; by working as his own most skilled compositor, and as corrector of the Press. At the end of the year the work done was accounted for, receipts balanced against outgoings, and the University financed the deficit on the operations of its 'public press'.

The other important initiative was that the University set up its own committee of management. In 1698 the Senate passed a Grace appointing Curators of the Press: a cumbersome body consisting nominally of the Vice-Chancellor, the sixteen Heads of Houses and the nine Professors *ex officio*, and twelve named members; the quorum was to be five only (a touch of realism). Three more names were added in October 1698 and seventeen in April 1699, to take the total to fifty-eight. This excessively large body soon resolved itself into groups which took monthly tours of duty, meeting weekly (at first, that is).

Notes made by Bentley in 1696, headed 'The design of ye Press by Dr Bentley', set out a kind of constitution and principles of operation. It is worth quoting in full:

1. That ye Chancellor, ye Vice-Chancellor, ye Regius and Margarett Professors of Divinity, ye Law Professor, ye Physick Professor, ye Mathematick Professor & ye Professors of Hebrew & Arabick, ye Greek Professor, & Dr Bentley ye present Library keeper to His Majesty, be constantly of ye number of Curators to govern ye Press; & if any other persons shall be thought necessary, they may be added to those aboue mention.

2. All Books that are printed with ye new Types may be licensed by three or more of ye Curators, who are to be very carefull in determining what Books shall be printed.

3. That under ye Curators, or by them, should be appointed an Architypographus, who may be ye Publick Library keeper for ye time being, or whom else they shall judge best qualify'd for that office, which may be held quamdiu se bene gesserit: his employment to be the constant inspection of ye Press, & ye immediate direction of ye Printer, Corrector, & all inferior officers; as also ye card of Matrices & Punchions, which are to be preserved carefully in a publick Chest for that purpose; All books to be printed with ye new types may be offer'd to Him by ye undertakers, & by Him to ye Curators before they are sent to ye Press.

4. The Architypographus may agree with ye Undertaker in ye name, & by ye Direction of ye Curators, for ye use of ye new types; & by their order may receive & expend such summs as they shall judge necessary for the service of ye Press, for which he may be accountable to them at their Meeting.

5. The Curators may determine ye Price of ye Copy between ye Publisher & ye Bookseller, if ye former be employ'd by them in ye Publication of any Book.

6. Those persons that are willing to put forth such Books as shall be approved by ye Curators, may receive by their appointment, an Encouragement suitable to ye Merit of their Undertaking, out of ye University Chest (besides what they have from ye Bookseller for their Copy) & out of the same Fund such an Annual Establishment as ye University shall think fitt, may be allowed to ye Architypographus.

7. Nothing to be printed off, after ye second review of any Book by ye Publisher, till it be again examin'd by ye Architypographus.

8. That ye Curators above mentioned, or any Five of them (whereof the Vice-Chancellor to be one) may meet two or three times every year (besides their usual meetings upon Ordinary Occasions) particularly to view ye condition of ye Press; to pass all acounts of Receipts & Disbursments relating to ye new Types; to enquire whether ye respectiue Officers perform their Duty, & whether proper Materials & able workmen are employ'd; & to add, alter, or retrench what they shall find convenient as may be most for ye Honor & interest of ye University.

Thirteen members attended the first meeting of the Curators on 23 August 1698, to consider the printing of quarto editions of Virgil, Horace, Terence, Catullus, Tibullus and Propertius to the order and at the expense of Jacob Tonson, who saw a market for elegant and correct editions of the major classics which ought to be in every gentleman's library, whether he read them or not, and which could be reprinted in a smaller format and in larger numbers for student use. These were to be set in the handsome type bought in Holland by Crownfield. A second meeting agreed that they were to be carefully proof-read in Cambridge by an 'inferiour correctour' – that is to say, a press-reader acting on behalf of the original editor. The whole venture was to demonstrate to the learned world of Europe and the polite world of England that there was a press in Cambridge which meant to rank with the scholar-printers of the continent.

Under these early auspices Terence was edited by Leng, one of the Curators and later Bishop of Norwich; Horace by Talbot, another Curator, and Professor of Hebrew; Catullus, Tibullus and Propertius by Annesley; and Virgil by Laughton. It was not until 1711 that Bentley's own Horace appeared, and when it did it impugned Talbot's edition with special care and vigour. It incorporated in the text between 700 and 800 emendations of the common text, and was 'unlike any edition of a Latin author ever before given to the world', according to Monk, Bentley's biographer. His edition of Terence (1726) was designed to supplant and extinguish that of Francis Hare.

Not surprisingly, Bentley published at the Press on his own behalf and at his own expense. Newton's *Philosophiae Naturalis Principia Mathematica* had been first published in London in 1687. It had been immediately received, not just in England but throughout Europe, as bearing out Newton's own claim: 'I have laid down the principles of philosophy; principles not philosophical but mathematical: such, namely, as we may build our reasonings upon.... From the same principles I now demonstrate the frame of the System of the world' – not a small claim, but justified and accepted. The book was out of print; and Newton's own mind had continued to move. There was an obvious case for a new edition of one of the two or three genuinely epoch-making works of science and philosophy, especially in Newton's own university, which was with commendable speed making his mathematics a staple of undergraduate teaching.

This enterprise shows Bentley in his best light. To the fore-sight which led him to undertake it, he added great care in its preparation, patience, and for him unusual diplomatic skill. Newton seemed cynical about Bentley's motives. He knew him well: '"Why" said he "he was covetous & loved mony & there-fore I lett him that he might get mony."' But then Newton him-self had a profoundly complicated character, and perhaps his denigration of Bentley was unconsciously designed to remove himself from inspection and criticism. In fact Bentley was both high-minded and immensely practical, as well as hard and driving. The care he took over the printing showed a genuine interest and a real eye for practical detail. In a letter to Newton enclosing a specimen page, he wrote:

I hope you will like it, and ye Letter too, wch upon trials we found here to be more sutable to ye volume than a greater & more pleasant to ye Eye. I have sent you likewise ye proof sheet, yt you may see what changes of pointing, putting letters Capital, &c I have made, as I hope, much to ye better. This Proof sheet was printed from your former Edition, adjusted by your own corrections and additions. The alterations afterwards are mine: which will show & justify themselves, if you compare nicely the proof sheet with ye finished one. The old one was without a running Title upon each page, wch is deformd. Ye Sections only made with Def. I. Def. II. which are now made full & in Capitals DEFINITIO. I &c. Pray look on Hugenius de Oscillatione, wch is a book very masterly printed, & you'l see that is done like this. Compare any period of ye Old and New; & you'l discern in ye latter by ye chang of points and Capitals a clearness and emphasis, yt the other has not: as all yt have seen this specimen acknowledg.

McKenzie, *Cambridge University Press* I, 168–9

Bentley found an editor to work on the text: Roger Cotes, a twenty-seven-year-old mathematician of great promise (Plumian Professor of Astronomy at twenty-three), who had both to incorporate Newton's revisions and to propose his own. Working carefully over Newton's results, Cotes was often able to propose improvements, and even to correct errors, as Newton rather gruffly acknowledged in letters to him. The new edition needed three years of correspondence and correction, being published finally in 1713.

Roger Cotes himself published in his lifetime a single work at the Cambridge Press, the *Harmonia Mensurarum* in 1722. It

# PHILOSOPHIÆ

## NATURALIS

# PRINCIPIA

## MATHEMATICA.

AUCTORE

## ISAACO NEWTONO,

EQUITE AURATO.

EDITIO SECUNDA AUCTIOR ET EMENDATIOR.

CANTABRIGIÆ, MDCCXIII.

The second edition of Newton's *Principia*, 1713, the fruit of Bentley's enterprise and Cotes's editing. The engraved version of the Cambridge emblem with angel supporters was made by Simon Gribelin for Bentley's venture, and was used as a colophon in the major editions of the time.

was reprinted in 1732. Posthumously published were his *Hydro-
statical and Pneumatical Lectures*. He was one of a relatively
small group of men of outstanding ability who turned their
attention to science in the wake of Newton. When he died young,
his promise unfulfilled, Newton said 'If he had lived we might
have known something'; but Cotes received neither payment
from Bentley nor public thanks from Newton. Indeed Newton
suppressed the preface in which on a first generous impulse he
had paid Cotes a tribute, and deleted a reference to him in the
text. Bentley's own accounts show that he ordered seven hundred
copies of the *Principia* to be printed at a cost of £117. By the
end of 1715 he had already made £200 in profit and had only
seventy-one copies left. The edition was pirated in Amsterdam
in 1714 and 1723.

The time taken to print works of learning when the author was
a perfectionist was a serious handicap to the prosperity of the
Press. Bentley passed the first sheets of his Horace in 1703, but
the whole book appeared in 1711. It was not held in type, since
the printer could not afford to have any part of his small stock of
type out of use for more than a few days. So the sheets were
printed off one or two at a time, and kept in store. If in a later
part of the book some change affected the earlier sheets, these
might have to be cancelled or even reprinted. Newton in particular would go on producing corrections and refinements long
after printing was completed.

The great example of Cambridge's ambition in these matters
was the edition of the Suidas Greek Lexicon edited by the German
scholar Ludolf Kuster. This was another of Bentley's initiatives,
but unfortunately he entrusted the venture to an intermediary,
John Owen, who was to supply capital and bookselling expertise.
The undertaking itself was very large: 1500 copies of three folio
volumes in double column, with Greek and roman type in two
sizes, and engraved headpieces and decorative initials. It is a
superb piece of printing, worthy of the scholar-printers of the
sixteenth century. It went through the press less slowly than
might have been expected, taking about four years to print.
While it was in the press Owen went bankrupt (though he continued to trade) and a London merchant-venturer, Sir Theodore

Janssen, was brought in as partner. By the time of publication in 1705 the Curators were faced with the problem of recouping the outlay, on their own behalf, and for Owen and Janssen (not to mention Crownfield, who had successfully piloted the work through a complicated printing process). The set of volumes was underpriced, but even lower prices had to be fixed for subscribers and favourable terms arranged for booksellers. Then, as earlier and later, it was discovered that sales overseas were usually by exchange, and therefore hard to turn into cash. The sale was slow, long-term warehousing produced stock deficiencies, and in 1733 a Syndicate (the first use of the term in connection with the Press) was set up to wrestle with the problem. In 1748 the University still owned three hundred sets in a London warehouse, and was paying annual storage charges. A kind of remainder operation took place in 1752: sets were sold to a Cambridge bookseller at a guinea each. It is a sad story, insofar as the work itself was more than creditable. The whole process was so long-drawn-out that nobody concerned with it at the outset was still there at the end; so it is doubtful whether any lessons learned could be applied, or even correctly stated.

The surviving accounts of the Press at this period show that there was an annual deficit – inevitably, given the way the operation was run. The cash payments from customers and the sale of books were regularly less than the year's wages; when the overhead was added the University found itself repaying Crownfield a substantial sum every year, and it seems to have occurred to nobody to take into account the payment from the Stationers. Trade declined in the 1730s, and by 1737 a new Syndicate was appointed to look into the Press. They reported in 1741 that between 1698 and 1738 the University's expenses had exceeded its receipts by £3000; and that the amount of work being done was decreasing and the annual loss therefore rising. Donald McKenzie notes that the actual recorded loss amounted to £1814.18.11½, so that the Syndicate was either exaggerating for the sake of effect or was including a notional interest charge; he also points out that over the same period the payments from the Stationers, properly invested and allocated to a printing and publishing account, would have more than met the loss. It would therefore have been theoretically possible for the University to run its 'public press' and balance its books, even on the unsatisfactory model devised in 1696.

But notional financial arrangements are one thing and able men, good arrangements and energetic policies are another. Too much was left to the skill and superintendence of Crownfield. He was a man of many abilities and great energy, but even he was tiring by the mid-1720s. He had been working for the Press since 1696 as Inspector, since 1705 as Printer. His failing energy was compounded by the fact that the other men who had launched the new Press with such enthusiasm thirty or more years before were also dead, dispersed, or elderly. Crownfield was pensioned in 1740, died in 1743, and was buried in St Botolph's church, where he was churchwarden.

The first Curators had set out enthusiastically. They were mostly chosen on grounds of seniority rather than suitability or genuine and lasting interest. They were too numerous to be an effective committee, but solved that problem by never appearing all together. The subcommittees which they set up to operate for a month at a time offered no real continuity of supervision, and the minutes showed that they busied themselves with small detail and not with policy. On 6 September 1699 it was agreed that Mr Crownfield be ordered to buy twelve gallons of linseed oil and a roll of parchment, and that the sashes be renewed. Printers did indeed need large windows, and these were commonly not glazed but made of oiled paper, which was translucent and weatherproof. They were renewed annually at Bartholomew-tide, and the occasion was marked by the annual wayzgoose or printers' feast. From then on work proceeded by candle-light. We can imagine the Curators learning this with interest in 1699. But it is hardly high finance or deep policy. The Vice-Chancellor was chairman *ex officio*, but Vice-Chancellors changed yearly and so never learned the business. The whole arrangement was bound to throw all effective management on to Crownfield, and to dissipate interest for lack of a sense of effectiveness. So the Curators – later the Syndicate – seem to have first lost momentum and then simply to have ceased to meet: there are no entries in the minute book between 1725 and 1737 when the new Syndicate was appointed. In short, the Press passed from a period of enterprise and enthusiasm into the stagnation of the mid-eighteenth century, in which the University itself lay becalmed, and which could hardly not affect its Press.

The most important parts of the output of the Press in this period have been touched on: Tonson's editions of the classics; Bentley's publications, including his own Horace and Newton's *Principia*; the Suidas Lexicon. During the period to 1705, Hayes was still printing almanacs, psalters and schoolbooks: from 1705 onwards Crownfield's productions are those of a learned press. There was still a considerable stream of controversial theology. The Press printed a number of books by William Whiston, a mathematician of some eminence and an acquaintance of Newton's. Newton himself was far from an orthodox thinker, and it may have been from him that Whiston acquired his heresies. As Richard Westfall writes:

Whiston did not share Newton's 'fearful, cautious, and suspicious Temper'. Having found the truth, he mounted the barricades to defend it. At the end of 1707, he made public confession in his Boyle lectures on the prophecies. Once he had taken the step, he forgot every semblance of prudence. He preached his views openly in Cambridge. He published a spate of theological works designed to shock orthodoxy and personally arranged to have them disseminated around the university. One of them, a collection of *Sermons and Essays upon Several Subjects*, reprinted a sermon of 1705 which ended with a prayer to Christ, 'To whom with the Father and the Holy Ghost, Three Persons, and One God, be all Honour, Glory...henceforth and for ever-more'. At the end of the volume, a single erratum directed the reader to the prayer: '*r* [read] in the Holy Ghost, *and dele* Three Persons and One God'. He could not have picked a more inauspicious time. The notorious Dr Sacheverell, who was then whipping up the paranoia of the orthodox for the greater glory of conservative politics, seized on the erratum as an example of blasphemy and irreligion. In the autumn of 1710, Whiston appeared before the vice-chancellor and heads to answer a charge of violating the statutes of the university by espousing Arianism. He chose to defend himself by attacking the proceedings. For his pains he found himself summarily stripped of his chair and banished from the university. Whiston appears to have seen himself as a new Luther who would lead a final Reformation. He spent the rest of a long life protesting the injustice done him, somewhat puzzled at the failure of the church to follow his lead. Newton had never deluded himself on that score. Now he sat by quietly, saying never a word as Cambridge drove out the successor he had selected. Bentley, master of Trinity, chose to absent himself from Whiston's trial.

Westfall, *Never at Rest,* 651

The Press found itself publishing both Whiston's mathematical and his theological works: his name appears as author of such publications in most years between 1702 and 1710: in 1708 there appeared both *The Accomplishment of Scripture Prophecies* and *A New Theory of the Earth.*

Knight's *Life of Erasmus* (1726) had classic status for over a century; Lyons's Hebrew Grammar (1735) continued the rather hesitant tradition of learning in Hebrew and Arabic started earlier with Ockley's *Introductio ad Linguas Orientales* (1706). Barnes's Anacreon (1705) and Homer (1711) were creditable editions and made use of Cambridge's elegant Greek type. The sort of controversy which Bentley naturally created about him broke out in 1721 when Conyers Middleton published in London a vitriolic pamphlet about Bentley's proposals for a new edition of the Greek New Testament. Bentley mistakenly thought the author was the Knightbridge Professor of Moral Theology, Dr John Colbatch, and answered in even more insulting terms, thus libelling Colbatch. Crownfield was prosecuted in the Vice-Chancellor's court, not for publishing the reply, but for selling it, and Bentley himself was summoned to appear but used his characteristic ingenuity to escape punishment in the end. Indeed the episode, though a minor campaign in Bentley's long wars against his colleagues, is characteristic. Colbatch woke one morning to find himself grossly libelled. Bentley was, at this stage, merely laying about him; perceived that in injuring Colbatch he had hit the wrong enemy; and suddenly became wonderfully on guard. The result was that Colbatch passed from being innocent victim into wrongdoer because his attempts to defend himself were clumsy and ill-conceived. In the end he found himself committed by the Court of King's Bench for a contempt of that Court in writing another pamphlet of his own contending that the University was not amenable to the authority of the Courts at Westminster. He was fined £50, and threatened with imprisonment unless he paid.

Bentley meanwhile, like the heroes of adventure stories, was free – not with one bound, but with a series of clever legal steps, leaving Colbatch to wonder for the rest of his life how his aggressor had transformed himself into the innocent party in the affair. But that was Bentley's gift – or one of them. He could start in the wrong, then catch his adversaries on the wrong foot, transform himself into aggrieved victim, and finally appear to his demoralised opponents as a passable imitation of the wrath of God. The Colbatch affair took place in the aftermath of the great struggle in which Bentley was for a time deprived of his degrees as a result of another dispute with Middleton. Here Bentley's tactics were deployed over several years of lawsuits, in which he won in the end. His inveterate enemy Middleton became University Librarian and published several books at the Press, including his *Origin of Printing in England* (1735). His earlier *Bibliothecae Cantabrigiensis Ordinandae Methodus* (1723) brought down on him the same fate as Colbatch's and on the same ground: he was adjudged in contempt of court; he was fined, committed and only released on paying the fine and giving sureties for his good behaviour for a year. We can imagine Bentley's satisfaction.

Crownfield had four presses in use, and employed up to seven compositors at a time. The Press was not a small enterprise by the standards of the time, and perhaps it is remarkable that it lasted so long, and, in its prime, did so relatively well. The practical credit must rest with the active Crownfield; but Chancellor Somerset and the extraordinary Bentley must be given the credit for the basic idea of a learned press, owned by the University, supervised by a body of senior members and aiming to publish only works of learning, to the greater credit of the University as a place of education, religion, learning, and research.

# 8

## THE EIGHTEENTH CENTURY

Professor Whiston lost his chair and was dismissed from the University in 1710, and felt himself hard done by. Between 1510 and 1610 he would have probably been burnt; and between 1610 and his own day he would have been very harshly treated indeed. Times were undoubtedly changing. Non-conformity with the tenets of the State religion remained a serious matter in Cambridge for more than a century after Whiston, so far as holding University office was concerned; but publication of one's views became progressively more common. This is partly because publication itself was less fiercely restricted. The first two centuries of printing were controlled with extreme vigilance by the State, and we have seen how hard Cambridge had to fight in order to exist at all as a printing centre: this was partly achieved by insisting on its ancient right as licensing authority. Having established the right to print outside London, it then had to establish the right to print books which were otherwise the monopoly of the Stationers.

The whole idea of monopoly was viewed with steadily decreasing sympathy in the eighteenth century as evidently a check on free trade. It would become more and more necessary for the two universities not to present themselves as partners in a ring; though the accommodations with the Stationers became more and more like that. Printing itself, with the lapse of the Licensing Acts in 1695, was free to spread outside London, and a provincial printing industry, mainly concerned with the popular trade in the local market, was established. Such restriction as there now was mostly took an economic or fiscal form: there were duties on some publications, and on paper. Concurrently the law of copyright began to move very slowly towards the concepts we now hold: it was recognised that authors as well as printers had rights, and the registration of copyright moved gradually away from the Stationers' Register. The mandatory deposit of copies in what became known as the copyright libraries had been established from 1665 under successive Licensing Acts: in turn this legislation was replaced by the Act of 1710 which specified nine such libraries. There was an Almanac Duty Act of 1711, and paper became subject to duty: the rate was raised from 5% to 10% in 1690, to 15% in 1700, and 20% in 1712. Similar legislation was repeated later in the century, but so was the important proviso that both universities could reclaim payments made in respect of paper used for books in Latin, Greek and the Oriental and 'Northern' languages. The copyright act was of course immensely important to the old university libraries; and the so-called 'draw-back' on paper recognised that the universities as publishers were engaged on work of public benefit. There was now an inclination to see university publishing as in the nature of a public service, and part of the national patrimony.

Yet in the 1730s the enterprise at Cambridge was in difficulties; and not surprisingly these were, at bottom, of an economic kind. By then Crownfield was old, and Bentley was locked in a succession of violent disputes with colleagues; so the two most active proponents of the revived Press of 1696 were moving off the stage. The Syndicate of 1737, which had plenipotentiary power over the Press, was appointed by a Grace which frankly recognised that the facility which had been set up forty years before for the use and benefit of the University was now so negligently administered that the University had lost much money by it. In a sense this was unfair, since the policy envisaged by the founders and pursued by the old Curators was not a commercial one. At least one of the recommendations finally made by the Syndicate in 1741 was shrewd, and constituted a change of policy. It gave this advice:

to undertake the printing of a Bible of such a Size as is of most general Demand, and this they did, 1. In order to serve the Public with a more beautiful and correct Edition than can easily be found. 2. For the Honour of the University, which would be advanced by such a work being well executed

CAMBRIDGE UNIVERSITY PRESS

at their Press. 3. That, by their being secure of constant Employment for them, they may be always able to retain a number of good Hands ready for any Work that shall be brought in. 4. Because they believe a considerable Profit may accrue to the University by printing Bibles. . . .

It will be remembered that the Stationers had bought peace with the University by a covenant of forbearance in 1706. The whole English Bible trade was for a time in the hands of John Baskett, who had a share both in the Royal Printer's Patent and in the Oxford privilege. He had produced some very splendid and some very inaccurate Bibles, including the celebrated 'Baskett-ful of printer's errors'. Indeed from 1709 the Baskett family took the place of the Barker dynasty as hereditary holders of the Royal Printer's Patent, which in 1772 passed to another dynasty, the Eyres. But the holder of the Patent was often prepared to assign his right temporarily to another person who acted as his deputy: this explains why some London-printed editions carry other printers' names as such 'assigns', and the Barkers and the Basketts were, as leading Stationers, willing at various times to enter into treaties with the Company and its Stocks. For the first forty years of the new century the three most common imprints were 'Bell and executrix of Newcomb', 'University Printers Oxford', and 'Baskett and the Assigns of Newcomb and Hills'. The first is a relic of a seventeenth-century Stationers' treaty; the second covers the period when the Stationers had succeeded in getting their nominees appointed at Oxford (more or less at the time when they controlled Hayes in Cambridge). The third form marked Baskett's dominance, from 1713 in London and 1715 in Oxford: in the latter year he printed a magnificent folio in Oxford as 'Printer to the King's most Excellent Majesty, and the University'. He had bought his post at Oxford for an annual payment. In London he had an agreement with the assigns of Newcomb and Hills. In 1716 he even obtained a share in the King's Scottish Printer's Patent, and after some litigation with the other shareholders appeared in the imprints of Scottish Bibles from 1726. Educated sentiment was not favourable to this kind of empire, and Cambridge's re-entry into Bible publishing must have been welcomed.

There was in this period a curious interlude. During the years

1730–8 the University, which had not leased its rights in the Bible to the Stationers, did lease them to 'Mr James and Company' – an enterprise which has a particular interest for the history of printing.

It will be remembered that the great advantage that the Bible sold in enormous numbers was offset by the disadvantage that it was a very large book which had to be reset every time it was printed. This was labour-intensive, but labour was cheaper than type, a form of capital which had to be constantly re-employed and could not be kept locked up, whereas the work of compositors and pressmen had to be kept in balance. The consequences for the text were serious: from printing to printing, old errors were more often repeated than corrected, and fresh errors were constantly introduced.

The problem was met head-on in Germany by the liberality of Karl Hildebrand von Canstein, who founded the Cansteinsche Bibelanstalt in Halle in 1710 (it still exists as a Bible Society). Canstein as a deliberate charitable venture kept the type standing and reprinted from it until it was worn out, correcting errors between impressions, and only resetting at very rare intervals. This was an evangelising enterprise, the selling price was kept low – and commercial publishers were of course undercut and driven from the market.

What 'Mr James and Company' had in mind was an early application of what later became known as stereotyping. A Scot called Ged had invented a process by which whole pages of type could be impressed in a mould, so that a metal cast then made from it could be used as a printing-surface. The type would be liberated for further use, and the whole process offered possibilities of economy such that a printer might offer Canstein's accuracy at something approaching Canstein's price without going bankrupt. A partnership was set up in London between Ged, a Stationer called Fenner, a typefounder called Thomas James, and his brother John. They were aware that Cambridge University could appoint three Printers, and that Jonathan Pindar, appointed in 1697, was a sinecurist. Pindar was persuaded to resign – for a consideration – and in April 1731 Fenner, who as a Stationer might be acceptable to the Company, took his place. In 1732 a house in Cambridge was rented, and men employed in the experiment. The plan was to print a Bible in small format and a Book of Common Prayer. Baskett got wind of this, and filed a Bill in Chancery against Fenner, but thought better of it and withdrew. In fact Baskett had no need to worry. The results of the new process were not good enough to sell, and Fenner died in debt in 1734. He did print a few books in Cambridge, and his unfortunate widow, inheriting his position, attempted to carry on his business. There was a lady somewhat similarly placed in Oxford who was said to know no more Latin than a cat; Mary Fenner knew only a little more English than a parrot, and wrote illiterate letters to the Vice-Chancellor promising to pay her dues. Quite astonishingly, she printed for Bentley – an edition of his Boyle Lectures (1735). She relinquished her lease in 1738, probably because she could not pay for it, and an interesting experiment petered out in wrangling between the surviving partners.

Baskett no doubt sensed that any attempt to suppress the revived Bible printing at Cambridge would fail, so he had to watch for a different opportunity, which duly arose. Meanwhile, the current University Printer, Joseph Bentham (appointed in 1740), printed a Bible in 1743, three Books of Common Prayer in small formats in the same year, a metrical psalter in 1744, and more prayer books in 1745. Another Bible followed in 1747. Given Baskett's command of the market, it is understandable that Bentham and the Press Syndicate, who were publishing at their joint risk, were more cautious than the Syndicate of 1741, which was merely envisaging a rosy future. Bentham appointed an agent in London – an important new development. Charles Bathurst in Fleet Street, London, is named on the title-pages of these books as sole agent; Bathurst found he could sell the Bibles as fast as they were printed, and became impatient with the caution in Cambridge.

Baskett's chance came in 1741. Bentham published an abridgement of the Acts of Parliament relating to the excise on beer, ale, brandy, vinegar and other liquors. (This was a practical concern in Cambridge, for the University was a licensing authority in this matter too.) Thomas and Robert Baskett filed suit, as King's

Printers, on the ground that their other monopoly was infringed, and were awarded an injunction restraining sale. The University fought back, and a long series of counter-actions reached the King's Bench. A decision was reached in favour of the University as defendants: it stated that the King's Printers were indeed entitled

> ...to the right of printing Acts of Parliament and Abridgements...exclusive of all other persons, not authorised to print the same, by prior Grants from the Crown.
>
> But we think that, by Virtue of the Letters Patent, bearing Date the 20th Day of July, in the 26th Year of the Reign of King Henry the 8th, and by Letters Patent, bearing Date the 6th of February in the 3rd Year of the Reign of King Charles the Ist, the Chancellor Masters and Scholars of the University are INTRUSTED, *with a concurrent Authority*, to print Acts of Parliament and Abridgements of Acts of Parliament, within the said University, upon the Terms in the said Letters Patent.
>
> (24 November 1755) Cooper: *Annals* IV, 301

At about this time the great jurist Blackstone was re-energising the Oxford Press, and Mr Justice Foster, one of the justices of the King's Bench, sent him a copy of this judgement, saying

> The Words underlined [italicised] were thrown in, by way of an Intimation to the University, that we consider the Powers, given by the Letters Patent as a trust reposed in that learned Body, for public Benefit, for the Advancement of Literature, and not to be transferred upon lucrative Views to other Hands. I hope both the Universities will always consider the royal Grants in that light.
>
> Cooper: *Annals* IV, 301, n

These were farsighted and penetrating remarks, picking up the prophetic observation of W.D. in the 1660s (p. 78). It was beginning to become clear that the old disputes had simply established rights; now the rights had to be given a meaning. Increasingly throughout the eighteenth century, the University in talking formally about itself was moving away from the aggressive stance in which it was merely asserting that it was an independent corporation, would not suffer the jurisdiction of the Bishop of Ely and enjoyed primacy over the municipality of Cambridge. It was now talking of itself as having a purpose: and that was to be a centre of learning which had to be preserved and increased, of education in which that learning was passed on to the young, and of religion, which was still inextricably connected with the service of the State at large. The right to print, which was based on the authority of the University as a centre of religious teaching and therefore of orthodoxy, which therefore made it a licensing authority, was now being given a wider significance. Bentley's endeavours and those of his colleagues had envisaged a learned press, which would without taint of commerce print, with worthy materials, technical skill and accuracy, the learned works written by the senior members of the University. At that time the rights established in the struggle with the Stationers, and which could be used to make an income, were leased back to the Stationers in a mixture of high-mindedness and shrewdness, and the receipts not placed at the disposal of the Press. Now it was being pointed out by the judges, who were as wise as they were learned, that if those rights were envisaged as a trust, the University and its Press could use them to perfectly proper advantage. The gentle rebuke about 'lucrative views' applied to the farming of the privilege by others for their commercial advantage. It could not apply to the use of those rights by the University if the receipts were turned to its own disinterested purposes, and especially to the publication of works of learning. These by their nature were expensive to produce, and had a small and slow sale to a learned readership which was not rich and could not afford the economic price. Such works needed therefore to be financed by some other undertaking which was not discreditable, so that the means should not corrupt the end or take priority over it. Nothing could be more creditable than the supply, to members of the national Church and others, of the Bible in the Authorized Version of that Church, or the Book of Common Prayer whose use had by Act of Parliament been made mandatory in 1662.

Baskett, as King's Printer, had been served notice that his activities as University Printer were an exercise of an authority concurrent with his activities as King's Printer, and that the authority of Bentham at Cambridge was of greater antiquity, and the ultimate source of his own powers at Oxford. It was not the end of all quarrels between the Royal Printers (the Stationers by now having lost power as a trading entity) and the two universities. But there was no serious challenge from now on, until in 1961–3 the Queen's Printer attempted to question the copy-right of the two universities in the New English Bible.

It is to Cambridge's credit that the advantage of the Bible privilege was accepted as implying a responsibility for the text. In 1629 and 1638 the Bucks and Daniel had made real attempts not only to print accurately but also to correct some of the inconsistencies in the London editions; and their work clearly entailed the activity of a learned editor who understood in principle what needed doing. In 1762 Bentham's folio Bible appeared. It was called the 'standard' edition because both Cambridge and other printers used it as the copy in later re-prints. It was carefully prepared by Dr F. S. Parris, Master of Sidney Sussex, and Dr Therond of Trinity. Apart from the correction of layers or generations of printing errors, the spelling and punctuation were revised, and the use of italics (for words not in the original language of the text, but necessary to the English sense) was made consistent. A quarto edition was pub-lished in the same year. A good deal of the stock of Parris's edition was lost in a fire, so that its influence was more limited than it should have been; but insofar as it was used by Cambridge and other printers to set from, it had a beneficial effect.

It was in order to print a folio Bible and an octavo Book of Common Prayer that John Baskerville sought and obtained appointment as University Printer. He exercised it for only about five years, so he was for that time co-Printer with Bentham, who served from his appointment in 1740 to his retirement in 1766. Baskerville's interests were aesthetic and technical. He began his career as a writing-master in Birmingham, and that obviously accounts for his interest in letter-forms and type design. He made a fortune in the trade in 'japanned' goods, and his knowledge of lacquers no doubt turned into an interest in ink manufacture and an almost fanatical concern with the finish of the printed page which transformed the uneven presswork of the old wooden press into something very much more modern-looking.

In 1757 he sent a specimen of type to a friend in Cambridge, explaining, with the same sort of practicality that distinguished Bentley's letter to Newton, that these types were meant to be readable by people who were beginning to have the usual middle-age problem of short-distance focusing but who did not like to fiddle with spectacles in church. He went on:

If I find favour with the University, & they give me a grant to print an Edition of a prayer book according to the specimen I would...send to Cambridge two presses, Workmen & all other requisites, but should be glad to take the chance of the Edition to myself, & make the University such Considerations as they should think fit to prescribe...My highest ambition is to print a folio Bible, with the same letter of the enclosed Specimen.

Baskerville negotiated with the University, and was appointed one of its Printers in December 1758. The main aim was to print the Bible and two prayer books; he was to obtain formal permission from the Syndicate if he wanted to print other editions; he was to describe himself as Printer to the University on no other books; his workshop was to be regularly inspected, and he had to pay the University £20 for each thousand copies printed of the larger prayer book. In May 1759 Baskerville wrote to the Vice-Chancellor (*ex officio* Chairman of the Syndicate):

I am taking great pains, in order to produce a striking title-page & specimen of the Bible which I hope will be ready in about six weeks. The importance of the work demands all my attention; not only for my own (eternal) reputation; but (I hope) also to convince the world, that the University in the honour done me has not intirely misplaced their Favours.

You will please to accept & give my most respectful duty to the University, particularly to the Gentlemen of the Syndick. I should be very happy if I could make an interest to a few Gent.[n] to whom the work would not be disagreeable, to survey the sheets, after my people had corrected them as accurately as they are able, that I might, if possible, be free from every error of the press; for which I would gladly make suitable acknowledgements.

'Making an interest' is eighteenth-century English for 'offering a payment' (in the nineteenth century payment of a fee was called a 'compliment'). The Syndicate may have used equally genteel language, but were quite tough. On second thoughts, they decided that Baskerville should pay £12. 10. 0 for every thousand of the smaller prayer book. Baskerville chafed somewhat at the payments and the difficulties, and wrote to Horace Walpole in November 1762:

The University of Cambridge have given me a Grant to print there 8vo and 12mo Common prayer Books; but under such Shackles as greatly hurt me. I pay them for the former twenty, & for the latter twelve pound ten shillings

# THE

## CONTAINING THE

# OLD TESTAMENT

### AND

# *THE NEW:*

Tranflated out of the

### AND

# With the former TRANSLATIONS

## Diligently Compared and Revifed,

*By His MAJESTY's Special Command.*

APPOINTED TO BE READ IN CHURCHES.

## CAMBRIDGE,

Printed by *JOHN BASKERVILLE*, Printer to the UNIVERSITY.

M DCC LXIII.

*CUM PRIVILEGIO.*

Baskerville's folio Bible, 1763 (much reduced).

the thousand, & to the Stationers Company thirty two pound for their permission to print one Edition of the Psalms in metre to the small prayer book: add to this the great Expence of double and treble carriage, & the inconvenience of a Printing House an hundred Miles off. All this Summer I have had nothing to print at Home. My folio Bible is pretty far advanced at Cambridge, which will cost me near £2000 all hired at 5 p. Cent. If this does not sell, I shall be obliged to sacrifice a small Patrimony which brings me in £74 a Year to this Business of printing; which I am heartily tired of & repent I ever attempted. It is surely a particular hardship that I should not get Bread in my own Country (and it is too late to go abroad) after having acquired the Reputation of excelling in the most useful Art known to Mankind; while everyone who excels as a Player, Fidler, Dancer &c not only lives in Affluence but has it in their power to save a Fortune.

The Bible appeared in 1763, the prayer books having come out in 1760 (two being reprinted in 1761). All were printed in Baskerville's own delicate roman and italic type, and the prayer books used his pretty type-ornaments. He printed on smooth 'wove' paper specially manufactured for him by James Whatman, not the rough 'antique laid' which was standard. The ink, very glossy and black, was manufactured to his specification. When the light type had been neatly impressed on the new kind of paper, the printed sheets were 'hot-pressed' between copper plates, which gave the same gloss as ironing a newly manufactured fabric. Since the effect of Baskerville's printing is the unadorned result of type, ink and paper, this attention to detail in type design, careful setting, presswork, paper and ink produces the classic beauty of pure printing. In the Bible it is delicate and graceful in detail, but imposing and austere in general proportion and in the abstention from all ornament. It is one of the great Bibles of all time: indeed the half-dozen or so folio Bibles of the same quality were printed mostly in the sixteenth century in France and Switzerland. Since Baskerville, only the Bruce Rogers Bible printed at Oxford in 1935 comes anywhere near him in authority and grandeur – though Rogers borrowed essential features of his design from Robert Estienne's great folios of 1532 and 1540.

While the University had leased a right to Baskerville, and charged him for it, it is clear that his own ambitions were not primarily commercial: it was his own (eternal) reputation he was seeking – that last infirmity of noble mind, as Milton had said. And indeed he did secure that reputation. But though he had secured 265 subscribers (their names are printed in the preliminary pages, and some – mostly booksellers – had ordered two, six, or more copies), the Bible seems to have been a commercial failure. After his death in 1775 the punches for his types were bought through the agency of Beaumarchais and went to Neuchâtel, but were identified nearly two centuries later and returned to Cambridge by the generous gift of the Fonderies Deberny and Peignot.

Bentham went on as Printer until 1766, and was succeeded by John Archdeacon, who was elected in December of that year at a salary of £140. Crownfield had been paid only £26, and even allowing for inflation the office was now clearly thought a substantial one. There are other signs that the Press in this period was prosperous. In 1765 the London bookseller Bowyer, being informed that for the previous seven years the University had made a surplus of £1300 annually, plus the £200 p.a. which they received from the Stationers for not printing almanacs, entertained the notion of becoming Printer and using Archdeacon as his manager in Cambridge. There was scope for 'opening the trade in new channels' and 'an immense fortune would certainly be raised'. Bowyer was being tempted to become a latter-day Baskett; but nothing came of the scheme.

The fortunes of the Press were undoubtedly founded on the Bible and the Book of Common Prayer. In the 1760s, 1770s and 1780s it was usual that at least one edition of the Bible was printed each year, and often more. All the formats were printed, from folio through quarto and octavo to duodecimo. The outlets must have been mostly through London booksellers, and there were now regular accounts with more than one agent: Edward Dilly, John Rivington, James Waugh, T. and J. Merrill. Archdeacon kept the books, and his accounts were approved and signed by members of the Syndicate.

On the other hand, the University had relinquished its right to print almanacs, and in 1777 a new contract was made with the Stationers which gave the University an annual income of £500 for twenty-one years in return for the Stationers' right to print without competition a number of schoolbooks including our old friend Lily's Grammar, still in use after over two hundred years. A similar agreement was made with Oxford; but both were upset by a certain Thomas Carnan, who was from all the evidence an exceedingly tedious person, but who managed in the end to give the two universities an unplanned benefit. Carnan was a bookseller in St Paul's Churchyard, and a litigious man: it was thought that by the time he died in 1788 he had spent £10,000 on lawsuits. The one which gave him the fatal taste would have put others off for life, but showed a fatal persuasion of the justice of any cause so long as it was his. It had to do with a favourite mare. It was first stolen, and he successfully prosecuted the thief. Then it died, but he became persuaded that it had been stolen again and that the report of its death was an attempt to deceive him. He 'repossessed' the horse, which was not his, was prosecuted, lost, appealed, indicted people for perjury, lost both suits, was prosecuted for malicious prosecution, lost, brought writs of error to the House of Lords, and lost again. Obviously not a born winner, he gets high marks for trying. With the Stationers' Company he had more luck because he had a better case. When he was prosecuted by the Company for printing almanacs, it was found in his favour by the Court of Common Pleas in 1775 that the right of printing almanacs was a common law right over which the Crown had no control. This was a severe blow to the Stationers, and the Company discontinued its payments to both universities, who were thus by Carnan's public-spirited action deprived of an advantage which had in recent years been used for the public benefit. The issue was debated for some time, and in 1779 Lord North, First Lord of the Treasury and also Chancellor of Oxford, moved leave to introduce into the Commons a bill to vest the sole right of printing almanacs in the two universities and the Stationers' Company. This would have restored the *status quo*, benefiting the universities – but also the Stationers, who could not themselves claim that the benefit was received in trust and put to disinterested use by a charitable body dedicated to the pursuit of learning. In the debate which followed it became obvious that monopolies were now offensive to public opinion.

The motion was defeated by sixty to forty, and the peroration of the closing speech by the Hon. Thomas Erskine of Trinity College, later Lord Erskine, Lord High Chancellor of England, is worth quoting. He appeared as counsel for Carnan:

And now Mr Speaker, I retire from your bar, I wish I could say with confidence of having prevailed. If the wretched Company of Stationers had been my only opponents, my confidence had been perfect; indeed so perfect, that I should not have wasted ten minutes of your time on the subject, but should have left the Bill to dissolve in its own weakness: but, when I reflect that Oxford and Cambridge are suitors here, I own to you that I am alarmed, and I feel called upon to say something, which I know your indulgence will forgive. The House is filled with their most illustrious sons, who no doubt feel an involuntary zeal for the interest of their parent Universities. Sir, it is an influence so natural, and so honourable, that I trust there is no indecency in my hinting the possibility of its operation. Yet I persuade myself that these learned bodies have effectually defeated their own interests, by the sentiments which their liberal sciences have disseminated amongst you; their wise and learned institutions have erected in your minds the august image of an enlightened statesman, which, trampling down all personal interests and affections, looks steadily forward to the great ends of public and private justice, unawed by authority, and unbiased by favour.

It is from thence that my hopes for my client revive. If the Universities have lost an advantage, enjoyed contrary to law, and at the expence of sound policy and liberty, you will rejoice that the courts below have pronounced that wise and liberal judgement against them, and will not set the evil example of reversing it here. But you need not therefore forget, that the universities have lost an advantage, – and if it be a loss that can be felt by bodies so liberally endowed, it may be repaired to them by the bounty of the crown, or by your own. It were much better that the people of England should pay £10,000 a year to each of them, than suffer them to enjoy one farthing at the expense of the ruin of a free citizen, or the monopoly of a free trade.

Cooper, *Annals* IV, 392n.

These wise words, elegantly and persuasively phrased, must have had their effect. In 1781 the Almanac Duty Act was passed, imposing a duty on almanacs, whoever printed them, and providing that out of that duty £500 should be paid annually to each of the two universities. The ground of this award was that in the past

the Money so received by them has been laid out and expended in promoting different branches of Literature and Science, to the great increase of Religion and Learning, and the general benefit and advantage of these Realms.

The sum payable by the Act was, by Grace of 11 June 1782, placed at the disposal of the Syndics of the Press for the publication of new works or editions of old works.

Almanac Duty itself was abolished in William IV's reign; but for two hundred years the Press received its annual £500 from the State. It was carefully allocated to named works of learning currently in production or recently published. It was the only benefit which the Press regularly received from an outside source. As its value declined it became principally a token that the State recognised that the presses of the two ancient universities managed without other regular subsidy to shoulder the major part of the burden of producing works of learning: a charge which might have fallen on the State if it were not so effectually carried out. Its discontinuance in 1981, on the two hundredth anniversary of its first payment, was received with regret as a kind of abandonment and a failure of recognition: it saved the taxpayer no noticeable sum of money and the civil service no burden of administration. It had a symbolic significance only, and should have been preserved for precisely that reason. Among the things it might have symbolised was gratitude that a cultural institution of proved national importance required no more help from the taxpayer, but had by its ingenuity, persistence and energy survived for four hundred years and grown into a characteristically English enterprise: unique, anomalous in that it is both charitable and independent, and very effective.

Archdeacon was Printer for nearly thirty years, being succeeded by John Burges in 1793. Richard Watts was Printer from 1802 to 1809, and then there began the long service of John Smith (1809–36) and John William Parker (1836–54). With the nineteenth century we are effectively in another age, and should pause a moment to look back on the century of activity which started under Bentley.

Inevitably the Press was at this time very much what the Duke of Somerset had imagined: the facility which enabled senior members of the University to commit to print their own intellectual productions. Somerset rather grandly called them 'those great, & excellent writinges, yt are so frequently published from ye

Members of yr own body'. Would that it had been so: but both the greatness and the frequency fell far short of his vision.

It is now too easy to see the ancient universities in the eighteenth century merely as a haven for plump clerics who did nothing but take the revenues of College or University office and, as Pope ambiguously put it, 'sleep in port'. It is true that this was the period of professors who mostly did not lecture, so that the pious Dr Parr, gazing benignly on one such, observed that 'the profound researches of Dr Waring, I suppose, were not adapted to any form of communication by lectures'. The University, having adapted its course of instruction and examination surprisingly rapidly in order to take account of Newtonian mathematics, seems almost to have exhausted itself intellectually in the effort, and most of its activity during the century was channelled into the College lectures and the University examinations, in which the medieval form received a Newtonian content. For many senior men their own active part in the dialectic of oral examination in Latin for higher degrees was their chief contribution. Apart from that main stream, individual scholars were free to engage in research, but since this was divorced from College teaching it was a lonely pursuit, often abandoned when the hitherto celibate don married and went off to a country living in the gift of his College. But a few persisted, and their research reached publication at the Press. The Professors of Chemistry were not inactive: in 1758 John Hadley published *The Plan of a Course of Chemical Lectures* – a detailed syllabus of forty-five pages. Hadley did give these lectures – for two years, at any rate. The first Lowndean Professor of Astronomy, Roger Long, Master of Pembroke, was appointed twelve years before the Statutes of that Chair were drawn up: they required him to lecture, to purchase instruments, and to make observations. He published a work on astronomy in two volumes at the Press. William Farish, a later Professor of Chemistry, delivered very popular lectures on the application of chemistry to the arts and manufactures of Great Britain, and the plan of these lectures was published in 1796 (evidently these 'plans', frequently published, enabled listeners to grasp the overall structure of the course). Of another Professor of Chemistry, Richard Watson, something is said below.

The study of Greek and Roman literature at Cambridge produced in Richard Porson a scholar of European reputation. His publications belong to the first years of the nineteenth century; a predecessor at Cambridge was Richard Dawes, whose *Miscellanea Critica* was published at the Press in 1745, and went through five editions by 1827: the two nineteenth-century editions were due to the influence of Porson and his pupils.

There were Cambridge dons who were not happy with the University's long intellectual sleep and its antiquated procedures. St John's College actually examined its undergraduates every year, and John Jebb (a respected Cambridge name) conducted a long campaign to make this a requirement throughout the University. He published his *Remarks on Education* at the Press in 1773; and there followed a running controversy in which others took part – for instance W. S. Powell's *Observations on Annual Examinations* in 1774.

But Jebb was the sort of campaigner who finally loses, not because his case is unsound but because he is. He had published an *Account* of his theological lectures in 1770 which revealed that he shared the then current Cambridge heresy, Unitarianism, so he was linked with early stages of the movement which led to the *cause célèbre* of the 1790s – that of William Frend, who was finally expelled from the University in 1793, to the great indignation of advanced young men like Coleridge. The most general aspect of these rumblings and occasional outbursts was the formal requirement of the University that its members should be orthodox members of the Church of England, and should declare as much by subscribing to a formula which included the Thirty-Nine Articles. This itself became a cause, and in the 'Anti-Subscription' controversy of the last quarter of the century Jebb also took part. His scheme for examinations was therefore contemptuously dismissed as the scheme of a fanatic.

Deeper than the issues of examinations and membership of the Church there lay fundamental political currents. The whole complex of intellectual trends and personal involvements may be illustrated by the case of Richard Watson, another Press author. He was a man of great activity and self-confidence. He was of course a minister of the Church of England, like virtually all dons

at the time. He had been Second Wrangler in the Tripos Examination, i.e. second in order of merit in the mathematical examination conducted in the Senate House which was the principal
exercise for a degree and which had only recently changed from
being conducted in Latin to being conducted in English. Watson
himself as Moderator improved the examination by taking candidates in groups selected according to merit, as shown by performance in the other exercises in the Schools, so he was the founder
of the distinction which later grew up between honours and pass
degrees. Looking for preferment, Watson's eye fell on the Chair
of Chemistry. He was elected to it in 1764. He knew absolutely
nothing of chemistry. What was perhaps more surprising at the
time, he learnt the subject in fifteen months, and began to lecture
on it. His *Chemical Essays*, published at the Press in 1781, were
reprinted, translated into German and won the approval of Sir
Humphry Davy. He improved the manufacture of gunpowder,
and saved the nation £100,000. Being a hard-headed man,
Watson secured a stipend from the Crown for his Chair – only
£100 a year, though. That was not enough for a man of his
ambitions, so he resigned the Chair of Chemistry and took the
Regius Chair of Divinity instead. In this capacity too he became
an author (as a cleric, he obviously had more of a start with the
subject). His *Theological Tracts* in several volumes appeared from
1785, and a succession of 'Addresses to Young Persons' and
'Charges to the Clergy' from 1787 onwards.

The Chair of Divinity was worth £300 a year initially, but
Professors seem to have been able to manage the endowments
of their Chairs, and Watson by good management raised his
stipend to £1000 p.a. – a very comfortable figure. He felt even
more comfortable as a Bishop, however, and became Bishop of
Llandaff. He appointed a deputy to give lectures on his behalf
in Cambridge so that he need not resign his Chair. It seems that
he did not disturb the Dean and Chapter of his diocese too much
either, for he resided mainly in London and in his native West-
morland, in a handsomely renovated country house, where he
carried out agrarian reforms. There, in 1793, he was the aston-
ished recipient of a long letter from a young Cambridge graduate
of no academic distinction, called Wordsworth, of St John's,

apparently a poet, who took fierce exception to a sermon which Watson had published in London. This touched on events in France, where the September massacres had taken place and the King had been executed, so that liberals such as Frend and Jebb and Wordsworth who had thought in a theoretical way that the Revolution was the dawn of a new era now had to wonder whether they really would be happy to see the same things happen in England. Wordsworth still was so minded – though already shaken by what he had seen in France. What specially irked him about Watson's immense complacency was that Watson had once been a liberal himself. He was now saying in his sermon that it was a sign of God's special providence that He had created both rich and poor; that the poor in England were well looked after and had no cause to murmur. But in the early years of his career Watson had not got on in the Church, and had perhaps been forced to profess chemistry to make a living, because he had been thought too radical by his fellow clergy. He had even welcomed the American Revolution in 1776 and the French Revolution in 1789. So he was a turncoat of an odious kind. The final irony, of course, is that in the end Wordsworth himself abandoned the illusions of his youth, and became a Tory. It would be charitable to assume that the agony he went through in that long change of mind also touched, however lightly, the more worldly Watson. The process which young Cambridge men went through between 1776 or 1789 and 1815 was an interesting parallel to what they went through between 1917 and the 1950s, and it is a mistake to be too easily amused at Richard Watson, or at the University as a whole in the period before the reforms of the mid-nineteenth century. Under the complacent surface there was a reforming turbulence: a great deal was being felt and thought and discussed.

Not so much was being published, however. Safely and perhaps salutarily mad, the poet Christopher Smart for several years won the Seatonian Prize, the winning poem being printed at the Press. The Seatonian Prize was founded by the will of Thomas Seaton, Vicar of Ravenston in Buckinghamshire and sometime Fellow of Clare Hall. He left an estate whose revenue was to provide a prize for a Master of Arts whose poem, in English, was judged the best by the Vice-Chancellor, the Master of Clare and the Professor of Greek. It was to be printed at the expense of the fund, and the subject was to be 'for the first year, one or other of the Perfections or Attributes of the Supreme Being, and so the succeeding years, till the subject is exhausted; and afterwards the subject shall be either Death, Judgement, Heaven, Hell, Purity of Heart &c'. During Smart's time the Attributes of the Supreme Being had not been exhausted as a topic, and in 1750 he wrote on the Eternity of the Supreme Being, in 1752 on His Omniscience, in 1753 on His Immensity, in 1754 on His Power, in 1756 on His Goodness.

Thomas Gray's Commemoration Ode, written for the installation of the Duke of Grafton as Chancellor, and set to music by Dr Randal, was printed in 1769. The study of botany in Cambridge was somewhat advanced during this period, and Thomas Martyn, the Professor of Botany, published a *Catalogue of the Botanical Garden* in 1771, his *Mantissa Plantarum* in 1772 and *Elements of Natural History* in 1775. For a time he was among the Professors who lectured, and to a sizeable audience, and in 1791 he considered that he had 'disseminated the knowledge of botany and of the Linnaean system' to more than five hundred people by word of mouth.

Perhaps the most ambitious publishing project of the second half of the century was the facsimile in two volumes of the *Codex Bezae*, 1793. The editor was Thomas Kipling, and the edition remained in print and in use for a century or more. The fifth-century manuscript, given to the University in 1581 by the great Swiss Calvinist scholar Theodore de Bèze, is one of the main sources of the text of the Greek New Testament, and its publication in this form is a clear sign that scholarship was not dead and the heritage of the heroic past not neglected.

# 9

## THE NINETEENTH CENTURY – I

THERE CAN BE NO DOUBT that the history of the University in the nineteenth century falls into two clear halves. At the end of the first, a Royal Commission reported to the Crown on the state of the University in 1852, and a further Statutory Commission was appointed in 1856 to revise the Statutes both of the University and of the Colleges. Its work on the University was completed and new Statutes in operation by 1861. Before the Commissions were imposed on the University it had already achieved a respectable measure of self-reform: indeed the first half of the century was marked by the struggle of men like Adam Sedgwick and William Whewell to persuade their colleagues to go as far as they could voluntarily, since certainly they could later be forced to go further. The whole process of reform, voluntary and imposed (though the Commissioners were mostly eminent Cambridge men) transformed the University, and was justified by the extraordinary outburst of intellectual activity which followed. The old studies, mathematics and classics (the only subjects for tripos examination before reform), were strengthened: and new triposes proliferated, in natural science, moral science, theology, history and so on; and first within the Moral Science Tripos and later as independent subjects, new studies such as economics, ethnography – indeed history itself – were fostered. When mathematics and classics were the only subjects examined for degrees, and when all formal teaching for the purposes of degree courses was done by the Colleges, lectures on other subjects by University Professors attracted a merely interested audience of amateurs and laymen: hence all those 'plans' of lectures, published at the Press, to attract the attention of possible hearers. When these other subjects were seriously pursued as courses leading to honours, the position of Professors was transformed, and so was their quality and their performance — also (from the publishing point of view) their interest as potential authors.

But in 1800 all that lay in the future. At this period the Press should be considered as a sizeable printing business whose fortunes were securely founded on the printing of Bibles and prayer books, for which a ready sale could be found, mostly through the London agents. The printing of the Bible was to remain throughout the century the central platform of the Press's fortunes, and its importance was greatly increased by two factors. The inauguration and growth of the British and Foreign Bible Society provided an ever-increasing outlet for cheap printings; and the technological development of printing itself made the supply of that growing market possible.

The Bible Society was founded in 1804. It was at first looked on somewhat askance in Establishment Cambridge because it was not a Church of England preserve. By statute, on its committee of thirty-six, fifteen places were reserved for the Dissenting Churches and six for European Churches. When therefore there was in 1811 a move among evangelically-minded undergraduates in Cambridge to found an auxiliary branch of the Society, there was opposition from senior members. Dr Isaac Milner, President of Queens' and also a Syndic of the Press, and the great evangelical Vicar of Holy Trinity Church, Charles Simeon (whose sermons were printed at the Press from the 1790s onwards), undertook to manage the necessary diplomacy with the University, and in effect took over the scheme. The Chancellor offered a subscription and accepted the Presidency, other sums were promised by noble Dukes and an Earl who was also a Bishop, and the Master of Trinity (Christopher Wordsworth, the poet's brother) and Milner agreed to attend the inaugural meeting. These encouragements were evangelically considered not just as signs of divine favour but virtually an apotheosis. 'Truly God shows that He reigns in the Earth', Simeon exclaimed. At the meeting itself he thought the unanimity was 'like the day of Pentecost' though it is not recorded that even upon the Master of Trinity there descended cloven tongues like as of fire, or that he spoke in other tongues.

The Society had started as a result of a plea for Bibles in Welsh. One such Bible had been printed at Cambridge in 1746, but the evangelical revivals of the later part of the century had increased the demand, while the poverty of many readers meant that it had to be supplied as a charitable undertaking. From that local beginning the Society grew into a national and then an international missionary enterprise, with its colporteurs distributing Bibles in other languages throughout Europe and then throughout the world. With translation work into non-European languages the Society and its daughter-societies (the American Bible Society was founded in 1816) became centres of remarkable linguistic expertise. From the point of view of one of the three presses entitled to print the King James Bible in England, supplying the Society was an important challenge in two respects. First, the Society as a charitable enterprise was committed to using its funds to supply purchasers at less than commercial prices, indeed at 20% below cost, or if necessary free: it therefore posed a potentially annihilating threat of unbeatable competition to the privileged presses. But since they were thus privileged, only they could supply the Society with its Bibles, and they were able to influence (within the limits of competition between themselves) the terms of supply. So a *modus vivendi* developed.

By an extraordinary coincidence there was developed at this very moment an improved technique of stereotyping which at last made it possible to avoid the two wasteful alternative methods of printing used hitherto: Canstein's, by which type was kept standing; or everyone else's, by which the type was reset every time an impression was needed. Stereotyping meant that a cast could be taken from the surface of a whole page of composed type, and the moulds kept. Plates could be cast from these, and re-cast when needed, so a single setting could be used to produce an indefinite number of impressions. The new process – an advance on Ged's – had been developed in 1803 by the versatile Earl Stanhope, a noted scientist and inventor, who gave the commercial rights to an entrepreneur, Andrew Wilson. Wilson communicated this to Cambridge for a substantial consideration,

THE

# NEW

# TESTAMENT

OF

## OUR LORD AND SAVIOUR

## JESUS CHRIST:

TRANSLATED OUT OF THE ORIGINAL GREEK;

AND WITH

THE FORMER TRANSLATIONS DILIGENTLY COMPARED AND REVISED,

BY HIS MAJESTY'S SPECIAL COMMAND.

*Appointed to be read in Churches.*

CAMBRIDGE STEREOTYPE EDITION.

*CAMBRIDGE:*

STEREOTYPED AND PRINTED BY R. WATTS,

FOR THE UNIVERSITY;

And Sold by Messrs. *Rivington*, St. Paul's Church-Yard; Mr. *Mawman*, in the
Poultry, London; and Mr. *Deighton*, Cambridge.

*July,* 1805.

The Cambridge Stereotype Bible; title-page of the New Testament,
1805. The first successful application of stereotyping to the printing
of the Bible. The edition was reprinted many times.

and the first stereotyped Bible was the Cambridge Stereotype Edition, of which the New Testament appeared in 1805, and the complete Bible in 1806. This was immediately purchased in quantity by the Bible Society, which held up its operations until it could use the new method.

The Press had now a brief commercial advantage, though the King's Printer and Oxford rapidly acquired the technique and joined Cambridge as suppliers of the Society's expanding needs. It would theoretically have been possible, or at any rate much more easy, to compete with the Bible Society by using the technological advantage. More sensibly the three privileged presses decided both to supply the Society and to attempt to maintain their own share of the market (inevitably, the middle and top end).

Stanhope also developed the printing-press itself, producing an iron press which was capable of a much greater and more even pressure, greater precision of register, and a longer and more trouble-free life than the old wooden press. The Fourdrinier brothers employed the British engineer Bryan Donkin to make the first practical paper-making machine in 1803, and by 1812 ten such machines were in operation in Europe, and machine-made paper became plentiful and cheap. Friedrich König came to London in 1806 and patented his printing machine in 1810. In collaboration with his compatriot Bauer he developed this machine, and on Tuesday 29 November 1814 the whole issue of *The Times* was printed by machine at the rate of 1100 sheets an hour. A very good team of pressmen in the handpress era might have been able to produce that number of sheets in a twelve-hour day, but it was rare. If Gutenberg had come back to earth one hundred, two hundred, or even three hundred years after his invention, he would have recognised printing as essentially the same process that it was in his time. Only after four hundred years would he have had cause to be surprised: but once the separate techniques began to change, they all changed rapidly within the course of the century. The application of steam-power to printing provided an obvious increase of power and acceleration of output. This took place in the 1830s. Mechanical typesetting and the mechanisation of binding were the last stages of the whole process, and they followed in the last quarter of the century.

In England these changes heralded the Education Act of 1870, which provided for universal education. But there was already a large reading public for some kinds of printed matter, and as in previous centuries the Bible was still the book which sold more copies than any other; and in the new industrial centres a virtually pagan population was being evangelised by a vigorous missionary movement. For the whole century, therefore, Bibles, New Testaments and prayer books were the staple output of the Press. It was in fact the smallest of the three privileged presses: Oxford had been large ever since Baskett's time, and the King's Printer maintained an even larger output than the universities because Royal Printers had always assumed that their Patent gave them the right to subcontract to other printers.

The University Printers of the time at Cambridge were Richard Watts (1802–9), John Smith (1809–36), and John William Parker (1836–54). John Deighton of the celebrated bookselling and publishing family was appointed Printer in 1802 and acted till 1811, but seems to have been a publishing agent in London and Cambridge rather than an active printer. It was Watts who had to introduce stereotyping, and the negotiations with Wilson for the use of the process involved complicated financial deals which almost certainly produced a loss in the first years of its use. At the same time the University was completely rebuilding its printing house, a quite large and expensive enterprise by the standards of the time. It is not surprising that in 1808 Isaac Milner and another Syndic were asked to examine the Press's accounts: a sign of concern. A pamphlet called *Facts and Observations Relative to the State of the University Press* appeared in 1808, and Milner and his colleague Wood must have been the authors, since the wretched Watts maintained his own position in a *Reply to the Report of Dr Milner and Mr Wood* printed in 1809. (In the days before typewriters and photocopying, the only way to circulate copies of a report was to print it. That is why our ancestors seem so formidably and publicly quarrelsome: it was virtually impossible to do these things privately.) It was the second such public washing of the Press's linen, following the similar negative autopsy in 1737 on Bentley's bold venture and its inevitable running-down. Watts resigned, no doubt feeling hard-done-by. The force of the charge against him was that the Press had made an average profit of £1500 p.a. before 1802, but none since then. In the circumstances, it is hardly surprising.

It will be remembered that the old printing house built in 1655 on the north side of Silver Street and at the corner of Queens' Lane had been in continuous occupation since 1707. It had been somewhat extended, but was at the limit of its useful life. The Press had actually crossed Silver Street in 1762 when it bought the site of the old White Lion Inn for a warehouse, which was built in 1786. In 1804 Watts was instructed to turn this warehouse into a printing office. A stereotype foundry was built adjoining it, and so was started the slow but steady process by which during the course of the century the Press gradually acquired virtually the whole site which runs back from the Pitt Building to Laundress Lane, with the exception of some houses and shops in Silver Street.

The most striking of these buildings is of course the Pitt Building itself, which, with its square tower, its pinnacles and other gothic ornaments, its oriel window above the doorway, its pleasantly warm-coloured stone facing, and its agreeable feeling of grandeur tempered by amenity, forms such a happy part of the Cambridge skyline and the procession of buildings between the Fitzwilliam Museum and the Waterhouse Building at Caius. It is still the symbolic and ceremonial headquarters of the Press, where the Syndicate meets and the Secretary has an office. It was not always kindly regarded. It is now thought one of the better nineteenth-century buildings, along with the New Building of St John's; but there was a time earlier in this century when persons of progressive taste shuddered at both, because the historical allusiveness was 'inauthentic' or 'unfunctional' (words of fear). Willis and Clark, tight-lipped, refer to the building as 'Late Perpendicular'. But the honest reaction of the tourist is admiration, and of the Cambridge inhabitant affection. The staff of the Press feel pride in it, as giving, in the historic centre of the town, an imposing yet agreeable symbol that the University

An early portrayal of the Pitt Building.

has its Press, a historic institution and an organic part of the architectural as well as the intellectual fabric of the whole. Those who worked in it until 1980 have a fond remembrance even of its severe inconveniences.

William Pitt the Younger, Prime Minister at twenty-three and great war leader against Napoleon, had died in 1806. He had been an undergraduate at Pembroke College, and was regularly re-elected to the Commons as what used to be called Burgess of the University (University seats in Parliament were not abolished until the twentieth century). At his death statues and memorials were erected. One public fund which had been started in his life-time to finance the erection of the statue of Pitt by Chantrey in Hanover Square had a substantial surplus left over, and the sug-gestion came from Cambridge itself that this money might be used 'for the Erection of an handsome Building connected with the University Press at Cambridge'. If the University for its part would acquire a site facing Pitt's old College, the Committee in London, as the Chairman, Lord Camden, wrote in 1824, would provide funds for a building 'on such a scale as to be a distinguished Ornament to the University, and tend to perpetuate the Name and memory of Mr Pitt'.

The University Press had already started to build on the island site between Silver Street and Mill Lane, and had its warehouse there. The erection of the Pitt Building was supervised in Cambridge by a Syndicate which organised the purchase of the land by the University for £12,000, and appointed as architect Edward Blore, best known for the house at Abbotsford which he designed for Walter Scott. Since the aim was frankly to build a memorial, it was more important that the building should have a tower, pinnacles, an oriel window, an imposing entrance, a ceremonial staircase (now replaced) and a handsome room behind the oriel window, than that it should serve the humble day-to-day purposes of the printing or any other business. No one now regrets this, though John Smith, the University Printer, may well have wondered what on earth he was going to do with the extraordinary present he was being given. But that was not the problem of the London Committee or the Cambridge Syndicate. They saw their dream-building erected. For a mere additional £1700 Blore also put up the north range of the brick-built internal court behind the Pitt Building in the severely elegant and quite practical Georgian style which architects and builders of the time provided without thinking about it: and this must have pleased Smith more.

The foundation stone of the Pitt Building was laid, with ceremony and speeches, in October 1831. The Building was opened, with more ceremony and more speeches, in April 1833. The ceremony was described by the Registrary Joseph Romilly in his diary:

*Tu. 30.* The grand procession to the Pitt Press where Lord Camden delivered up the key to the V. Chr – Ld Camden spoke with a loud clear voice, but from attempting to talk after his ideas were exhausted decidedly broke down. Dr Webb in reply made a long wordy mouthy speech in praise of Billy Pitt: –

it was delivered awfully slowly & not worth hearing – saw Ld Camden &c work off [i.e. print on a hand-press] impressions of a Latin description of the work of the day. – Good lunch in the Syndicate rooms – Went with Lord Bayning to the top of the Press: a very good view of Cambridge: N.B. – a splendid day.

Romilly always enjoyed a lunch (a 'cold collation' on this occasion, according to Cooper) more than a speech: so do most of us; and he had a radical tinge which made him unsympathetic to 'Billy Pitt'. The official records may have groomed the speeches somewhat: they strike an edifying note which can now be taken seriously enough. Lord Camden (soon to be Chancellor) said, in part:

> The Committee, animated by a personal respect and affection towards their contemporary, have endeavoured to cause to be erected on this site, such a building as might prove an addition to the other great improvements already perfected in this place, and which, from its peculiar destination, will unite the name of Mr Pitt with all those works of religion, morality and science, which will in future emanate from it, and diffuse throughout the world the connexion of his name with erudition and learning.

The Vice-Chancellor in reply gave some cause for Romilly's reaction:

> What more appropriate monument then could be erected to the memory of Pitt than this building, the chief purpose and object of which is to send forth to the world the Word of God; and could he, with prophetic eye, when residing in yon neighbouring college, whose proudest boast is to number him amongst her sons – could he have beheld such a structure, bearing his name, raised for such a purpose, and erected by such friends, even his own eloquence would have scarce sufficed to express the feelings of his heart. My Lord, the edifice with which you have adorned this university, and the illustrious name it bears, will add a fresh stimulus to our exertions in the dissemination of truth, the extension of science, and the advancement of religious knowledge; and I humbly trust that nothing will ever issue from these walls but such works as may conduce to the furtherance of these important objects.

The building had cost £10,711. 8. 9. When it was completed and available, and people had to think what to do with it, they could find no easy answer. The rather dark ground floor was available to the Printer for storage. Elsewhere rooms were used for other kinds of storage: Whewell kept his mineralogical collection there; the Mesman collection of pictures was hung in the Oriel Room until the Fitzwilliam Museum was ready for them.

Romilly himself then acquired the room as the Registrary's office, and the University archive was kept in the tower. It was not until the 1930s that the new University Library building liberated space in the Old Schools for the Registry; the Pitt Building was then in 1937 at last converted into offices for the Printer. In 1963 when the Printer moved to his new building, the Oriel Room itself was finally used for the purpose for which it was designed: the Press Syndicate began to meet there; and found, final irony, that Blore's ceremonial gothic vault absorbed all sound so effectively that Syndics could scarcely hear each other across the hollow square of tables round which they sat. A temporary system of hangings on the walls improved the acoustics.

Behind the Pitt Building there was now forming a Cambridge 'court'. Two sides of the rectangle, the west and north ranges, were built in 1826 and 1831–2, and a house for the Printer was built in Mill Lane at the same time. The whole site was further developed as the century went on, to form the rambling complex of buildings, on three floors, with communicating yards and stairs and bridge, which formed the printing house until 1963. It became intolerably inconvenient in terms of work-flow; the floors would scarcely bear the weight of modern machines, the site offered no possibility of expansion, and it was very hard to get lorries in and out in modern traffic conditions. It was more like a 'printer's quarter' in a medieval town – as indeed it was – than an effective factory. But from the 1830s onwards, people walking down Silver Street would hear, especially before the increase of motor traffic, the steady tramp and thrashing of the old reciprocating cylinder-presses in the machine-room. It was like the breaking of mechanical waves, short, rapid and regular. It was a natural part of the life of the town, and reassuring.

In the 1830s, the Vice-Chancellor was quite correct in saying that the chief purpose and object of the Press was to send forth to the world (and especially to the British and Foreign Bible Society) the Word of God. Watts's successor as Printer, John Smith, served from 1809 to 1836. He inherited the unsatisfactory and no doubt costly working arrangement with Andrew Wilson, Stanhope's deputy in the matter of stereotyping; and indeed Wilson had a nominal post as Printer until 1811, acting as a kind of agent and partner in London. But there were disputes with him over the profit-sharing agreement, and it would seem that stereotyping never became easy – and therefore potentially profitable – until the original delicate and brittle plaster moulds were replaced by the much more flexible and easily used papier-mâché mould invented in Lyons in 1829. (The French called the mixture *flan*, and this was anglicised as 'flong'.) This meant that from the 1830s onwards Bible printing could become faster and more profitable, especially since steam-power was introduced at the same period. In effect, the Press was beginning to face some of the problems of a modern business, aiming to supply a mass market with a standardised product. The capital being steadily invested in buildings and equipment was getting unprecedentedly large. Technological innovation was making economical production possible, but the business needed to be run professionally if the plant was to be effectively used and there was to be an adequate return on the investment, and it seemed increasingly important to have an agency in London. Like Watts before him, Smith found himself criticised, and he printed the inevitable pamphlet in 1829, called *Observations Relating to the Affairs of the Press*.

He made some remarks which will be all too familiar to his successors: for instance that academic authors delivered copy late, or in irregular batches, and rewrote their books in proof, so that the corrections bill was ruinous; and that the greatly increased number of examination papers caused a seasonal surge which held up other work. He pointed out that when he was appointed the Press had only eight presses, and he had raised this to thirteen by 1813; but that he was under-equipped, and hard-pressed to supply the British and Foreign Bible Society with the increasing flow of Bibles which they ordered through the agency of the London firm of Rivington. He also presented a statement showing an average annual profit of £3191 from 1809 to 1827.

It seems that his statement was not accepted. The Syndicate asked Clowes of London, head of the printing and bookselling dynasty, to examine the Press and advise them. Clowes sent his very capable London overseer, John William Parker. As a result of their report Clowes himself was appointed Superintendent of the Press, on the understanding that he would supervise the London business, while Parker as his deputy would come to Cambridge and superintend the printing. Smith remained Printer until 1836, when he retired, and Parker then succeeded him. He commuted between Cambridge and London; his house in the Strand became in effect the Cambridge depository and agency – mainly for the sale of Bibles and prayer books, of course. Books were still usually published under an arrangement which stemmed from the eighteenth century; a partnership or 'conger' of Cambridge or London booksellers would commission and finance a book and then dispose of the edition between them. In such cases the Press was merely the printing facility. In other cases Parker himself would be one of the publishing partners. In a few cases, mostly books of high scholarship, the Press itself was sole publisher; and classical editions would use the old formula 'typis ac sumptibus...' (with the types and at the expense of...).

It was in Parker's time that steam-power was introduced; a Syndicate minute of 13 June 1838 resolved 'that it appears expedient to introduce machinery into the Pitt Press'. Parker's obituary in *The Bookseller* of 1 June 1870 records:

After a great deal of opposition he succeeded in introducing steam power; but for many years the Bible Society resolutely set their faces against books so printed. Mr P. seeing that the prices of bibles must be greatly reduced, prepared a large edition of the nonpareil bible at about two thirds of the price then charged, and thinking that he would find a welcome reception with such a boon at the Bible Society, took a dozen copies to the Manager, Mr Cockle, but soon found out his mistake; he however pointed out the advantages offered to the Society, but found more than his match in the Manager, who as soon as Parker's back was turned, sent for the binder and told him that the Cambridge people had very kindly prepared some cheap bibles, printed by machinery, but he found 'from the smallness of the margins they would not fold up evenly, and was not sure that, as a cheaper ink had been used, they might not set off when pressed'. Strangely enough, all these predictions were verified; when the books came home from the binder they were unreadable; some of the pages were rough, while others had whole lines cut off, and...the Committee would not sanction the purchase of 'such rubbish'. Two or three years later the cry for cheap bibles arose; the whole of the rejected bibles were purchased by the Society, and marvellous to relate, not one set off in binding, nor was there any difficulty in the folding!

The annual production of Bibles rose from a steady 30,000 or so copies in the 1810s and 1820s to near 50,000 in 1830 and 175,000 in 1840. But the Syndicate still felt that they were managing what Bentley and his colleagues had once called a 'public press'. What was now a very large facility, already a major employer of labour in the town, was subject to the will of those outside persons who might or might not give it work. True, the Bible and prayer book offered a valuable staple trade. But there was fierce competition with the Queen's Printer and with Oxford, who were larger, both for the retail trade and for the supply of the Bible Society. This itself had tended to drive prices down; and there was trouble in store from another direction. The Queen's Scottish Printer's Patent had lapsed in 1839, and had not been renewed. Printing of the Bible in Scotland was made free, subject to licensing and supervision by a Board. Hitherto neither English nor Scottish printers had too openly invaded the other national territory but now Scottish Bibles began to seep into northern England, starting a process which culminated when in 1858 William Collins set up an office in London, and began openly to sell his Bibles there. He was not impeded. The overall result was that prices of Bibles in England fell by half, and it became very difficult to sell the better quality product which Cambridge produced. It seemed good advertisement for free trade, but meant that the margins secured by the competitors in this market were now almost as thin as the paper they used, and standards declined; and the university presses, who could reasonably represent that they needed something like the Bible if they were to accept losses on scholarly publishing, were less able to feel that the Bible was a support that they could rely on.

It had occurred to the Syndicate that the Press might itself be a publisher. Indeed, in a very small way it always had been, or rather the University always had been; for in commissioning from the Press a handbill, a volume of congratulatory poems or a volume of statutes, it was acting as publisher; and it had always been a Bible publisher, since the right to print the Bible was vested in the University itself, and exercised by the University Printer only by virtue of his office. The Syndicate itself resolved on 25 May 1838:

At a meeting of the Syndicate held this day it was agreed, that the following be the form of an imprint for the New Edition of Wilson's Illustrations etc. of the New Testament and that the same be adopted as the imprint in all such books as shall be retained as the property of the University:

Cambridge, printed at the Pitt Press
by J. W. Parker, Printer to the University

This makes it quite clear that the concept of the University as publisher existed; but who was to perform the actual executive role: the Syndicate themselves? Inevitably it would devolve on Parker; but as publisher he was acting on his own behalf, as all University Printers had felt free to do from the beginning. If he had a good idea for a book, he would publish it, either on his own as 'J. W. Parker, West Strand', or in collaboration with the Deightons in Cambridge and Rivington in London, or such other backers and partners as he could find.

The books published in Cambridge in the first half of the century are not numerous, because so much of the printing capacity was taken up by the Bible, and among these books it is hard to find many which were published by the University itself, for the reasons touched on above. The period is a kind of limbo between the eighteenth century and the rapid and very heartening expansion which marked the second half of the nineteenth century and especially the years after 1870. Some important books were published, however.

The greatest classical scholar of the period was Richard Porson, who held the Chair of Greek. An early disaster for him was the loss of his Fellowship at Trinity. He was a freethinker and would not be ordained, and felt the College had cheated him out of one of the two Fellowships open to laymen. He was elected Professor, however, and held the Chair while living (and, alas, drinking) in London. His editions of Euripides began to appear there, but the *Medea* and *Hecuba* were printed in Cambridge, and his pupils also produced his *Adversaria*, *Aristophanica*, four tragedies of Euripides, a *Praelectio* on Euripides reprinted from the *Adversaria*, and, late in the century, his *Correspondence*. The type-face used for the texts was called the Great Porson Greek, and was an important departure from the old-style wiry Aldine cursives in almost universal use hitherto.

It is also satisfactory to see that the Press published for the University reformers of the first half of the century – especially Whewell and Adam Sedgwick among the scientists, Peacock among mathematicians, J. S. Henslow the botanist, and the Liberal Anglican historians Connop Thirlwall, John Grote, Julius Hare, and later F. D. Maurice. Men like these initiated the changes in the University curriculum which were finally enforced by the Royal Commission. They also began to loosen the constrictions of Anglican orthodoxy. Whewell was, like Newton and Bentley before him, and like Watson and Wordsworth, a northern grammar-school boy of exceptional force of character. He had to become an Anglican priest, indeed a Doctor of Divinity, as a matter of course and a necessary apprenticeship. But, as Sydney Smith said, his forte was science, his foible omniscience. He was Professor of Mineralogy, but then he was also Knightbridge Professor of Moral Theology: he published treatises on moral philosophy and its history, on mechanics, architecture, mineralogy, astronomy, and a *History of the Inductive Sciences* in three volumes; he also translated Schiller; and he was deeply interested in international law. There were sermons, of course; also addresses to the British Association when it met in Cambridge. He fell out with his opponents, naturally enough; but also with his allies. Some elements in his character and career are pure eighteenth-century; but his overall disinterestedness and idealism made him a true reformer; while the sheer overflow of personality, like Bentley's, made him seem like a force of nature. Of the books published at the Press perhaps the most locally influential was *Of A Liberal Education in General; with Particular Reference to the Leading Studies of the University of Cambridge*. This was published by Parker in 1845 – being no doubt too contentious for the Syndicate to sponsor.

It was in the same general vein as Adam Sedgwick's *A Discourse on the Studies of the University*, printed by Smith in 1834 for the Deightons and Parker. Older than Whewell, but like him a Trinity man, Sedgwick was also a controversialist, though less robust. He became Professor of Geology, knowing little of the subject, but became a highly respected geologist as well as a reformer. He was Secretary to the Chancellor when Prince

Albert held the office: indeed it was he who thought of the Prince for the Chancellorship, and he was a valuable intermediary between the University, the Crown, and the Government. He became one of the Royal Commissioners, and in that capacity became one of the most effective of all the reformers.

Whewell and Sedgwick, for all their breadth of interest, were essentially scientists. It was demanded of them that they be Anglicans; it was a natural step in their careers that they were Wranglers, since Anglican orders and the Mathematical Tripos were the linked channels to University preferment. Hare and Thirlwall were also Anglican priests, but not mathematicians. Their orientation was towards history, and towards German scholarship. They translated Niebuhr's *History of Rome*, which was printed at the Press in two large volumes. This symbolised the liberation of the German tradition of theological scholarship and interpretation – at that time much more advanced – into the intellectual life of the University and of England.

J. S. Henslow was a pupil of Sedgwick's, and Darwin's teacher at Cambridge. In a move characteristic of the time, he left the Chair of Mineralogy, in which he was well informed, for that of Botany, of which he knew as much as anyone else in Cambridge at the time (i.e. very little). But he was a genuine naturalist at a time when it was still possible to know all that was known in several fields, and he became a distinguished botanist. He had a real gift for illustration, for lecturing and for administration, and he carried through the transfer of the Botanic Garden from the old site (the present New Museums Site in Pembroke Street) to the present one: a process which took fifteen years, from 1831 to 1846. Henslow's publications at the Press were partly reforming pamphlets, partly plans of lecture courses, and an *Address* (1846) on the needs and the future of the Garden. But these were important, as maintaining an enlightened view of the subject in the days before the Natural Sciences Tripos, founded in 1861. Henslow is one of the more important members of the tradition of Cambridge botanists, from Ray in the seventeenth century, through Thomas Martyn and James Donn in the eighteenth, to the great expansion and the various transformations of the subject in the nineteenth and twentieth centuries. Martyn's *Catalogue*

(1771) and *Mantissa* (1772) and Donn's *Hortus Cantabrigiensis* (1796: thirteen editions to 1845) began as lists of plants in the Cambridge Garden, and broadened in Donn's hands into lists of all plants in cultivation in English gardens.

Three factors at least meant that by the end of the 1840s the Press was once more in difficulties. The expenditure by the University on the Press's buildings and equipment had been very heavy. The confident expectation, with the acquisition of the secret of stereotyping, that Bibles and prayer books would provide a steady sale at reasonable margins was constantly threatened by the cut-throat condition of the trade, with the Bible Society always present as a charitable missionary enterprise which supplied below cost, and the Scottish competition threatening other levels of the market. The Press was to a large extent the supplier of printing to other publishers, and might at any time be owed considerable sums by them. It did not at this time consider itself as in any substantial way an initiator of its own publishing projects. Where it did, it felt quite rightly that its first obligation was to Cambridge and to learning, and it had a natural tendency to sponsor works of scholarship which no commercial publisher would touch, because they would make no profit (for instance the observations of the new Observatory: a regular series, of scientific but not of commercial value).

It is important also to note here that the brothers Daniel and Alexander Macmillan came to Cambridge in 1843, and ran a bookshop at 17 Trinity Street. Two years later, they took the shop at 1 Trinity Street which is now the shop of Bowes and Bowes. Daniel died in 1856 but Alexander carried on until the publishing business went to London in 1863; and well before Daniel's death Macmillans had become a very active publishing house. 'Young persons' or 'juveniles', to use the Victorian terms, did the main work in the shop: the Macmillans may have seemed only to stand about, but they had a great gift for engaging their customers in conversation, and they entertained the same people out of business hours. They came to Cambridge partly because they had a veneration for F. D. Maurice; they knew Hare, who helped them with capital; Maurice introduced them to Kingsley. Before long practically every talented author in the University was making his way to Macmillans, who had a free run for nearly thirty years. Their books were very often printed at the Press – especially the more important ones – and so far as the Press was considered to be mainly a printing house, that was a good arrangement; the Press was serving local authors in a very practical way. But it was a long time – too long – before it became clear how disastrous this arrangement was for the development of Cambridge publishing. It is not extravagant to say that it was set back by an indefinite number of years – several intellectual generations, in some subjects.

It was another factor, at this stage a small one, but increasingly a large one, in the imbalance in the Press's activities. From the 1840s onwards there were signs that things were beginning to go badly, largely for lack of effective control at Cambridge. Parker lived in London and ran his publishing from his house in the Strand. After his early period of superintendence it is reasonable to assume that he came to Cambridge less and less often. A Mr Harvey was dismissed in 1843 for keeping the books badly. The Syndicate had to look into the matter itself, concluded that there was some dishonesty, but also revealed a state of great confusion in the accounting which was wasteful and ultimately damaging.

A sign of some early concern was a proposal from the Regius and Norrisian Professors of Divinity, both Syndics, who in 1844 prepared a list of standard works in theology which could be reprinted 'in order to provide against the loss which the want of full employment for the workmen at the University Press frequently occasions'. It would also have a beneficial long-term effect, since it would 'acquire a copyright interest in certain important books which would ultimately prove a permanent source of income'. Inevitably, they thought at their own level: they proposed worthy but very serious books – Knight's *Life of Erasmus*, Stillingfleet's *Controversial Writings against the Romanists* and Cosin's *Scholastical History of the Canon*. These and other such books were among those which had to be remaindered in the 1850s. Parker loyally supported the venture, offering to take four-fifths of the edition immediately, and the last fifth when he had sold the rest, on terms which seemed to offer a profit. He pointed out that the scheme would enable the Syndicate to select works for publication and to appoint their own editors; it would furnish work for the Press at comparatively little outlay, would 'yield a proprietary profit' and was guaranteed against loss. Parker engaged 'to put himself into direct communication with every competent bookseller in England, and through agents in Edinburgh and Dublin with those of Scotland and Ireland also, and thus secure the cooperation of the whole trade of the United Kingdom in their circulation'. Alas for such misplaced enthusiasm and energy: the books chosen could hardly engage the whole-hearted support of the trade; they sold very slowly indeed.

As the 1840s wore on, other signs of trouble began to appear. In 1848 a special Sub-Syndicate found that the Press had too many bad debts: some £6690 was owed. Several debts were more than three years in arrears; Parker himself owed money. The Sub-Syndicate reported in 1849, and its recommendations throw light on the business procedures, which were still those of the previous century. The Vice-Chancellor was still the chairman of the Syndicate for the good reason that *ex officio* he ran all the University's business, and received all moneys and made all payments on its behalf. The Sub-Syndicate recommended that he pay all wages, rates, taxes, insurance and other ordinary outgoings due during his year of office, and pay all bills for paper as well as all tradesmen's bills and all salaries up to Michaelmas, when he left office. After 3 November all sums received were to be paid to the new Vice-Chancellor; all sums so paid were to be carried by him to the Press account of his year of office, and this was to be audited before the end of the next Michaelmas term; and that a schedule of all balances due to the Press at Christmas and remaining unpaid at the time of the following audit be laid before the auditors (themselves Syndics) and the Syndicate. It was a system which was bound to fail, and to be shown to be increasingly inadequate to the new times.

Another Sub-Syndicate reported in May 1849, having been appointed 'to consider whether any reduction ought to be made in the present working staff of the establishment'. Their report too encourages reading between the lines:

...they commenced their enquiry with ascertaining the actual cash balances paid over to the Chest by the Press during the period 1820–1847.... The whole Press receipt during the above period amounts to £619,580.2.0. Also that the balance in favour of the Chest amounts to £50,471.19.9. and that the balances against...amounted to £10,337.10.2, leaving a balance of profit...of £40,134.9.7., i.e. an average yearly balance of profit [actually the simple excess of income over expenditure] on the 28 years of £1433.7.5....

They learned from Mr Parker that...the presses, machinery etc. had been almost entirely renewed and everything connected with the establishment placed upon the best and most improved footing. The whole expense...has been defrayed out of the current profits of the Press... The stock of printed books...has been very considerably increased. Mr Parker estimates the value of the apparatus and stock of the Press to be at a very moderate computation £10,000.... Mr Parker further estimates the amount of good debts ...at £2000.

Your Sub-Syndicate...cannot refrain from expressing the opinion that the result of their enquiry...is highly satisfactory in itself and very creditable to Mr Parker.

That, as we say today, was the good news. The bad news followed:

As regards the future prospects...the average annual balance paid to the Chest during the years

| | |
|---|---|
| 1820–26 inclusive amounted to | £2047.1.3. |
| 1827–33 | £1714.13.11. |
| 1834–40 | £1319.16.10. |
| 1841–47 | £651.17.11. |

...the rapid diminution of profits indicated by the above statement deserves the serious consideration of the Syndicate.

The Sub-Syndicate went on to note 'a serious and progressive falling off of pressman's work' paid by the piece, but noted that there were staff on fixed salaries amounting to £3917. 18. 8 a year – in other words the overhead was becoming an increasing proportion of a diminishing turnover. The agency accounts (that is, the sale of Bibles, prayer books and books to the London booksellers, including Parker) showed there was a 'considerable falling off in this important branch of business [the publishing side] which ought also to form a subject of serious consideration for the Syndicate'. The Sub-Syndicate recorded on the other hand that Parker's account as publisher was nearly double the amount of the three next largest agents; that it was the only account that had not declined; and that he had contributed some £1600 annually by commissioning printing. The total payments to the Press which came through Parker as agent, publisher and 'Commission Printer' were a quarter of the total gross receipts.

The Sub-Syndicate concluded that the Syndicate were:

already aware that the business of printing Bibles and Prayerbooks is at present far from being as remunerative as it has been in former years, and that there is not only no increase but rather a diminution of Author's work [i.e. authors approaching the Press with a book to be printed on their own account, or in collaboration with a bookseller].

Parker was consulted, and made drastic suggestions. On 18 May it was agreed 'to reduce wages and the number of people employed, as proposed by Mr Parker'; and to report to the University. The report said that the Syndicate had determined 'to place the Establishment upon a reduced footing'.

Other measures included continuing but not well-conceived attempts to develop the Press's own publishing. Dr Corrie, Master of Jesus and a Syndic of the Press, offered to edit the *Homilies*, and presented the copyright of the book to the Press. Whewell, also a Syndic, offered to edit Sanderson's *De Obligatione Conscientiae Praelectiones decem* ('The book appears to me to be an excellent moral treatise, so much so that I have appointed it as one of the special subjects of examination for the Moral Sciences Tripos in 1852'). Other such initiatives were Field's edition of St Chrysostom's *De Sacerdotio*, Humphrey's *Theophilus and Athenagoras*, Holden's *Minucius Felix*. An edition of Barrow's works was also approved. In 1852 Whewell offered to edit Grotius's *De Jure Belli et Pacis*. Some of these works too were sold off cheaply in later years, a clear sign that they had not fulfilled their purpose. Nonetheless this was an early attempt by the Syndicate to initiate a publishing programme, as distinct from offering a printing service to others who knew what they wanted to publish; so it represents a positive movement. By 1852 these efforts were becoming more systematic: another Sub-Syndicate was considering editions of the Greek and Latin classics. It was bound to be clear to teaching members of the Syndicate that there were 'students of limited acquirements', especially men reading for the pass degree, and they, more than others, needed help. In December 1852 the Sub-Syndicate reported that it was desirable to publish editions of 'parts of such works as might be selected for the Previous Examination and the Pass Degree'. It recommended ten such books: editions of Euripides, Cicero, Xenophon, Demosthenes, Isocrates, Plutarch, and Ovid.

It was at this moment, one of the recurring low points in this history, that the Royal Commission into the University included the Press in its survey of all the University's activities. On 24 November 1851 the Vice-Chancellor transmitted to the Syndicate the questions framed by the Commissioners. The Syndicate appointed a Sub-Syndicate to draft the replies, having secured a Grace authorising an official reply. In a statement covering the eventual replies, the Syndicate withheld details of profit and loss, saying:

The Syndics assume that the information furnished to Her Majesty's Commissioners will, in some form, be laid before the public. Whilst therefore the Syndics would have willingly furnished to your Lordship and your Colleagues the fullest information respecting the present position of the University Press, they felt themselves precluded from communicating the same information to their rivals in the trade and the public at large.

The Syndicate informed the Commissioners that there were eighteen Syndics, who met fortnightly during term, with a quorum of five, one of whom must be the Vice-Chancellor or his deputy, and the average attendance was just over seven; and that the only financial privileges enjoyed by the Press were the 'drawback' of $1\frac{1}{2}$d per pound weight on paper used for learned printing, and the Government Annuity of £500, on which tax was paid. They went on to say that the business of the Press consisted of the printing of Bibles, Testaments, and prayer books; of printing work for the University and Colleges; of printing books edited for the Syndics; of book- and job-printing for the members of the University; of printing works published by learned societies (the Cambridge Philosophical Society, the Parker and the Selden Societies, for instance); and of 'such Bookwork as subject to the imprimatur of the Vice-Chancellor may be offered by Publishers and other connexions of the Press'. They concluded:

It does not appear to the Syndics that any change of management could produce greater profits than are now realized; if indeed any change whatever could be made without destroying the efficiency of an establishment which for the purposes of the University must necessarily be kept up on a considerable scale.

The half-despondent, half-defensive note in that sentence reflects the feeling of a body which had repeatedly faced a problem but not seen a solution.

The figures supplied to the Commissioners, and published by them in their Report in 1852, are interesting. The University had spent more on the purchase of sites and the erection of buildings for the Press than for any other of its departments: between 1821 and 1833 £27,658 had been spent in this way. The estimated annual return to the University over the previous seven years was £895. The University spent £182 a year on printing reports and notices at the Press. The plant consisted of frames and other equipment for seventy compositors; presses for fifty-six pressmen; eight printing machines requiring fifty men and boys to mind them; a ten-horse steam engine occupying four 'hands'; a steam milling machine, hydraulic and screw hot presses at which '100 men and boys might be employed if necessary'. The Syndicate showed that the Press had between 1810 and 1850 supplied Bibles, New Testaments and prayer books in the numbers given in the table below, which tell their own story of a high point followed by a decline:

| | Bibles | Testaments | Prayer books |
|---|---|---|---|
| 1810 | 29,500 | 56,500 | 24,900 |
| 1820 | 28,750 | 40,250 | 38,000 |
| 1830 | 48,000 | 65,000 | 68,000 |
| 1840 | 195,000 | 243,500 | 55,000 |
| 1841 | 125,000 | 108,500 | 19,000 |
| 1842 | 41,250 | 146,000 | 50,000 |
| 1843 | 57,250 | 94,100 | 54,000 |
| 1844 | 38,000 | 43,500 | 27,500 |
| 1845 | 57,000 | 34,500 + 5000 Greek | 45,500 |
| 1846 | 78,000 | 72,500 | 20,000 |
| 1847 | 32,500 | 80,000 | 10,000 |
| 1848 | 76,500 | 94,000 | 20,000 |
| 1849 | 31,000 | 75,000 | 1,000 |
| 1850 | 31,000 | 35,000 | 3,000 |

The Syndicate also pointed out that:

for several years past arrangements have been made...for reprinting, as circumstances might warrant, standard works in theology and general literature in order to provide against the loss which want of full employment for the workmen would otherwise occasion.

The Syndics have from time to time engaged the services of distinguished members of the University for the purpose of preparing and superintending their publications.

What the Syndicate could not see, it could not point out. With hindsight one can say that the figures presented to the Commission permit a diagnosis. There was over-capitalisation in the sense that the plant and machinery were under-occupied. There was however a shortage of the working capital which would permit a remedy. There had been over-employment. The recurrent dissatisfaction which the Syndicate had felt with their printers – Watts, Smith, and now the hard-working Parker himself – was a symptom of a condition that neither party had fully analysed and which required a mental leap into another dimension. The Commissioners, who reported on this branch of the University's activity as on every other, noted the lack of a commercial element in the government and administration of the Press, and suggested that matters would improve if this were introduced. They concluded:

It is only by associating printers or publishers in some species of co-partnership with the University, or leasing the Press to them, that any considerable return can hereafter be expected from the capital which has been invested in it.

We see here a recurrent phenomenon. At any time when the Press was going badly, before or after 1852, the eye of the critic would fall, inevitably, on the physical structure of the Press, on the buildings, the machines, the staff, the whole considerable apparatus now owned by the University, and into which a great deal of money had been poured. The lack of 'return on capital' was in fact only an indicator, a symptom, of what was lacking. In any case, a return on invested capital is the proper objective of a commercial firm, not of a university press, which does not exist to make money, but to fulfil a scholarly objective. But it seems clear now that the organisation of the Press was indeed defective:

in that respect the Commissioners were right. What were fundamentally lacking, however, were coherent policies and objectives. The printing and the publishing should have stemmed from a concept of the function and nature of a university press. An adequate concept would have led to the development of publishing policies and programmes which would have reflected that concept. Better financial viability would have followed. But such developments required the arrival of the people who would have the ideas; and they would appear only when the need for them was itself felt. The Commissioners were halfway there when they said:

We are satisfied that no Syndicate, however active and well chosen, can replace the intelligent and vigilant superintendence of those whose fortune in life is dependent upon its [the Press's] success.

That is to say, the University now needed to move entirely away from the notion that it could have a 'public press', that it could appoint successive competent persons as University Printers, and these persons could for a time move in and exploit the facility so provided, while doing a little bookselling and publishing on their own account, while the Syndicate itself merely guaranteed that nothing disgraceful was printed; passively received, as governing body, reports and accounts; and from time to time descended into management at an inappropriately low level, or tried to sort things out when they had gone badly wrong. That was essentially the eighteenth-century, even the seventeenth-century, pattern. The Press was now a large printing works, a factory, capable of producing a great deal of printing. It had to be managed successfully. But, more important in the long run, in the period when the Macmillans and to a lesser extent Deighton were, without effective competition, calmly and successfully exploiting virtually every publishing opportunity which the University offered, the Press had first to discover the difference between being an old-style bookseller and a modern publisher, then to discover the specific publishing role of a university press, and finally to rethink its constitutional and statutory nature. This was not an easy or short process: in a sense it never ends. But in the 1850s the University found that it had developed, over many years and in a natural and organic way, an organisation which bore all the surface features of an industrial and commercial enterprise, which was at that moment painfully adjusting itself to the nineteenth century. A first priority would be to leave the eighteenth century behind, especially its relationships (based on the economics of hand-production and of distribution before modern times) between booksellers and printers, and its financial relationship with the University which made it merely one of those miscellaneous and not yet very important activities which each successive Vice-Chancellor supervised during his single year of office, monitoring payments into and out of the Chest. It was then a natural temptation to think simply in nineteenth-century commercial terms, of capital employed, of return on capital, of profit; and to run this large printing business as if it were any other. The Syndicate, loyally coping with this problem, almost inevitably felt it had to drop into the thought-processes and the received ideas of the commercial world outside, and the Commissioners themselves strengthened the temptation. They were at any rate more effective thought-processes, and a kind of discipline. But the risk involved in surrendering to them entirely was that one would lose sight of the essentially academic and altruistic *ends* of the whole enterprise, and there were now several earlier episodes of a similar nature which demonstrated that it was not enough, every generation or so, to trim the ship and get the 'profits' in the right ratio again. It was more than time to start thinking of a specific function; to define it and fulfil it. Fortunately this process began, for reasons to do with the changing nature of Cambridge as a University. In the last half of the century it was not possible to lose sight of intellectual aims when all around they were being so vigorously pursued. That ferment was bound to be reflected in the Press before very long. If at the opening ceremony of the Pitt Building the sardonic Romilly thought that Lord Camden and the Vice-Chancellor, being ordinary men, were also 'wordy' and 'mouthy', the things they were pointing to were not touched by their weaknesses (or Romilly's). The dissemination of truth, the extension of science, and the advancement of religious knowledge will outlast all sorts of mockery, and there was, fortunately, a great deal of all three going on after the 1850s.

# 10

## THE NINETEENTH CENTURY – II
## CHARLES JOHN CLAY AND
## THE PARTNERSHIP

THE REPORT of the Royal Commission was acted on after some deliberation. In February 1854 a Sub-Syndicate was appointed 'to consider whether any steps should be taken to manage the business of the Press either by means of a Partnership, or by employing a Superintendent remunerated by a percentage on the profits of the business done; to enquire whether means can be found for making such an arrangement....'.

The Sub-Syndicates of the time acted with such speed that one is tempted to conclude that the members had little else to do and enjoyed the excitement which the Press brought into their lives. This group reported in the following month that they had 'conferred in the first instance with Mr Parker...and afterwards... proceeded to London where they had interviews with the Secretaries of the Bible Society and the Christian Knowledge Society and also with Messrs Rivington and Mr Seeley [important booksellers with publishing interests]. They were assured by all the persons with whom they conferred (including Mr Parker) that the plan of managing the business of the Press by way of partnership with one or more persons practically acquainted with the trade is the one most likely to prove advantageous. They have also reason to think that persons of this description and possessing sufficient capital might be found.' They concluded that they proposed to make further enquiries and to enter into negotiations with 'suitable parties'.

These enquiries and negotiations went with equal speed. On 31 May a Grace proposed to the Senate a partnership with Mr George Seeley of Fleet Street, London, Bookseller, and

Mr Charles John Clay, M.A. of Trinity College and of Bread Street Hill, London, Printer.

Parker had been given a broad hint of the way the wind was about to blow. He seems to have offered disinterested advice, and then to have moved out of the way by resigning as Printer. In the following year he also lost to Seeley the agency for the sale of Cambridge Bibles and prayer books and the Syndicate's books.

Seeley, as a prominent bookseller with a Cambridge connection, was an important intermediary. He was very inclined to act himself as agent for the sales in London, but firmly advised that the Press also needed an active resident Printer: these two working together could first increase the output and then sell the product, playing into each other's hands. He also happened to know a 'suitable party', and put the Sub-Syndicate in touch with the Clay family.

The elder Clay, Richard Clay I, founder of both the printing business and the dynasty, had been born in Cambridge in 1789, had gone to the Perse School, and been indentured apprentice in 1803 to Richard Watts, then University Printer. This was the time of the development of stereotyping at the Press, and Clay learnt the process, which was to be important in his own business. He set up in London in 1817, and by 1854 was the patriarchal head of a very large printing business in a Victorian factory built in a grim renaissance style. His elder son, Charles John Clay, was born in 1827, and went up to Trinity in 1846. He was a scholarly boy, and thought of following the still routine path of reading theology, taking orders, and becoming a don. But he failed to get a Fellowship at Sidney Sussex, and went into the family business. In 1854 he was about to get married, was tempted by the possibility of the job at Cambridge, and he or Seeley persuaded Richard Clay to advance the capital needed to set the young man up in business in Cambridge as University Printer and Partner. To the University it was obviously a consideration that Richard Clay had an old Cambridge loyalty, and that C. J. Clay was a member of the University with an intellectual bent, and able to talk to senior members as one of themselves. Indeed, long after, when James Cartmell, Master of

Christ's, retired in 1878 after years as the first of the Deputy Vice-Chancellors who became in a serious way and for an extended period Chairman of the Syndicate, he replied to a farewell message from the Syndicate, telling them how much they owed to Clay, and thinking it proper to interject that 'Mr Clay's culture and gentlemanly feeling eminently fit him for his position'. Something of this must have been evident in 1854, when he was appointed at the age of twenty-seven, and immediately embarked on forty years of very remarkable activity.

Cartmell himself became a Syndic in 1849, was a member of the Syndicate which recommended the partnership and Clay, became Deputy Vice-Chancellor in 1854, became member of another Press Sub-Syndicate (the predecessor of the later Business Sub-Syndicate and the present Finance Committee) and was the leading spirit on the Syndicate until 1878. In effect, he and Clay reconstructed the Press; or Clay did it with Cartmell's wise guidance and support.

The deed of partnership with the University was to run for fourteen years from July 1854. There was to be an advance of capital: the University was to provide £10,000 (in the form of the buildings and plant); Clay and Seeley were to provide £5000 each. So the University had a half-share in the business, and each of the other partners a quarter-share. The partners would jointly occupy and operate the printing works, on which no rent was to be paid; but rates, taxes and so on were paid out of the partnership account. Seeley and Clay were to 'transact the whole business', with Seeley as sole agent in London. Clay was to be Managing Partner in Cambridge and University Printer, at a salary of £400 p.a. The Syndicate could have its own books printed at the Press at normal rates, paying the partnership. The University could have its printing done at the Press, also at normal rates. Each partner was to receive from the business a 5% return on capital; any 'clear profit' remaining was to be divided, half to the University, half to the other partners.

This was a more business-like arrangement than anything in the past history of the Press. It was based on the assumption that the University's 'capital' in buildings, machinery, staff competence and goodwill, and especially the University's position as privileged printer, were capable of much more effective exploitation than they had had in the past. This assumption was proved correct. At this moment Clay may not have had precise ideas about the development of a publishing policy: he could see that the Syndicate accepted each year a small number of scholarly books, sometimes having illusions about how well they would sell. This constituted a steady stream, if not a large one, of printing orders which he could count on. He could count on even more orders, and larger ones, from Macmillans, who were busy publishing the more interesting and saleable books being written in Cambridge. As an educated and enterprising man, it would soon occur to him that there was scope for development here. Meanwhile the overall nature of the partnership agreement meant that Seeley and Clay were looking for a return on capital, and also a 'profit' – properly so-called, since they meant to take it out of the business. The University for its part felt a kind of duty to use its printing facility effectively; the measure of effectiveness was 'profit', and this might either be employed as further capital, or used to finance learned publishing – though in the age before state-funded tertiary education the University had its own needs, and it did in the nineteenth century look to the Press as a source of funds. So both partners were prepared to take money out of the business, the University for its own purposes, which were charitable, and the partners as a straightforward return on capital and a reward of enterprise.

In July 1854 two accounts were opened at Mortlock's Bank (now Barclays). One was the University Press Partnership Account, where cheques were to be signed by the Vice-Chancellor (still) and Seeley or Clay. The other was the University Press Syndics Account – cheques to be signed by the Vice-Chancellor. So began the process, not a mere accounting process, of considering the Press under the various aspects of its different activities: at this point printing and 'other'. It was an immense step, as the first such step always is: metaphysically it can be considered an essential departure from the eighteenth century.

Meanwhile the partners, as new brooms, swept various departments clean. Clay began at once to purchase machinery and type and put to press new Bibles and service-books. The prices of a

number of books in stock were reduced, and Seeley was authorised to sell off bulk stock of others (a remaindering operation).

The Syndicate itself was reconstructed. It was heavy with
Heads of Houses, and the term of office was indeterminate.
A Grace was proposed to the effect that it was 'desirable that the
services of members of the Senate who may be willing and able
to devote attention to the subject, should be engaged successively
in superintending the management of the Press'. It recommended that the Syndicate should consist of the Vice-Chancellor
and fifteen members; that five should retire each year and be
replaced by five other persons. Essentially this gave a three-year
term, without possibility of immediate re-election. As the years
went by, it was considered first that it was desirable that certain
members should be re-elected because of their value as Syndics,
and then that the term of office was too short. The Vice-
Chancellor remained a member *ex officio*, and can be found acting
as Chairman at specially important meetings for many years; but
the system grew up of having the Vice-Chancellor appoint a
named Deputy as Chairman, and Cartmell was the first of these.
Indeed, until the appointment of a Secretary of the Syndicate, the
Chairmen carried out many executive duties. One can recognise
their hands as writers of the minutes of Syndicate meetings, and
it is clear also that they wrote much of the correspondence relating to the publishing business until it became too much for
them, and Clay took over the function.

Seeley withdrew from the partnership in 1856. Perhaps he had
only meant to see it well established before leaving. At any rate
the University had no hesitation in making a new partnership
with Clay only, the University taking three-quarters of the profits, having increased its share of the capital. New agents were
appointed in London, one for the sale of books, the other for
Bibles and prayer books.

In the first few years of the partnership, Clay concentrated
on producing and selling Bibles and prayer books, and recovering
the share of the market which Cambridge had lost in the late
1840s. The books already commissioned in the previous period
duly appeared, and indeed they constituted the basic element
of the Syndics' first catalogue in 1875. The best-seller (if the

phrase is allowable) was Pearson's *Exposition of the Creed*. This monument of Anglican orthodoxy appeared in two versions, one edited by Temple Chevallier (second edition, 7s. 6d.); one, for the use of the students of Bishop's College, Calcutta, 'with some additional matter occasionally interspersed' (fourth edition, 5s.). But the other works, Isaac Barrow in nine volumes, and the Latin works of the Fathers, went much more slowly: it took a century to sell Barrow out; so when Whewell in 1858 offered to edit Barrow's mathematical works, a decision was deferred 'in consideration of the large sums now invested in proprietory works'.

In the same year it was agreed that Clay should send review copies of 'books published by the Syndics to Editors of some of the principal periodicals from time to time'. The list as it then stood would not have prompted very exciting reviews, and in November 1863 Rivington, who had become London agent in 1861, frankly recommended that stock be reduced by public auction, especially of Barrow's works, Wheatley on the Common Prayer, Smith's *Select Discourses*, Kemble's *Anglo-Saxon Gospel of Matthew*, Whewell's Grotius, and Hey's lectures.

In 1866 the partnership was renewed. In recommending this course to the Senate, the Syndicate reported:

During the last ten years the business of the Press has greatly increased and has attained a considerable magnitude. Large additions have been made to the Machinery and Plant, which, the Syndics have reason to believe, are now in excellent working order and of a very valuable character.

Mr Clay considers that the Press now produces four or five times as much work as it produced when he first undertook the management.

A new deed of partnership stated the capital was now £33,000. Clay's salary was raised to £675 (it was a charge on the partnership before the division of profits, so Clay paid his quarter-share).

In the late 1860s the publishing policy remained passive and cautious. Peter Mason's *Rabbinic Reading Book* was accepted, and W. W. Skeat's *Gospel of Mark in Anglo-Saxon*, Walker's translation of Gaius's Commentaries, Seeley on Pterodactyls, and Mullinger on the early history of the University. The *University Reporter*, founded by Rivington, was taken over in 1872, and the indefatigable George Forrest Browne appointed editor.

(Of him it was said that knowledgeable dons, when asked the classic Cambridge tourist's question, 'Where is the University?' were tempted to place the enquirer before Browne, saying 'Here it is.' He was Secretary to the second Statutory Commission, had been a Proctor, was a member of the Council of the Senate, and was for some time Secretary of the Local Examinations Syndicate where he fostered the growth of the Extra-Mural Board, before passing into a higher sphere as Bishop of Bristol.)

Other books accepted at this time were Skeat's edition of (what else?) *The Gospel of Luke in Anglo-Saxon*, Todhunter's *History of the Mathematical Theories of Attraction*, and a new edition by Sandys of Bentley's *Phalaris*. These were not venturesome publications, but the seventies begin to show a distinct quickening of the pace of publishing, including two large ventures of great importance.

The first was the Revised Version of the Bible. The New Testament was not published until 1881 and the Old Testament not until 1885; but the work of revision was of course lengthy, and began in 1870. It will be remembered that Collins had set up as Bible publisher in London in 1858. The Queen's Printer's Patent itself lapsed in 1859; and by this time there was sufficient public feeling against the continuance of the Bible monopoly to cause the institution of an official enquiry by a Committee of the House of Commons, followed by a report of evidence given to it. One witness pointed out that the result of Collins's incursion had been a drastic reduction of prices. Others pointed out that neither supervision in Scotland nor privilege in England had been a guarantee of absolute accuracy. Two-and-a-half centuries of reprinting had produced thousands of small variants between the texts accepted as standard by the privileged presses, and these disparities had, since early in the century, produced a movement, especially at Cambridge, for a return to the supposed original purity of the text of 1611 (itself of course corrupt). This was a tangled matter for the ordinary churchgoer to get hold of, but it produced a feeling that the system of privileged printing was a characteristic English historical anomaly without the benefits such anomalies were usually supposed to bring. The Committee recommended that the Royal Patent be not renewed as not in the public interest; but since it was only the casting vote of the Chairman which produced the majority of one for the recommendation, the Patent was quietly renewed in 1860.

The Cambridge Paragraph Bible of 1873, edited by F. H. Scrivener, was in effect a critical edition of the text of the Authorized Version, in which Scrivener had laboriously followed the whole history of that text in order to provide a proper recension. Indeed he had treated it as any editor should treat any text. It provided a standard for future printings of the Authorized Version, and was the most effectual answer to those who wanted to go back to 1611. Scrivener showed why that would have been a bad thing to do, and his text provided the considered alternative. It is the culmination of the Cambridge tradition of care for the text initiated by the Bucks and Daniel in 1629 and 1638, and continued by Dr Parris in 1762.

This obvious service was the nineteenth-century vindication of the University's right to be an exception to the Royal Printers' monopoly rather than a justification of that monopoly and the system of privilege. When in 1870 the two universities heard that a new version of the Scriptures was being prepared, considered that it might become the new Authorized Version, and thought how dependent their fortunes were on the existing one, they frankly conceded that their deepest interests were at stake, almost their existence. The new version would be a new copyright; and it was essential to them to own it. It was agreed at the Syndicate meeting of 1 July 1870 to make an offer for it, and in August (at a special Long Vacation meeting) to combine with Oxford and the Queen's Printer. Negotiations with Oxford and the Revisers were opened, conducted by Cartmell and Clay on behalf of Cambridge, and lasting until May 1871. It was then recommended to the University that (the Queen's Printer having dropped out) the two university presses should defray the costs of revision in return for the copyright. Oxford and Cambridge were each to provide £1000 per annum for up to ten years.

The second great enterprise was the virtual foundation of the Press's list as publisher for schools. During the second half of the century the University itself became outward-looking. It recognised a duty to the schools of the country, and not only to those which sent boys (and soon girls) to be educated at Cambridge. It took its part in the national examinations system, and the scheme of Local Examinations was supervised by Cambridge as one of the main centres from 1858. The Secretary of the Local Examinations Syndicate was G. F. Browne (mentioned above), and it occurred to him in drawing up syllabuses for examinations in English, modern languages and classics, that the Press might be asked to undertake to supply the editions of texts which his Syndicate prescribed. He made the suggestion formally in March 1874, needing the books for December of that year. Very remarkably, they were provided. By June editors had been found and the texts edited, and the editions were put to press. The first five titles of what was soon after called the Pitt Press Series for Schools were

*Lascaris* and some easy poetry in French, edited by Masson
*La Métromanie,* by the same editor
Kohlrausch: *Das Jahr 1813,* edited by Wagner
Vergil: *Aeneid XII* edited by A. Sidgwick
Xenophon: *Anabasis IV,* edited by Pretor.

An early volume in the Pitt Press Series.

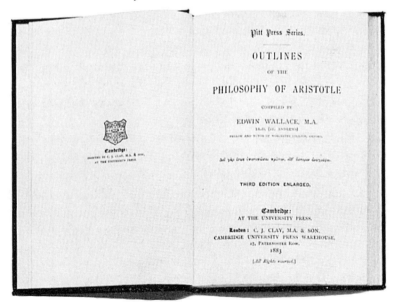

Fifteen hundred copies of each book were printed, the books were stereotyped, the prices were fixed at two shillings (except *Aeneid XII*, which was 1s. 6d.) and the editors were paid £25, or £35 for a longer book. Browne had warned the Press that the number of candidates in Greek was 280, German 390, Latin 1400 and French 2800, but it was some time before it was realised that since the markets for books were of different sizes, this should be reflected in the edition size and the price. Eventually the Pitt Press Series consisted of over two hundred volumes.

Important innovations now began to follow in rapid succession. We need to go back two years, to 1872, to find that Rivington, the London agent, gave notice in November. It will be remembered that from Thomas Thomas's time a printer in Cambridge could not possibly make a living from the sales of books in and around Cambridge, and absolutely had to have a London outlet. It is only in our own time that it has been possible to avoid this, partly because the transport network now makes it easier to supply the English sale from any part of the country, partly because the sale for academic books has become international rather than national, and the English sale has long ceased to be the dominant consideration. From 1584 until 1872 Cambridge was dependent on London agents for the diffusion of its books, and this was almost certainly an inhibiting factor. It was now decided, and it must have been on Clay's advice, that the Press (that is to say the partnership) would no longer have agents, but would conduct its London business in an office of its own under the supervision of a paid manager.

An office was found in Paternoster Row, in the old bookselling part of London. The Cambridge Warehouse, as it was called until well into the twentieth century, opened on New Year's Day 1873, with a staff of four. The trade grew, and the publication of the Revised Version New Testament put a heavy strain on both the people and the accommodation. The Warehouse moved to larger premises in Ave Maria Lane in 1884, in time for the publication of the Old Testament and the complete Bible in the new version. C. J. Clay visited the Warehouse every week, and every week he was sent a report of the sales of Syndics' books. For the first ten years this consisted of one folded sheet of foolscap, with the main titles printed, and the slow sellers added by hand as occasion arose. There was one traveller, James Massett How, a stout middle-aged man who wore loud check suits, and had a Napoleon III moustache and imperial. He was a great reader – of Dickens perhaps, for in him nature seems to have followed art. If his orders were thought small he would say 'My dear Sir, remember that I have to overcome an Augean stable of prejudice!'; and at Christmas he would say to his colleagues 'Sir, I wish you a superabundance of those domestic felicities which we associate with the festive season of Christmas.' Those colleagues wore chimney-pot hats and morning coats as marks of respectability; but the manager once wondered aloud whether Mr Clay would like to see them going about dressed like gentlemen.

In 1874 another important decision was made, though it was slightly equivocal. A Syndicate minute of 17 October reads:

The correspondence with Authors and Editors respecting the publication of works undertaken by the Syndics having much increased of late, so that the assistance of an official Secretary has become very desirable

And Mr Clay – who has for some time past virtually managed these matters for the Syndics as well as the publishing affairs of the Cambridge Warehouse in London – having offered to undertake without salary the duty of Secretary in such manner as may be most convenient and agreeable to the Syndics

It was agreed that Mr Clay be appointed Secretary to the Syndics of the Press, the duties of such office being subject to the control of the Vice-Chancellor and the appointment not conveying any right to be present at the meetings of the Syndicate.

The partnership with Clay was renewed in March 1876, and his salary was increased, with an additional sum for managing the London Warehouse, so his new functions were in fact recognised. The report to the University recommending the renewal was full of satisfied confidence and spoke highly of Clay. So of course did James Cartmell in his farewell message to the Syndicate in December 1878:

Every member of the Senate must rejoice both in the recovery of the Press from the low point to which its fortunes had fallen 26 years ago: and also in its continually increasing prosperity now.

This I attribute almost entirely to the good fortune which the University had in connecting itself with Mr Clay as the Managing Partner of the Press, to whose honourable principle, ability, skill and efficiency I gladly take this opportunity of bearing my testimony. . .

For the last few years, in addition to his ordinary duties as Managing Partner he has voluntarily undertaken without remuneration the office of Secretary to the Syndicate. Without such help from him the labour of the Chairman of the Syndicate would be increased manyfold and the publications of the many useful works which are now being issued from the Press would be impossible.

Cartmell could look back on one other important venture which had just been embarked on: The Cambridge Bible for Schools. This was a series of small volumes of commentary on the books of the Bible. It was edited by J. J. S. Perowne, later Bishop of Worcester and formerly a Syndic of the Press. It was what the French call a work *de longue haleine*, since the last volume was not published until 1918, by which time some of the earlier volumes had been revised, and everyone first associated with it was dead. But it had a very long life, not only in schools, but at a higher level. (At one of the sessions of the Literary Committee of the New English Bible, meeting in Oxford in the 1960s, I remember a discussion turning on some point of interpretation in Exodus. One of the members of the Committee turned to Sir Godfrey Driver, saying, 'What does it say in The Work?' Sir Godfrey consulted a small blue book and gave a ruling. It was the CBS edition of Exodus, edited by his father S. R. Driver.)

On 24 February 1877 the Syndicate declined to publish what later became the Oxford English Dictionary. All publishers expect to make wrong decisions, and can only hope they are small mistakes. This was possibly the largest wrong decision in publishing history, but we can only say that with hindsight. For many years Cambridge must have congratulated itself for not being burdened with that apparent white elephant, especially in the years when the Press was committed to heavy payments for the revision and the production of the Revised Version.

The story begins with a letter of 23 December 1876, which Clay must have read on Christmas Eve. It had a printed heading 'From F. J. Furnivall', and began:

My dear Sir

I want you folk at the Pitt Press to take up a big thing that'll ultimately bring you a lot of profit and do you great credit, tho' there'll be considerable outlay at first. I've written to Mr Aldis Wright [a Syndic] about it...

Clay was an unbending man, it seems; and even in the festive season these breezy colloquialisms would have misfired with him. One can almost see the eyebrows lifting. The letter went on:

The work is now in such a state that if the Press will advance £600 a year for 3 years, for an Editor & 2 Subs, the work can be finished and printed to I, & the issue of it in 5/– or 10/– parts begun, to provide for the editorial charges, & begin to repay the paper and print. The whole Dicty could be completed in 10 years, in 4 vols 4to of 1500 or 1600 pages each, with abridgements in 4to, 8vo, square fcap 8vo for schools, 5/– and 2/6 and 1/–...

As we now know very well, that account was either ludicrously optimistic, or as Clay might have been inclined to say, a fraudulent prospectus. Furnivall added

The Press would have to lay out say £4000 or £5000 before money came back. If this is too much for 'em, I'm sure that Trübner or H. J. King would go shares...Macmillan wants us to publish with him...He knows what a success the book must ultimately be, but wants to screw us [the Philological Society, which sponsored the Dictionary. Furnivall was Secretary]. We resist; and before going to Oxford I try you, as I'm sure the book would ultimately prove *a grand thing* for the Press. See Skeat if you will. He knows the real value of our material, & Murray's capabilities. Please tell me who are your leading Syndics, that I may apply to them

Very try yrs    FJF

Murray, of course, was the great editor who very effectively resisted Furnivall's attempt to cut the Dictionary down to Furnivall's proposed dimensions, and who further for many heroic years resisted the efforts of the Oxford Press to do something similar in order to limit their expenditure and the Dictionary's size. And of course he was right; but for years Cambridge men must have looked over to Oxford and sighed with relief that they did not have *that* to contend with. It is highly unlikely that Cambridge could have afforded the Dictionary, until very recently.

In any case the main trouble with Furnivall's proposal, in Cambridge eyes, was Furnivall himself. Aldis Wright and Skeat (of the Anglo-Saxon Gospels) knew about him: they probably told Clay that he was a scoundrel and a mountebank. That is a rather summary judgement of an engaging character, but in the austere Cambridge of 1877 it is the judgement most likely to have been made: do not have anything to do with that awful man. So the Dictionary was declined, after Clay had talked to Furnivall in London, sized him up, and advised him to write a more formal letter to the Chairman of the Syndicate. There is no record of any discussion at the meeting: the decision seems to have been made briefly and as a matter of course. It would be a cautionary tale, if publishers did not know the moral from their own experience, and if it were possible to guard against being monumentally wrong by any simpler method than always being right.

Meanwhile changes were steadily taking place. Turquand Young were appointed accountants in 1881: not just a sign that the old system of internal audit was past, but also a symbol of modern business practice. A warehouse in Glasgow was acquired in 1881, and was run by the Scottish traveller with one boy to keep the shop while he was away. The London Warehouse moved to Ave Maria Lane in 1884. This was in good time for the publication of the RV in 1885: very soon the first and second floors were full of stock of this Bible, but on the ground floor in one room a set of pigeon-holes was at first quite enough to house the London stock of the 'Syndics' Proprietary Books'. There was a 'counting house', with two clerks. The work of binding the books, which came from Cambridge in sheets, of sending out review and presentation copies, of placing advertisements, and printing prospectuses, of taking London orders over the 'trade counter' and sending travellers through the country – all this began to take on the recognisable shape of a publishing business.

The first catalogue of the 'proprietary works' had appeared in 1875; it occupied sixteen pages, and was printed in some of the books themselves. It listed Scrivener's Cambridge Paragraph Bible, the Greek–English Testament, the Anglo-Saxon Gospels, the editions of the Fathers and the English theologians, and the editions of the classics. There was also a work in Sanskrit and one in Arabic. There was the beginnings of a scientific list: Thomson's *Treatise on Natural Philosophy*, Thomson and Tait's *Elements of Natural Philosophy*, Tait's *Elementary Treatise on*

*Quaternions,* Fourier's *Analytical Theory of Heat* translated by Freeman; Sedgwick's *Synopsis of the Classification of the British Palaeozoic Rocks,* his *Catalogue of Silurian Fossils,* a catalogue of osteological specimens in the Anatomical Museum, and the Cambridge Observatory's *Observations.* In law there were the Commentaries of Gaius and the Institutes of Justinian, translated by Abdy and Walker, and Whewell's Grotius. In history J. R. Seeley's great work on Stein was announced as in the press in the 1876 reprint of the catalogue; Mullinger's History of Cambridge and Baker's History of St John's were listed; and Willis and Clark on the *Architectural History of Cambridge* was in the press (also 1876). There were catalogues of MSS in Cambridge libraries and the University's Statutes and Ordinances. In the Pitt Press Series there were in 1876 three Greek, five Latin, four French, three German, and three English texts. It was a small list, but it was a serious beginning.

It was outweighed, for the time being – indeed it was almost swept away – by the Revised Version. Six editions of the New Testament were published simultaneously in 1881, in various formats and types. Of the smallest and cheapest 100,000 were printed, and almost immediately reprints of 50,000 and then three of 100,000 were ordered in 1881 alone. Publishers can come to fear runaway best-sellers because of the cash demands they make: an immense amount has to be spent, and always in advance of receipts. But there seems to have been no crisis: a tribute to Clay's financial management.

There were, however, some signs of strain. In October 1883 a Sub-Syndicate was appointed to consider ten years' accounts. Their report concluded that the publishing business had over this period lost £5705. 6. 9. Receipts had been £42,000, outgoings £26,000. The £16,000 balance had been absorbed in the printing and publication of the 'proprietary works', together with £5000 from the Government Annuity Fund. £8500 had been paid to the Revisers. So £21,000 had been 'sunk' in publishing. It had contributed to the profits of the printing business, and there was an asset in copyrights, stocks, and stereotype plates. 'But there still remains a large portion which cannot be looked on as in any sense remunerative.'

The Sub-Syndicate classified the publications in four groups: the Revised Version itself; the Pitt Press Series; the Cambridge Bible for Schools; other books. The first would definitely be profitable. The second produced mixed results: the French books showed large profits, the German ones fair profits, the Latin paid their way; the Greek and English made losses. The Cambridge Bible for Schools, at an early stage, was not in sight of profit. The other books consisted of those which could never have been expected to make a profit, and those that could have been. The Syndicate recommended

that a sharp line be drawn in future between books undertaken with the expectation of a profit, and those which are not so undertaken, and that more care be taken in undertaking books of an unremunerative character... [that] definite sums be voted for the purpose of covering the expected deficit, and a record be kept.

This was the beginning of a system which was followed for many years. But there were elements of unreality in this effort to be more realistic. Alas for 'sharp lines'! They can be drawn, but they interrupt an infinitely finely shaded spectrum; and they are drawn at a certain moment in a process which is itself changing. If they are drawn before publication they represent no more than a guess at what will actually happen. These predictions are regularly falsified. Indeed the Sub-Syndicate went on to recognise this, without drawing the conclusion:

Books have been undertaken as likely to be profitable which have not proved to be so...Estimates [should] be prepared of the probable cost of production of the books proposed and of the probable return from their sale... no book [should] be accepted which, unless stereotyped, will not on that estimate clear its expenses on the sale of three fourths of the first edition [stereotyping was a cost often charged to the second impression].

The Sub-Syndicate went on to say that prices had sometimes been fixed too low, payments to authors had been in certain cases too large, there had been too little control of authors' corrections: there should be a clause about this in the agreement with them. There should be more or better publicity: a small Sub-Syndicate was appointed 'to confer with Mr Clay on the best means of bringing the publications of the Press before the notice of the public'.

Who was being criticised here? Was it Clay? It is hard to say. Clay as Managing Partner no doubt advised the Syndicate, and as Secretary he presumably prepared the business for the meetings, which from February 1883 were held regularly once in each fortnight during term-time on Fridays at 2.15 p.m. (as they are now). But Clay's main concern was running the large printing business, which he did well and profitably, and running the London Warehouse, which mainly existed in order to sell very large numbers of Bibles and prayer books: this too went well. The publication of books was still a very small matter – something which was floated by the other activities. To Clay these other activities were the main end of the whole enterprise; he would gladly help the Syndicate to lose a *little* money each year on their learned publishing. That was, so to speak, their affair, but he would be worried if the loss on publishing threatened the health of printing and Bible selling. In fact the relationship between the two businesses was already beginning to change: the current loss on publishing was partly a result of inexperienced optimism, but partly the first result of wise long-term thinking: and some of both must have been Clay's. He was at once University Printer and in an anomalous way Secretary of the Syndicate. He was the executive conducting the publishing which would eventually require a change in the structure of the partnership, and then its dissolution.

Meanwhile it was agreed in February 1884 that there should be formal agreements with authors, binding both parties to specific terms, and Clay was to sign them on behalf of the Press. At the same time a standing Sub-Syndicate was set up to consider all business details respecting books. This became a working committee to which Clay could present the estimates now demanded, and which could recommend terms of publication. From June 1884 prices and payments to authors became its province.

In November of that year Clay received a letter which was as characteristic as Furnivall's:

Gentlemen,

I am recommended by learned & scientific friends to lay you [sic] before you a work long (six years) in preparation which is the record of my Travels in Arabia now ready for publication. As in it is the sole account and the mere verity of some of the most interesting regions of Arabia where I long travelled and dwelt & was the first European since the Roman times & that in it are some great acquisitions to Epigraphy, Geology, Geography it is a book I believe which Oriental Scholars would not have lost. Who would know what is Arabia Deserta may taste it in my book without the bitterness of Travel.

As regards the style I believe examined of your English Scholars you will find it not unworthy of a University. I am a philologist in all the Germanic Scandinavian and Romance languages since 20 years & have made a bold stand in the midst of the torrent of jargon & mist [?] for a right Anglicism: this is necessarily but imperfect so is every singular attempt.

Some friends praise it and some blame me & would have it recast by a *littérateur*, that is by one who probably knows less of English & of Arabia than the author. What savour would be left in it of Arabia!

Your obdt servant<br>
C H A S  M.  D O U G H T Y

(Doughty's hand, like his style, resists comprehension. The word 'mist' is a conjectural emendation.) It might be said that the letter gives fair warning. The experienced publisher's heart would first rise and then sink on reading it: probably an important book, certainly a difficult author – trouble.

The most interested Syndic was the great William Robertson Smith, who had just become Professor of Arabic at Cambridge after the tremendous stir caused by his dismissal from his Chair at Aberdeen for what was called the 'advanced' character of his Biblical articles in the ninth edition of the *Encyclopaedia Britannica* (i.e. for heresy). He had studied in Bonn and at Göttingen with Ritschl. His *Kinship and Marriage in Early Arabia*, accepted by the Press in 1885, was one of the foundations of ethnography: if an outsider wanting to be malicious were to say 'Aren't you very sorry not to have published Frazer's *Golden Bough*?' (it went to Macmillan) a Press editor would do well to reply 'I would rather have published Robertson Smith.' The ordinary reader has not heard of him, of course; but that is another matter. Robertson Smith recommended publication of *Arabia Deserta*, and the Syndics accepted it as a two-volume work, of which 1000 copies were to be printed. A condition of publication was that Doughty should accept Robertson Smith's proposals for revision 'to render the work intelligible to ordinary English readers'. The forecast of sales was rapidly halved, and Doughty asked to contribute £200, plus the cost of any printing in excess of 1200 pages, plus excess correction. Doughty made trouble over the revision, and then corrected mercilessly in proof. By publication in 1888 he owed £730, and was genuinely surprised to hear that the Syndicate meant what they had said. He failed to pay, was sent a solicitor's letter, and in the end surrendered the copyright instead: it could revert to him after the first impression on payment of £200.

In 1886 Clay was approaching sixty. He had been Printer and Managing Partner for more than thirty years, and had been Secretary for twelve. His son John Clay (a graduate of St John's) had been taken into the partnership in 1882, and was assisting him. A younger son, Charles Felix Clay, was also of age to enter the business, and the Syndicate agreed that it was 'willing to recommend the introduction of Mr Charles F. Clay into the partnership provided that he bring with him a practical know-ledge of the publishing business as carried on by the best firms'. It was an indication of the current preoccupation.

The old deed of partnership expired, and a new one was drawn up after 'extensive consideration'. The Syndicate had to balance the hitherto satisfactory conduct of the business under Clay against the fact that he was ageing and that the prospect of a dynasty was now before them, which might be a good or a bad thing. Were the younger Clays men such as their father had been? Probably not, since he was exceptional. The partnership was renewed in 1886 on tougher terms. C. F. Clay was included, but the partners now had to pay rent of £800 for the buildings as well as rates and taxes. On the other hand, an additional £200 was to go to the Managing Partners in consideration of the increased business in London and Glasgow, and £200 towards the rent of the new premises in Ave Maria Lane. These payments all came out of the profits before division.

In 1887 R. T. Wright, Fellow of Christ's, joined the Syndi-cate, and went straight on to a number of Sub-Syndicates. In 1887 the term of office of Syndics was increased from three to five years, an indication that more time was now needed to under-stand the business. In March 1888 it was agreed to appoint a Sub-Syndicate to 'consider the best means of affording assistance to Mr Clay in conducting the correspondence in connection with the publishing business of the Syndics and to confer with Mr Clay upon the subject'. In May it was reported that 'Mr Clay had withdrawn his application', a cryptic remark which was no doubt well understood by those who read it. Plainly minds were moving, and equally plainly the thinking was about structure and control, with special emphasis on publishing. It seems possible also that there was some unease, or even dissatisfaction. A different indicator was the opening of a third bank account in 1889; so that three separate functions were now recognised. The two recognised in the 1850s had been 'printing' and 'everything else'. The three now coming into focus were 'printing', 'publishing' and the original or controlling interest of the Syndicate as a separate entity which chose to take part in those enterprises with a partner, Clay. The Syndicate in that 'pure' capacity (to use the mathematical term) was the arm of the University called the Press. This sharpening of focus would put in question Clay's status in relation to the third entity. Subsequent events make it seem likely that the thinking here was Wright's. The ground was being prepared for a decisive change.

Before we come to that, it should be pointed out that in the 1880s Clay was acting quite enterprisingly as publisher, though it is likely that he was given very valuable advice by a distinguished band of Syndics. The great historian F. W. Maitland became a Syndic and an author at this time, and in 1885 the Syndicate accepted the first of his books on the history of law. The scientific publications proceeded slowly but steadily, and names begin to appear which are still familiar. Fenton's *Qualitative Analysis* was accepted in 1883; the first of the mathematical textbooks of S. L. Loney (*Dynamics*) was accepted in 1885. These were the first of many standard Cambridge textbooks with an extraordinarily long life: they went on being reprinted and reprinted, forming part of the active backlist which any publisher needs in order to pay his overheads and finance his new publications. A. W. Verrall was invited to write a volume of Essays on the Greek Drama in 1888, and to edit the *Ion* in 1890. Mr Clay was 'authorized to treat with' Edmund Gosse and J. W. Hales for books on literature with some popular appeal: so the notion of actively commissioning books was now accepted. It was a long way, mentally, from the remark made in a letter by W. E. Heitland in 1874: 'As therefore I have found out that the University Press accepts books I venture humbly to offer this [Cicero: *Pro Murena*] to the consideration of the Syndics...'.

In November 1889 it was agreed to ask Mr Verity whether he would edit for the Syndics 'some portion of Milton's Poetical Works other than *Paradise Lost*'. He agreed, and there was started an immensely fruitful partnership. Verity went on to edit more of Milton, and then Shakespeare. It is a safe estimate that his editions sold several millions of copies in all, being reprinted regularly for sixty or seventy years. It is indicative of the difficulty of drawing 'sharp lines' that at one quite early point his request for a larger fee was refused on the ground that it was not clear that the work was very profitable. One only knows that at the end of the day; and Verity's day was a long one. He became a *bête noire* of literary critics in the 1930s, partly because generations of schoolchildren, myself included, learned from him how to do 'character studies' – being required by the School Certificate examiners, also reared on Verity, to do so. But the rest of Verity's matter, though dry, is firm. If you want to know what he has to tell, he has a lot to tell.

In short, by 1890 the Press was recognisably becoming a modern publisher, though on a small scale. It had the beginnings of a scholarly list, a scientific list, a schoolbook list. It had begun to take initiatives and to commission books. It still depended primarily on the printing business, and its printing and its sales were still mainly of Bibles and prayer books. It had in Charles John Clay a man who had served it for many years with very great energy and distinction, who had retrieved its fortunes and taken it to an assured position. But the future now had to be provided for, and another restructuring was needed.

# 11

## R.T. WRIGHT AND THE
## SECRETARYSHIP

R. T. WRIGHT was re-elected as Syndic in 1890 for five years, but before he had served that term his position, and Clay's, had radically altered. Some signs of strain, or at any rate signs of fundamental thought, have already been mentioned. One such sign is the Syndicate minute of 12 June 1891:

It was agreed on the proposition of Professor Robertson Smith that a Sub-Syndicate be appointed through whose hands shall pass the MS of all works to be printed for the Syndics.

This does not sound now like a very practical or workable proposal; it could only have been made as the result of a feeling that things were not being done that should be done.

A sharper note is sounded in a minute of 16 October:

Mr R. T. Wright resigned his place on the Sub-Syndicate appointed on May 15 1891 to edit the catalogue of Books published by the Syndics, on the ground that a new catalogue had been issued without consultation with the Sub-Syndicate.

Here an issue is plainly being forced, and by Wright himself. Another minute of the same meeting reads:

The Chairman undertook to inform the Syndicate at their next meeting how many books...had been put in hand in the Long Vacation without having passed through the hands of the Sub-Syndicate appointed on June 12, 1891.

And at the next meeting on 30 October:

It was agreed that a Sub-Syndicate be appointed to consider the existing arrangements for supervising the publication of the Syndics' works and to report to the Syndicate.

Pausing only to decline A. E. Housman's offer of some notes on Propertius, thought more suitable for journal publication, the

R. T. Wright, Secretary of the Press Syndicate 1892–1911. From
the portrait in the Pitt Building.

Syndicate approved on 13 November this report, which, in the history of the Press at any rate, must be considered epoch-making, for it marked the beginning of the end of the partnership with the Clays. The recommendations were as follows:

1. The publishing business of the Syndics involves a great deal of work which has nothing to do with the printing and warehouse departments.

2. Many parts of this work cannot be properly done by the Syndics at their meetings, but require prompt attention from day to day and individual labour.

3. Hitherto the Syndics have received much help in such matters from Sub-Syndicates or from individual members of the Syndicate who have charged themselves with special pieces of work; but a very large amount of work which in an ordinary publishing firm would be performed by a partner or a paid member of the staff has hitherto been undertaken by Mr Clay as unpaid Secretary to the Syndics. This work has been purely voluntary on his part and belongs to a department which lies outside the partnership between Messrs Clay and the Syndics.

4. The Sub-Syndicate are of opinion that the publishing business of the Press is now too large to be economically and effectively managed in the way described, and that the Syndics ought to have the help of a paid Secretary in that part of their work which is distinct from the printing and warehouse business.

5. The following is a provisional list of duties with which in the opinion of the Sub-Syndicate the Secretary should be charged:

    a. To keep the Minutes of the Syndics and prepare Agenda for their meetings

    b. To correspond with authors and prepare agreements

    c. To receive authors' copy and, with the approval of the Syndicate, to transmit it to the printer

    d. To supervise arrangements for illustration, maps, etc.

    e. To assist the Syndics in such matters as title-pages, bindings and other details of the external form of publications

    f. To supervise the list of Press and presentation copies

    g. To advise the Syndics about advertisements and to see to the form of advertisements, extracts from reviews, announcements of forthcoming works etc.

    h. To supervise the catalogue of the Syndics' publications.

6. The Secretary should be provided with an office within the buildings of the Press. The Syndicate room might be temporarily used for the purpose, but a proper office should be provided as soon as possible.

7. The Syndicate recommend that the salary of the Secretary be £300 per annum, payable half-yearly.

The recommendations of the Sub-Syndicate were accepted, with the rider that 'the Secretary should in no case be a member of the Syndicate': which meant that if a Syndic were appointed he must resign and move (so to speak) to the other side of the table. It was also agreed that the election should be made at the next meeting, so it is quite clear that the whole matter was speedily resolved because it had already been thought through.

On 27 November 1891 it was

Agreed that the office of Secretary be offered to Mr R. T. Wright, with an expression of the desire of the Syndicate that he should enter on office on the 1st of January next, and that the Sub-Syndicate appointed on October 30 be requested to confer with Mr Wright and Mr Clay upon further details of duties of the office.

At the last meeting of 1891, on 11 December, a minute read:

The Chairman having informed the Syndics that Mr Clay had expressed his acquiescence in the appointment of a paid Secretary made...after consultation with Mr Clay, and had consented to retain his office as Secretary to the Syndicate,

It was resolved that Mr Clay be requested to conduct as theretofore all correspondence relating to the Revised Version and to undertake such other duties as may not be entrusted to the recently appointed Secretary.

That the Syndics having taken steps to relieve Mr Clay of a portion of the arrangements for the publication of the Books of the Syndics, the work in connection with which has now become very onerous, desire to place upon their Minutes a record of their sense of the valuable services voluntarily rendered by Mr Clay since his appointment as Secretary in 1874.

Undoubtedly Clay was hurt: it must have been this change as much as his age which caused his resignation at the end of 1893. It is easy to feel for him now, but no doubt thoughtful people, including Syndics, felt for him then. But surely they were also increasingly feeling that the partnership, so valuable in 1854 and after, was now becoming perceptibly anomalous. The process of dismantling it was slow; it did not end until 1916. The anomaly can best perhaps be described by saying that in 1886 Cambridge had three University Printers: Charles John Clay, John Clay and Charles Felix Clay. So the terms of the ancient charter of 1534 were being literally applied, three hundred years after the appointment of Thomas Thomas. Like him, the Clays were all M.A.s of the University: educated, loyal and thoughtful men.

But the printer's imprint began 'printed by C. J. Clay M.A. and Sons', and the publisher's imprint began 'London: C. J. Clay and Sons'. The names sounded too much like those of the partners in an ordinary commercial firm, and were a reminder that, all other differences apart, the University was still, after three hundred years, in the fundamental position of licensing printers and 'stationers or booksellers' to administer its imprint. Moreover the deed of partnership recognised that the outside party, having advanced capital, was in the business for the purpose of making a personal or private profit. The time was being reached at which this type of arrangement was thought improper and repugnant, but it could be ended only when the University was in a position to administer the entire Press itself. This could no longer be done by the Vice-Chancellor or his Deputy, busying himself about the Press in addition to his other duties. Nor could it be done by the Syndicate themselves, or the endless Sub-Syndicates which proliferated in the nineteenth century. It emerges very clearly from the record that these small committees, of three or four people, represented bursts of activity: they concentrated on one problem and found an *ad hoc* solution in a remarkably short time; then they went back to teaching.

Two essential stages had now been reached. The theory, or one might even say the theology or metaphysics, of the Press could now be stated: the Press Syndicate, representing the University, were in fact the University's printing and publishing arm. They could also be considered under two separate practical aspects: printing and publishing. An awful – in the eighteenth-century sense of the word – comparison was possible. In the early part of the century, Porson (a notorious unbeliever) explained to a friend as they walked down the street his special difficulties with the doctrine of the Trinity. A cab was passing, with three passengers. 'There you are', said the friend: 'Three men in one cab.' 'No', said Porson, 'It would need to be one man in three cabs.' If they had lived at a later time the friend might have confuted Porson by pointing to the Press where one entity, the Press, had three aspects: the Syndicate, the Publishing business, and the Printing business.

I surmise that it was Wright's special distinction to have made this analysis and then to have started to draw the practical conclusions; but he might have been helped by Maitland's acute legal and constitutional mind. At any rate the priorities were surely right. Constitutional change must come from the centre and the top: the Syndicate themselves had to have their own executive, or they would forever be at a disadvantage in dealing with those who were actually doing the day-to-day business. More important, the Syndicate had to have a clear sense of their own role as the constitutional source of all executive action. The new kind of Secretary became their representative or embodiment, at least in respect of publishing, in dealing with staff, customers and authors. It was obviously a momentary oddity that as well as three Printers the Syndicate had two Secretaries; but that was a historical legacy which would speedily pass away.

On 22 January 1892, at the first Syndicate meeting of the new era, Wright's name is listed among those present, though Clay's never had been. It seems hardly conceivable that he never attended; but it had been made clear to him that he had no constitutional right to attend, and the events of 1891 suggest that much was decided in his absence.

At that first meeting the Syndicate accepted Cunningham's second volume on the *Growth of English Industry and Commerce* (the foundation of the list in economic history, which is now one of the subjects in which the Press is pre-eminent); Verity's *Paradise Lost XI and XII* (2500 copies and stereos), Dowdell's Ovid: *Metamorphoses I*, and Love's *Elasticity* (one of the Press's favourite titles, and a textbook with a life of three-quarters of a century). Perowne offered to resign as Editor of the Cambridge Bible for Schools, but it was agreed that he be dissuaded; and new buildings were discussed, especially the new office for the Secretary.

In the rest of that year the Syndicate accepted, among other books, the first of E. G. Browne's studies of Persian literature (once more, a notable list being founded); the indefatigable Verity was invited to edit 'three or four volumes of Shakespeare'; Jebb's one-volume Sophocles was taken, and so was Loney's *Trigonometry* (another long-term best-seller). In 1893 Pollock and Maitland's great History of English Law was accepted (still in print, in paperback), so was Wyatt's *Beowulf* and Ewing on the Steam Engine – almost as long-lived. The Syndicate also instituted two large-scale ventures. It was decided that the Pitt Press Series was not to be the sole publication for schools: it provided set texts, but children also needed good course-books. A Sub-Syndicate recommended a series, with books on English history, the modern history of other countries, a 'commercial' (i.e. an economic) history of England, an English grammar, a book on Elizabethan drama. Not all of these suggestions came to fruition, but most did, often in a revised form by an author other than the one first proposed. The second large venture was to be a biological series edited by Shipley: it was to contain Harker's *Petrology* (in print until very recently), an introduction to anthropology, a book on the vertebrate skeleton, one on paleobotany by A. C. Seward, and the *Elementary Botany of Plants* by Francis Darwin.

Two very distinguished names were added to the scientific list: J. J. Thomson was 'invited to write a book on Thermodynamics and the kinetic Theory of Gases', and C. S. Sherrington offered *Experimental Pathology*. The Press was in the process of publishing the collected papers of a number of great scientists and mathematicians: Lord Kelvin (previously W. Thomson), Lord Rayleigh, Clerk Maxwell, Reynolds, Stokes, Tait, Sylvester and Cayley; but inevitably such collections were retrospective, and rather like monuments. The genuinely exciting work now going on in Cambridge, initiated and symbolised by the establishment of the Cavendish Laboratory of Experimental Physics in 1871 with Clerk Maxwell at its head, meant that the Press ought also to be looking for the monographs which gave classic summaries of very recent advances. J. J. Thomson was one such author, and the first of many, though it became noticeable in the twentieth century that the chosen form of publication for important scientific work was less and less often the book or treatise, and more often the journal article. It therefore became important to publish journals, and the Cambridge list was founded in 1893 when the *Journal of Physiology* was published on commission. In the same year the Syndicate accepted Thomson's *Elements of the Mathematical Theory of Electricity and Magnetism*.

In 1894 it accepted A. C. Haddon's report on his study of the Torres Straits Islanders, a pioneering work in anthropology.

The next stage in the constitutional evolution of the Press and the gradual dismantling of the partnership was soon reached, in 1894. A Sub-Syndicate on 'Partnership arrangements' reported. There was on the horizon the need to renew the partnership – perhaps on different terms – when it expired in 1896; and the report of the Sub-Syndicate can be seen as a consolidation of Wright's position vis-à-vis the Clays. Its recommendations were adopted on 10 June 1894. In addition to the duties already prescribed (which mainly had to do with the business of the Syndicate meetings and the seeing of books through the press), Wright was now required to examine the partnership printing accounts, so far as they referred to the books published by the Syndicate, and to prepare cheques for signature by the Chairman for payment of those accounts, of royalties, and of shares of profits to authors. He was to give more direct supervision to advertisements, and to visit the London Warehouse about once a fortnight. His salary was increased, as recognition of this increase of responsibility. As a visible symbol of his function, at the end of the Long Vacation 1894 he took possession of his new office: the neat little red-brick building in what might be called 'Dutch Queen Anne' style which still stands on the Mill Lane side of the Old Press Site, with a later bridge to the Pitt Building on one side, and (originally) a green baize door to the old printing works on the other. At first it had only one storey. It contained a large Syndicate room for meetings, with shelves all round being now quite rapidly filled with the new publications, a William Morris carpet, and a big fireplace which roasted the Chairman's back at Syndicate meetings. Next door there was an office for the Secretary and one for his clerk; and that was all. The Syndicate met in their new and very pleasant room on 12 October 1894, admiring, no doubt, the equally new electric light (though it was not thought desirable to have telephones until 1902). They went on meeting there until 1963, when the building – its second storey had been added in 1927 – was passed to the University along with the old Printing House site. In 1894, however, Clay in the Printer's office could look across to the new Secretary's office, and reflect on the changes he had seen: this one he had not brought about himself. (They faced each other, incidentally, across a pleasant grass court with a walnut tree in a rectangular flower-bed – all now asphalted over for the inevitable carpark.)

A report to the University by the Syndicate on 23 November 1894 reminded the Senate that in 1886 an agreement had been made for ten years, and that it was now time to consider its renewal. But it was not recommended that it be renewed unchanged.

On November 20, 1893, Mr C. J. Clay communicated to the Syndics his wish to retire from the position of Managing Partner at the close of the present year, if satisfactory arrangements could be made for carrying on the work of the Press under the management of his sons, Messrs J. and C. F. Clay.

The Syndics learned with great regret that Mr Clay felt it necessary to terminate his connection with the Press which has lasted for a period of 40 years and has been characterised throughout by loyal devotion to the interests of the University....

The Syndics consider it desirable that the present partnership should be dissolved by mutual consent as from the 31st day of December next.

The Syndics consider it desirable that separate and distinct Deeds of Partnership should be made between the University and Messrs J. and C. F. Clay relating respectively to the Printing business in Cambridge and the Publishing business in London and elsewhere for a period of ten years from January 1 1895.

It is proposed that the provisions of the new deeds of partnership shall continue to a large extent the same...the principal alterations being as follows:

1. That definite portions of the capital of the present Partnership be assigned to the Printing and Publishing Partnerships.

2. That the share of the University in the capital and profits of each Partnership be increased from three-fourths to five-sixths, and that the remaining one-sixth...be supplied in equal parts by Messrs J. and C. F. Clay.

3. That the rent paid by the Printing Partnership to the University shall be increased from £800 to £1200 a year....

4. That the payment by the Syndics of the annual sum of £200 towards the rent of the London Warehouse be discontinued, but until the sales of the Syndics' proprietary books reach a certain definite amount [actually £21,000 p.a.] the Syndics contribute a sum not exceeding £200 a year towards the expenses of the Publishing business.

The Grace was approved, but by a vote: for fifty, against eleven.

Lord Acton, Regius Professor of Modern History and first editor of the *Cambridge Modern History*.

F. W. Maitland, Downing Professor of the Laws of England and a Syndic of the Press.

It may seem that the changes were small; but they were a beginning. The separation of the businesses was now represented in the deeds of partnership, and the Syndicate were also demonstrating the distinction between themselves as partner in the operation of two enterprises and themselves as finally the owner of the two enterprises. They had increased their share in the partnerships; and by raising the rent and discontinuing the payment towards the warehouse rent, they had raised the charges on both businesses before profit could be declared, so that the Clays on both counts took a smaller proportion out of the business.

It happened that in 1895 the gross sales of the Syndicate's publications amounted to £22,000, of which £1800 came from sales in the USA through the agency of Macmillan (instituted in 1890) and £160 from India. No contribution was therefore payable towards the expenses of the London Warehouse. Wright did some sums in 1896 which tended to show that over a number of years the receipts from books compared with their costs showed a balance in favour; but he managed this only by including a notional value of copyrights and stock on the 'receipts' side. In fact the publishing was showing a small annual loss, for two reasons. The first was that it was just not big enough; the second was that the Syndicate recognised a duty to accept some books regardless of considerations of profit and loss; and this element of their publishing would always affect the overall outcome. It was reckoned that in the 1890s between eleven and twenty-one books were accepted in each year in the 'certain' knowledge of a loss on each. (Alas again for such certainties! Verity had been thought a doubtful case a few years before: and now the new universal history to be edited by Lord Acton was included among the certain losers.)

What we now know as the *Cambridge Modern History* arose from an initiative of Wright's, developed in consultation with Maitland. On 13 March 1896 it was minuted

That Prof. Lord Acton be asked whether he would consider the possibility of his undertaking the general direction of a History of the World in case the Syndics decide to publish such a work; it being explained to Lord Acton that the Syndics have not yet decided that it is desirable, on financial grounds, to undertake such a book.

One can very easily be frightened by one's own ideas: sometimes quite rightly, as here. On 8 May a further minute showed that a practical way had to be found of taking the great venture step by step:

The proposal for a Universal History to be edited by Lord Acton was further considered in a modified form, it having been suggested that the scheme should include Modern History only, beginning with the Renaissance. A letter from Lord Acton as to this form of the proposal was read and it was ꞏꞬꞏꞌꞝd to appoint Dr Maitland and Mr Whibley a Sub-Syndicate to consider together with the Secretary with Lord Acton with the view of reporting on a detailed scheme.

On 22 May

It was agreed 1. That the Syndicate undertake the publication of a Modern History of the World provided satisfactory arrangements can be made as regards a detailed scheme.... 2. That the Syndicate desire to express their thanks to Lord Acton for the readiness with which he has approached the question and request him to prepare a detailed plan of the work.... 3. That Lord Acton be informed...that the Syndics think it would be desirable that he should write some portion of the work himself.

In October Acton's report was received and approved; he was appointed general editor of a history in twelve volumes. Contributors were to be paid 10s. per page, and Acton was to get £300 for general superintendence and £100 for each volume. Acton resigned in 1901 on grounds of ill-health, and A. W. Ward, G. W. Prothero and Stanley Leathes were appointed co-editors (they were all knighted for the work). In February 1902 the first volume was published in an edition of two thousand copies at 15s. Ward was a remarkably efficient editor, and all twelve volumes were published by 1912.

In 1895 the Syndicate accepted McTaggart's *Hegelian Dialectic*, and the first work of R. A. Nicholson: *Selected Poems from the 'Dīvāni Shamsi Tabrīz'* (still in print, in paperback). Browne and Nicholson were the twin pillars of a growing list in Arabic and Persian Studies which became very distinguished indeed. The first work by the great A. N. Whitehead was his *Generalised Algebra*, accepted in 1896. His partner in *Principia Mathematica*, Bertrand Russell, approached the Press in the same year with a work 'on the foundations of geometry'. In 1898 Sandys's *History of Classical Scholarship* was accepted.

By 1898, apart from the books which the Syndicate accepted one by one on their academic merits, the active publishing of the Press was being carried on through eight series: the Pitt Press Series, the Series for Schools and Training Colleges, the Cambridge Bible for Schools, the Smaller Cambridge Bible for Schools, the Greek Testament for Schools and Training Colleges, the Historical Series, the Geographical Series and the Natural Science Manuals. All these series provided textbooks, for use by students in secondary schools, teacher-training colleges and universities. These series were founded in the expectation that the books would ultimately make a surplus, and this must finally have been the case, but it took time; and in June 1898 the Financial Sub-Syndicate reported that after payment of interest the printing business showed a profit in 1897 of £2799, but the publishing had lost £354. These losses were effectively borne by the partners, necessarily including the Clays, and here was plainly a potential source of ill-feeling: for the Clays, very effectively managing the printing, could reasonably say that they were carrying the publishing business, which was now conducted by an upstart or interloper without business experience, but who had, as they did not have, the ear of the Syndicate. It must therefore have been an urgent priority for Wright to remove the loss on publishing, and that could be achieved only by doing more, and doing it well.

The loss on publishing was reduced to £80 in 1898, became a profit of £80 in 1899, and a profit of £420 in 1900. Wright could therefore look the Clays in the eye with the confidence of a man whose business was growing and was evidently well conducted; but for many years yet the printing business remained the largest part of the Press's entire operation, and the publishing was looked on as a new and doubtful enterprise, or, more bluntly, as a way of gambling with the money made on printing. It must also be said that until 1970 the Secretary of the Syndicate went on being also the head of the publishing business. There was a possibility of bias here, or a possibility of conflict that could produce personal strains, until the restructuring introduced in 1972 by Lord Todd as Chairman and Geoffrey Cass created the post of Chief Executive of the Press, above and in charge of the heads of the two businesses.

There were small practical changes in the relationship with the Clays. In 1898, they pointed out that the loss on publishing came at the point at which the turnover reached the agreed amount at which they also lost the contribution to the expenses of publication, and that the commission they were left with did not cover the costs. It may have been Wright who put into the minds of the Syndicate that the Bible trade, which was supposed to supply the deficiency, was itself not making a sufficient profit; so that though the Clays were given a larger commission they were also asked to look at the prices of Bibles. In the following year the interest to be recovered on capital before the profit was declared was reduced to three per cent.

In 1900 the first typed document in the central archive appears. It is a report of the Business Details Sub-Syndicate, about 'arrangements for the future conduct of the business of the Press'. While it shows an important development, reflecting expansion, some of the details make odd reading today to Wright's successors:

When Mr Wright was first appointed, it was understood that his duties would only require his presence in Term time. Though not bound to do so by the terms of his appointment, Mr Wright has frequently been in attendance during the vacations.... Definite provision should now be made which would secure the presence of the Secretary...or some other responsible officer at those periods in the vacation when business arises for consideration.

Since Mr Wright's appointment there has been a steady increase in the work of the Secretary... to such an extent that it seems desirable in the interests of the Press that assistance should be given...[in the form of] an additional officer...not a merely clerical secretary, but an Assistant Secretary.

...additional attendance will be required of the Secretary [whose stipend was raised to £700. He]...may be expected to give throughout the year whatever time and attention are required for the management and development of those parts of the business of the Press for which he is responsible and be in residence for a considerable part of the vacations as well as during term.

It was recommended:

That it be the duty of the Secretary and the Assistant Secretary to attend at the Press as a rule during some portion of each day during Full Term and at such periods, not in Full Term, as the Syndicate may from time to time direct: and they shall arrange so that between them such attendance shall be secured for a large part of the business day....

That the hours of attendance of the Assistant Secretary at the Press be such that he is left free to do a certain amount of other work such as e.g. lecturing.

It had been formally established in previous years that Wright had power without reference to the Syndicate to ask prospective authors to send in manuscripts, to find referees in cases of urgency, and to pay them a fee of not more than three guineas. In Long Vacations he had power to fix prices. These specific provisions show that the Syndicate still felt able – and wanted – to do a lot of the business themselves; but it was a phase which was bound to pass as the volume of business increased, and in particular as the urgent decisions were seen to pay no heed to the University calendar and the cycle of meetings. It must already have been the case that Wright was doing far more than his official brief specified – perhaps at first in consultation with the Chairman of the Syndicate. As the new century went on it became more and more necessary that executive decisions be taken day by day in the office, while the Syndicate became a deliberative body which considered and approved larger matters.

There were eighty-eight candidates for the post of Assistant Secretary. Leonard Whibley was appointed. He had been a Syndic, like Wright, was a Fellow of Pembroke, and lectured in classics and taught for his College – indeed he was the tutor of the young S. C. Roberts, who went up to Pembroke in 1907. Whibley did not occupy the post for long: he obviously wanted to extend the duties, and Wright and the Syndicate seem not to have been ready for this yet. When he pressed them, he was told that they were willing to *reduce* the hours of attendance, so that he could do other things: he could come in for two hours a day instead of three in term-time, with ten weeks' attendance in vacation, four days' attendance in each week. The Syndicate was also willing to engage a clerk. Whibley resigned, but it seems to have been an amicable exchange; he went back on to the Syndicate – and that was probably a good thing, since he could exert there a continuing pressure for change and expansion.

A. R. Waller took his place as Assistant Secretary in 1902. He had experience of London publishing, and was something of a scholar as well, having edited several English poets. He had worked for Duckworth and Dent, both 'coming' firms at the time. He was a business-like man, with a good head for figures. By being more patient than Whibley, he slowly built up his own position, and in due course became Wright's successor as Secretary. One of his early assignments was the supervision of the transfer of the London Warehouse from Ave Maria Lane to Fetter Lane in 1905, the much larger premises being a sign of the increased publishing business. Waller was introduced to the Press by A. W. Ward, Master of Peterhouse and editor of the *Modern History*, and Ward and Waller together edited the *Cambridge History of English Literature*, which appeared between 1907 and 1916.

Acceptances in these early years of the century included J. J. Thomson's *Conduction of Electricity through Gases*, E. T. Whittaker on Mathematical Analysis, Kenny's *Cases in Criminal Law*, Bateson on Mendel's Theory of Heredity, the first of H. M. Chadwick's books on the heroic literatures, G. E. Moore's *Principia Ethica*, and Jane Ellen Harrison on Greek Ritual (the first of an important series of books linking classics with wider thought about religion and philosophy). Among schoolbooks, in 1902 two mathematics masters at Harrow called Godfrey and Siddons were invited to write an Elementary Geometry. The 'Harrow connection' produced an extraordinary list of mathematical schoolbooks, forward-looking for their time, which went on being published until the 1960s: Siddons was variously partnered by Daltry, Price, Hughes, Snell, Lockwood and Morgan; his venerable figure was last seen at a party celebrating fifty years of publishing; and Kenneth Snell in retirement went to teach in Ghana, where he produced an African adaptation of the final course. The four-figure mathematical tables produced by Godfrey and Siddons were regularly reprinted in hundreds of thousands, and its sales over the years must make 'Godfrey and Siddons' the only publication of the Press to come anywhere near the Bible or the Book of Common Prayer in total sale.

In the last years of the nineteenth and the first of the twentieth centuries some notable books in the sciences and mathematics were accepted, both in and outside of series. A Physical Series founded in 1902 included Thomson's *Conduction of Electricity* and Rutherford's *Radioactivity* (1904, with subsequent editions metamorphosing into Rutherford, Chadwick and Ellis: *Radiations from Radioactive Substances*). A Biological Series included early editions of Willis's *Dictionary of the Flowering Plants and Ferns*. The famous Cambridge Tracts in Mathematics were founded in 1905; G. H. Hardy was one of the editors, and his *Pure Mathematics*, first published in 1908, is still in print. Whitehead and Russell's great work, *Principia Mathematica*, was published in three volumes between 1910 and 1913.

There is in the archive, now in the University Library, a small black notebook, whose contents are headed 'very private, for the Syndics of the Press only'. It is a lucid statement of the constitutional position in 1901, and was probably used as a sort of catechism for incoming Syndics who might have been in Porson's frame of mind about the metaphysics of the whole operation. After a brief resumé of the history since 1854, it sets out the current terms of the partnerships. These were described as the 'A Partnership' which covered printing, and the 'B Partnership' which covered the publishing operations carried out in London. In both, the Press had a majority share in the capital, and took an equivalent share of the interest and profits. It was pointed out that the B Partnership dated from 1895:

This business publishes and sells Bibles and Prayerbooks, buying them in quires from the A Partnership, binding them and selling them to retail booksellers.... The B Partnership also publishes on commission the Syndics' books.... The capital of this Partnership is £14,000.... At present the rate of interest is by agreement fixed at 3 p.c. only: the profit or loss after payment of interest is divided between the partners in the same proportion as the A Partnership [five-sixths to the University and one-twelfth each to the two Clays].... In the case of both Partnerships, while the detailed management is left in the hands of the Messrs Clay, the sanction of the Syndics has to be obtained on important points....

The third term in this trinity is 'C. The Syndics' books'. The Syndicate accepted the books of their choice, employing the A Partnership to print and the B Partnership to publish and sell to the trade, repaying sums actually expended by the B Partnership, and paying a commission, currently twenty-two per cent, on sales.

The capital in the hands of the Syndicate (as distinct from that held by the partnerships) consisted of the Press buildings in Cambridge, other property in Cambridge, investments, stock of books in Cambridge and London, stereotype plates and copyrights. There was also the income of £500 from the Government Annuity Fund. Summing all this up, the document reads:

Roughly speaking, the net proceeds of the sales of the Syndics' books about cover the printing bill and the payments to authors. For the three years 1897, 98 and 99, the average amount of the net sales (after paying for advertising, binding and commission) was £14,823; the average printing bill was £10,567 and the average of the payments to authors £3,606; this appears to shew a surplus of £650: but the average of the Syndics' miscellaneous expenses for the same three years was £445 apart from the Secretary's stipend and the payment to the A Partnership for clerical work.... It would seem that there is an annual deficit of about £950, against which must be set any increase of the capital locked up....

To meet this apparent deficiency the Syndics have an income from various sources which may be roughly calculated thus:

| | £ |
|---|---|
| Interest on capital in the A and B Partnerships | 2440 |
| Profits (average) say on both Partnerships | 1500 |
| Rent of Press premises | 1050 |
| Rent of house property | 450 |
| Interest on investments | 100 |
| | 5540 |

or after allowing for the deficit of £950, a surplus of £4590.

The sum of £4500 may therefore be taken roughly as the margin at the disposal of the Syndics, but it cannot be counted on with any certainty, as sales fluctuate considerably and as occasions for large and unforeseen extraordinary expenditure arise frequently.... For these reasons it seems very desirable that a considerable fund should be kept in reserve.

That was a shrewd conclusion: the first statement of a recurrent concern which has remained a pressing one ever since. The writer went on however to point out that

In the past the profits of the Syndics have been largely used in extending the business and in the purchase of adjoining property, but considerable sums have been transferred to the University Chest. Within the last 25 years the sums so transferred have amounted to £31,000.

The University had therefore used the Press as a milch-cow. It is a great tribute to the Clays' management that so much had been produced, so that the Press itself had grown and the Syndics' publications been financed, while the University and the Clays had also been able to take money out of the business. But the analysis showed this to be an improvident proceeding, especially in a publishing enterprise which was now committed on a considerable scale to long-term and uncommercial academic publishing, and which had no source of external support other than the Government Annuity. Simply to assume that the printing business could for ever generate the business on which all else depended was obviously unwise. The publishing business was being rapidly developed, but would always carry with it its own handicap – the learned books at the 'top end' of the list. It was becoming increasingly clear that these books were the justification of the whole enterprise, precisely because they were the books which no other publisher would contemplate. They provided the Press with its *raison d'être*. That function was the obligation which the University and the academic world laid upon the Syndicate; it required to be underpinned by an endowment such as the Colleges themselves possessed, and to be managed as a trust, as the Colleges were by their governing bodies.

The document of 1901 thus revealed a danger, and even an impropriety – at least an improvidence: both the University and the Clays were taking out of the enterprise money which should have been used to secure its position, and without that endowment its position only *seemed* secure. If Wright was the author of the document, as seems very likely, he had added a new analysis to those he had already carried out; and in making the position clear to new Syndics, he must also have caused some of them to think that further changes were necessary.

And indeed these followed. In 1904 the Syndicate reported to the University that the partnership would need to be renewed in 1905, and proposed a new arrangement, with John Clay only, for the management of the printing house; Clay's share of the capital should be one-tenth, i.e. an increase for him personally, since he had previously shared a sixth with C. F. Clay, but now the University was increasing its share from five-sixths to nine-tenths – a step towards total control.

The proposal for the publishing business was more radical, and shows the University taking complete control: so one more very important stage had been reached. The report said:

At present the publishing business is conducted partly in London and partly at Cambridge. The London Warehouse undertakes the sale of books; the arrangements for their production are made at Cambridge. The books undertaken by the Syndics are published on commission by the London Warehouse. This necessitates keeping two distinct sets of accounts and there have in fact been two distinct businesses. The Syndics think it will be a substantial improvement for these two branches to be consolidated and form a single business.

A difficulty...arises from the fact that the publishing business cannot be looked at solely from a commercial point of view. The Syndics consider that the publication of works which cannot prove remunerative but which are regarded as valuable contributions to learning is one of the most important functions of a University Press; they could not recommend any change which would hamper them in undertaking works of this class. The Syndics therefore do not feel able to recommend that any partner should be associated with the University in the publishing business consolidated as explained above. They consider that it is important in the interest of the University to retain the services of Mr C. F. Clay and propose to ask him to accept the post of London Manager with duties similar to those he at present discharges. The Secretary to the Syndics would continue to act, as at present, under the direction of the Syndicate; thus the joint management of the publishing business would be in the hands of these two gentlemen.

As a last step in this reorganisation it was proposed that the Syndicate itself should consist of the Vice-Chancellor or his Deputy, and fourteen members, two to be appointed annually for a term of seven years, and not being re-eligible except by special Grace.

Another epoch had been reached. The University, represented by the Syndicate, was now a publisher in its own name, and without any intermediary agency, whether printer, bookseller or stationer, to use the old terms. It was a mark of extraordinary continuity, or a sign of strangely slow evolution in the book trades, that there existed in Cambridge until 1904 this age-old arrangement. For more than three hundred years the University had had associated with it up to three stationers or printers or sellers of books. The three Clays in 1884 were lineal successors of Thomas Thomas and all the printers, booksellers, agents and publishers in between. There had been two decisive intrusions into those coherent strata: the attempt of Bentley and Somerset to push the balance towards control by the University, and the external pressure from the Commissioners of 1852 to push the balance towards a commercial partnership. The second had been more successful and long-lasting, and there can be no doubt that one of the heroes of this story is Charles John Clay, who served the University as well as he served his own family. But the other hero is Wright, the second Secretary in one sense, but the first one in reality. Wright's contributions were three: the analytical power to see that the constitutional situation was wrong; the political skill to put through the successive constitutional changes which improved the situation; and the ability as publisher to build up the publishing business by a series of editorial and business decisions which enabled it to take off. Wright had to 'correct' a situation which was on the face of it outstandingly successful. He had to inflict a rebuff on, and take the place of, a man who had done the Press much good. He had to build up, from a quite small beginning, and against the entrenched success of Macmillan, a publishing business which had to cease to be a kind of parasite on the printing business, and which had to become an equal partner. And he had to do this while accepting the obligation to publish books which could not possibly pay their way.

By the changes of 1904, Wright had reduced the partnership's role to having a very small share in the capital and profits of the printing business, and the managing directorship of that business. It is significant that of the Syndics who signed the report, Leonard Whibley dissented from the proposal about printing. That could mean only either that he thought it was unfair to the Clays to reduce their share, or that he thought it should have been eliminated. His history shows that he must have wanted them removed altogether; but he always wanted to move faster than Wright and his fellow Syndics. In fact, John Clay died in 1916, and Wright's successor, Waller, was in a position to steer through the last stage of the dismantling of the partnership. J. B. Peace, a Syndic and an engineer, was appointed University Printer, and the University at last had total control of all elements of the University Press, after sixty-two years of partnership with the Clay family. C. F. Clay continued to manage the London Warehouse at Fetter Lane until 1925.

Wright's last year as Secretary was clouded by the affair of the *Encyclopaedia Britannica*. The eleventh edition of 1910 is a very good edition, still worth consulting on many topics. The *Britannica* had passed into American ownership, and the active promoter was Horace E. Hooper, who was in the process of setting the English book trade by the ears in a number of ways. He was a pioneer of book-clubs and of direct selling, both good ways of marketing encyclopaedias; but his energy and his methods had already upset the trade before the *Encyclopaedia* was mooted. Hooper persuaded Wright that the new edition was a worthy one, that the University's imprint could be put on it without shame, and that some of the printing could be done at Cambridge. The Press did not have to finance the whole scheme, but was asked to publish on commission. It seemed a good idea, but Hooper's promotion simultaneously upset the book trade, which was being bypassed, and the University, which thought that its name was being exploited by a fly-by-night vulgarian. This was hard on Hooper, who was convinced that he was just doing 'a good selling job', having done a good editorial job. He believed in his product. But the University was very strait-laced, hated his advertising, and showed its disapproval by threatening to non-placet the election of any Syndic who had been concerned with the publication. The nomination of the useful A. C. Seward was duly withdrawn, and a scandal averted. The touchy Whibley, now an ex-Syndic, was prominent among the critics.

# 12

## WALLER AND ROBERTS AS SECRETARIES: LEWIS AS PRINTER

WRIGHT RETIRED at the end of 1911, and was succeeded by Waller. It became immediately necessary to have a new Assistant Secretary, and S. C. Roberts was appointed. The Press, as publisher, was now embarked on a steady upward course, with its constitutional position and its structure remaining virtually unchanged from the dissolution of the partnership in 1916 until 1972. During that period publishing first came to rank equally with printing in terms of size and economic importance, and then to surpass it; but at the beginning the Printing House was still the larger employer of labour, and the more important centre of activity.

The division of the publishing business between Cambridge and London produced some unintended results. The Cambridge editorial office was tiny: the Secretary, the Assistant Secretary and a clerk were the entire staff. The London office went on being called the Warehouse long after it had effectively become the accounting, marketing and sales office of the Press, where the books were bound and sent out for review, advertisements were designed and placed, authors' accounts kept and royalties paid, travellers briefed and their orders and booksellers' orders taken, and the books sent out from 'forward' stocks. One consequence of the small size of the Secretary's office and its proximity to the Printing House was that until the 1960s it depended on the printing staff for many services: not just clerical help, but also design, estimating, progress control – all the processes which were in other firms being taken over by a publisher's production office. For many years therefore it must have seemed to the more departmentally minded of the Printer's staff to be little more than a small agency for the conducting of printing work towards the major department of the Press. The Printing House for many years had a greater capacity than the Syndicate publishing could fill; and the balance was secured by the Printer's putting on his bowler hat and going off to the London publishers for work.

The Warehouse staff, however, cut off in London from the mysterious deliberations of the Syndicate, and visited first by the Olympian C. J. Clay and then the no less Olympian Wright, felt isolated and subservient initially, and then, when they acquired self-esteem, inevitably tended to have a separate sense of identity which easily fell at times into the classic 'us-and-them' mould characteristic of any departmentalised organisation, exacerbated by fifty miles of separation, and a residue of resentment.

The full development of these tendencies lay in the remote future. It was Waller's main function to keep the Press on course through the disruption of the First World War. The principal consequence of the War was a rise in post-war wages, which meant that Waller found himself insisting that book-buyers would have to get used to prices much higher than they had been before the War. He had inherited from Wright the conviction that the Press needed an endowment fund to secure it against abrupt or prolonged changes of circumstances, but the irony of his situation was that by 1914 he had made no more than a start, and then saw the War operating as just such a change, long and severe enough to dissipate the funds set aside.

During the War, John Clay died and J. B. Peace became Printer, so it was one of Waller's achievements to complete the process started by Wright – though it may have been somewhat frightening in the middle of that cataclysm, with its unforeseeable economic consequences, for the Press at last to launch out completely on its own. But according to Roberts, Waller was another hard-headed Yorkshireman with strong nerves. He had just finished editing the *Cambridge History of English Literature* with Ward, and was wrestling with the problem of the *Cambridge Medieval History*, which had a timid and unsystematic editor quite unlike Ward, where the central European contributors had had their contracts revoked on patriotic grounds, where it was hard to find worthy substitutes, and where progress was inordinately slow. Two volumes had been published before the War but the last volume did not appear until 1936. The *Cambridge Ancient History* was also planned in Waller's time: though it was published after his death, it went smoothly and relatively fast, the twelve volumes and five volumes of plates being published between 1923 and 1939.

The *Cambridge History of British Foreign Policy* was also planned at this time; and it too was edited by Ward. He was eighty-five when the first volume came out, but kept up his unperturbed editorial work until he died in 1924, at the age of eighty-seven. He had been a Syndic from 1905 to 1919, and Chairman for much of that time; his partnership with Waller was like that of Cartmell with Clay, and of James Porter with Wright. A photograph shows him at his desk, very obviously writing and not just posing. The silky white hair brushed back, and the silky white moustache and imperial carefully combed out, make him look like so many other Victorian and Edwardian eminences – groomed as if for some intellectual Cruft's. Roberts remembered him in the 1920s, moving in his brougham from the Lodge at Peterhouse, in morning coat and silk hat, somewhat deaf but very courteous. The courtesy helped him with his more ruthless editorial duties – and so his histories got published, while the gentle and ineffectual Whitney, editing the *Medieval History*, wrung his hands at the mere thought of having to tell a contributor to get on. F. E. Adcock, the organising editor of the *Ancient History*, had Ward's gifts: he enjoyed the politics and logistics of large-scale editing, and liked taking what he called 'statesmanlike' measures.

An important change was the appointment of G. V. Carey as another Assistant Secretary in 1913. Both he and Roberts went off to France in the army, and both were wounded. Returning, Roberts was made responsible for bindings and jackets, and for advertisements and publicity as well. He found that while he had been in France the first steps had been taken in what is sometimes called the Press's typographical renaissance, which is dealt with below. He also found himself dealing with some of the authors whom Waller had attracted to the Press, notably Q (one now has to explain that this was Sir Arthur Quiller-Couch, the King Edward VII Professor of English Literature) and John Dover Wilson, the great Shakespearean scholar. Q had published with the Press some of his very popular lectures (*On The Art of Writing*, for instance, which contained a much-quoted lecture on 'Jargon'). Dover Wilson had published in 1911 his *Life in Shakespeare's England*, which was even more popular and had a longer life. Waller persuaded these two to co-edit a new edition of Shakespeare, one play to a volume, and Bruce Rogers's design for this was one of the first fruits of the new movement in typography. Three comedies appeared in 1921, but the last play in the New Shakespeare (as it came to be called) was not published until 1966. Q before his death had left the venture to Dover Wilson, who, as he touchingly wrote in the 'postscript' to the preface of the *Sonnets* volume, by the time it was in proof could no longer see a line of print. In the final volumes of the plays he had other scholars as assistants or as volume-editors. Considering how much of the work he did himself, forty-five years is not a long time in which to edit some forty volumes of Shakespeare; but by the time he had finished, textual and bibliographical knowledge had so far advanced – with the help of men like himself – that it was time to start again. In the year in which this History is published, the first volumes of a New Cambridge Shakespeare will appear: a sign that the work of scholarship is unending, and that it is only academic publishers who expect to be about and active for a very long time who can seriously entertain projects of this duration and then start again. Waller's initiative progressed in its stately way through the Secretaryships of Roberts and Kingsford into the term of office of Richard David, himself a Shakespearean scholar. All who had to do with 'Dover', as he was called, loved the old man, who would argue courteously with brash young men prepared to think him old-fashioned yet finding he had a touch of greatness. The New Shakespeare itself started as a row of pretty little volumes bound in brown cloth (Roberts's choice: Waller disliked it). The text was reprinted, without introduction and notes, as the Cambridge Pocket Shakespeare (not very successfully), and then very successfully paperbacked. It can now be seen, well printed and cheerfully bound, as a big single volume in stores like Boots and Marks and Spencer, as a final accolade.

It is no accident that that digression has taken us from the First World War to 1984. Such is the continuity of university press publishing. One might appropriately slip in here the notion that Wright's vision of a universal history, based on reading Acton and talking to him and to Maitland, takes us from 1896 to the end of this century. For the first step, the *Modern History*, with the *Ancient* and *Medieval Histories* as natural complements, was followed by Histories of India and of the British Empire, by the great *Economic History of Europe* (nearing completion), and after the Second World War by Histories of Islam, of Iran, of Africa, of China, of Japan, of Latin America (the first volumes of the two last should appear in 1984). I was about to say that with the completion of the last volume of the last History, Wright's vision will have finally been realised in the course of a century; but reflect that the *Modern History* has already been replaced with a *New Modern History*, the *History of India* is to be replaced also and the *Ancient History* is being revised. It would be rash also to say that the process is endless, since a new kind of history will one day replace the notion of the Cambridge History itself; but it will have lasted for at least a hundred years, which is a pretty solid contribution to the world's learning. Any residual soreness about the Oxford Dictionary is also somewhat assuaged; without knowing it, Wright's Syndics undertook something which has proved to be as large and as long-continuing. If they had known in 1896 that they were embarking not on twelve but ultimately on two or three hundred volumes, their courage might have failed them. They took the first step, and the rest followed.

Another tradition which Waller started was a small one, but peculiarly 'Cambridge'. Cecil Torr was a Cambridge man, a Devon landowner with a scholarly bent who had published some books on commission at the Press in the 1890s. When he sent in *Small Talk at Wreyland* for printing, J. B. Peace read it, enjoyed it and persuaded the Syndicate to publish it. Puzzled reviewers first wondered why on earth the Press had taken on this oddity, and then persuaded their readers to buy it as a unique record of

S. C. Roberts, Secretary of the Syndicate 1922–48. From the pencil
portrait by Francis Dodd in the Pitt Building.

something passing out of English life. It was this book perhaps which prompted George Sturt to send the Press his classic *The Wheelwright's Shop*, and his autobiographical *A Small Boy in the Sixties*. Roberts saw that this was a tradition in the making, and encouraged Frank Kendon (a later Assistant Secretary) to develop it with books by Walter Rose (*The Village Carpenter* and others) and Eric Benfield (*Purbeck Shop*) and others. Kendon's successors accepted Miss M. K. Ashby's biography of her father, *Joseph Ashby of Tysoe*, and commissioned a two-volume selection from Sturt's journals. Kendon extended the vein by producing 'countryside' books illustrated by artists such as C. F. Tunnicliffe: so that what started as an inexplicable or inconsistent phenomenon became a recognisable Cambridge University Press 'line'. It also acquired, in the hands of others, ideological overtones: F. R. Leavis saw Sturt as the chronicler of an 'organic society'; others would see it as part of 'the world we have lost', in which they took a more quantitative interest than Sturt did. In publishing at large this is now called 'nostalgia', and there was a little boom after the publication of Blythe's *Akenfield*. Peace and Waller started the tradition, and Denys Thompson's anthology, published at the Press in 1980 and called *Change and Tradition in Rural England* is a summation of the whole body of writing, with a special place given the books published in Cambridge.

Waller died in office in 1922. Roberts, still only thirty-five, was appointed Secretary. He immediately proposed that Carey should be appointed Educational Secretary, a new post which recognised the crucial importance of the educational list. The books in this list were still for secondary schools only, with a strong leaning towards public and grammar schools – publishing for the more academic type of education preliminary to university entrance being naturally appropriate to the Press at first. In those days successful schoolbooks had what now seems an immensely long life: they would go on being reprinted for twenty to fifty years, or even longer. Securing such books and then successfully promoting them was an obvious way of providing the traditional mainstay of any publisher's activity, the secure backlist. Carey and his successors built on Clay's and Wright's foundations: to the Pitt Press Series, the Cambridge Bible for Schools and Verity and Siddons, they added history, geography and English courses, more texts in French, books about teaching. The other components of the backlist were university textbooks (such as Kenny's *Cases*, Borradaile and Potts on *The Invertebrata*, Hardy's *Pure Mathematics*, Harker's *Petrology* and many more) and the steady sellers among the learned and scientific books (such as Browne and Nicholson from the Oriental list, Maitland and Tanner in the history list and 'the big blue mathematical books' mentioned below). The great beauty of these books, from the publisher's point of view, was that they went on and on selling. Every year, from the hundred or so books published, a few reached this category, and the number added was larger than the number going out of print. A university press by its nature deals with books which have a long life; if the sale is very slow, an obvious stock problem is produced – the list grows larger each year, and so does the stock, which may get out of balance with the sale and represent a huge past investment but a dwindling future asset. This danger was averted in the period between the wars by the buoyancy of the backlist: the books which went on selling produced a steady, and it seemed forever reliable, three-quarters of the total annual sales. The stock of recent books needed to be watched, but once they had become 'reprints' the sale was remarkably stable for years. In the period before 1939 Roberts was therefore able to build up a balanced list in a period of relative stability, not drastically affected by the economic fluctuations of the 1920s and 1930s. If one asks why this was so, one possible answer is that neither the schools nor the libraries, university students and staff whom the Press supplied at that time were as dependent as they now are on public money. The market was smaller than now, and less international, but it was less perturbed by the decisions of central authorities.

Roberts's personal contribution was a very active willingness to commission books, and to extend the range of what was published. Genial and sociable, he made friends with authors, and from that position fed them with ideas. Sir James Jeans, the astronomer, was one such friend. He had first published with the Press in 1908, when his *Mathematical Theory of Relativity* was accepted. His *Astronomy and Cosmogony* followed in 1928. These were 'big blue books' – the familiar name given in the Press to mathematical and physical treatises in large format (usually royal octavo), chastely bound in very dark blue, and printed, in the later years, with enormous skill and – for those with eyes to see it – a real beauty. It was the beauty of very good setting, with superb handling of the mathematics, which made the Press at that time the finest printer of mathematics in the world. The 'big blue books' can be taken to start with Lamb's *Hydrodynamics* in 1879 and to stretch to Griffith's *The Theory of Transition-metal Ions* in 1961, by way of *Principia Mathematica*, Whittaker and Watson's *Course of Modern Analysis*, Eddington's *Mathematical Theory of Relativity*, Condon and Shortley's *Theory of Atomic Spectra* and A. H. Wilson's *Theory of Metals* (1936), and others no less distinguished. The sight of this noble range of volumes on the shelf causes the cool Cambridge heart to beat a little faster with justified pride, since it represents both the highest form of publishing (fundamental contributions to knowledge by first-rate scientists) and the finest achievement of printing. It also gave Roberts a fruitful idea. Whitehead and Eddington had shown a gift for lucid exposition: the Press had published White-head's *Concept of Nature* in 1920, and his *Science and the Modern World* in 1926; Eddington's *Nature of the Physical World* had followed in 1928 and his *Expanding Universe* in 1933. There was a large readership for such books, which were the publishing equivalent of extra-mural teaching, with the advantage that the authors were great authorities on their subjects. Roberts saw the same gift in Jeans, capable of extension to a more popular level of exposition, and so an even larger market. He confessed in his memoirs that he had underestimated the potential sale of *Science and the Modern World*, and he found that Eddington was unapproachable, but Jeans could be talked to. His *The Universe Around Us* (1929) was the result of such conversations. *The Mysterious Universe* (1930) was an expansion of a Rede Lecture, and in the first month of publication reprinted three times, selling 1000 copies a day, and provoking cartoons in the London evening papers, reproduced as advertisements in the Underground. It was the best-seller in a succession of best-sellers, and the popular scientific expository book became another Cambridge line, with books by Schrödinger, George Gamow and others continuing the tradition into the period after the Second World War. Sir Charles Sherrington's *Man on His Nature* is a favourite with many readers, though it never got Jeans's appropriately astronomical sales. These successes helped to create a new public for D'Arcy Thompson's *Growth and Form*. First published in 1917, it was revised in 1942, and was several times reprinted. In its way it ranks with Whitehead as one of the high points in this genre.

Such books are an extension of, rather than a diversion from, university press publishing in its pure form. Roberts presided over the steady acceptance, year after year, of scientific and scholarly books. For instance, four new scientific series were founded: the Cambridge Psychological Series, the Cambridge Comparative Physiology, the Cambridge Series of Physical Chemistry, and the Cambridge Physical Tracts. The last, reborn after the Second World War as Cambridge Monographs on Physics, is still in existence. The growth of experimental psychology in Cambridge produced one classic: Sir Frederick Bartlett on *Remembering* (1932).

In history the Press was especially active. G. G. Coulton, the combative medievalist, founded the Cambridge Studies in Medieval Life and Thought (still active in its fourth series, having been edited by Knowles and Ullmann after Coulton). Economic history produced the classic works of Sir John Clapham. Eileen Power, like Maitland's pupil Mary Bateson in the 1890s, died before she had achieved all that was expected of her, but she published one book, *Medieval English Nunneries* in 1922, and a posthumous publication, *Medieval Women* (1975), made available a text she had been working on at her death. Tanner's works on constitutional history were used as student textbooks. In 1929 the Press published the first work of a young Fellow of Trinity, Steven Runciman, and in 1940, with the Battle of Britain in progress, there appeared *The Monastic Order in England* by Dom David Knowles. The times could hardly have been more unwelcoming, and Knowles was asked to provide a subsidy. It was not realised then that this was the first volume of one of the great historical works of the century: *The Religious Orders in England* appeared in three volumes after the War and Knowles himself joined the Syndicate. Runciman's later works, especially the *History of the Crusades*, also in three volumes, displayed a marvellous narrative gift straight out of the nineteenth century (a compliment) and corrected Western European cultural chauvinism. Thousands of readers were taught to think of Byzantium and the Islamic world as more civilised than the barbarian invaders from the Catholic west.

These were movements that Roberts started and his successors inherited. He also made friends with Housman, who had a sociable side behind his morose persona as poet and his savage mask as scholar. The second edition of his Juvenal appeared at the Press in 1931, and Manilius from 1932. The Press also published his lecture on *The Name and Nature of Poetry* in 1933; and saddened English dons recognised that it had set their critical cause back by ten years.

In English studies, the record is less distinguished; and this seems odd in the era when Cambridge was to a large extent inventing the modern academic study of the subject. It is true that the Press published H. M. Chadwick's *The Growth of Literature*, a great book of permanent value; and George Sampson's *English for the English*, a pioneering tract on the place of English in schools. Jessie L. Weston's *From Ritual to Romance* is now known to thousands as one of Eliot's sources for *The Waste Land*. But the publications of the most lively members of the new Cambridge faculty went to other publishers. An important influence here was Ian Parsons, who had read English at Cambridge, went to Chatto and Windus, and very enterprisingly sought out the best critical work which came from Cambridge-trained writers. The Press remained important in Shakespeare studies, however, with Dover Wilson's books, Caroline Spurgeon on *Shakespeare's Imagery*, and the Harrison and Granville-Barker *Companion to Shakespeare Studies*. A. J. A. Waldock's *Paradise Lost and the Critics* was, F. R. Leavis said, the best book on Milton he had read. The great achievement in Roberts's time was the completion in 1940 of the *Cambridge Bibliography of English Literature* edited by F. W. Bateson. Again, it was heartening at that particularly black moment to bring out a massive work of useful scholarship.

But it is increasingly difficult and misleading in the twentieth century to pick out publishing 'plums' in this or that subject. In 1876, the Syndics' proprietary books numbered about thirty. By 1900 there were five hundred books in the catalogue. With acceptances at a steady hundred or so a year, and given the longevity of Cambridge books, that total rapidly rose by a straightforward arithmetical progression. In 1921 Roberts reckoned that there were 2500 titles in the catalogue. The number of people employed at Fetter Lane had risen to 110 (there were 280 in the Printing House) and the size of the staff was an indication of the relative importance of the publishing business. By the time Roberts retired the catalogue must have contained four thousand titles (the Second War had somewhat depressed the total: fewer books had been published, and paper rationing had also restricted reprinting). It now stands at something like seven thousand. It needs to be judged as a whole – difficult though that is – and not just by the most visible peaks.

Publishing therefore moved to a position of parity with printing and then surpassed it. There began a very long-term and at first very slow decline in the importance of the Bible, which was masked for many years by increasing access to a large American market. This was successfully cultivated from 1930 by a special agency arrangement with Macmillan set up by Roberts and from 1931 headed by Ronald Mansbridge. Macmillan also handled the academic books, and American sales became an increasingly important factor. In the mid-thirties the publishing staff in Cambridge had risen to seven, with one part-timer: the Secretary, two Assistant Secretaries, the late Mr Woods (still affectionately remembered for a charming manner, a totally bald shining nut-brown head, and a passion for the theatre), who took dictation and typed; Mr Parsons, who wrote up the Syndics' minutes in longhand in a huge blue leather-bound book; the Secretary's personal assistant and secretary; and 'the mysterious, bearded and ultra-polite Mr Pond', who may have done the agreements and the insurance but does not seem to have been over-burdened. Dividing his attentions between the

Secretary and the Printer there was the formidable and grudging caretaker Mr Keetch, who could be persuaded to supply things like blotting-paper, and who also had a stock of the paper-knives given free with sets of the *Encyclopaedia Britannica* and, for jubilees, the fairy-lights which had been used on the Pitt Building in 1897 (since Keetch served the Press for seventy years, very old man and very young boy, he inevitably saw several jubilees). Keetch was a sort of infernal porter, who locked the Press doors three minutes after opening and closing hours and was then (literally) deaf to latecomers; his grandest function was to brew the very strong tea at Syndicate meetings.

At Fetter Lane, C. F. Clay was succeeded by E. B. Diver, an ex-bookseller. The real work was done by R. J. L. Kingsford, first as Assistant Manager and then as London Manager. He had started in Cambridge as Assistant Secretary in 1922, replacing Carey. In 1938 the London office moved to Bentley House in the Euston Road, planned by Kingsford as a purpose-built publisher's office, with administrative and accounting departments arranged in a square around a central ground-floor warehouse. It was one of the first such buildings (publishers had usually just taken over a pleasant old building in a London square, and squatted picturesquely but inconveniently in rooms meant for living in). It had a striking uniformity of 1930s style in its furniture and fittings; and the beautifully panelled library-cum-showroom was used for entertaining. In this efficient, attractive and stylish building, Kingsford also created an *esprit de corps* among the slightly overawed former inmates of the Warehouse – though with the continued isolation from Cambridge the new building could do little to halt the tendency towards polarisation between the two centres of activity.

By 1938, when Bentley House was finished and opened under Kingsford as London Manager, a pattern was set which lasted some forty years. Most of the publishing staff were in London, now the centre of an organisation which increasingly looked to the whole world as its market. In particular, sales in the USA began that steady expansion which continues today. But that was not all: in the days of the British Empire, when secondary education was being introduced on an increasing scale and conducted in English on lines set in English schools, the sales of English schoolbooks overseas became an important consideration for British publishers. This happened first in India, where ever since Macaulay's famous memorandum, education in English had begun to create an elite of public servants. The same process began in Africa, and Cambridge was a name in many parts of the world because pupils learned from Cambridge books before taking Cambridge-organised examinations. The new Education Secretary, Charles Carrington, was for a time stationed in London, first at Fetter Lane, then in Bentley House, and began the process of visiting schools in search of authors – including schools in overseas territories. The ordinary reader who thinks that publishers produce novels, plays, poetry and biography never realises that this is the proverbial tip of the iceberg, and that the publishing of 'literature' actually rests on the foundation provided by a much larger activity. Bibles and almanacs and Lily's Grammar were the supports of the University's printing and publishing in earlier centuries. The Bible has slowly declined

Bentley House, 200 Euston Road, London NW1: the Library of the former London publishing house, 1938–80.

during the twentieth, but was still very important as an export for most of the time; and the old schoolbooks were now replaced by Verity, and Loney, and Godfrey and Siddons. These were now regularly reprinted by the twenty thousand, except for the Mathematical Tables which, in the days before electronic calculators, were regularly reprinted in hundreds of thousands.

In Cambridge the tiny staff received and produced the hundred or so new books published annually. Roberts himself liked to be an active publisher, in the sense that he was unwilling just to sit in his office and wait for books to be submitted. He would write or speak to likely-seeming potential authors, and it was his special endeavour to get books which 'lightened the list' or gave the travellers a 'bag-opener': books of a somewhat more general nature which would provoke a look of recognition in the eye of a cultivated non-specialist reader. He also wanted to prove that the Press could sell these books as well as a general publisher would. But again, to vary the cliché, this was the icing on the cake. The staple Cambridge products, as they must always be, were the learned monographs and the university textbooks; and these books regularly outlasted the more ephemeral general books, except for occasional classics like Sturt. All the books, whatever the subject, were 'handled' in Cambridge by the two Assistant Secretaries, who were in a rudimentary way editors. Richard David tells of the occasion when he had to insert all the punctuation marks in a work on appendicitis: the author had never gathered which stop to use in which place, but he wrote well, and the stops just fell into place. I remember (in the later days when there were three Assistant Secretaries) inserting all the part- and chapter-divisions in a long work on archaeology which arrived as one huge undivided outpouring.

The Assistant Secretaries were also their own production controllers and (in the 1950s) their own designers in some matters, since they took over bindings, which had been designed in London by Kingsford in the 1930s (and his bindings were superb); and also jackets, which had been designed by Frank Kendon until they grew too many and his health failed. The conferring of these design functions on the Assistant Secretaries rested on an assumption about the kind of design they would –

at that place and in that time – produce. There was a feeling that an ethos of Cambridge design had been created over the years, and that any intelligent person would absorb it by aesthetic osmosis, and turn out respectable variants of the Cambridge approach.

The so-called typographical renaissance would be better described as the application to academic printing and publishing of design principles learned as the Press made increasingly good use of the Monotype keyboard for setting, and the use of Monotype faces in 'display' work. It was a great achievement, but it would be a mistake to identify it with ordinary 'fine printing'. Of course it owed a certain amount initially to William Morris as the original propagandist and highly visible practitioner, but Morris's influence on typography was equivocal, in the sense that while you admire his books as pieces of decorative texture convincingly carried out with good materials, you would not want to have to *read* one of them. Morris's types were archaising, and initiated the tendency to escape from the nineteenth century by plunging rather desperately into the past, in search of some ideal period of the hand-crafted. So Morris's books looked like illuminated manuscripts transferred into black-and-white.

The prestige of the Arts and Crafts and private press movements, and the undoubted beauty of the objects they produced, concealed their inconsistencies, and various well-meaning manufacturers began to imitate elements in both. Dent's first books in the Everyman's Library had imitation Morris bindings and endpapers, with entirely ordinary printed texts (very sensible: but the dichotomy was a criticism of Morris). In 1901 at Cambridge a minute had read, 'A scheme having been suggested by Mr Clay for the purchase of a new fount of beautiful type for printing limited editions or special books on very good paper, the Syndicate gave a general approval.' The dread words 'beautiful' and 'limited editions' appearing at the outset, suggested the preciosity and the inevitable failure of the enterprise. In September 1902 M. R. James and Aldis Wright were the Syndics deputed to suggest the books to be printed this way.

Some editions of English texts were produced. The type itself was a photographic reproduction and regularisation of a late fifteenth-century roman, and fairly ugly, though 'different', of course – mostly different from the rather light, rather character-less types of the late nineteenth century, with their grey colour on the page and their remorseless readability. The new editions – quartos on hand-made paper – failed to sell: Roberts remembered being invited to help himself to copies when he came to the Press in 1911, before they were remaindered or pulped. It was a much more significant decision that the Press made in 1913; for then, with much hesitation, the Monotype composing machine was introduced. Hitherto all setting had been by hand; and at first the only distinguishing features of Monotype were that it substituted machine composition; that it did this by casting fresh type for every piece of setting; but that it still cast type in single characters, not in whole lines. Everything about its intelligent use had to be learned afresh, as with every new technology; and the immediate result was no doubt a drop in standards.

The apprentices and craftsmen and overseers were the men who really carried out this change; and in the end it was they who were so versed in what the Monotype machine could do that they had in their mind's eye and at their fingertips the un-spoken criteria of a Cambridge style. Nonetheless leaders and thinkers were also needed. The first of these was the American typographer Bruce Rogers, who came to England in 1916. He was working with Morris's colleague Emery Walker in London. Sir Sydney Cockerell had been Morris's secretary, was now Director of the Fitzwilliam Museum, and had been in recent years one of the most informed critics of the Press's typographic style, or lack of it. He now put Rogers in touch with the Press.

This happened at an opportune moment. Criticisms by people conscious of their own possession of taste were becoming more frequent, indeed very widespread. M. D. ('Manny') Forbes, the celebrated eccentric organiser of the English Faculty, travelling to Ceylon on a Japanese ship, found on his table at dinner a peculiarly awful printed menu. He sent it back to a friend in Cambridge, scribbling on it 'Printed at the University Press?' There were even formal representations in the Senate House, from Stephen Gaselee in 1915. The Syndicate, disturbed, asked a committee to report in 1916; the report was commented on by

Waller as Secretary and by Clay as Printer. They pointed out that 'in view of the special nature of the Syndics' publications, not much scope for variation exists and that...in the case of scientific and educational works...many utilitarian factors have to be taken into consideration'. The comment showed a failure to see the real point, but that point could be properly put only later, when the new technology had been so developed that it was possible to give an ostensive definition: do it like this.

John Clay died almost immediately after the report, being replaced by J. B. Peace, who was not a printer by training, but an engineer. Presumably he had an open mind and an interest in the new process; at any rate it was Peace who employed Rogers as typographical adviser. The most important results of Rogers's two years at the Press were not the rather pretty little books which he designed during the time, with their tendency towards historical pastiche. Nor was it the report which he wrote for the Syndicate, but rather the practical example which he gave to the men he worked with in the Printing House, and especially F. G. Nobbs and J. A. Scott, who ran the Monotype department. Nobbs later became Overseer of the Monotype composing room, and he and his successors were in important respects guardians of the tradition which was forming.

Rogers's report made two main points: first, that it was almost unbelievable that an important printing house could go on with such a poor repertory of typographic material; second, that the object of the Press should be to secure that all its products should have a distinctive character – it should be clear to the informed eye that Cambridge books were products of a Cambridge tradition. This required the continuous supervision of every detail, since a printed book is actually an aggregate of many small details. That kind of consciousness would in practice and after a while make it possible to say that in this matter or that the Cambridge house-style was such and such.

Rogers produced his few books – notably the design for the New Shakespeare – and left, having made a great personal impression, and implanted important ideas. His report, which must have made painful reading, was shelved: but the painful reading perhaps had its own effect in time. And certainly it

Walter Lewis, University Printer 1923–45. From the pencil portrait by Francis Dodd in the Pitt Building.

influenced Roberts himself. Rogers designed Roberts's own book *The Story of Dr Johnson* (1919), and it was rather striking that on his departure Roberts started to design books himself: Frank Kidson's *The Beggar's Opera* has the full Rogers treatment: drop initials in ornamental frames; ornamental rules above and below the headings; title-page and chapter headings in large sizes of upper and lower case; lots of 'swash' italics; all sorts of little 'period' touches. The book was quarter-bound with decorated paper boards, a paper label on the spine, and a canary-yellow jacket. It was pretty, but it was not serious, since the 'style' was stuck on as decorative touches and would hardly transfer to titles like *The Mathematical Theory of Relativity*. That transference had to come more slowly, and to come from the development, by trial and error, of the best ways of treating mathematics, chemical formulae, footnotes, quotations, the matching of exotics (Greek, Hebrew and so on) with roman type; and the treatment of chapter headings, sub-headings, running-titles, and title-pages themselves when you could not appropriately make them pretty or give them a period flavour. This was the true Cambridge style, developed since 1922 and still alive, though now facing the challenge of conversion to yet another technology.

The next impetus was given by the appointment of Walter Lewis in 1923, as Peace's successor as University Printer. Peace's death in January followed Waller's by less than six months, and so Roberts, the new Secretary, was faced within weeks of his own appointment with the need to organise the succession at the Printing House as well. There was no deputy within the printing department itself. By March the search had led to Lewis, and he was appointed. He remained Printer until 1945. It was he who recommended the appointment of Stanley Morison as typographical adviser in October of the same year. Morison was later to advise *The Times* as well as the Cambridge Press, and he also advised the Monotype Corporation itself, being largely responsible for the design of the succession of type-faces for book-printing marketed by the corporation during his time. He was able at the Press to supervise early – sometimes the first – uses of these types in bookwork, while for *The Times* he also supervised the design of Times New Roman and the associated faces.

Stanley Morison in about 1930.

He combined great scholarship and an encyclopaedic knowledge of the history of letter forms from Roman times onwards, with historical insight of a cheerfully tendentious sort (he had been a pacifist, an atheist and a Marxist, and converted to combative Catholicism). In his later life he also enjoyed a ringside seat in politics: he was a great friend of Lord Beaverbrook, and moved as freely in the world of newspaper magnates as in that of the Church and the world of printing itself. Lewis and Morison became an extraordinary partnership. Lewis was bluff, friendly though tending to puncture pomposity, free of speech (to put it mildly) and apt to talk to you with a fag-end in his mouth while he did something practical which got ink on his fingers. He was immensely vigorous and active, amazingly untidy, a born leader and a good man without mystery. Morison on the other hand seemed sacerdotal: something austere seemed to cloak him until he twitched it aside and revealed the mischief in him. He always wore black: black shoes, black socks, black suit, black tie, black hat, black overcoat, black attaché case. The white shirt, white hair when I knew him, and the occasional light sprinkling of dandruff were appropriate parts of the printing image: the black was inky, and the white was the paper itself. He was very dogmatic, but also loved being contradicted. He had a high tenor voice, and a wild laugh; and young Assistant Secretaries hearing a fierce slap and a sound somewhere between a donkey braying and the high melisma with which Muslims are called to prayer, would realise that it was not a punishment going on, but SM striking his thigh and laughing in the Secretary's office. 'Ah, Morison's here', they would say.

The partnership was completed by Nobbs, a tall redhaired rawboned man who was curmudgeonly until excited, when he became virtually impossible. One of his talents was for arguing on both sides of a question with great heat: a sure way of baffling the opposition. But Nobbs was the main repository of all the unspoken 'know-how'. Morison would specify type-face and sizes; he would do a sketch-like layout for the title-page; in the hands of Nobbs and his compositors a battery of understood conventions would come into play; and there in the proofs was another Cambridge book. One of the great skills, and one which can never be codified, is the mastery of spacing: knowing when and how to keep the texture tight, and when and how to let in air at the articulatory places. After the Second World War the Cambridge style was codified in a style-sheet and in other ways, partly because the Printing House pioneered work-measurement and payment by results, so that many operations needed to be standardised, and partly because in the end Cambridge books became too numerous for the Printing House itself, and had to be subcontracted. The outside printers had to be given instructions, and this came at a moment when the whole process had become a conscious one: yet there were still things which could not be said, only pointed to. Either you saw it or you did not.

An uncovenanted benefit was the enthusiasm communicated to the publishing staff. Roberts himself had fallen in love with design. As an Assistant Secretary he had had to design jackets, finding them initially to be simple 'dust-wrappers'. A sheet of blue-grey paper was wrapped round the book, with the title printed on the spine in black. That was that. Roberts used half-tone pictures, with the title and author's name displayed on the front board. He used coloured inks and coloured papers, to the dismay of the old generation of Printing House staff. Kingsford's bindings of the 1930s, whether they use bright Sundour cloth and foil labels and ornaments, or whether they use the simplest lettering, are uniformly excellent, indeed collectors' pieces. The seasonal lists, in which the new books were announced, were sometimes used as the first application of a new type-face: they were individually designed (some of the first ones by Kingsford) and like all ephemera are even rarer collectors' pieces. Assistant Secretaries proposed designs for their books to Lewis and Nobbs, and had their ideas tactfully knocked into shape. They had love-affairs with particular faces: Richard David remembers a brief liaison with Bodoni, while Frank Kendon was faithful over many years to Bell, in which this book is set.

All this passed into the bloodstream, so to speak, and became almost like an instinct. Cambridge books of the 1920s and 1930s have a recognisable air rather than a single style. Lewis was a blunt man and Morison an austere one; yet the books often have a delicacy, even a daintiness about them. There followed the war period when paper was rationed and its substance and texture much changed. Its hard surface and thinness made for slim books, and as much of the surface as possible had to be printed on so as to make best use of it. It was obviously done with skill, so that even these books have an attraction. The strength of the tradition was shown after the war, when Lewis retired and Morison too was less active. Under Lewis's successor, Brooke Crutchley, and in the hands of John Dreyfus as Assistant Printer and Nobbs's successors as Composing Room Overseer, the books were as well designed as ever. And now as previously, though the Printer did work for the Nonesuch Press and other houses appealing to the connoisseur, the staple product of the Press had nothing to do with 'fine printing'. In the 1890s this had meant using a 'private press' type on handmade paper, perhaps with illustrations. In the 1930s it came to mean printing *Daphnis and Chloe* in Perpetua, in combination with slightly lubricious wood-engravings and coloured drop initials. What was printed never seemed to matter, since it was not meant to be read. The quality of the Cambridge product depended on the fact that an important text – essential to some group of scientists or scholars – was being produced in a manner which gave it a clear structure and made it comfortably legible and easy to refer to; the conventions were designed to assist the reader, and they had as much to do with a kind of applied experimental psychology – the psychology of perception – as with any canon of aesthetics. They also took specially complex material – the transcription of documents, the display of formulae, the arrangement of catalogues, the arrangement of some kind of taxonomy – took it and printed it in such a way that the intellectual structure inherent in the document itself was rendered visible and comprehensible. All this was done with elegance and sobriety, the qualities most closely connected with efficiency of use. It was still sometimes pretty, when a book lent itself to allusive period treatment, but it was more often beautiful in an austere way, sometimes with a touch of grandeur, always inventive and effective. If the reader had been conscious of the ways in which his path was smoothed, it would have been a defect. Many small conventions withdrew from sight, except to the experienced eye. All most readers could say was that it looked 'nice' (even 'beautiful') and read easily, and the book 'worked' in that all its elements served their functions. The hallmarks, in the Monotype period, were the setting – even and close – and the presswork, where the type pressed into the paper, imprinted a sharp image which neither went too deep nor was too light: the even colour of the inking throughout the book and the perfect register on both sides of the paper were the final display of disciplined competence.

It was surprising how many authors said and still say: 'I have always admired the Cambridge type.' There is no Cambridge type: they were thinking perhaps that since Oxford had the Fell types, Cambridge must have something similar, and they liked the idea. But a good many authors came to the Press because of the quality of the printing. They got phenomenal accuracy from the compositors and readers. Housman would feel it necessary to draw attention to anything he had had to correct in the proofs; he once wrote to a colleague that 'the Cambridge Press cannot be trusted implicitly', and was so far from thinking accidents inevitable that, his startled eye falling on a turned letter, he sent an indignant letter about 'this horseplay on the part of the printer'. You can take that line only when errors are so rare that they seem deliberate. Such accuracy was taken for granted. The authors also got a specific service: the individual nature of an important book was analysed and its structure displayed. The design would reflect that nature and structure, so that it was not a matter of applying decoration or 'style' as a superficial thing; the form grew outwards from within.

In a history like this, the characters who stand out in the early days are likely to be famous men like Bentley and Richard Watson and Whewell – people about whom records are kept. The less well-known tend to disappear, though there must have been interesting and colourful personalities among them: and this is sadly true of the craftsmen who actually did the work of printing the books. Their records would have been the reminiscences of friends and colleagues, which can become folklore, but which tend to die when the circle of direct acquaintances itself disappears. Until recently there were men who joined the Press at fifteen, and worked for fifty years; and in the days when men started work at twelve or thirteen, and there was no fixed retiring age, this sort of folk memory went back for almost three-quarters of a century. Keetch for instance, having worked at the Press for over seventy years, lived to be ninety-one. How much he must have remembered which is now lost! But fortunately some reminiscences do survive, giving a unique flavour of the old days of the Clay dynasty, when men worked a fifty-five hour week for a wage of thirty-six shillings.

The legendary characters were men like Alfred Mason, the head of the counting house and effectively works manager, who was so heartily disliked that stories about him became common currency and circulated for years. Even his appearance has been perpetuated: short, stooping, and with quick stealthy movements; his cropped white hair and beard and glinting glasses gave him his nickname, Frosty. He looked over the glasses at his subordinates while he made them writhe under his sarcastic tongue. He particularly liked to come up silently behind people and catch them doing something wrong, and then to make them ridiculous before their colleagues. He loved this ascendancy over others; he could not learn too much about the private lives of staff or customers, so as to know their weaknesses. He worked at a desk which overlooked the front steps, so that he could watch all comings and goings. He would question travellers and other outsiders to build up his store of knowledge. He had come to the Press in Charles John Clay's time, held him in veneration, and as an older man had a kind of added power over John Clay by being quick to tell him in any situation what his father would have done. He had no great knowledge or love of printing, which was simply a craft which had acquired all its age-old practices and went on using them unthinkingly; this meant that he feared and distrusted the Monotype keyboard when it came, and even did what he could to make it fail. He used to spit, almost religiously, when he passed the casters.

To the outside world, especially to the University, he appeared civil, indeed urbane, presenting a smooth face and a bland manner to superiors. He revered position and success, and his greatest respect was for those who had made money (the directors of the

Cambridge Building Society were 'All five-figure men', he said once to Roberts: the Victorian hall-mark). But he was no re-specter of persons behind their backs: indeed, once, watching the venerable departing back of Henry Jackson, O.M., Syndic of the Press and Regius Professor of Greek, he turned to Roberts and said 'There he goes: and not the only learned fool who's wasted my time this morning.' He died in office during the First World War, aged seventy-six and nearly senile: still respected by some and feared by more.

Perhaps Mason helps us to understand one side of Nobbs, who had a phenomenally quick mind, intense individuality, and energy, the three qualities in combination bordering on genius. At thirteen he came into the Press, where all the working prac-tices were ossified custom. He learned and turned out his own work so fast that he always had time to spare, and his surplus energy then merely got him into trouble. To Mason and his fellow authoritarians, Nobbs must have been just a nuisance; while Mason and the other old men must for Nobbs have stood for the world – which he was against. He may therefore have decided that Monotype was going to succeed just because they did not believe in it, and it would please him to prove them wrong. He may also have been impressed by Bruce Rogers because he too was a lone voice crying in the typographical wilderness of 1916: so 'layout' became a cause alongside the Monotype itself.

Nobbs's demonic aspects were well recorded by his younger colleague George Willers, who understood him very well, ad-mired him, and was one of the few whom Nobbs actually helped or encouraged. Willers saw that even Nobbs's sporting activities were part of his nature. It was he who pointed out that Nobbs in a football match acted as if he were the only player: his own team, like the other side, were mostly in the way, and he had to win the match by himself, charging all over the field for the entire match, yet easily deprived of the ball by any cool-headed player. He liked cycling because it was a one-man activity, and he could go faster and further than other people. He cycled from Oxford to Cambridge in five hours; and when (either for company or in order to have people to be up against) he joined a club, he showed how he despised the capacity of other members. 'Is that

The tower of the Pitt Building and the old Printing House buildings from the river. Gwen Raverat's wood-engraving shows a scene which has hardly changed since the 1880s.

all?' he said, when they had completed a nice little ride to Linton and back: he went straight out again and did Bishop's Stortford and back to finish off the day's riding. Even his eating was demonic. He once ordered a breakfast at some sporting event for five people: the other four failed to arrive, so he ate the whole table-load, including twenty fried eggs. Yet the books he laid out have a delicacy which seems feminine. Willers summed up that gift of his in a single telling phrase: he had an extraordinary capacity to think in type.

The other great character was Harry Hagger, known as 'Buck'. He was a general cleaner under Keetch's often distracted supervision, was immensely strong, and made a great show of being simple, though he was capable of a kind of calculation as well as a kind of acting. He wore a white coat, a very loud waistcoat, and John Clay's cast-off bowler hats. He cleaned the abominable lavatories, and also swept the pavement before the Pitt Building, with much farcical activity, including presenting arms to passers-by, using his broomstick as rifle. He became known as one of the sights of Cambridge, and was appreciated as a free show. One had to be careful with him, though: two undergraduates passing in a chaise once said something derogatory, whereon Buck stepped into the road and neatly overturned the chaise.

Keetch was a kind of *chef de protocol* of the University; other people with flagpoles would watch the top of the tower of the Pitt Building to see when the flag should be flown. On one occasion the flag got tangled in the pulley at the top of the pole, and on Keetch's order Hagger climbed up hand over hand to free it. Arrived at the top he realised what a splendid view of Cambridge it gave (and perhaps what a splendid view of him it gave to Cambridge). So he pulled himself on to the truck and remained there, while Keetch begged him to come down. Eventually he did, having been promised a new pair of boots: Keetch honoured the promise.

Mrs Hagger used to send Buck his lunch at the Press. One day – it must have been a Monday – she sent a bowl which purported to be a rice pudding. Buck was eating this, and suddenly looked thoughtful. He leaned over to a friend, and said 'Teddy, this looks like starch.' The friend leaned over, looked into the bowl, and said 'It *is* starch.' Buck paused a moment, and then said 'Never mind. I've started it, and so I'll finish it.' The inner fortification seems to have done him good, though one hopes Mrs Hagger saw her mistake before she put the rice on the washing.

There are other such anecdotes: of Thomas Ayre, an old, decrepit and rather foul-smelling reader, known as the 'comma fiend' because he inserted so many commas, to the disgust of the apprentices who lost time making the corrections. Another reader, 'Knocker' Toombs, always got drunk on Friday night.

Once in that state he won a duck, plucked and trussed for the oven, in a raffle. Carrying this towards home, he got to Hobson's Brook, looked at his prize as if seeing it for the first time, and put it in the water, saying 'Here, ducks can swim: I've carried you far enough.' On another Friday night, on his way home to Ely, he stopped in front of St Catharine's, turned his unfocused gaze on the front court, and began to pull the chain which keeps pedestrians off the grass. He explained that he was trying to get the ferry to come over from the other side.

In some ways this is a now-lost world, and in most ways that is for the good. In particular a great deal of Victorian respectfulness based on simple fear has since disappeared. It is crystallised in one last little vignette. Keetch was a good billiards-player; so was John Clay. Leaving the office at the end of the day, Clay would sometimes say to Keetch that if nobody was coming to dinner, he would like to have a game; he'd let Keetch know. If he had not rung by eight o'clock Keetch was free. Keetch would then hang around in the court until 8 p.m., so that he could hear the office telephone which might or might not summon him to Clay's house. He was so far from being resentful of this treatment that he thought it uncommonly condescending that he was allowed to leave the house by the front door. Another aspect of this attitude was the men's fear and hatred of Mason. The whole era ended with the advent of J. B. Peace, who treated people in a completely different style: it must have been for this that he was so mourned at his death despite a quite short term of office.

# 13

---

## FROM 1945 TO 1972

ROBERTS retired to become Master of Pembroke College in 1948. Lewis had reached retirement age in 1943, but stayed on until the end of the War and Brooke Crutchley's return from service at the Admiralty. So by 1948 the Secretary and the Printer had both changed, after more than twenty years during which the world itself had greatly changed.

The war years subjected the Press to heavy strains, some expected, some not. International trade was itself disrupted, and that mattered because by the end of the 1930s academic and educational publishing in the English language had become international. Within the United Kingdom itself, under siege from 1940 onwards, publishers had to cope with bombing, which destroyed stocks (Bentley House escaped, not being in the old bookselling area round St Paul's, which was flattened); and also with paper rationing, which made it very hard to replace stocks, or even to print such new books as were written. There were unexpected results: the hunger for reading material meant that everything in print or everything newly published was bought unhesitatingly, and such stocks as were not bombed were sold out. This produced a surge of cash, which could not be spent either on buildings or machinery or on substantial reprinting or on new-book publication. Some books did get written nonetheless, and were accepted for publication at some future time when their turn in the queue would come; so that Cambridge entered the post-war period with a safe-full of manuscripts waiting for printing – and in the immediate post-war period, when shortages of materials got worse rather than better, that pile of commitments grew. (Among my duties in 1951 as a new Assistant

Secretary was the maintenance of a printed Commitments List, presented to the anxious Syndicate at every meeting. It recorded what was added at the last meeting, and what had gone for printing in the same period. Another duty was to get the type-scripts out of the safe, and put them in hand one by one, over many months.)

During the War two important decisions were made. Faced with the accumulation of cash, Roberts persuaded the Syndicate to donate £49,000 to the University to found the Pitt Professor-ship of American History in 1944. It was in one way an imagin-ative gesture, good for the University's relationship with the USA, and it brought a succession of distinguished scholars to Cambridge to fill this visiting Chair; but the War was scarcely finished before Roberts's successors were groaning at the thought of how essential needs might have been met with that money.

The gift must have sprung from a strange kind of euphoria: Roberts knew of the constant and compelling need for an endow-ment fund from Wright and Waller; Chairmen of the Syndicate whom he admired, such as Sir Hugh Anderson and J. F. Cameron, had repeatedly urged it on him; he knew it well enough from his own experience. The one advantage of the War was that it more or less enforced saving: and here was a very considerable sum almost lightly given away.

A year or two earlier, it had been suggested that the Press, as part of the University and, since 1916 and the end of the partner-ship, no longer subject to partial profit-taking by the Clays, ought to be exempt from income tax. This too was an important consideration. In truth, the Press had no outside source of funds. (The Government Almanac Annuity of £500 could hardly be considered significant.) Its printing and publishing, in good years, produced surpluses, though not large ones. These sur-pluses were the only source of new funds and reserves: if they were depleted by tax, the future security of the whole operation was to that extent put in question. But in 1940 – as those who were alive then will remember – it was a patriotic duty to give to the war effort: rich people would present a whole warplane to the nation, and poor people would buy a few bullets for its machine guns. It is understandable that the Syndicate, meeting resistance from the authorities, were unwilling to press the case; it was less understandable that the case was allowed to rest for over thirty years, at the end of which relief from corporation tax (as it had become) was an urgent necessity.

Those, one can now say, were mistaken judgements. One of Roberts's last actions was a triumphant success. This was to approve Kingsford's scheme, proposed in 1948, to turn the Cambridge sales agency at the Macmillan Company in New York into a fully-fledged independent Branch of the Press in new premises of its own on Madison Avenue (since 1951 at 32 East 57th Street). Ronald Mansbridge, who had run the agency, naturally became the first Manager, and he continued in the new American Branch to develop the sales of Cambridge books, ably assisted by his Financial Controller, Jack Schulman, who succeeded Mansbridge as Manager of the Branch in 1971. At first it was primarily a marketing organisation, and conspicuously successful at selling the list, but in the mid-1960s editors were added to the staff, and in the 1970s a production department; so that it became a microcosm of the whole Press, and the hitherto small stream of books by US authors became a substantial flow.

Kingsford became Secretary in July 1948, and retired in 1963. During that period the post-war time of shortages turned into the ten or twelve years of boom which preceded 1969. Publishers who had once thought that their business was simply to choose good books and sell them well had to learn pressing economic lessons, for it turned out that coping with a period of expansion was only slightly less difficult than coping with recession: in both cases special forecasting, financial and management skills were needed. In particular, the publishers of books with a long life had to be more farsighted than the producers of commodities with a rapid turnover, since, as we shall see later, the insidious weakening power of inflation was easy to ignore.

At the beginning of the 1950s, the Press as publisher produced about 130 books a year, nearly all of them printed at Cambridge. This figure had varied little since early in the century, but the quality of the backlist had produced a steady growth of turnover. In 1936, 38 % of this was exported. That percentage dropped during the Second World War, but in 1947 returned to the pre-war figure. In 1951 exports passed 50%, and in 1962 60%. The number of titles published grew slowly; after the war-time decline it returned to 100 in 1946, and stood at about 130 throughout the 1950s; but the numbers of copies printed of each book began to rise as governments throughout the world devoted more funds to education. There was therefore a substantial growth beginning, and it was export-led.

The 1960s saw the foundation of new universities and other centres of tertiary education, in both the developed and the developing countries. It was said that at one time during this period a major library was opening every week in the USA, and, as in the War, it became easy for academic publishers to sell their books: print-runs grew, and reprints followed. Future economic historians of the book trade will be able to demonstrate that never since Gutenberg had edition-sizes of learned and academic books been so large, or the market so receptive. It was a golden age, in which, as Shakespeare said, people 'fleeted their time carelessly'. There seemed no reason why it should not last for ever. But it imposed severe strains on cash management while it lasted; it was marked throughout by inflation, at first slow and then frighteningly fast; it lasted only about twelve years; and was followed by a recession which lasted longer and increased the strains many times over.

The period was also marked by a number of publishing successes. The most important was the publication of the New English Bible (New Testament 1961, Old Testament and Complete Bible 1970). The two university presses played again the role they had played with the Revised Version. They supported the work of translation, and since this started in 1948 and went on until publication, the cost was very great indeed. Translation and publication costs exceeded one and a half million pounds. But the presses were able to support it, and it was natural that the Joint Committee of the Churches which sponsored the New English Bible should have turned to the university presses as non-profit-making publishers with centuries of experience, a commitment to the Bible and theological scholarship, and a developed marketing network throughout the world, especially in the USA. There was a special service at Westminster Abbey to mark publication, with representatives of all the Churches and The Queen Mother present. The long procession was led by officers of the Cambridge and Oxford University Presses. When the New Testament was published it was received with enormous interest, and the sales were very large.

It will be remembered that the Queen's Printer had in the 1870s decided not to take part in the publication of the Revised Version. In 1961 it may have seemed as if the New English Bible was going to be officially 'authorized' for use in the Church of England, and indeed its use was recommended, though not made mandatory. The Queen's Printer felt that his historical prerogative was being infringed or endangered, and decided for a last time to test the powers of the Royal Patent. This was not done, as in earlier times, by attempting to restrict printing at Cambridge and Oxford, or the sale in London and elsewhere. Instead, the Queen's Printer in effect challenged the copyright of the university presses; without seeking permission he issued a paperback text of the Gospel of St John. Cambridge and Oxford took out an injunction, and so once more the three presses royally empowered to print Bibles were in legal contention with each other – the last battle in the long war which since 1591 had erupted at intervals like a volcano with periods of dormancy. In 1963 Mr Justice Plowman declared that the royal prerogative could not be construed to cover all translations of the Bible, and that the New English Bible was a common-law copyright.

Two million copies of the New Testament were sold in the first two months after publication, and the complete Bible did comparably well in 1970. Cambridge supported the NEB with an important initiative, replacing the old Cambridge Bible for Schools with a complete commentary on the whole Bible in the new version. The Cambridge Bible Commentary, in over fifty volumes, was published between 1963 and 1979 – a very remarkable piece of editing. The more frequently studied volumes (e.g., C. F. D. Moule on Mark's Gospel) immediately became steady sellers.

At the school level the Press secured successors for Siddons and his colleagues. In 1964 was published the first volume of the School Mathematics Project, one of the most successful curriculum reform schemes ever undertaken in Britain. The 'SMP' under its director Bryan Thwaites remained in being and revised its early publications, keeping abreast of changes in schools, and responding to criticism of its product. It also extended its operation, enabling the Press itself to enter primary-school publishing with the SMP's middle- and primary-school schemes. There were also overseas adaptations, for East Africa and Australia; but naturally the main sale was in the United Kingdom itself. The Project was so successful that it became the most-used mathematics course in English secondary schools, and still represents a significant portion of the Press's UK business.

Another feature of the 1960s was the development of publishing for African secondary schools, based initially on a new scheme for examinations in African History sponsored by the Cambridge University Local Examinations Syndicate. Textbooks on African history by J. D. Fage, Roland Oliver and others had a very large sale in Africa, and contributed to the developing sense of cultural identity in the newly-independent nations. An uncovenanted benefit was that these publications at the school level helped the development of the Press's list in African history at the tertiary level, leading to the *Cambridge History of Africa*, edited by Fage and Oliver, now nearly complete in six volumes, to the *Journal of African History* and *Journal of Modern African Studies*, and to a monograph series. The Press also published the first French course for African schools; and an imaginative programme of little 'readers' featured tales of African interest by African writers, including Achebe and Ekwensi. These too have sold many hundreds of thousands of copies.

The African experiment sprang from a feeling that Cambridge, especially through the Local Examinations Syndicate (despite its name, a University institution now providing public examinations throughout the world), had acquired an obligation to make the last stages of English influence in the former colonies thoughtful and positive. But producing books for a single market was to be less and less the Cambridge pattern. There was a conscious decision not to engage so far in overseas territories that a large local trade could be supported only by local publication, often in local languages at the primary-school level. That was the pattern followed by other major publishers, and there was always a risk that it would turn their publishing empires into a set of powerful provinces, each headed by a sort of pro-consul developing the territorial trade at the expense of the books produced back in England. That kind of centrifugal tension was dangerous, and in any case many of these local markets were at the mercy of nationalist sentiment, which resented neocolonialism, or the fluctuations of world trade. The one market which presented stability in the face of those fluctuations was the USA. At the highest level, academic books, especially in the sciences, are international; and at that level the world language is English. It became increasingly clear in the 1960s that there was an international role for academic publishers in English, and that the books produced in Cambridge would sell throughout the world. The largest single market was undoubtedly the USA, since it was the richest and most powerful country, educated a high proportion of its population at tertiary level, was engaged in pure and applied scientific research on a scale no other country could match, was itself a potential source of more authors than any other country, and was basically the strongest and most productive economy of all. There could be no doubt where the priorities lay: the development of the American Branch was the key to the future.

At this point in this History it is increasingly difficult to pick out outstanding titles published, not because they are few but because they are many: they are mostly still in print and their authors mostly still alive; and the borderline between history and advertising is now too easily crossed. Yet it would be wrong not to mention a few. Kingsford's Secretaryship saw the publication of the *New Cambridge Modern History*, for instance: the twelve volumes were published at a brisk rate, to be followed later by an Atlas and a Companion Volume. In 1956 appeared *Documents in Mycenaean Greek*, a sober title for a book which revolutionised classical archaeology: it was the *compte rendu* of Ventris and Chadwick's decipherment of the Linear B script, giving texts of three hundred clay tablets from Knossos, Pylos and Mycenae, with a translation and commentary. It is also a monument of Cambridge printing skill. In 1952 appeared the first edition of Clapham, Tutin and Warburg's *Flora of the British Isles*, the first complete and up-to-date flora for at least fifty years. Richard David, first as Assistant Secretary and then as London Manager, played an important part in its compilation and publication. A botanist of professional standing, he helped to ensure that the information in it was well arranged and easy to refer to. The system of graded headings and cross-functioning of keys established a pattern which was to become the standard. Once more, it was an example of the skilled use of the Monotype keyboard. It is not an obviously beautiful book, but it is a remarkable piece of learned printing. The tradition of publishing in taxonomic botany made the Press in the 1970s the natural home for the *Flora Europaea*.

Nor could one fail to mention the greatest single-handed piece of inter-cultural interpretation ever undertaken – Joseph Needham's *Science and Civilisation in China*. Volume I appeared in 1954; Volume V, Part 5 in 1983; and Volume VII, the scheduled end, will appear in due course. This *is* a beautiful book: Frank Kendon designed the printed boards and the jacket; John Dreyfus designed the page, with its two layers of footnotes in roman and Chinese characters. It is also one of the modern world's great intellectual enterprises, conducted by one man with a few devoted helpers.

Kingsford retired with the satisfaction of seeing the printing business finally moved from the old site behind the Pitt Building to the new University Printing House in Shaftesbury Road. For years Lewis and Crutchley had been hampered and frustrated by the inconvenience of the old buildings, with their many levels, their cramped space, their island site with the river on one side and two narrow medieval lanes as the only approaches. After the War, the problem for years was finance. As the economy began to expand in the late 1950s, this situation eased; a site could be bought from Clare College; planning permission obtained; loans secured. Crutchley directed this major move, and in 1963 the new building was opened by the Vice-Chancellor. The acquisition of the twenty-five-acre site was of enormous future advantage to the Press, and later made it possible to contemplate another radical change, which also came to be an

The University Printing House, 1963.

urgent necessity. Publishers were now finding London expensive and no longer convenient: in particular it began to seem absurd to use sites in central London for what was largely a warehousing and accounting function. The publishing business was divided geographically in two. Perhaps some of the London operations could be moved to Cambridge?

As the successor of Wright, Waller and Roberts, Kingsford united in the office of Secretary at least three functions. He was simultaneously the Syndicate's chief coordinating officer, head of the publishing business, and editorial director. The publishing business was run as a collaboration between the Secretary and the London Manager, who was himself not only the head of that large separate unit in London but also what we should now call marketing director and director of operations. That duumvirate worked successfully while the publishing business was relatively small. It was the equivalent of a partnership in a family firm, and until the 1960s the Press was like a fair-sized family firm. Similarly, printing businesses were still, at that date, quite often linked to publishing businesses: as with the Clays, some members of the family would run one business, and some the other. Relationships could be kept informal as long as neither business grew too large. But the boom of the 1960s led to an expansion of publishing which made this part of the Press's activities the greater of the two. A new stage of evolution became inevitable, and it was given urgency by the change in external economic conditions which turned strain into crisis.

Already in the late 1950s the Press's publishing business was using other printers. It was not so much that publishing exceeded the capacity of printing as that the backlog of unstarted work could only be liquidated in a reasonable time in that way. At first work was subcontracted through the production office of the printing business, and new staff were taken on by the Printer for that purpose. The Printer still supplied the design service, progress control, press-reading and subediting.

This last function was an important development. Until after the Second World War it was the general practice to give 'copy' (still often in manuscript, and often, as Lewis once wrote on Dover Wilson's script, 'bloody') no more than a 'technical mark-up' in which type-sizes and headings were specified. The compositor set the book, maintaining extraordinary faithfulness to what was given him. The reader then went through the proof critically, often marking queries. At this stage authors were in the habit of 'getting things right', and, partly stimulated by the reader and partly because they had checked their sources, they would correct drastically in proof. As labour became more expensive, this became foolish and wasteful. Subediting was meant to do two things: to avoid that waste by asking the questions early, and to facilitate the analytical Cambridge design procedure which did not impose an off-the-peg treatment, but worked outwards from the internal structure. The subeditor could explain the structure to the designer, alert him to special features, and even propose improvements to the author which would help the designer and ultimately the reader. This essential service was initiated in Crutchley's time as part of the Printing House's functions; for it will be remembered that in the 1950s the old system of Assistant Secretaries in Cambridge provided a minimal staff on the publishing side, which needed either to be supplemented in this way, or to be developed into a proper editorial office.

This latter development occurred under David. He divested himself of the editorial function exercised hitherto by the Secretary, and appointed a Chief Editor (myself) in 1965. An editorial staff now began to grow. and to take a more active role in commissioning new books, and especially in entering more subjects. The strengths of the Press derived from the traditional curriculum at Cambridge; mathematics, classics, theology and philosophy were followed by the sciences, oriental studies and European literary studies, in much the same order as these had become teaching subjects. But now linguistics and sociology and the new area studies were being added to the range; anthropology was becoming more important as a key to other studies; political science was developing rapidly; it was important to make up lost ground in economics and in English, and in every subject seriously pursued it was necessary to take an active role. Scientists no longer wrote books as a matter of course: they had to be persuaded. The editors had to leave the office and travel round the universities, talking to the potential authors who were being courted assiduously by competitors. In the 1930s the Press had published a little in a remarkably wide range of subjects just by being there and saying 'yes' to the right offers. Now the situation was reversed: many books had to be asked for. And if it had been decided in principle that (for instance) linguistics was here to stay and good books in the subject must be found, then a systematic list had to be built as a conscious construction. It would consist of a monograph series called *Cambridge Studies in Linguistics*; a journal – more than one if possible; other monographs published independently of the series; textbooks; reference books, and books for a wider public. All these books would be written in the UK, in the USA, or wherever the talented authors happened to be; so the staff editor carrying out that policy would have to travel the whole world.

Another major overseas development occurred at this time. For many years, Cambridge University Press books had been sold in Australia through the agency of Georgian House of Melbourne. Press Bibles had been sold through the Australian branch of the Lutterworth Press. Arrangements were made in 1969 to acquire the sales, distribution and agency business of Georgian House, and to make it into the Press's own Australian Branch – at first with company status – under Brian Harris, the Branch's first Manager. At the same time, the Press took over the Australian business of the Lutterworth Press, so bringing all Press publications under one roof.

The general expansion of Press publishing that now began to take place was itself dependent on the appointment and training of a new kind of editor. There was nobody to train the first generation, who had to learn by doing. Then, when the books came in, in increasing numbers, it became necessary to take over the supervision of their production. A production department was therefore set up under a Production Manager, Peter Burbidge. The subeditorial department had already moved across to the publishing side. The move to the new Printing House in 1963 inevitably severed the imaginary umbilical cord which had gone on linking the publishing function to the printers while it was so easy just to cross the court and speak to the right person. The publishing business now had to do for itself with its own staff what had been done for it (and well done) before. Moving into the Pitt Building, vacated by the printing business in 1963, the new editorial and production departments found themselves rapidly filling it. The seven-and-a-half people in the Secretary's office in 1935 (Richard David's recollection) had become only a dozen by 1951 (my recollection), but in the 1960s they multiplied.

In 1964 the Syndicate accepted 150 books; in 1967 the figure passed 200; in 1969 it was 225 and the rise continued through the 1970s. It should be remembered that the number of copies printed was rising much faster, so that the global output, considered as units printed, quadrupled during this time. This was the era when a monograph sold its 2500 or 3000 copies and sometimes reprinted in a year or two; when the experiment of paperbacking academic textbooks succeeded, and it was unexceptional to print a first edition of 2500 in hardback and 10,000 in paperback. Schoolbooks were routinely launched in editions of 20,000. If successes were larger, failures were also large, and a programme of active commissioning is always more risky than passive acceptance of safe offers. The 1960s therefore presented a period of increasing cash outflow as production costs – and stocks – rose with inflation as well as with the larger numbers printed.

Towards the end of his period of office, David faced the kind of situation which had been faced before in the Press's history – in 1852 for instance. But this time the Press was a sizeable enterprise; the two businesses employed nearly a thousand people; and the Press's management structure was now far from ideal for the tackling of a threatening cloud of problems which had been gathering for some years. The Press was ripe for a major structural and financial reorganisation.

The potentially disastrous effects of high rates of inflation had crept up on publishers almost unnoticed – and indeed any manufacturer whose products had a significant 'shelf life' before they were purchased by the consumer was insidiously affected. The long-term rate of inflation in the United Kingdom had been about $2\frac{1}{2}\%$ for some years. Between 1960 and 1965, the annual average rate rose to $3\frac{1}{2}\%$; and between 1965 and 1971 rose further to $6\frac{1}{2}\%$, actually reaching $9\%$ in 1971. This rate was alarmingly high, although it had not yet reached the almost continuous double figures of 1974–81. Publishing costs in any one year were soaring, but three-quarters of the income for the year came from books which had been in stock for many years – in the case of the Press, for ten, twenty-five, or even fifty years. New books tended to have prices which reflected current costs, but books from the 'backlist', sold from existing stock, had prices which bore no relation to current replacement costs – and three-quarters of Press annual sales were of such books. Publishers throughout the United Kingdom were slow to realise that it was essential to ensure, in a time of high inflation, that the prices of backlist books were regularly uplifted in line with current costs. This requirement was particularly crucial for the Press since its backlist was bigger than the average publisher's, and its annual income was therefore more dependent on backlist sales. The result was that as the Press's costs rose, its net income fell. In an attempt to counteract this effect, nearly all United Kingdom publishers increased the prices of their new books still more, instead of equalising price rises over all their products including the backlist, and a pronounced gap developed between new book prices and backlist prices. This had the effect of depressing new book sales.

There were also ominous signs that the publishing boom of the fifties and sixties was in any case coming to an end. Educational markets were beginning to be short of cash, and higher new book prices did not help. In 1969–70 there was a marked fall in book purchases in the United States library market, as spending budgets were cut in schools and libraries, and in scientific research. Sales per title of scholarly books began to drop: but the Press was slow to adjust its printing numbers accordingly, so its stocks of unsold books began to rise, and financing them put extra pressure on funds. High prices, declining purchasing power, reduced sales per title, and inadequate pricing policy began to interact in a vicious disabling spiral. Expenditure on staff and general overheads was still geared to the boom period of the sixties, and this made matters worse. The result was that by 1969 the Press's cash resources had been totally depleted, and a large overdraft had begun to grow which was alarming the Press Syndicate, the University Financial Board, and Barclays Bank.

Clearly, drastic action was needed, but the management structure which David had inherited had weaknesses which made clear-cut action difficult. It was not simply that a rather 'scholarly' mode of management was having to grapple with a large-scale business crisis. Changes in the scale and location of Press operations in the sixties had exacerbated the problems of structure and location already mentioned, accentuating the centrifugal tendencies of the different segments of the business and placing strains on the executive structure.

This structure was geographically rather than functionally based. This fostered the tendency towards polarisation, prevented unified and focal decision-making and encouraged a departmental approach. The current economic problems promoted a proliferation of committees, discussions and paperwork, and hindered real decision-making and indeed even a full appreciation of the seriousness of the business situation although David himself was well aware of it. The Press Syndicate, uncomfortably conscious of the financial problems, but lacking the business experience to resolve them, themselves asked for more and more information and documentation, putting even more pressure on management.

At this stage, in 1969, David rightly decided that it was no longer possible for one man to be simultaneously both Secretary of the Press Syndicate (i.e. the Syndicate's chief coordinating officer) and also head of the publishing business. Steps taken five years previously to improve the coordination of the printing and publishing businesses, for example by instituting joint committees, had not proved successful. There were crises from time to time, and some mutual lack of confidence. David felt that a University Printer might more easily accept the control of a chief officer who was not at the same time the head of the Press's other business; also that the Press's operations had grown so much in scale and complexity that each role had become a full-time job. The Press Syndicate concurred. Early in 1970 David withdrew from the post of Secretary of the Syndicate to be full-time head of the publishing business, with the new title of University Publisher. The two businesses were officially decentralised and put onto an 'arm's-length' business relationship with each other. The post of Secretary of the Press Syndicate was passed, for the sake of continuity, to the University Treasurer, Trevor Gardner, who in that position was to play a very important role in the next two years; and the Press ceased for the moment to have a chief coordinating officer at the head of its executive staff.

At the same time, two Sub-Syndicates were created by the Syndicate to supervise the two businesses: a Publishing Sub-Syndicate and a Printing Sub-Syndicate. The Syndicate's concern with business problems also led to the dividing of the Syndicate Meetings into two: Business Meetings and Editorial Meetings. The first Business Meeting was held on 13 March 1970. Two businessmen from outside the University were coopted onto the Sub-Syndicates. Sir Alan Wilson, FRS, then Chairman of Glaxo, had as Fellow of Trinity and Lecturer in Mathematics been the author of the classic *The Theory of Metals*, mentioned above as one of the 'big blue books'. He joined the Printing Sub-Syndicate in 1970. Sir Robert Taylor, then Chairman of Costains, the large construction firm, joined the Publishing Sub-Syndicate in 1971. Some of the elements necessary to the resolution of the Press's problems were assembling, and David's statesmanlike move had opened the way for a restructuring, but two major elements were still missing.

In the meantime, anxiety about the Press's financial position had been steadily growing, as the overdraft borrowings mounted. The Statutes and Ordinances of the University require that each year the Financial Board appoints one or more (usually two) of its members as representatives to examine the Annual Accounts of the University Press, and to confer with the Press's Auditors, who are appointed by the Board. The representatives discuss the Accounts in detail with the senior executives of the Press, and then make a report. The representatives appointed to consider the 1969 Accounts were John Bradfield (Bursar of Trinity) and Christopher Johnson (later Bursar of St John's). Two of the most able financial men in the University, they saw at this relatively early stage what was going wrong. They commented:

The figures show that the profitability is seriously inadequate. This is the more disappointing because the efforts of the Press to increase gross profit have met with some success, but rapidly increasing overhead expenses have largely offset this improvement. It was very clear to us that publishing businesses are particularly prone to suffer from the effects of inflation because of the deferment of their profits and the high overhead element in the profit and loss account.

They concluded that the Press needed to make a profit of at least 5% of sales to plough back into the business. Their argument ran as follows:

(1) A commercial publishing and printing business has the simple aim of maximising profit.

(2) This is inappropriate to the Press because of its duty to publish scholarly works, and to do a great deal of printing for its owner, the University.

(3) But there must be *some* kind of aim to serve as a guide over the attitude to be taken to worthy but unprofitable proposals, and over the pricing of sales where there is little or no direct commercial comparison.

(4) An aim of 5% for ploughing back seems minimal having regard to the considerable needs of the Press itself for new finance, the fact that the University is unlikely to be able to provide further capital, the difficulty of long-term funding from non-University sources, and the extent to which bank accommodation has already been used.

This shrewd analysis, as well as diagnosing the Press's ill-health and suggesting some of its causes, brought into focus three vital concepts: the need for viability self-financed through the generation of surpluses; the distinction between the Press's altruistic activities and those of commercial publishers – which was later to be the main ground for the recognition of its charitable status; and the increasing difficulty which the University would have in coping with the financial needs and vicissitudes of this growing giant, and the eventual impossibility of doing so.

Once again, it was one thing to diagnose the situation; quite another to rectify it. Anxiety about the Press's financial position continued to mount.

A Syndicate Minute of 17 February 1970 referred to the constant exceeding of overdraft limits, and another of 9 October 1970, commenting on the 1969 Press Annual Accounts, read:

The Syndicate expressed concern at the inadequacy of the net income, and in particular at the amount of the income that had been paid out as interest on borrowings. The continued increase of these borrowings also gave a cause of anxiety.

It was pointed out in the same Minute that in 1969 the bank had financed 25 % of the Press's total assets but had taken 51 % of the Press's total income in overdraft interest.

In 1970, the position deteriorated further. The year-end overdraft, usually by no means the annual peak, increased by another £256,000, and was equivalent to nearly 20 % of annual sales, but overdraft was rising faster than sales. It was already within £16,000 of the upper limit fixed by the Financial Board. The official report accompanying the 1970 Annual Accounts said:

It must be remembered that, on each of the last three occasions of the annual meeting with the Bank the Manager has asked for some assurances that the Press is taking steps to reduce its dependancy upon the Bank. In good faith, these assurances have been given but not kept. On these figures, and with the knowledge of what has happened during 1971, it is apparent that at the next meeting in April 1972 the Press is going to ask for an increased borrowing limit, which may also exceed that at present imposed by the Financial Board of the University.... Should the Bank, or the Financial Board, refuse this increase, the Press could find itself in a most embarrassing position. Unless urgent steps are taken to rectify the position either by an improvement in profit margins providing an increasing proportion of new money from that source, or by pruning some aspects of the Publishing activity, a very critical situation is bound to arise.

After considering the 1970 Press Accounts, the representatives of the Financial Board (Bradfield, and Eric Ceadel, the University Librarian) struck a similar urgent note:

Still struggling. The loss on Syndics' books is alarming. A substantial turn-round in U.K. profitability is urgently needed. The heavy overdraft situation, combined with the low level of profitability on the publishing side, creates a problem of much anxiety.

The Financial Board quickly communicated to the Press Syndicate its concern at the dangers inherent in the situation. Problems were by no means confined to the publishing business. The printing business had also had a difficult year in 1970, with high wage claims and work getting scarcer. Substantial capital expenditure would be needed for the transition to computer-aided composition: but that transition was to take longer than expected. The majority of books were not handled by computer-aided composition until 1978, and journals were even later, although the target for both had been 1974. The Financial Board representatives who examined the 1971 Accounts commented on the inadequate volume of work, and the 'slump in demand for high-grade printing in the printing trade in general', concluding:

Moreover, the volume of work in the printing division has worsened further since the end of 1971, and there is not much hope of improvement in 1972 in this respect.

There were many signs that the printing business's traditional concentration on fine quality in Monotype printing needed to take more account of changes occurring in the market place. There was a great demand for cheaper composing methods – slug or typewriter – not only for straightforward text but for complicated work, including mathematics. Cheap litho houses were being used for reprints previously done from rotary-letterpress plates; Bibles were being transferred to web-fed machines, of which the Press had none; and there was a move from cased to paper binding, and from sewn cases to unsewn. There were also signs of a reduction in University work, which had not been positively encouraged during the previous few years; and the publishing business was making greater use of outside printers – partly for technical and cost reasons, but partly through lack of confidence in the printing side. A tougher market required greater attention to financial and commercial factors. The necessary change from letterpress to lithography had started, but was going too slowly. Printing problems were further exacerbated by a national shortage of skilled craftsmen.

The Financial Board representatives were even more gloomy about the publishing business: 'Unhappily the 1971 Accounts show no improvement but instead a deterioration . . .'. The Press was floundering; and it was an additional misfortune that Sir Frank Lee, the Chairman of the Press Syndicate, was seriously ill, and died in the spring of 1971.

At this dark moment the Press had a great stroke of good fortune, and one key element necessary to its recovery fell into place. Lord Todd of Trumpington, Master of Christ's College and Nobel Laureate, became Chairman of the Press Syndicate. He writes in his autobiography:

Following the death of Sir Frank Lee in the spring of 1971 I came under heavy pressure from the Vice-Chancellor and the University Treasurer to succeed Sir Frank as Chairman of the Syndics of Cambridge University Press. They were most insistent and particularly as I had refused to allow myself to be nominated for the Vice-Chancellorship, I felt I had to accept. Already on my first visit as Chairman to the offices of the University Press I was horrified; the Press was to all intents and purposes bankrupt, with a soaring overdraft and with sales and receipts dwindling, so that they were unable to cope with rising costs. I believe that only the knowledge that behind the Press stood the University with its great resources had kept the bank from calling a halt.

*A Time to Remember*, 189

Todd was from the start a shrewd, decisive and courageous Chairman, and very much the man to handle the Press's crisis. He chaired his first Business Meeting of the Syndicate on 14 June 1971. It is clear from his autobiography that he thought that the members of the Press Syndicate, as academics, were trying to run the Press as if it were a University department, and was critical of their tendency to want Press staff to be as far as possible academics themselves, remunerated on university academic scales without reference to the rates paid in the world of business. He had both to dispel any remaining complacency among the Press's officers, and to move the Syndicate itself in new directions.

A special Committee on the Location and Management of the Publishing Business was quickly set up under his chairmanship. It reported to the Syndicate on 5 November 1971. The Report identified a number of weaknesses in the pattern of the Press's publishing operations. It called attention to the current size and complexity of the business, and to the inadequacy of the manage-ment structure. It also criticised the geographical dispersal of publishing activities:

In particular the existence of two distinct 'centres of gravity', operational in London, policy-making in Cambridge, makes it difficult to establish and maintain common objectives and shared assumptions throughout the organisation.

It recommended more centralisation in Cambridge (although it proposed a warehouse in north London, and the retention of a central London 'presence'), and the formation of a Board of

Management for the publishing business, to broaden the executive structure. By far the most important proposal was that a senior appointment should be made from outside the Press to manage the relocation of publishing facilities and to plan the long-term future of the publishing business.

The second key element necessary to the recovery of the Press was about to fall into place. There was now a strong Chairman. What was needed in addition was a strong chief executive officer. A happy combination of circumstances led to the availability at that very moment of Geoffrey Cass, who had been Managing Director of the publishers George Allen and Unwin Ltd. A graduate of Jesus College, Oxford, Cass had successfully reorganised the London office of the Press, as a management consultant with Personnel Administration Ltd in the early sixties, while David was London Manager; and Cass and David had enjoyed working together. An article in *The Times* about Cass gave David and Todd the same idea simultaneously.

The Press approached Cass, and the challenge appealed to him. Todd, David and Gardner negotiated with him, and on 21 December 1971 Geoffrey Cass joined Cambridge University Press, taking office as Managing Director of the publishing business on 1 January 1972. His brief was to rescue and revive an ailing organisation.

Todd had moved very fast, indeed at a pace quite untypical of University activity. He had clearly decided what to do at an early stage. He comments in his autobiography:

Fortunately there were some members of the Press who realized the position and were looking for a lead which could only come from the top. I had a busy few months at the start but was lucky enough to get things on the right lines quickly. In these initial moves I received great help and encouragement from R. W. (Dick) David, the University Publisher, who was well aware of the problems and who, quite unselfishly, sought with me to reorganize the Press, even if it detracted from his own position of authority; I shall always be grateful to him for his help. It was evident that the first essential was to appoint a really first-class managing director/chief executive with experience in commercial publishing. Since it was obvious that to get such a person one would need to pay the going rate in competition with commercial publishers, I decided that the best thing to do would be to engage the right man and only tell the Syndics about it after the deed had been done. In this way I was able to appoint a really brilliant executive in Geoffrey Cass...He took office with us on 1 January 1972 and from that day the Press never looked back. Within a year it was back on the rails and by the time I had to resign (with great regret) my chairmanship at the end of 1975 when I became President of the Royal Society, we were not only making very substantial surpluses but had built up an extremely strong cash and assets position. Although the success was undoubtedly due to Geoffrey Cass, I like to think that I played some part in what was an important rescue operation for the University and for academic publishing.

*A Time to Remember*, 189–90

Todd's characteristically brisk and modest summary of the events of the next few years provides the outline of the next chapter.

# 14

RECOVERY: 1972-4

Lord Todd had played a vital part which probably no one else in the University would have had the judgement or the confidence to undertake at that time. The appointment of Geoffrey Cass marked the beginning of a massive reorganisation, first of the publishing business, then of the Press as a whole. During most of 1972, Cass worked as Managing Director of the publishing business. The challenge was a daunting one. The financial state of the Press was bleak; bank borrowings were rising at an alarming rate; and the morale of the staff of the publishing business was low. Few members of the staff or of the Press Syndicate believed that a recovery was possible.

The Financial Board of the University, considering the finances of the Press in December 1971, had said that before it would approve an overdraft limit for 1972 it would require to have a report on the general financial position of the Press. Cass started with an analysis of the cash position and of the cash forecasts for 1972 and 1973. The result was an urgent visit to Barclays Bank to negotiate an extension of the overdraft facility. The Bank agreed 'to provide a breathing space for the review that you are carrying out with your colleagues'. The Press Syndicate had set up a special financial Sub-Committee, on 28 January 1972. At the beginning of April 1972, that Sub-Committee reported to the Syndicate and to the Financial Board, telling the Board:

The inevitability of increased overdraft facilities, and their implications for the long-term financing of the whole Press, together with the general unsatisfactory position of Press finances at the moment, led the Publishing Sub-Syndicate to propose, and the full Syndicate to accept, that the main financial strategy of the whole Press should in future be handled by a special

[ 246 ]

Sub-Committee of the full Syndicate, consisting of Mr Geoffrey Cass as executive member, reporting to Lord Todd, Sir Alan Wilson, Sir Robert Taylor and the University Treasurer.

The report revealed that the Press's borrowings from the bank were likely to exceed its overdraft limit in April 1972, and to go on rising throughout May. The Sub-Committee believed that

...assumptions that the Press...had the credit resources of the University behind it, have led in the past to the acceptance of a break-even, or near break-even, basis of operation, and to a degree of unconcern about the overdraft position and the general financial situation.

The Sub-Committee laid it down that targeted surpluses were essential, particularly during a period of high inflation. (With stocks and debtors rising, results that appeared to be 'break-even' in profit-accounting terms were illusory, and disguised a serious drain of actual cash.) The Sub-Committee's analysis ended with a warning that an urgent formal approach to the bank was needed for increased overdraft facilities, and with a request that the Financial Board should approve an increased overdraft limit for 1972. The Sub-Committee also listed the steps which Cass was taking to bring the publishing overdraft under control.

The Financial Board considered the Sub-Committee's report and replied to the Press Syndicate on 20 April 1972 in sober terms:

The Board expressed grave concern about the continuing increase in the overdraft limit and noted that if the present trend were not checked the overdraft would very quickly reach unmanageable proportions.

You will appreciate that the Financial Board's anxiety has regard to the fact that the Press's overdraft is part of the liabilities of the University, and that the University would be responsible for meeting the Press's commitments if, at some stage, the Press itself was unable to do so.

The Financial Board agreed to the increase in the Press's overdraft limit, but only on several conditions, the principal one being that:

The business affairs of the Press would continue to be run under the supervision of the special Sub-Committee appointed by the Syndicate.

This was a significant condition, advised no doubt by the University Treasurer, Trevor Gardner, who was *ex officio* a Syndic of the Press as well as the principal officer of the Financial Board. It will be remembered that he also held the title of Secretary of the Press Syndicate. In that capacity he had been instrumental in persuading Lord Todd to take on the chairmanship of the Syndicate in 1971. His wisdom and foresight were added to Todd's clarity of mind and sheer nerve; and the Press owes no less to him. The Financial Board's reply initiated a major development in the way in which the Press Syndicate handled its financial and business affairs.

The Syndicate had no alternative but to accept the Board's conditions. Indeed, Cass secured the overdraft needed for the payment of royalty cheques in 1972 only two days *after* the royalty cheques were due to be sent out. Brian Jackson, the manager of the Cambridge branch of Barclays, who must have enjoyed supporting a recovery in a period when affairs were usually going the other way, wrote:

Dear Mr Cass,

I am writing to confirm that we have arranged an increased overdraft limit of £1,750,000 on the account of the Press, to run for eight months, to provide the additional breathing space that you require for the reorganisation.

Geoffrey Cass had already begun that reorganisation in January 1972. Once the overdraft facility had been secured, he gathered together the seventy most senior staff in the publishing business, gave them a very frank briefing about the financial plight of the Press, and told them how he proposed to rectify the situation. He had been given complete and sweeping powers by the Syndicate, but he had determined not to use dismissals and redundancies as a means of saving large amounts of money, even though he saw, and told the management of the publishing business, that the business was heavily overstaffed. He took the view that the management was basically responsible for over-staffing, so that crude measures placing the burden of recovery on ordinary staff would be unjust, and should be used only as the last resort. He had seen that redundancies usually occurred in business because management had not been tough enough in holding staff and other overhead costs to proper levels at all times. Rigorous staffing and expenditure policies were unpopular when there was no crisis in sight; but weak management created crises by allowing overstaffing and overspending to occur, and then overcame those crises by arbitrarily dismissing large numbers of staff.

Accordingly, he restricted his own general action to placing a complete embargo on new recruitment and the replacement of leavers, although it must have been very tempting in that financial crisis, and with an eight-month deadline, to save a lot of money immediately by jettisoning excess staff.

At the same time, Cass imposed strict controls on general overhead expenditure, instituted tough measures to reduce production costs and control printing numbers, reduced stocks, tightened up credit control procedures, and began to analyse the pricing strategy of the publishing business, its marketing capability, the management structure, and the calibre of management. For a short time, a target 'return on capital' was specified to act as what the Syndicate Minutes called 'an emergency yardstick'. This had been requested by the Financial Board, and it was a concept familiar to the Board and to the staff; but it was soon pushed into the background as inappropriate.

He left editorial policy virtually untouched, except that he encouraged growth. He believed that to cut back on publishing, particularly during a period of high inflation, would be short-sighted. He made it clear that he had a high opinion of the Press's list, that he regarded the Press's scholarly output as paramount, and had no intention of expediently altering its nature as a solution to the Press's financial problems. The Minutes of the meeting of the special Sub-Committee of 19 June 1972 record:

Mr Cass emphasized that it was no part of his strategies to change the fundamental publishing policy of the publishing business. It seemed that some people thought that, in some way, more 'commercial' books and fewer 'academic' books would emerge from the Press. He emphasized that his proposed solution to the immediate and longer term financial problems did not lie in that direction at all. He hoped to be able to *strengthen* the Press's ability to publish books which would not normally see the light of day in a commercial press, by making the Press as a whole stronger and more viable.

This is what was achieved over the next ten years. It is clear that, coming to the Press from a commercial firm, and seeing it with fresh eyes, Cass was struck by its unique nature. That perception made him want to make its nature clear and to strengthen it, not to turn it into an imitation of the kind of general publisher he had just left.

His analysis of the Press's pricing policy convinced him that the prices of the backlist titles had not kept pace with inflation, and that this had seriously undermined the income side of the Press's financial balance. He initiated a major programme of repricing the thousands of titles in the backlist. There was some opposition now and later to this measure, which he met by re-stating the analysis of the effects of inflation on products with a long 'shelf life' before sale. Cars, for instance, are produced for sale in a relatively short time-period; virtually all costs and income actually accrue within that period, and those costs, prices, and income necessarily reflect the current value of money. A university press incurs all of the year's *costs* at the current value of money, but three-quarters of its annual *income* comes from prices fixed in earlier years before inflation had reduced their real value. Those who could not understand why a price fixed on the basis of known costs, ten years ago, should now be changed upwards were well answered by being asked whether any sensible person would sell his house at the price he had paid for it when it was newly built twenty-five years earlier; that price would be reasonable only if there had been no inflation since. One sells one's house at the current price, not the historic price, in order to be able to buy another. Current book prices had to reflect replacement costs, not original costs.

The Minutes of a 1972 management meeting make Cass's philosophy clear:

We need not feel ashamed of strategic entrepreneurial measures to make ourselves more viable. We need not be faint-hearted in defending our new policies. We have a higher proportion of books in our list, that would never normally see the light of day in a commercial press, than any other university press. If we are to continue to produce economically marginal books because they are academically desirable, then we must have money to be able to do that. We are not interested in maximising profits; we have no proprietors, no shareholders, we pay no dividends. There is no-one into whose pockets money pours if we increase our prices. All our measures will be aimed only at securing our ability to continue to be a genuine, effective, viable university press. Our defence against criticisms is total.

These thoughts show how Cass's mind was moving. It struck him as soon as he entered the Press that it was undoubtedly a charitable institution. He frequently reminded the Syndicate and his colleagues of the integrity of the Press's funds, the total ploughing-back of surpluses without any external distribution of earnings, the absence of private monetary interests, the clearly charitable objectives, the complete controlling ownership of the University of Cambridge, and the gratuitous professional control exercised by the (unpaid) Press Syndicate. His official Report to the Press Syndicate on the Press's 1972 Annual Accounts is evidence of the way in which his ideas had crystallised:

It cannot be emphasized too often that the aim of the Press is not to make profits. Our overriding objective is to publish works of scholarship and education because they make a worthwhile contribution to human knowledge. The goals of a university press are vitally different from those of commercial presses. However, all our efforts in 1972 have been devoted to ensuring that the Press is at least as efficient as any commercial press, and that it produces enough funds to safeguard its continuing ability to discharge its duties to the University and to scholarship.

Another indication of his views on the status of the Press was his early abandonment in the accounts of the Press of 'profit' and 'profit-accounting', as inappropriate and positively misleading, both internally and in the outside world. The University Press existed to disseminate knowledge, not to make money, and certainly not to produce 'profit on turnover' or 'return on capital'. The Press's capital was not a financial investment but the means of achieving the diffusion of scholarship and education. The operations of the Press *were* the Press's purpose; they were not the means to some financial purpose. The Press was a trust governed by the Chancellor, Masters, and Scholars of the University of Cambridge. It merely had to remain financially viable in order to discharge altruistic operational objectives: and of course it had to ensure its viability in the future. This way of thinking was endorsed by the Financial Board. Its representatives, after examining the 1972 Press Accounts, and urging further fund-generation, explained:

We do not suggest that profits be pursued for their own sake as in a purely commercial undertaking. The case is rather that only a sound financial basis will permit the continuance of a conscious policy of giving help where help is most needed to ensure that works of merit in scholarship are made available to the world.

Cass was very conscious that the Press had entered its 1971 crisis with no cash reserves at all. He was deeply convinced – and his involvement in the affairs of the Royal Shakespeare Theatre had reinforced the conviction – that substantial cash reserves were essential to the survival and integrity of any great charitable institution, whether educational or artistic.

The distinction between cash reserves and working assets had not been very clear within the Press when he arrived. For instance, he had found that a number of people felt that the Press's overdraft could be eliminated by the sale of Bentley House, the Press's London office. Indeed, a report in the late sixties had said that it might be argued

. . . that future capital receipts, e.g. from the sale of Bentley House, would more than adequately provide for all foreseeable cash needs during the next few years.

In 1972 Cass saw the re-location of the Press as a low priority: and he did not believe that a growing cash drain could properly be stemmed by the sale of an asset. Bentley House had outlived its usefulness, and there was every reason to think that the Press would be better united on a single site in Cambridge, but Bentley House was an operational asset, not a 'nest egg' or a reserve, and its sale could be no answer to the Press's underlying problems. Basic financial viability and a strong, cohesive management team were the first priorities. He also rejected the idea of converting the overdraft debt into long-term funding. Overdraft was the cheapest method of finance until the Press could be made self-supporting. He informed the Financial Board of his views on 10 April 1972, concluding:

Similarly, the sale of Bentley House could not be regarded as a sensible method of getting rid of the overdraft. This would be putting a finger in the hole in the dam rather than structurally repairing the dam in a proper manner. The Press should organically rectify the cash-generating power of the publishing business, not use temporary first-aid. Bentley House might well need to be sold – but only as part of an overall strategic plan for the future operations and location of the Press.

The Financial Board representatives accepted these views, and the question of disposing of Bentley House was pushed into the background, while Cass concentrated on halting the outflow of cash.

He immediately took steps in 1972 to make cash the key factor in terms of which all operational targets were to be expressed. Simple and reliable cash forecasts were instituted, and financial performance was primarily judged by success and failure in cash generation. 'Profit' and 'surplus' were completely discarded as measures of success. He felt that the confusion in the minds of many Syndics and Press executives between accounting 'profit' (a merely notional figure) and actual cash generation (money in the bank) had been a major cause of the 1971 crisis. In 1970, publishing and printing had made a combined 'profit' of over £200,000, but there had been an outflow of cash (and an increase in overdraft) of £256,000. From 1972 onwards, Cass's main long-term financial goal was the building of a substantial reserve fund to act as a buffer against crises like the one which arose in 1971. He realised that the size of the Press meant that the University itself would find it virtually impossible to rescue it if disaster befell: and universities were in any case growing increasingly short of funds. His policy of building reserves was wholeheartedly endorsed by the Financial Board; its representatives were to remark in a later year:

The financial scale of the Press operation is of the same mathematical order of magnitude as that of the University itself which can not therefore act as a financial cushion. The Press has to generate its own reserves...

In the meantime, Cass had been assessing the strengths and weaknesses of the management team and the effectiveness of the management structure. There were able people in the Press, but he urgently needed immediate general management support in the areas of pricing and operational decision-making. His first move was to recruit Anthony Wilson, who had worked with him at Allen and Unwin. Wilson was a graduate of Corpus Christi, and his first job when he returned to Cambridge to join the Press in March 1972 was to carry through the repricing strategy, which he did with skill and determination. Repricing of the backlist was completed just before the Government imposed a general price freeze as part of its counter-inflation measures.

1972 was a year of remarkable change. The Press's financial situation rapidly began to improve as the new measures started to take effect. Costs were cut dramatically, and income began to increase. The overdraft stopped rising, then began to fall. Between 1969 and 1971, the publishing cash position had been deteriorating, and the overdraft mounting, at an average rate of about £25,000 per month. In May 1972 it reached the highest peak ever recorded; then the recovery measures began to bite, and the cash position started to improve at the rate of about £90,000 per month. By 31 October 1972, the overdraft had been reduced by nearly £450,000. Lord Todd, on behalf of the Finance Committee, was able to report to the University Financial Board:

The Committee is pleased to report a most satisfactory improvement in the affairs of the publishing business, resulting in a substantial reduction in overdraft. These figures reflect the policies initiated by Mr Cass and the vigour with which he has applied and continues to apply them.

By the end of 1972, the publishing overdraft was only one ninth of the forecast figure, and less than one fifth of the overdraft at the same date in the previous year. By January 1973, the Publishing Division had a positive bank balance, and by April the whole Press was back 'in the black'.

After considering the 1972 Press Accounts, the two University Financial Board representatives were able to say:

It is gratifying that the measures introduced and vigorously pursued in 1972 have so rapidly produced such a radical change in the financial position of the Publishing Division.

Taken as a whole, the profitability and financial strength of the Press improved vastly in 1972 and this improvement has continued into 1973. The Syndics and the staff of the Press merit warm commendation on this substantial achievement.

During 1972 there was much discussion between Lord Todd, Geoffrey Cass, and Trevor Gardner – who were the Cambridge members of the special Sub-Committee – about the management structure of the Press as a whole, which still lacked a chief co-ordinating officer. Sir Gordon Sutherland, the Chairman of the Printing Sub-Syndicate and Master of Emmanuel, and Professor Brian Reddaway, the Chairman of the Publishing Sub-Syndicate, were involved in these discussions. The two businesses were still operating 'at arm's length', which, in view of the current crisis, seemed even less sensible than before.

On 11 April 1972, Todd presented to the Syndicate a short paper on 'The Organisation of the Cambridge University Press' which began:

I have been giving a good deal of thought recently to the organisation of the Press. The recent death of Mr Arthur Gray [Printer Designate, who had been going to succeed Brooke Crutchley] and the impending retirement or resignation of several members of the Printing and Publishing Sub-Syndicates makes this a peculiarly appropriate time to look at the whole question of organisation and decide the lines on which we wish to proceed before making any new appointments. Our present system is clearly unsatisfactory owing largely to a lack of definition of function of the various bodies and individuals concerned, and, consequently, a diffuse management structure. The main object of the Press, as I see it, is to publish works of scholarship as part of the educational function of the University. The Syndicate must remain very concerned that this primary object is always kept in mind, and they must continue to exercise the supervision which they have traditionally maintained over editorial policy. But recent events have made us uncomfortably aware of the necessity of running the Press efficiently as a business if we are to have the resources to carry out this function and indeed to expand it as we would all hope to do. While, therefore, I envisage that the Syndics must maintain a firm grip on editorial policy, I believe it is in everyone's interest that the business side should be run on competent business lines.

Our basic difficulty is that the Press Syndicate tries to do two things at once – to act as book-choosing Committee on the one hand and a Board of Directors handling financial and policy matters on the other. Its constitution makes it, on the whole, much more effective in the first than in the second capacity. This has, of course, led to the creation some months ago of a Finance Committee consisting of myself as Chairman, with the University Treasurer, Sir Alan Wilson, Sir Robert Taylor and Mr Geoffrey Cass to handle the business affairs of the Press as a whole and to report to the Syndics. The fact that this Committee had been established by the Syndics was, incidentally, very helpful in persuading the Financial Board to underwrite a much needed increase in our overdraft facilities. The Committee has, I believe, been working effectively and, suitably enlarged, it could, in my view, fulfil the role of a board of directors for the business side of the Press while remaining subject ultimately to the authority of the Syndics to whom it would formally report. The delegation of such authority as is needed by the Finance Committee is already permitted by existing ordinances, but it would be necessary for the Syndics to authorise the appointment of a

Managing Director/Chief Executive of the Press who would carry the ultimate executive responsibility for both the Publishing and Printing Divisions.... it is suggested that Mr Geoffrey Cass would be an excellent, and indeed obvious, choice for the position of Chief Executive.

Todd went on to propose the formal establishment of a Publishing Division and a Printing Division, each with an Executive Board:

These two Divisions should be separate in the sense that they should separately be accountable for their actions and their results. The Divisions cannot really be regarded as completely separate companies; they are in fact wholly-owned subsidiaries of the parent C.U.P. and are involved in much inter-divisional trading.

He suggested that the need for Printing and Publishing Sub-Syndicates would disappear, but proposed that their respective Chairmen, Sir Gordon Sutherland and Professor Reddaway, and also the University Publisher (Richard David) and the University Printer (Brooke Crutchley) – as the heads of the two Divisions – should become members of the 'Finance Committee', as the special Sub-Committee had come to be called. He proposed a number of resolutions to the Press Syndicate, of which the principal ones were:

That the Syndics confirm the delegation to the Finance Committee of authority to control the financial and business affairs of the Press and to supervise the Publishing and Printing Divisions, in accordance with policies laid down by the Syndicate.

That Mr Geoffrey Cass be appointed Managing Director and Chief Executive of the Press with executive authority over both the printing and publishing sections of the business.

The Chairman's proposals were approved by the Press Syndicate on 22 September 1972. The proposals were also supported by the representatives of the Financial Board who examined the 1971 Press Accounts on 10 November 1972:

These developments are of vital importance and we endorse the need for them to be pursued vigorously in order to reach a stable financial position. We have already drawn attention to the very welcome reduction in the 1972 overdraft compared with the forecast.

The success of these developments... is clearly of the greatest importance for the future of the Press.

Once again the Press had a chief officer, but the overall executive authority of this new post of Chief Executive of the Press was much more inclusive and more clearly defined than at any previous time. As the Syndicate's report of 1 November 1972 to the Financial Board put it:

> ...executive responsibility for the entire business of the Press [is] in the hands of Mr Cass as Chief Executive....

The title of 'Secretary of the Press Syndicate' was not considered appropriate for a proper executive head of the Press, and this title continued to be held by the University Treasurer, until it was added to Geoffrey Cass's title, in 1974.

The Publisher, Richard David, and the Printer, Brooke Crutchley, now reported to Geoffrey Cass as Chief Executive, and were responsible to him for the operations of their Divisions. Each of them chaired a Divisional Executive Board of Directors. The two Sub-Syndicates were dissolved, and the Syndicate delegated supervision of the business and financial affairs of the Press to the Finance Committee. A sound structural foundation had been laid – both at Syndicate and at executive level – not merely for the resolution of the crisis but for the expansion of the Press which was to take place over the next dozen years. The framework had been strengthened; but the edifice remained the same.

Members of the Press Syndicate were probably relieved to be able to withdraw from direct detailed involvement in the Press's executive affairs and to concentrate more on editorial matters: and with evidence of improvement in the Press's financial state already visible, they would have been even more relieved if they had been able to foresee the full extent of the general economic recession of the seventies which was even then beginning to confront printing and publishing in the United Kingdom. Reorganisation had come in the nick of time. External economic conditions worsened, and the 1970s saw a series of sharp recessions accentuating a long-term decline in world trade which affected every one of the Press's markets.

Indeed it is hard to see how the Press could have survived that deterioration if it had not been forcefully turned round before

things became too bad. It could not have been completely fore-
seen in 1972 quite how bad they would be; but it was calculated
in 1983 that over the previous decade the world market for
academic monographs, which had perhaps doubled in the boom,
had then been reduced by a factor approaching three, so that the
market, having first been stronger, then became weaker than it
had been in living memory – weaker than in the War, or during
the Depression before it.

It is interesting at this point to reflect how effective had been
the role of the Financial Board in helping the University Press
out of its crisis. By Statute and Ordinance, the Press Syndicate
has total control over the running of the Press, and the University
in effect treats the Press as a trust, with a distinct identity,
operating within the University. But the University has always
preserved its sovereignty by retaining ultimate powers to control
the Press's borrowing, and as a last resort to dismiss the members
of the Press Syndicate – whom of course it also appoints. It is an
excellent system for allowing a major business (if an altruistic
one) to operate successfully within a great and ancient university.
It works by exception. While the Press runs successfully, the
ultimate powers lie dormant: but if the Press runs into financial
trouble, Press borrowing rises, and the University Financial
Board's powers to limit borrowing are activated. Controlling the
purse-strings of debt gives the Financial Board even greater
powers, since it is in a position to insist on other measures as the
price for credit – as it did in 1972. Since the Board reviews the
Press's Annual Accounts each year, and since the Board's chief
officer, the University Treasurer, is *ex officio* a member of the
Press Syndicate, the Financial Board is in a good position to see
financial trouble begin to arise and to comment on it – as it did
in the early seventies.

Towards the end of 1972, Geoffrey Cass had finalised his
proposals for a new publishing management structure, and for
new appointments from outside the Press; and he presented them
to the Finance Committee. He proposed

...to get away from the geographically determined structure which had
led to the artificial division of operations between Cambridge and London,
and had inevitably produced a serious degree of polarization and tension

and he intended to give

...more managerial power and responsibility to the acquisitions editor...
and to restore the individual book to the centrally important unifying role
which was the dynamic theme and focus of most successful publishing houses.
The broken-up, departmentalized approach killed initiative, enthusiasm, and
decision-making. The mainsprings of publishing were manuscripts and books
and the excitement surrounding them – not methods, and procedures, and
departmental committees.

He had found that decision-making concerning the individual
book tended to be dispersed departmentally. He believed that
most large publishing houses were over-administered and over-
departmentalised, particularly in the USA, resulting in the
blunting and neglect of the entrepreneurial drive which created
vital publishing houses in the first place – the interest of individuals in the whole process of bringing particular types of books
to the market. The personal involvement and commitment of an
acquisitions editor over the lifetime of a book were essential –
and particularly so in a university press.

The 'global' administrative approach to publishing was rarely
successful. Cass believed that publishing success sprang from
taking right decisions at the 'micro' level, in respect of each
individual book. If entrepreneurial decisions at the 'micro' level
were correct, business success at the 'macro' level was far more
likely to follow. However, it was vital that decision-making
should be consistent and resolute over the whole range of the
Press's publishing. Anthony Wilson was appointed to the new
post of Publishing Operations Director, to oversee and coord-
inate all decisions on prices and print numbers – a move which
proved very effective.

Cass had also concluded that there was

...simply insufficient general management capacity at the highest operating
level capable of tackling the major problems of re-location, re-organization
and computerization....

Cass and David decided that the Publishing Division urgently
needed a Managing Director and a Marketing Director, and it
was felt that these two posts could be filled only from outside.
A Printer Designate was also needed to succeed Brooke Crutchley,
who was due to retire in two years' time.

The Finance Committee approved these plans, and so did the full Syndicate on 1 December 1972. The Syndicate 'authorized the Chairman and Mr Cass to conduct any negotiations and to take any action that might be necessary to implement them'.

Cass regarded new top management appointments as essential to the revival of the Press. If an altruistic enterprise was to be self-financing, in direct competition with commercial companies, then it needed a core of executives with entrepreneurial flair. Administrative abilities alone – even of high calibre – were not enough. The Press did not, like most other charities, simply administer funds which had been gathered through donations, subsidies or fund-raising. It had to earn every penny of its income through its business enterprise in the market place. It needed entrepreneurs who could adjust their business approach to take account of the special objectives and problems of a charitable enterprise, and who could live happily with them.

The first new appointment was that of David Knight as Marketing Director in February 1973. An Oxford graduate, Knight had extensive high-level international marketing experience with McGraw Hill, Allen and Unwin, and Weidenfeld and Nicolson. This was quickly followed by the appointment of Philip Allin in October 1973 as Managing Director of the Publishing Division. Allin, a graduate of Trinity College, Cambridge, had like Cass been a management consultant with Personnel Administration Ltd in the sixties, but joined the Press from the Components Group of International Telephone and Telegraph (ITT) in which he had been Regional Director for the United Kingdom, Scandinavia and Iberia. To assist the integration of the new 'Publishing Division', Allin based himself in the London office. He at once began to tackle three important objectives: to unify and motivate the new Publishing Division team, to plan the re-location in Cambridge of the Press's London operations, and to accelerate the progress of computerisation in the Division.

The other stage in strengthening the management structure was the appointment, in April 1973, of Euan Phillips as Printer Designate. Phillips was a graduate of Emmanuel, and joined the Press from Unwin Brothers, the printers, where he had been Managing Director.

The end of 1972 had seen a massive improvement in the Press's situation. The Press Syndicate watched with something approaching awe as a dangerous situation which had seemed quite intractable was resolved. They had given Geoffrey Cass sweeping powers, and had not known quite what to expect, but to their relief there had been no great dramas, no mass redundancies or closures, editorial policy had been unaffected, and scholarly publishing output was actually increasing. After examining the 1972 Press Accounts, the Financial Board representatives commented:

We noted with satisfaction that the improvement in profitability was secured without detriment to the publishing programme; indeed the Press increased its output of new books in 1972. We understand that C.U.P. is the only major academic press which achieved this in a year which...was a very bad period for academic publishing in general.

The Chief Executive was now able to turn his attention to matters other than mere survival. At the beginning of 1973 he effected a complete restructuring of the Annual Accounts, with the assistance of Peter Hodgson – soon to become Financial Director of the Press – and introduced a new version of the Annual Report, measures which were regarded by the Syndicate's Finance Committee as giving 'a fresh understanding of the total structure and the financial framework of the Press'. To strengthen the links between the Publishing Division and the Printing Division, he arranged for Philip Allin to be a member of the Printing Board, and for Euan Phillips to join the Publishing Board. This provided an authoritative voice from each Division at the meetings of the other.

In 1974, Brooke Crutchley retired as University Printer and was succeeded by Phillips. Crutchley had built a great reputation in the world of printing, and his period of office had seen the vital move of the Printing House to its new premises on the site in Shaftesbury Road, which was soon to be the home of both businesses. Phillips inherited the difficult set of problems mentioned earlier. There was still an acute shortage of printing work, and the printing business was overstaffed, given the market conditions. The real value of the Press's printing sales (at constant prices) had fallen by 17 % between 1971 and 1973. The numbers printed of individual publications were falling rapidly throughout the industry, and shortage of craftsmen made it difficult for the printing business to react properly to the imbalance between composition and printing and binding.

Richard David also retired in 1974. His unselfish vision had served the Press well, and the transition to a new management had occurred on his initiative, and with his cooperation and friendship. All who manage a historic trust – and the Press is such a trust, like the Colleges and the University itself – must want at the end of their trusteeship to leave the enterprise in a better state than that in which they found it: and the decisive action taken in 1971 and 1972 had secured that.

David retired as University Publisher – head of the Publishing Division – and now a further organisational change took place. Philip Allin became head of the Division (under his existing title of Managing Director) and Chairman of the Board of the Division. The title of University Publisher, which had existed for only a few years, passed to me, and was now used to describe the editorial director, and not the head of the Division. The University Publisher was given an additional direct reporting link to the Chief Executive outside the normal command structure, to reflect the special importance of the editorial function in the operations of the University Press.

In 1973, the rate of inflation in the United Kingdom began to rise alarmingly. Publishers, and especially academic publishers, were caught between the pressures of high costs and high prices. The Press began to develop its policy to meet the inflationary threat. In the 1973 Annual Report, Philip Allin as Managing Director of the Publishing Division of the Press, wrote:

The market for academic books is now more difficult than at any time since the war. Characteristically the university press book appeals to a small audience dispersed throughout the world. Price rises due to inflation mean that the individual purchaser relies more and more on the library, but the same price rises mean that libraries which bought freely in the 1960s now pick and choose much more carefully. It has been clear for several years that sales are affected by this development, especially in the second and sub-

[ 262 ]

sequent years after publication – the 'backlist' years which have in the past produced a high proportion of the Press's turnover.

[The Press] will have to work harder to produce other books less dependent on institutional sale, that is with an individual academic sale, or a semi-popular, or a classroom sale. More specifically it is also intended to increase publishing in the sciences and social sciences, and reorganisation and new appointments are being made to that end. Our largest single export market is the USA, and it is proposed to increase the number of books coming from US authors...

Globally, the strategy remains what it has been: to have a central editorial policy which actively seeks books with a potential international sale, presents them to the Syndics in Cambridge, and then markets them throughout the world.

1974 and 1975 were significant years for the Press in many ways. The rate of inflation moved into double figures in 1974 and actually reached 16%: yet even this figure was dwarfed by the 24% of 1975. Some printing and publishing costs were increasing by more than these figures, by up to 30% or 40%. British industry was at a very low ebb. Many concerns were facing liquidity crises, and a lot were forced out of business altogether. Publishers and printers were having a particularly hard time of it, and cash shortages were forcing most publishers to cut their publishing programmes. The Press had generated cash reserves just in time. The problem now was how to retain the ground that had been gained, while confronting cost inflation which far exceeded normal sales growth. Geoffrey Cass outlined the future policy of the Press in his Annual Report on the 1974 Accounts:

No organisation has a magic way of maintaining its viability in the face of 20% to 40% increases in costs. The gap between average growth in sales income of 10% per annum and increases in costs of 20% to 40% can only be bridged by either retrenchment or real growth. Inflation cannot be countered by pricing policy alone, particularly since the UK inflation rate is higher than in most other parts of the world in which we sell. Prices could not automatically follow current costs in book publishing, either in timing, or size, or frequency. Retrenchment – although adopted by many publishers – is neither a dynamic nor a long-term answer. In any case, retrenchment would be the last resort of a university press dedicated to the spread of knowledge. The only acceptable solution consistent with the objectives of the Press is real growth accompanied by an increase in productivity. The Press is accordingly planning for real growth in titles published and in numbers of books sold. While we have the cash resources we must tackle the inflationary problem with positive rather than negative measures. The long-term strategy is one of growth.

This policy had in fact already begun, and it was to continue to dominate the operations of the Press throughout the seventies and into the eighties. After their examination of the 1974 Press Accounts, the representatives of the Financial Board were already able to remark:

It would not have been surprising, albeit disappointing, for us to have found the Press suffering from the ills besetting so many concerns at this time. The contrast was startling. For instance, while the liquidity problems of much of industry and commerce are notorious, the Press has a large, and growing, positive cash balance. Or again, while other publishers are busy cutting back their lists, the Press is actively increasing the number of titles it is publishing.

The importance to the academic world of the expansion of the output of the Press when it is more and more difficult to get scholarly work published needs no emphasis.

During this period, the Press continued to take on more and more of the burden of scholarly publishing in the United Kingdom, while other UK publishers were curtailing or ceasing their efforts in this area because of the cash losses involved.

# 15

## CHARITABLE STATUS RECOGNISED

ATTENTION could now be given to major strategic considerations which hitherto had had to take second place. The Press
had been restored to financial health, its management had been
restructured, with new talent recruited from outside, and its
operational plans for the immediate future had been determined.
Cass now began to consider the taxation status of the Press.

It had always been clear to him that the Press was operating as
a charitable trust, and that it satisfied all the requirements for
tax exemption – yet it was subject to Corporation Tax. In one
sense this was very surprising: yet, in another, it was not, for he
had quickly discovered not only that people outside Cambridge
were largely ignorant of the nature, constitution and ownership
of the Press, but also that members of the University and even
of the Press itself knew less than they should about its history and
nature. Indeed, during the 1971/2 crisis he had been hard put to
find many people, either inside or outside, who realised that the
Press was an altruistic national educational institution which was
worth saving. Ironically, the fact that Cambridge, unlike Oxford,
had restricted itself rigorously to scholarly and educational publishing seemed to have contributed to the general ignorance
about the philanthropic nature of its activities. Inside the Press,
he had found a curious ambivalence of attitude, even among some
of the more senior officers. On the one hand they knew that there
was something 'special' about the Press, but on the other they
wanted to be regarded as the equivalent in effectiveness and
vigour of any general publisher. That in itself was reasonable;
what was unreasonable was that they seemed to fear that charitable status would somehow be seen as 'unbusinesslike', or that

it would be taken by others as giving the Press an unfair advantage.

Cass thought this view was illogical, and deprived the Press of its rights. Cambridge University Press was indeed virtually unique, but that uniqueness should be its strength. In his view, the Press was entitled to freedom from tax, and had been paying tax needlessly, at least since 1916 when the partnership had ended. Statutory provisions had been specifically provided by Parliament for the exemption from tax of the trading of charitable organisations, for good reasons based on the special nature of charities. Charitable privileges were not something to be ashamed of, or sensitive about. A charitable organisation was entitled to tax exemption, provided that its trading satisfied the strict provisions of the law. Cass examined the various reasons advanced for not seeking tax exemption and regarded none of them as valid, and most of them as pusillanimous. It had been variously argued that there might have to be legal proceedings which would draw unfavourable attention to the Press or to the University; that tax exemption would be bad for the standing of the Press (and its officers) in the printing and publishing trades, and that this would damage relations with other organisations; that charitable status would limit the Press's field of activity; that seeking tax exemption might endanger the University's funding from the government and be a threat to the University's own tax immunity; and, finally, that the Press had tried to secure exemption from tax in 1940, had failed, and therefore hadn't a case. All these reasons had been voiced at one time or another in Press Syndicate meetings, and there was evidence that similar gloomy views had been expressed at Oxford in respect of Oxford University Press.

Over the years since the war, scarcely anyone had actively supported the idea of positive action, one of the few exceptions being Trevor Gardner. The Press's professional advisers tended to favour the idea, but no one had taken any purposeful steps. Lord Todd proved to be another ally, and he supported Cass's determination to obtain freedom from tax for the Press. As a preliminary investigation preceding possible new copyright legislation, the Whitford Committee on Copyright had sought submissions from publishers. The Press had a special interest in the matter because of its privileged position under the Letters Patent as Bible publisher, and in 1974 Cass submitted to the Committee a detailed statement which necessarily rested on an analysis of the constitution, the nature, and the history of the Press – the essential core of the earlier chapters of this book, and starting from the Letters Patent of King Henry VIII granted in 1534. That analysis also proved to be the starting point of the more fundamental analysis which occupied Cass for a significant part of 1975.

On 25 October 1974, he got the Press Syndicate's authority to challenge the 1972 Corporation Tax Assessment on the Press, and to contest the decision made in 1940 by the Special Commissioners of the Inland Revenue. On 29 October 1974, he informed the Vice-Chancellor of this move, as a preliminary to possible litigation. In this way the Press embarked on the final step in the clarification of its nature and status: resolving the last anomaly which had remained undisturbed since 1916, and which had been lived with for so long that it had come to seem natural. That dangerous complacency was now dispelled.

Examination of the 1940 case showed that the Special Commissioners had denied the claim for exemption on the ground that, since the Press was printing and publishing for the outside world and not simply for the internal use of the University, the Press's trade went beyond the purpose and objects of the University and (in terms of the Act) was not exercised in the course of the actual carrying out of a primary purpose of the University; though the Commissioners conceded that the publishing so conducted was 'specialized and devoted to the production of works of learning'.

The decision was evidently based on a set of misconceptions, and readers of this history are in a position to wonder how a University activity, devoted to the advancement of learning and religion, first instigated and then continuously controlled by the University for nearly four hundred years, in accordance with the Letters Patent granted in 1534 at the University's own request, could fail to be within the purpose and objects of the University. Furthermore, the whole history of Cambridge since the Commissions of the nineteenth century was of a body which in science and the humanities served the cause of research and learning, which is not domestic but international. The old formula, 'education, religion, learning and research', necessarily carried a missionary implication in schools, in parishes, in other universities, in libraries, in research establishments; and books and journals were the primary communications which supplemented and made permanent the spoken word of teaching. Moreover, the Press had from its earliest times recognised as a prime function the general publication of learned works which commercial publishers would not undertake.

However, there is some excuse for the Special Commissioners' classic misjudgement. In 1940 the case had been presented half-heartedly, with little in the way of supporting evidence or constructive argument, and with virtually no reference to the long history of the Press, to its charters, or to relevant legal decisions registered in the Press's favour over the centuries. The Press was advised by Counsel in 1940 to appeal against the decision, but did not, partly for the patriotic reasons mentioned earlier, and partly because the Press did not wish to appear to be 'claiming an unfair advantage' over other publishing houses during the war.

Cass could only see the 1940 case as a false start, too easily discouraged. Clearly, the definition of the University's purposes which was implied in the Commissioners' decision was wrong – and it would be relatively easy to prove that. The Commissioners had not been made sufficiently aware of the Press's history, which was itself the best way of showing how it had reached a status which should give it exemption.

Exemption from Corporation Tax is available under the Income and Corporation Taxes Act for the profits arising from any trade carried on by a charity, provided that the profits are solely applied to the purposes of the charity and provided that the trade is exercised in the course of the actual carrying out of a primary purpose of the charity. For the purposes of the Act, a 'charity' means any body of persons or any trust established for charitable purposes only. Cass's initial analysis, made between 1972 and 1974, had identified in his own mind several features of the

Press's constitution and operations which brought it within the ambit of the Act.

First, it was wholly owned by, and an integral part of, the University of Cambridge – itself a charity. The Press was established and governed under the Statutes and Ordinances of the University.

Second, from the constitutional and legal point of view the Press itself had no separate corporate status, apart from 'the Chancellor, Masters, and Scholars of the University of Cambridge'. 'Cambridge University Press' was therefore simply the style under which the University of Cambridge printed and published.

Third, the University of Cambridge had carried on the trade of printing and publishing for nearly four hundred years, and there had been an unbroken succession of University Printers since 1534. The Press was, so far as could be ascertained, the oldest press in the world.

Fourth, the governing body of the Press – the Press Syndicate – was quite unlike any board of directors in ordinary commercial life. It was appointed by, and dismissible by, the Council of the Senate of the University. The members of the Press Syndicate were unpaid; they governed the Press as representatives of the Chancellor, Masters, and Scholars of the University, and had done so since 1698. Before that, the Press had been directly governed by the Vice-Chancellor and the College Heads. Members of the Syndicate had no private financial interest in the Press, and represented the ultimate in gratuitous professional control. They were Masters of Cambridge Colleges, Professors and senior academics of the University. As at all meetings of important University committees and Syndicates, at meetings of the Press Syndicate academic gowns were worn both by members of the Syndicate and by the executive officers of the Press to signify that they were conducting the University's business. The Vice-Chancellor of the University, or his Deputy, chaired the Press Syndicate, and the University Treasurer was also a member of the Syndicate, *ex officio*.

Fifth, every publication of the Press had to be individually presented to and approved by the Press Syndicate on behalf of the

University before it could be printed and published. This was no mere formality, since the appraisal was academically rigorous. The process was the modern equivalent of approval by the Vice-Chancellor and three doctors, required in 1534. The officers of the Press had power to reject publications, but they had no power to accept them.

Sixth, publication by the Press Syndicate was approved on the ground of the contribution which the Syndicate judged that publication would make to the advancement of knowledge, education, or religion. It followed that the publications of the Press were exclusively scholarly, educational, or religious. The Press complemented and extended the research and teaching activities of the University by making available world-wide, through its printing and publishing, an extensive range of academic and educational books, learned journals, Bibles and prayer books, and examination papers. On this analysis, the objectives of the Press were patently charitable. 'Profit' as such was not considered or required by the Syndicate. They were concerned only with the viability of the Press, now and in the future, as the condition of its ability to continue to pursue its scholarly objectives.

Seventh, the Press had since 1916 had no partners, shareholders or investors who stood to gain financially from its operations. All funds held by the Press, all funds received by it, and all funds generated by it, were ploughed back into further scholarly, educational, and religious publishing. There could not now be any distribution of 'profit' or assets to any persons or bodies of persons: therefore no commercial motive or motive of private pecuniary gain intruded. Moreover, the Press's integrity was fully protected by its constitutional status. It could not be bought or taken over.

Eighth, even the University itself now made no call on the Press's funds, though any such call would itself have been charitable. The last significant contribution of the Press to the University had been the foundation of the Pitt Professorship in 1944, and that obviously charitable gesture had been on its own initiative. The printing and publishing activity of the Press *was* its prime purpose. That activity was not carried out to secure 'profit' or funds, even for some other charitable purpose – not even to secure funds for the parent University. The University chose to perpetuate and finance the charitable printing and publishing activity out of the funds raised from that activity. In effect, these were wholly at the service of the world-wide academic and educational community for the dissemination of knowledge and religion through the printed word.

Ninth, the Press was self-financing. Apart from the historic and by now merely symbolic annual grant of £500, it received no government income or regular grants or subsidies of any sort. It had to generate its own funds in order to pursue its objectives. The Press's activities were entirely for public benefit, but it was not a drain on public funds.

Tenth, the American Branch of the Press was in fact exempt from all US taxes.

On all these grounds, Geoffrey Cass felt convinced that the University Press could only be considered a self-financing charitable trust, established and controlled by, and existing within, another charity – the University of Cambridge – but with a distinct self-contained identity and financial integrity of its own. The Press's own objectives were clearly charitable, and its activities also directly fulfilled the University's wider primary purposes, and had been recognised to be doing so for centuries. The Press, charitable in itself, and also part of a greater charity, seemed nonetheless to lie in a curious no-man's-land. Though an integral part of the University, it was treated as a separate entity, as a 'company', by the Inland Revenue for taxation purposes. The 1940 claim had failed, unreasonably, on the judgement whether the activities of the Press were carrying out a primary purpose of the University, not whether the activities themselves were intrinsically charitable or were in pursuit of a primary charitable purpose. The judgement had taken a very narrow view of the University's own purposes. But the absurdity was that the Commissioners' views had the effect (within the law) of rendering the Press's relationship to the University an actual handicap; for the Press's own primary purpose was charitable, and its activities carried out that primary purpose. In other words, the Press, viewed alone, qualified for exemption even in 1940. Much of course depended on exactly what case the Inland Revenue was asked to consider. Cass suspected that, because of the particular way in which the exemption clauses were framed in the legislation, the Press's 1940 appeal against tax might have been attempting the more difficult of what he saw as *two* possible routes to the deserved exemption – more difficult because there was no formal statutory definition of the University's purposes.

To check his own opinions about the Press's position, Cass took preliminary advice from the Press's solicitors, who made helpful suggestions. They too believed that the Press had a strong case, and they had discussed the issue with the Press's auditors, who also thought the Press should contest its tax status. Cass then retired to the University Archives for weeks, where he worked both on the Press's history and on key material relevant to a study of the University's own objectives.

The product of his research was a submission to the Inland Revenue. It described itself as a 'preliminary statement' rather than a formal submission of the Press's case; nonetheless it was a fairly massive document. The District Inspector of Taxes, who was the initial addressee, must have quailed a little when he received some sixty typewritten pages, dated 21 November 1975, and a little more when he read, at the end of Geoffrey Cass's letter:

This letter is not our formal submission: but there seems to me no reason nevertheless why it could not provide a basis for an Inland Revenue decision to exempt the Press, at this stage. Our formal submission, when completed in the Spring, is likely to be several hundred times bigger than this letter. Yet the complete dossier of evidence and historical documents will, in the main, merely reinforce each of the key points of this letter a hundred times over. I have extracted for this letter the crucial items which would determine the case.

As that extract suggests, the submission took the form of a detailed legal and historical argument in which the nature of the Press's activity was analysed both as something given from the very beginning and as something which had evolved. In essence the historical account was a summary of the archival material now used in the early chapters of this book, and it quoted crucial documents, such as the charters, and the comments of contemporary observers. The legal argument was designed to provide a completely new approach to the crux of the 1940 case, which was whether the Press's trade was exercised in the course of the actual carrying out of a primary purpose of the University.

Cass set out to advance two main theses. The first was concerned with this crux, considered the University itself, and was divided into two arguments. The first of these was that the activities of printing and publishing scholarly and religious work for markets outside Cambridge were, *de facto*, a primary purpose of the University of Cambridge, because the University had as a matter of historical fact pursued such activities for nearly four hundred years, on royal authority, confirmed at various times during the four centuries by legal decisions at the highest levels. The second argument was that the trade of printing and publishing scholarly and religious works was exercised in the course of carrying out the University's wider primary purposes: the advancement of education, religion, learning and research, including the dissemination and diffusion of knowledge beyond the confines of the University itself. Those purposes could not be confined to what happened 'within the walls' of Cambridge, and never had been. The general dissemination of knowledge was a necessary part of the advancement of education and learning.

The second main thesis broke away from the ground of the 1940 case altogether, and considered the Press by itself: this particular argument did not rely on relating the activities of the Press to a primary purpose of the University. It contended that the primary purposes of the University Press itself in respect of its printing and publishing, quite apart from the Press's connection with the University, were themselves wholly charitable. They fell within the second head (the advancement of education and learning), the third head (the advancement of religion) and probably the fourth head (other purposes for the benefit of the community) of the recognised charitable purposes established by the preamble to the Charitable Uses Act of 1601 as re-stated by Lord Macnaghten in Pemsel's Case (1891). The Press was clearly established 'for charitable purposes only', and therefore already qualified for charitable status. It was entitled to tax exemption in its own right. Furthermore, if the Press had had corporate status distinct from the University it could without difficulty have obtained independent registration as a charity. If it had been a separate charity, the question whether it was carrying out a primary purpose of the University would not have been an issue. It would however be absurd for part of an existing charity to have to seek separate charitable registration solely in order to secure tax exemption for patently charitable activities which were in any case prime purposes of its parent charity – which itself qualified as a charity under the same charitable heads.

The submission had three main sections: one consisted of evidence and argument bearing on the history and role of printing and publishing within the University and on the objectives of the Press throughout that history; the second comprised evidence and argument about the objectives of the University of Cambridge; the third outlined the key features of the Press's constitution and operations. Other sections cited relevant legal judgements in support of the Press's case, outlined the differences between the Press and other publishers, analysed the physical output of Cambridge University Press, compared the tax status of its overseas branches, and drew final conclusions. The whole was supported by evidence and quotation from the historical record.

Cass assembled a dossier of items of evidence from royal, legal, constitutional, parliamentary, and University documentary sources. The historical analysis naturally began with the royal charters: the Letters Patent of 1534, and the later grant of 1628. Of the first Cass said:

...it was never envisaged for a moment by either the University or the King that the University's publishing and printing was only for the 'internal use of the University'. The Royal Charter specifically referred to...books being sold 'as well in the same University as elsewhere in our realm, wherever they please'. Furthermore, the University's Stationers and Printers could only print books ('omnimodos libros' – 'all manner of books') that had been approved by the Chancellor of the University or his Vice-Chancellor and three doctors. In relation to the question of establishing whether printing and publishing works of learning for use outside the University is a prime purpose of the University, and whether dissemination of knowledge by printing and publishing works of learning is in general a prime purpose of the University, it would be *impossible* to find more compelling evidence than this Royal Charter speaking to us across 441 years of history. It is an authority which has been effective since what the lawyers refer to as 'time out of mind'. If this is *not* an incontestable establishment of a prime purpose, it makes nonsense of the concept. There is, however, no doubt at all historically what view the Courts – from the House of Lords downwards – have taken of this Royal Charter over the last four and a half centuries.

He went on to point out that when, on 6 February 1628, Charles I had granted further Letters Patent to the University under the Great Seal of England, it was 'to advance learning and end all controversies'. The King had 'ratified and confirmed unto the Chancellor, Masters, and Scholars of the University of Cambridge, all and every of the Privileges and Immunities by the said Letters Patent of 20th July 1534 Henry VIII to them granted'. These Letters Patent contained a significant amplification, empowering the University's stationers and printers to sell their books 'as well within the said University *as elsewhere within any of his Majesty's Dominions*'. The clear statement that the issue was concerned with the advancement of learning was linked to a direct indication that the output of University printing and publishing was not confined within the walls of Cambridge.

Naturally, the submission quoted the important comment of William Dillingham, who introduced the word 'trust' into the whole discussion:

The University'es priviledge is looked upon as a trust for the public good...

Another crucial quotation used the words of Mr Justice Foster of the King's Bench, writing in 1755 (p. 109):

...we consider the Powers given by the Letters Patent as a trust reposed in [the University], for public Benefit, for the Advancement of Literature. ...I hope both the Universities will always consider the royal Grants in that light.

Cass also quoted James I, who in confirming Henry VIII's Letters Patent (which had been ratified and confirmed by Elizabeth) accepted

...this policy of our ancestors as being both salutary for the commonwealth and favourable for the advancement of knowledge.

Another source was the Almanac Duty Act of 1781. Referring to the use made by the University of this money (then a substantial sum) in printing and publishing, the Act of Parliament read:

AND WHEREAS the money so received by them has been laid out and expended in promoting different Branches of Literature and Science, to the great Increase of Religion and Learning, and the general Benefit and Advantage of these Realmes. . . .

The reader will remember that the charitable nature of the Press had been stressed at the opening of the Pitt Building. Cass also quoted the speeches made at the earlier laying of the foundation stone: for instance, Lord Camden, reflecting on the future of the building, had said that he trusted

. . . that it will be the means of diffusing more generally the knowledge which the Press of Cambridge University has hitherto been so pre-eminent in doing . . . [and that] . . . the knowledge diffused will be planted on the foundations of true religion, and of all those sciences for which this University has long been so distinguished.

The 'public interest' was also in the mind of Lord Eldon, the Lord Chancellor, in 1802 when he gave judgement in favour of the University in its dispute with the then Royal Printers about the printing of the Bible. After considering the construction put by Courts of Law upon the Letters Patent of 1534, he concluded:

my opinion is that the public interest may be looked to upon a subject, the communication of which to the public in an authentic shape, if a matter of right, is also a matter of duty in the Crown, which are commensurate. The principle of the law is that this duty and this right are better executed and protected by a publication of Books of this species in England, by persons confided in by Letters Patent under the Great Seal of England.

It was a necessary part of the Press's submission that the dissemination of knowledge beyond Cambridge itself had always been one of the University's purposes. It was evident that the creation and advancement of knowledge and then the transmission of it merely to a select few would be self-defeating. Cass quoted President Butler, of Columbia University, in his 1917–18 Report:

A university has three functions to perform. It is to conserve knowledge; to advance knowledge; and to disseminate knowledge. It falls short of the full realization of its aim unless, having provided for the conservation and advancement of knowledge, it makes provision for its dissemination as well.

He went on to quote the words of Dr A. W. Ward, later Sir Adolphus Ward, Master of Peterhouse, editor of the *Cambridge Modern History* and the *Cambridge History of English Literature*, Syndic of the Press and Vice-Chancellor's Deputy as Chairman of the Syndicate, in his speech at the end of his term of office as Vice-Chancellor of Cambridge University on 1 October 1902:

> The researches and studies single-mindedly pursued inside and outside our laboratories and libraries by resident members of this University and by students and scholars whom this University has trained form the chief motive element in its intellectual life and the most potent factor of its national and international significance. Nor have I any hesitation in adding my belief that the University Press, as a main agent in making the results of these researches and studies known within and beyond our local limits, will in future become of more importance than ever as an organic branch of our academical activities.

Two years later, in 1904, Ward had inevitably taken part in the formal discussion in the Senate House of the Report of the Syndicate on the future of the partnership with the Clays. Speaking now as representative of the Syndicate, he came naturally to the theme of 'the advancement of learning' as part of the topic of discussion, namely,

> the management of one of the most important of the agencies which [the University] has at its command for this very purpose.

Ward went on to say that there was one thing 'which for my part I consider fundamental – that it is the duty of the University to utilise the Press for the publication of contributions, as such, to the advancement of science and learning'. And he referred to the University Press as directly affecting 'some of the highest and widest of the purposes which the University desires to serve'.

Cass also quoted the University's own view of the charitable nature of the University Press's activities, as made clear in a Joint Memorandum submitted to the Secretary of State by the University of Cambridge and the University of Oxford in 1911. The Joint Memorandum referred to 'the benefits arising to education and learning through the agency of the University Presses', adding:

The Universities have built up great organisations for the production and sale, not only of [Bibles and prayer books] but of books that promote the general cause of education and learning...

...as they do not work for private profit they are able to devote year after year considerable sums to important works which are not immediately remunerative or not remunerative at all, and which no other publisher would undertake unless with the assistance of a subsidy...

...[the Presses] have discharged their obligations faithfully and to the public advantage....

The submission dealt elsewhere with the Special Commissioners' implicit contention of 1940 that the University of Cambridge could not be concerned with 'printing and publishing for the outside world'. Cass dismissed this, saying:

The primary concern of Cambridge University for the general advancement of knowledge and learning, rather than for simply local teaching, is manifest in all the historical evidence. Cambridge University is not, and never has been, a factory for producing students with degrees...

History clearly shows that Cambridge University itself has throughout been concerned with the advancement of learning in the noble, global sense – rather than in the sense of educating its own scholars. The history of the University is utterly consistent on this point. The purposes are always expressed in the broadest, most comprehensive terms; and there is not the slightest suggestion in seven hundred years of history that the pursuit of them is geographically confined within the 'walls' of Cambridge University. The local education of students is merely one of the University's functions.

He supported the contention with this firm statement from the Report of the 1922 Royal Commission on Oxford and Cambridge Universities:

The University has two main functions to perform. It must provide the best possible teaching for [its students]...and it must also make provision for the advancement of knowledge.

From his study of the history of the University, and the attitudes adopted towards it and embodied in statutory documents by successive monarchs, judges, commissioners and parliaments, Cass then attempted a definition of the University's prime purposes. The reordering of the words in the traditional central phrase was meant to reflect modern emphases:

...the acquisition, advancement, conservation and dissemination of knowledge in all subjects; the advancement of learning, education, research and religion; and the advancement of literature and good letters.

He argued that the Press's activities were a necessary, as well as a *de facto* part of the attainment of these purposes; and the Press's printing and publishing directly satisfied them.

The submission then examined the anomaly of the taxation of the Press from several different angles. For instance, the American Branch of the Press – far bigger in terms of sales than any American university press – was exempt from all American tax: yet its income was taxed in the United Kingdom when it was transmitted back. American tax law treated income from a university press as exempt in the ordinary case precisely because 'it would be derived from an activity that is substantially related to the purposes of the university'. It had always been accepted by the US authorities that the principal purpose of the activities of Cambridge University Press was 'to further the purpose for which the [university] is granted exemption'. Cass commented:

It is faintly amusing that the Press of the ancient University of Cambridge can obtain exemption for its publishing activities in the United States of America yet does not possess such privileges in Great Britain; and that a foreign country can perceive for tax purposes, and act upon, fundamental features of an organization which remain unrecognized in its native land.

The submission then went on to cite relevant legal judgements to support the charitable nature of the Press's printing and publishing activities. Extracts from the Court of Appeal judgement of 1971 in respect of the appeal for registration as a charity by the Incorporated Council of Law Reporting were particularly important, since the points at issue in that judgement were virtually identical to those in the Press's case:

The element of unselfishness is well recognized as an aspect of charity, and an important one. Suppose on the one hand a company which publishes the Bible for the profit of its directors and shareholders: plainly the company would not be established for charitable purposes. But suppose an association or company which is non-profit making, whose members or directors are forbidden to benefit from its activities, and whose object is to publish the Bible: equally plainly it would seem to me that the main object of the association or company would be charitable – the advancement or promotion of religion.

(Lord Justice Russell)

Secondly, it is clear that the mere fact that charges on a commercial scale are made for services rendered by an institution does not of itself bar that institution from being held to be charitable – so long, at any rate, as all the profits must be retained for its purposes, and none can enure to the benefit of its individual members.

(Lord Justice Sachs)

Where the purpose of producing a book is to enable a specified subject, and a learned subject at that, to be studied, it is, in my judgement, published for the advancement of education, as this, of course, includes as regards the Statute of Elizabeth I the advancement of learning.

(Lord Justice Sachs)

For the present purpose the second head [the advancement of education] should be regarded as extending to the improvement of a useful branch of human knowledge and its public dissemination.

(Lord Justice Buckley)

...the members of the council, who are not more than 20 or so in number at any one time, are precluded by the council's constitution from obtaining any profit or benefit as members from its activities. The council's publications can be bought by the general public and are, as the evidence shows, bought by a wide variety of users, including academic bodies, commercial and industrial bodies (including public utility undertakings), public authorities, government and public departments and offices, trade unions, and a wide variety of libraries, professional institutes and miscellaneous bodies, as well as a great many bodies and persons concerned with the administration and practice of the law, and all of these not merely in this country but also in many other countries within the Commonwealth and elsewhere.

(Lord Justice Buckley)

Although the objects of the council are commercial in the sense that the council exists to publish and sell its publications, they are unselfregarding. The members are prohibited from deriving any profit from the council's activities, and the council itself, although not debarred from making a profit out of its business, can only apply any such profit in the further pursuit of its objects. The council is consequently not prevented from being a charity by reason of any commercial element in its activities. I therefore reach the conclusion that the council is a body established exclusively for charitable purposes and is entitled to be registered under the Act of 1960.

(Lord Justice Buckley)

Since every one of those remarks could with great aptness have applied to the University Press – or rather to the Press Syndicate – Cass believed that they pointed to the wholly charitable nature of the Press's activities, and also supported his thesis that the

Press, had it not been part of the University, could easily have obtained its own registration as a charity, and that for the purposes of the Income and Corporation Taxes Act, the Press Syndicate was a body of persons (or a trust) established by the University for charitable purposes only, and therefore qualified for tax exemption by reference to its own primary purpose. However, he was also confident that the submission proved that the Press's charitable activities fell squarely within the University's primary purposes.

Cass did not know which of his two theses might carry the day, but he believed that he had provided more than sufficient evidence in his sixty-page letter to demonstrate that there was no possibility that the Courts would uphold the 1940 decision of the Commissioners. The virtual uniqueness of the Press meant that a decision in its favour would create no general precedent. Because of this, and in view of the strength of the Press's case, he hoped that the matter could be settled without legal proceedings. He concluded his letter with his genial threat to overwhelm the Inspector with several hundred times more evidence, and as a neat final historical touch, added this envoi, as a last sheet to the letter:

Forasmuch as learning hath antiently had this spetiall favour and priviledge, that upon any occasion of grievance, or complaint offered unto the Two Universities of this Realme, whensoever they have made their immediate recourse to the King or his Councell for speedie redresse and for avoyding length and charges of suit in an ordinary legal proceeding of Justice, they have never beene refused, but allwayes gratiously accepted.

> From an Order of the Lords of the Privy Council, in favour of the Vice-Chancellor of Cambridge University, October 21st 1612. Confirmed by Decree of the House of Lords, May 12th 1647.

Fortunately, the 'formal submission' was never needed. Throughout the case, the Inland Revenue officials were most courteous and helpful. Geoffrey Cass met the District Inspector. A further letter of a mere twenty-three pages, dated 18 December 1975, clarified certain details. The whole matte. was then passed up to the Inland Revenue Policy Division at Somerset House in London, and the Revenue's own legal advisers began to consider the case.

A letter from the Inland Revenue Policy Division, dated 9 November 1976, gave Cass the momentous news that the Inland Revenue had decided to accept in principle the claim to charitable status. A further letter of 3 December confirmed the details. It seemed that Cass's second thesis had won the day. The Inland Revenue had recognised and accepted the charitable status of the Press and accordingly made tax exemption under the Income and Corporation Taxes Act available to the Press Syndicate. In terms of the Act, the Inland Revenue had accepted that the Press Syndicate was 'a body of persons or a trust established for charitable purposes only'.

The acceptance that the Press's activities were indeed charitable and exempt from tax was not only historically important. It had the practical effect of clarifying in the minds of the Syndicate and its senior officers what they were trying to do overall, so that it had value as a guiding principle in business and editorial policy. As the Chief Executive remarked in his Annual Report on the 1976 Accounts:

The second most important element [in effecting the recovery of the Press] has been the analysis and clarification of the nature, philosophy, objectives and role of the Press. It was this analysis that led to the unswerving pursuit of freedom from tax for the Press: and it was this analysis that has provided an effective reference framework for the whole of the Press's operations.

From the Press's point of view, the tax decision had three invaluable advantages: it finally removed any element of ambiguity regarding the Press's nature; it was implicitly – if belatedly – an admission that the Press was a national cultural asset; and it gave a vital boost to the Press's financial viability, liberating funds to serve the world of learning far more effectively, and assisting the long-term enterprise of building up the reserve fund which Wright and Waller and their successors had longed for, and the lack of which had at the end of the 1960s alarmed the University itself, and caused the Syndicate and staff to think that they might soon be looking into the abyss. Nothing in the Press's operations or constitution had significantly changed for some sixty years, so the decision also confirmed that the Press had possessed all the qualifications for charitable status since at least 1916.

Oxford University Press meanwhile had been cautiously waiting to see the outcome of the Cambridge case. Soon after the result was known, after consulting Cambridge, Oxford presented their own submission and eventually received similar exemption.

# 16

---

## FROM 1974 TO 1984

At the end of 1975, Lord Todd became President of the Royal Society, and resigned the chairmanship of the Syndicate. He was succeeded by Dr Morris (later Sir Morris) Sugden, F.R.S., Master of Trinity Hall, who served until his death in January 1984. Morris Sugden's period of office was also a notable one: it saw considerable expansion in the number of titles published annually; further strengthening of the Press's management team, and, more important, the new University Statute which provided a further charter for the Press; and the consolidation on a single site in Cambridge.

On his appointment as University Printer in 1974, Euan Phillips had resolutely confronted the problems besetting the Printing Division. He had recognised the threats posed by cheaper methods of composition, shortage of skilled craftsmen, and the increasingly widespread use of offset printing, and had begun corrective action. In 1975, Geoffrey Cass brought in Harris Myers, from commercial printing, as Managing Director of the Printing Division and Deputy University Printer. When towards the end of 1976 Jack Schulman retired as Director of the Press's American Branch, Phillips moved to New York to replace him. He was succeeded as University Printer by Myers, who did a great deal to bring the Printing Division into the new technological and business era, making it more efficient and more competitive. He accelerated the introduction of computer-aided composition and offset printing – both of which were badly needed. He improved the commercial awareness of the Division, particularly in respect of pricing and date-keeping, and strengthened the Division's marketing capability.

Administrative offices were moved onto the shop floor to make possible better contact and co-operation.

The installation at the University Printing House in 1978 of the Lasercomp – a phototypesetter which generates, on film or bromide paper, digitised versions of the best Monotype hot-metal typefaces – continued the trend towards modernisation, while maintaining the Press's high standard of typography. In the 1978 national book design and production exhibition, there were no fewer than seven Cambridge books amongst the fifty titles which were chosen for commendation. Only three of these were set in hot metal and printed by letterpress; the others were all produced by the latest methods. The new technology was clearly enabling the Press to maintain its high standards of design and production, while facilitating the considerable expansion in publishing output which marked the whole period after 1972. That expansion had been continuing apace. Plans to increase the volume of publishing in the sciences and social sciences were beginning to bear fruit. In 1977, for the first time, the number of scientific titles accepted by the Syndicate exceeded a hundred.

There was a further important development in the status of the Press as international publisher. European academics were beginning to want to reach a world readership, and recognised, however reluctantly, that this meant that they would either have to write in or be translated into English, or at least be published by a publisher with access to the worldwide English-language market. From the Press's point of view, Europe had now to be treated not just as a market but as a source of authors. An important step in 1977 was the establishment of a formal agreement between the Press and the Maison des Sciences de l'Homme, a government-sponsored institute in Paris, directed by the great historian Fernand Braudel and administered by Clemens Heller. Under this arrangement the Press became in effect the official publisher of a leading French intellectual agency, with an international network of scholarly relationships, sponsoring important authors in the humanities and social sciences. Books were to be published in European languages as well as in English. This proved to be a very fruitful arrangement contributing significantly to Anglo-French and Anglo-European academic entente. The output of this joint imprint had risen to ninety-two publications by the end of 1983, and the arrangement provided a model which is likely to be replicated with scholars and agencies in other countries.

Implementation of the plan to increase the number of books by American authors was also progressing well. The New York editorial department founded in the mid-1960s now began to grow more rapidly; two new appointments were made in 1977, and two Cambridge editors were seconded to New York in the autumn of 1978, starting a pattern which could include a tour of duty as well as permanent secondment.

The conscious development of the Branch reflected both its intrinsic importance to the Press and its proven effectiveness. Well founded and directed by Ronald Mansbridge and Jack Schulman, it was one of the sections of the Press which had been in good shape at the onset of the financial crisis in 1971. Jack Schulman, then Manager (later Director) of the Branch, had been a shrewd businessman, and he had soundly reinforced the structure built by Mansbridge's entrepreneurial flair. In the 1970s, the Branch was becoming a publishing house in microcosm, as the editorial function grew. And it was a very substantial microcosm, since for many years its sales in America had been considerably greater than those of any American university press.

Contemplating the Press as a growing worldwide organism, and especially the Branch's rapid expansion in the 1970s, Cass felt it particularly important that the unique character of the Press should be maintained. He saw the Press as a unitary entity, with its centre in Cambridge, however widely its activity was now directed. The University was the centre, the heart from which the University Press's operations radiated. Neither he nor his senior colleagues envisaged the Press as an ordinary multinational organisation in the commercial mould. From the Press's viewpoint, the world was not a set of discrete national commercial markets to be exploited profitably by autonomous companies or shared in collaboration with local publishers; it was a single global academic and educational readership, served by a unitary organisation. This marketing approach was an extension of the editorial concept that the world of learning was a single world. It was not consistent with the nature of a true university press that foreign units of the Press should have corporate status in overseas countries and lead semi-independent lives of their own. The constitutional strength of the Press, and a main source of its uniqueness, was the control of the University's imprint by the Press Syndicate, operating on behalf of the Chancellor, Masters, and Scholars of the University. Cambridge, the centre of the Press's activities, had more than mere geographical significance. It was the place where the worldwide editorial policy of the Press was created and directed; and where the manuscripts of authors from all over the world had one standard applied to them at the meetings of the Press Syndicate. If the Syndicate accepted a manuscript, the resulting book was published worldwide from, and by, the University of Cambridge.

The nature of the Press meant that it was neither possible nor appropriate simply to give overseas branches financial targets or even operational targets and just let them get on with achieving them. Such an approach was possible, and very often desirable, in the case of the overseas companies of a commercial multi-national enterprise. The common denominator of a commercial company's overseas units was *profit*; operational independence could often be granted provided that financial targets were achieved; from the commercial and strategic point of view, such overseas units might very well operate quite differently in different countries and no harm would be done to the operating ethos.

In the case of the University Press, the academic aim, the intellectual standard and the editorial strategy were paramount. The University could not maintain the character and consistency of the Press's operations worldwide if the Press's overseas branches had operational autonomy. Nor could quantified financial or operational targets be an appropriate touchstone for the Press. Neither profit nor volume was the objective, but the dissemination of knowledge to a known standard of excellence, set and approved by the University through the Press Syndicate.

Geoffrey Cass believed that this objective could only be achieved by recognition within the Press itself, throughout its worldwide operation, that Cambridge University Press was a single tree, with branches. The roots and the trunk were in Cambridge, England. Alternative analogies such as a collection of federated states or empires, or a group of companies in a multinational commercial conglomerate, were totally inappropriate.

It followed that the only suitable status for an overseas unit of the Press was that of 'branch': it was out of character to seek separate incorporated 'company' status in the overseas country. That status would automatically create constitutional and legal separation, independent local objectives and loyalties, and publishing and printing goals perceivable as different from those of the University of Cambridge. Furthermore, it would not be the Chancellor, Masters, and Scholars of the University of Cambridge who were legally operating in that country. So that the proper overseas status was that of a *branch* of the Chancellor, Masters, and Scholars of the University operating through the Press Syndicate. Being a branch did not imply inferiority but complete membership of the unitary Press organism.

And indeed the Press's American Branch had always been such a branch from its foundation. It had no separate corporate status in the USA, unlike the American wing of Oxford University Press. However, the Press's Australian marketing unit had been established in 1969 as a company in Australia. This was an anomaly, and it was rectified in 1982 as a final logical step in the constitutional review and restructuring which took place during the whole period from 1972.

With the American Branch expanding, becoming more and more important as a component in the worldwide publishing operation and more and more like a large publishing house on its own account, with all the associated functions – editorial, subeditorial, progress control, marketing, distribution, and accounts – there was a real danger that there might be unthinking conventional demands for more independence, particularly from new staff more familiar with commercial companies, and unaware of, or unable to identify with, the unique history and the consequent constitutional structure of the Press. These tendencies are common enough in overseas subsidiaries in the commercial world, especially if the subsidiaries are large and important. They produce another variant of the 'us and them' polarity, so dangerous to the coherence, vitality and morale of any organisation.

Fortunately, Jack Schulman had always been a great believer in the 'one family' concept. He had been with the Branch from its foundation, had seen it become more than a marketing and distribution agency and had kept it on course. As the expansion continued after 1976, it became a matter of real concern to ensure that the physical growth of the Branch was accompanied by increased awareness of the real nature of its status and role in the Press's worldwide operations. In its turn, the University became more and more conscious that its American Branch was a senior and crucially important member of the Press family, and one whose stature would continue to develop and grow.

As an example of that growth, in 1977 the Press Syndicate accepted thirty-two projects sponsored by the Press's editors in America. By 1983, the American acceptances had risen to 180. A measure of the Press's status as publisher in the United States is the number of prizes won by Cambridge books in the USA. In 1981 Cambridge books were crowned as 'the most significant book in early modern European history'; 'the best work on modern European history'; 'the best book in British history published in the previous five years'. Another book received one prize as 'the most significant book in American history' and another as 'the best book by a woman historian'. In 1982 the American Historical Association gave prizes to Cambridge books as 'the best book in European diplomatic history', and 'the most significant book on Indian history'.

Meanwhile, in England, the long-contemplated project of cen- tralising in Cambridge the whole of the Press's activities in the United Kingdom was beginning to crystallise. In 1977, the Press Syndicate gave Geoffrey Cass and Philip Allin general per- mission to go ahead with the construction of a very large new building adjacent to the University Printing House on the Press's extensive site at the end of Shaftesbury Road. This building was to be an office and warehouse complex which would house the whole of the Press's Publishing Division.

HRH The Prince Philip, Duke of Edinburgh, was, like his ancestor Albert the Prince Consort, Chancellor of the University. An active Chancellor, he visited the University frequently, and on one such visit, in November 1977, he came to the Press. Cass was able to broach with him in conversation the possibility that the new Publishing Division headquarters should be named in his honour and be called the Edinburgh Building, and formal consent followed.

Planning and co-ordinating the construction of the Edinburgh Building was the task of Philip Allin, the Managing Director of the Publishing Division. The IDC Group of Stratford-upon-Avon were chosen as the designers and builders of the new complex, though senior executives of the Press were involved in the design at all stages. The new building offered a splendid opportunity to reconsider the physical organisation of work in the Publishing Division. Allin and his colleagues saw the opportunity to make the physical environment reflect the movement away from 'horizontal' organisation by functional departments and towards a vertically integrated 'group' method of working, so that all those involved in the publishing of the individual book – in editorial, subeditorial, design, progress control, and publicity – would find themselves working closely together in both senses of the phrase. The general aim had already fostered the formation of publishing 'groups', and the Edinburgh Building was designed with this working structure in mind. As the photographs show, the editorial floors have jutting bays. Each of these outlying 'pods' holds a group, while, towards the centre of each floor, common services support all the groups. The large warehouse building holds the entire United Kingdom stock of Cambridge books, previously dispersed in various locations. Particular care was paid to the design of these warehousing facilities. In the early 1960s, the Press had pioneered methods in its distribution warehouse in London which were recognised as producing the fastest service to booksellers in the UK. For the next fifteen years, despite the Press's considerable growth, the independent 'league tables' of UK publishers' distribution

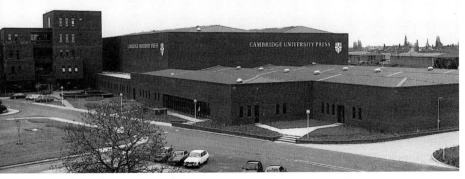

The Edinburgh Building. The upper photograph shows the projecting bays or 'pods', which house the groups. The lower photograph shows the office block on the left and the warehouse on the right.

performance had continued to show the Press as among the fastest suppliers, and it was vital that the standard of service should be maintained from the new Edinburgh Building.

Work started in the summer of 1978. In the spring of that year, it had already been decided to move the London operations of the Press to Cambridge before the end of the year, well before the Edinburgh Building was actually completed. Philip Allin wanted to split the massive relocation into two stages, to minimise disruption, and to remove time pressure from the proper completion of the Edinburgh Building. This proved to be a wise decision, and undoubtedly avoided many of the traumas associated with major relocation of businesses. Temporary office accommodation was found in various buildings in the centre of Cambridge, and a floor of the University Printing House was also made available. The distribution warehouse moved to leased premises on the outskirts of Cambridge. The actual transfer from London to Cambridge took place over two consecutive weekends in October 1978, the warehouse first, and then the offices. Normal distribution service was resumed within a very short time.

The first stage of the Edinburgh Building – the warehouses – was completed and occupied in 1979. The final stage – the office block – was completed and occupied towards the end of 1980. When the second move had been made, the now-united staff of the Publishing Division could at last see itself for what it was. Most key members of the management had moved to Cambridge, though some more junior people had not wanted to leave London. It was now possible, in the Edinburgh Building, to walk around and see the whole publishing house functioning as an organic entity. For everybody this was a new experience and a heartening one. For some it was also a little awe-inspiring: they had not realised that they belonged to so impressive an operation.

1981 was the first complete year since 1873 to be spent by all the staff of the Press in the United Kingdom on the same site. After a century in London, the move from Bentley House was attended by no trading or geographical disadvantage, but brought immediate substantial benefits in terms of general efficiency and unity of purpose. Specific advantages were immediately gained in communications, staffing, general overheads, internal operating structure, and interdivisional transport and communication. The 'group' method of working proved its worth at once; and it is hard to imagine that the growth in the number of titles published since the early 1970s could have been achieved by any alternative, functionally-departmentalised, arrangement.

The highlight of 1981 was undoubtedly the official opening of the Edinburgh Building on 29 May by Her Majesty The Queen, accompanied by His Royal Highness The Duke of Edinburgh, as Chancellor of the University. The spring of 1981 was disastrously cold, grey and wet, and as 29 May approached, the thought of an outdoor event in the worst of English weather caused some anxiety. But when the day came it was dry, if not warm, and spirits rose. The Queen officially opened Robinson College in the morning, and in her speech at the opening reminded her Cambridge audience of earlier events:

My great-great-grandmother came here at a time when *her* husband was Chancellor. Queen Victoria recorded in her diary that the Loyal Address was read by 'my beloved Albert', looking 'so splendid in his robes'. By a happy coincidence Queen Victoria went on to dine at Catharine Hall, where on this occasion it will be the Vice-Chancellor who will read the Loyal Address.

Before the day is out, we are looking forward to our visit to the University Press, another integral part of the University whose origins go back so many hundreds of years that this University can claim a longer history of continuous printing and publishing than any other university in the world. I feel great satisfaction that its new building will bear the name of my husband and your Chancellor.

The Vice-Chancellor, Professor Sir Peter Swinnerton-Dyer, Master of St Catharine's, was also a Syndic of the Press, so it was a happy arrangement that the Vice-Chancellor's lunch, given in the hall at St Catharine's, linked the morning and the afternoon celebrations. The Queen was welcomed at the Edinburgh Building in a brief speech by Geoffrey Cass, and then unveiled the handsome commemorative plaque in the entrance hall. A tour of the Edinburgh Building and University Printing House then led to the afternoon's main event, a garden party on the large playing field beyond, where some 2750 guests awaited the royal visitors. They were representatives of the University and the City, authors, editors, advisers, other printers and publishers, and that large category 'friends of the Press'. Above all, there were members of the staff and their families. The traditional skills evolved to handle these royal occasions were deployed: as if by magic the large crowd shaped itself around an elliptical space; down one side the Chancellor, and down the other The Queen slowly progressed, chatting informally to the many people who were presented to them. They were seen by all, were photographed by most, and talked to many. The informality made it a relaxed occasion; but the vivid green of the grass, the white of the marquees and the colours of the ladies' dresses more than made up for the grey English sky. It remains in the memory as a bright and colourful day.

There was also a satisfaction for the historically minded. The Press has two royal charters, of 1534 and 1628. By some ingenious means (it would be good to know how) John Legate and Cantrell Legge had each printed a work by a reigning monarch. But this was the first official royal visit to the Press; and it was fortunate that it should have come at a moment when the Press was celebrating so much: primarily and obviously the opening of the new building, but also the completion of a phase of reconstruction which had been informed throughout by an analytical consciousness of the nature of the Press which was founded on a sense of its history. The consolidation of the whole United Kingdom publishing staff in a single large and impressive modern building showed the University and the world that the Press was indeed a major force in publishing. When it is reflected that the cost of building – several millions of pounds – was financed out of the Press's own operations, that this was done in the depths of the continuing recession, and that just over ten years earlier the whole idea would have been thought inconceivable, indeed a bad joke, we have one measure of the transformation in the Press's fortunes achieved since 1972.

Another source of satisfaction was a further culminating moment in a decade of change. 1981 also saw the approval of a new University Statute for the Press. In 1979, the Council of the Senate had set up a special committee to consider the relationship between the University and the Press, and to review the

The opening ceremony, 29 May 1981. Her Majesty The Queen talking to guests at the garden party.

(left to right): HRH The Prince Philip, Duke of Edinburgh, Chancellor of the University; Philip Allin; Dr T. M. Sugden, Chairman of the Press Syndicate; Her Majesty The Queen; Geoffrey Cass.

Statutes and Ordinances by which the Press was governed. At that time, there was no single Statute which dealt with its establishment and government. The many references to the Press scattered throughout the Statutes and Ordinances had never been co-ordinated and consolidated, with the result that ambiguities and inconsistencies had arisen with respect to the position of Press officers within the University, and the rules governing the sale of Press property. Over the years, special provisos and exemptions had evolved in University legislation to enable the Press Syndicate to operate a business enterprise effectively. The special powers and discretions, and the exclusions from rules primarily designed to regulate normal academic University departments, had been incorporated into the University Statutes and Ordinances piecemeal; but now they badly needed systematic examination and reorganisation. Moreover, the seemingly casual and dispersed references to the Press gave no indication whatever of its scale and importance in the University. although the Press was by far the biggest component of the University in terms of size of staff and annual budget. Nor was there any statutory definition of the purpose or objectives of the Press.

Geoffrey Cass and Anthony Wilson were appointed to the reviewing committee together with two Syndics, Professor Gareth Jones and Professor Sir Peter Swinnerton-Dyer (chairman of the committee, and later Vice-Chancellor). The committee determined to bring together the scattered references, eliminate inconsistencies, clarify the nature and objectives of the Press, show explicitly the powers and duties of the Press Syndicate, and as far as possible state all this comprehensibly in a single new Statute, supported by one section of Ordinances.

The committee made its recommendations to the Council of the Senate which then, with the full agreement of the Press Syndicate, proposed to the Senate on 6 February 1980 a Grace for a new Statute J. *The Report of the Council of the Senate on the constitutional arrangements for the University Press* informed the University that:

The Council of the Senate, after discussions with the Press Syndicate, have reached the conclusion that a general revision of the legislation relating to the Press, both in Statutes and in Ordinances, is required. The main change proposed is to introduce a new statute, Statute J, relating to the University Press, which will include certain of the provisions now included in Ordinances which the Council consider would be more appropriately embodied in a Statute. No amendment is being proposed to the powers of the Press Syndicate as at present exercised. . .

It is proposed that the new Statute J should include at the beginning a statement setting out the objects of the Press and the responsibility of the Press Syndicate for the direction of the affairs of the University Press. The objects clause has been worded so as to be the same as that which was used by the Press Syndicate in claiming charitable status for the Press in respect of tax liabilities. The proposed Statute includes provisions concerning the composition of the Press Syndicate and clarifies the powers of the Syndicate in relation both to property and financial matters generally and to the terms and conditions of service of their officers and employees. . .

As the Council was careful to point out, the new Statute and the consequentially-amended Ordinances gave no new powers to the Press Syndicate; rather the wide powers of the Syndicate were directly revealed in Statute and Ordinance for the first time, instead of indirectly and obscurely through a proliferation of exemptions, exceptions and long-established custom and practice. For that reason, this was a moment of some tension for the Press Syndicate and its officers. They watched a little anxiously to see how the University would react to this piece of frankness, though they also felt that it must ultimately be for the benefit of both the Press and the University, and for the relations between them. Readers of this History and especially the chapters covering recent times will appreciate that it is not surprising that a unique institution – an ancient business of a quite special nature, with its charitable aims achieved through effective trading activity – does not fall easily into the pattern of other departments or institutions in an ancient university. Few if any University departments or Colleges spend tens of millions each year, and none of them has to generate the whole of that from competitive trading in the commercial market place. The way in which this cultural enterprise had come to be governed by its parent University had evolved organically over the centuries, and, particularly in 1972 and after, had been shown to work exceptionally well. But the University as a whole was not aware of the mechanisms, as it was not aware in detail of recent history; and some members might be surprised at features of the revealed structure. They were now being given the opportunity to comment. The Council's Grace was important enough to produce discussion as a matter of course. There was lively debate in the University, reflected in the formal Discussion in the Senate House. Discussion centred mainly on the mechanism of University control, the Press Syndicate's powers over the Press's funds, accountability, and the publication of accounts.

On these last two concerns, what had been University practice for very many years seemed fresh and strange when discovered for the first time; and few people grasped the extent to which accountability to the University had long been firmly established. It is of course implicit in the whole story of the crisis of the early 1970s, related above, and is worth repeating.

The Financial Board of the University endorsed the existing arrangements for the accountability of the Press as wholly effective. Those arrangements were (and still are) as follows. All the Press's financial affairs, annual budgets, and Annual Accounts are discussed in full by the Finance Committee of the Syndicate, and the detailed minutes of that Committee are circulated to each member of the Press Syndicate. Each member of the Syndicate then receives copies of the Annual Accounts and of a most detailed financial Annual Report. These are thoroughly discussed – like all major financial and business matters – at meetings of the full Press Syndicate, who then formally approve the Accounts and the Report. The Financial Board of the University then nominate two of their members to meet the Chairman of the Press Syndicate, the most senior officers of the Press, and the Press's Auditors, to discuss the Annual Accounts and Annual Report in detail. The two Financial Board representatives submit a comprehensive report which is presented to the whole of the Financial Board. The Financial Board discusses the Press's Accounts and Report at a meeting at which a complete set of Press Annual Accounts is tabled, the Press's Annual Report having been individually distributed to each member of the Board. The Financial Board's comments are then communicated formally to the Press Syndicate. We have seen how effective this procedure was in the early 1970s: it was in fact the mechanism by which the University set in motion the corrective measures which rescued the Press.

The members of the Press Syndicate pointed out to the Council of the Senate that they themselves, as the University's trustees of the Press, constituted a pretty fair representation of the University and the Colleges. The eighteen Syndics at that moment happened to include both the Vice-Chancellor *and* his deputy, and the University Treasurer, *ex officio*. The other members of the Syndicate were all appointed by the Council of the Senate; and the then Syndicate included both a present and a past Vice-Chancellor, at least one future Vice-Chancellor, five Heads of Colleges, ten Professors, two University Readers, two Heads of Departments, and four Chairmen of Faculty Boards. There were also five members of the Council of the Senate, and three members of the Financial Board. Alternatively considered, they were eighteen Fellows of eleven different Cambridge Colleges, and eighteen members of the Regent House and of the Senate. The fact that the eighteen Syndicate members combined between them all these roles was sufficiently indicative of their distinction and fiduciary reliability.

As for the question whether the Press's accounts, which were fully disclosed to the Financial Board, should be generally published, one Syndic who was also a member of the General Board (Gareth Jones, Downing Professor of the Laws of England) wrote at the time:

In the commercial world it may well be that corporate accountability cannot be achieved without publicity. But the Press is not a business in that sense. It is a charitable business which is part of the University: and it is, as such, very effectively accountable in financial matters to the University through the Press Syndicate and the Financial Board.

As a charity operating in commercial markets in the present-day industrial and governmental environment the Press needs every special competitive advantage it can muster, if it is to continue both to serve scholarship and remain ·financially viable.

People like to think that phenomena follow general rules, and that institutions have common patterns of behaviour, preferably familiar ones. The unique nature of the Press, and the difficulty of explaining this at much less than the length of this book, undoubtedly accounted for some of the questioning of the Council's proposals. Senior members were being asked immediately to grasp the concept of a trading charitable trust which is part of an exempt charity, and which is using neither public money, nor University money, nor shareholders' money, nor investors' money. They were also being asked to accept that the methods of accountability which were already in operation in respect of the Press were perfectly effective, very appropriate, and to the advantage of both the Press and the University.

The formal Discussion in the Senate House produced three useful suggestions which were incorporated as amendments in the Council's final proposals. These were embodied in a Notice on 10 March 1980 which summarised the Council's considered view:

The Council have considered the remarks made at the Discussion on 19 February 1980 of their Report, dated 4 February 1980, on the constitutional arrangements for the University Press, together with the comments of the Financial Board and of the Press Syndicate on those remarks.

The Council wish to repeat what they have already said in their Report, that the proposed Statute contains very little that is new. It is designed to consolidate powers and duties which are at present scattered, some in Statutes, some in Ordinances, and some, where the legislation is either not explicit or not clear, only in customary practice. It also does away with some inconsistencies; and it rectifies some unintended side-effects of the abolition in 1974 of the distinction between University offices and posts, which have only recently come to light. Despite what was said at the Discussion, the Report was not intended to make major changes in the constitutional position of the University Press; nor does it in fact do so.

Nevertheless, because of the wider issues raised at the Discussion, the Council think they should make clear in this Notice how they see the Press both as a part of the University and as a business enterprise, and what they see as its value to the University.

The prime purpose of the Press is to publish works of scholarship. Every book that is published by the Press has to be approved by the Syndicate, which (apart from the Treasurer) consists entirely of distinguished academics from within the University. The Syndicate's decision whether to accept or reject a book is based almost entirely on the merits of the book as a contribution to learning, and commercial considerations play little part in the decision. Certainly, many of the books which the Press publishes, though academically desirable, are ones which no commercial publisher would consider. The undoubted advantages of printing and publishing in the name of the University, with charitable status, contribute to the ability of the Press to publish such books.

But the University cannot afford to subsidize the Press, and if the Press got into financial difficulties the result for the University could be extremely serious. This means that the Press must be run as a business, and a successful business, because it is in direct competition with other businesses. The analogy with other departments of the University is wholly unsound, because other departments of the University are not in the market place. The officers of the Press need to have the same financial freedom as the management of any other business. The Financial Board keep a close watch on the accounts of the Press, to assure themselves that the financial state of the Press is sound; but they ought not to interfere with the financial management of the Press except in a crisis – and it is precisely that for which there is provision. Nor should the Press be regarded as a potential source of income for the University; indeed, such a suggestion would gravely damage the function of the Press as a non-profit-making (though also non-loss-making) institution, on which depends much of the goodwill which the Press enjoys.

In summary, the Council believe that the Press must be academically the servant of the University, but financially independent and self-sustaining.

The Notice continued:

The Council have accepted the advice of the Financial Board that publication of the accounts of an organization such as the Press would be in the interests neither of the Press nor of the University as a whole.

The Council agreed to amend the proposed Statute to require an Annual Report from the Syndicate, in order to keep the University more fully informed about the activities of the Press. Such an Annual Report has appeared in respect of each year since 1980.

At the suggestion of the Syndicate, the Council also responded to the Discussion in the Senate House by proposing to include a specific reference to printing and publishing in the objects clause. The Council added that they understood 'the word "printing" to carry the broadest possible meaning, and not to be tied to any particular technology'.

In the democratic way of the University, a ballot on the Council's proposals was called for. The vote by the Regent House, on 12 and 13 May 1980, resulted in a very substantial majority for the new Statute. Statute J was subsequently approved by The Queen in Privy Council in 1981, and so became the law of the land.

The new Statute was not a revolution, but a ratification. It re-affirmed and consolidated the unique nature of the Press. It was the constitutional coping-stone of the whole structure as it had evolved in course of time. The only completely new feature was a precise statement of the Press's charitable objectives; and Statute J explicitly confirmed that the income and funds of the Press could be used only in pursuit of those objectives.

The objects clause now serves two vital purposes. It provides a permanent statutory foundation for the Press's charitable status; and it imposes a firm control on the nature of the Press's activities, preventing any diversification which might not be consistent with University objectives.

Statute J is therefore in a sense the most recent 'charter' of the Press, succeeding and complementing the instruments of Henry VIII and Charles I of 1534 and 1628. The Statute, which is printed in full as Appendix II (in updated form, to 1999), begins:

There shall be in the University a University Press which shall be devoted to printing and publishing in the furtherance of the acquisition, advancement, conservation, and dissemination of knowledge in all subjects; to the advancement of education, religion, learning and research; and to the advancement of literature and good letters.

This is a comprehensive statement of the charitable aim, which combines a modern breadth of view with traditional elements (Erasmus and Thomas Thomas would have recognised the last phrase in its Latin form).

The period from 1980 to 1982 saw an important restructuring of the Press's company in Australia. This had been established in 1969 in order to strengthen the Press's ability to reach effectively one of the most important English-speaking academic markets and an increasingly valuable source of authors; and to provide a better service to that market by making books actually available to it from within Australia. Stockholding in Australia helped to overcome the problems of delay and cost caused by distance from Cambridge. The business of the company, painstakingly developed by the brothers Brian and Kim Harris, was at first exclusively in marketing and distribution, but editorial initiatives are now being taken in Australia and are likely to increase. The main premises are in Melbourne, with a small office in Sydney, but the Press outgrew its original offices and warehouses in Melbourne and in 1984 found purpose-built accommodation just outside the city.

When the Australian company was freed from Australian taxation as a charity in 1980, and then converted to 'branch' status in 1982, the Press's worldwide operating structure was finally rendered fully consistent. The unique nature of Cambridge University Press, even by comparison with Oxford University Press, now manifests itself in four particular aspects: all authors worldwide are contracted with the Chancellor, Masters, and Scholars of the University; all publications worldwide are approved in advance by the University through the Press Syndicate; all Press operations worldwide are tax-free; and all overseas units of the Press have branch status and are not incorporated in the country in which they operate.

Ever since the times when the Printer to the University found himself printing Tripos Verses, Assizes of Bread and Ale, labels for the University Library and a host of small jobs for the dons, the Press has found itself required to provide some form of local jobbing-printing service, which in the past has had to be accommodated within the main printing works – an arrangement which benefited neither the service itself nor the mainstream printing being carried out in the works. During 1982, to solve the problems of providing an effective service, the Press established a jobbing-printing unit in the Pitt Building. The new unit, deliberately located in the centre of the city for the convenience of its potential users, was specifically designed to give a fast, low-cost service to the University and its associated institutions and to the Colleges. It was given the name of University Printing Services.

It was not intended to be a money-maker but was established entirely as a useful service to the University and the Colleges – to be what Bentley would have called a 'publick' service. A substantial volume of work is needed to make it fully viable, and its long-term success will depend on the extent to which it is used by the Colleges and by University departments, clubs, and societies.

In its small way, this provision of a practical domestic service to the University is symptomatic of the modern spirit of the Press. The business revival achieved since 1972 has been characterised by two principal features: a transformation of the Press's perception of itself by understanding its historical growth and its role, and a re-integration of the Press into the life and purposes of the University. It was wounding and discouraging to hear suggestions, at the time of the discussion of the Statute, that the Press was trying to distance itself from the University. The whole thrust of Cass's stewardship had been to bring the Press consciously closer to its parent University both in spirit and operationally, to prevent it from becoming simply another large general international publisher, and to keep it a true university press, proud to be part of the University, and complementing and extending worldwide the activities of the University. The role and constitutional significance of the Press Syndicate have been defended and strengthened; and the Syndicate, its Finance Committee, and the Financial Board of the University have been provided with regular and reliable information about every aspect of the operations of the Press. The business structure of the Press overseas has been reconstructed to preserve the charitable academic nature of the Press and the sovereignty of the University. The Press's dealings with the outside world, and all the Press's literature, publicity, and letterheads – indeed, everything which concerns the stance of the Press and the nature of its operating – have been brought into harmony with this approach. The final symbolic act was physically to bring all the Press's operations back into Cambridge. The new Statute was the constitutional seal on this policy.

The Printing Division in 1984 is still re-shaping itself to respond to the sweeping changes recently affecting the printing industry. The development of computer-aided photo-typesetting and the move away from hot-metal setting necessitated the retraining of many staff. Virtually all printing is now produced by offset lithography. Hot-metal setting is now little used, but the Press can still provide it, together with letterpress printing, if it is required. Most setting is now carried out on micro-computers linked to a main computer, but the Press is changing to a new system based exclusively on micro-computers linked by a data ring to give increased flexibility. The Press produces its own computer systems and pro-grammes (its 'software') to meet the needs of specialised printing, and is well equipped to handle data provided by a wide variety of sources which will in future no doubt include authors and publish-ers. Print numbers of specialised academic books were severely reduced during the recession, so the Division has given particular attention to the problems of short-run printing, using special machinery to reduce setting-up times compared with running times. The effects of many modern problems are common to both Divisions of the Press, and there is now closer liaison and under-standing between them than there has ever been.

Growth continued in the Publishing Division. The great increase in academic output since 1971 had been organically gener-ated within the Press, and not brought about by acquiring other publishing houses. In 1984 it transpired that the Press issued one thousand publications. 'Publications' include such things as second editions, simultaneous paperback editions, the University's official publications, and the cassettes and other supplementary material which accompany many modern textbooks. Actual new titles were around nine hundred. Sixty-seven learned journals were issued in their several parts; there were special editions of the Bible; and about one-and-a-half million examination papers were produced. The Press created and sent out in 1984 about eight million units of book, Bible and journal printing and publishing.* All told, they made the Press the largest purely academic publisher in the United Kingdom. The output is composed of publications in almost every academic subject, at every level from the primary school to post-graduate research. New projects in new fields for new markets are constantly being undertaken. For constitutional reasons, the Press does not engage in 'general' publishing, so that the total service to education and learning which is comprised in this very large flow of publications may be considered unmatched. And, once again, to contrast this actual 1984 output with the Press's prospects as seen in 1972, when a scaling-down of the whole operation was seriously talked about as a possibility, is to give a measure of the advances made in the period 1972–1984.

* In subsequent years, statistics for Press output continued to increase dramatically.

# 17

## CONCLUSION

THIS has been a characteristically English story, combining a long history with a continuous evolution, imperceptibly slow over long stretches but with episodes of rapid change – culminating in an entity which the English themselves take for granted but which foreign observers find unique. What in another country might be carried out by an official agency – perhaps administered by a ministry of education or culture – is in England the function of a chartered private body (one thinks of the Royal Society) or a chartered corporation (like the Royal Shakespeare Theatre) or a chartered department of a university, as in the case of the two ancient university presses. These bodies take pride in their antiquity, their charters and their independence. In the case of the presses, not a penny of public funds is now involved, and the idealistic aim is if anything increased by removal of any constraint which might be implied by official support. The total absence of a political dimension is an enormous benefit.

During its history, the changing pattern of the book trades in England and the development of a modern publishing industry provide some of the forms which have moulded the Press at various times: but the history of the University is just as important, since the University has always been the sponsoring body, providing the ethos which its Press has had to follow.

In 1583, puritan Tudor Cambridge saw the possibility of having its own press, based on its charter, and not subject to the licensing powers of metropolitan Anglicanism. It found in Thomas Thomas a Cambridge-educated scholar-printer who was prepared to undertake a venture which was partly commercial, partly intellectual and political. As a working printer he was able to fit into the traditional pattern – the licensed stationer working in and for the University. That pattern extends, substantially modified but unbroken, from the medieval *stationarii* to the Clay family, whose last link with the University was dissolved in 1916. For that whole time the basic arrangement was that the University first licensed, and then entered into partnership with, tradesmen or professionals who had the skills of printing, and often binding as well, and who had access to the bookselling world in London and the English provinces, and ultimately to the world outside England. Over those three hundred years, the differences between Thomas Thomas and Charles John Clay are much less striking than the similarities.

But during the centuries there were also decisive shifts within this kind of relationship. The first notable one was Bentley's initiative. It was he who saw that the University must have a capital holding, and exercise a control beyond mere licensing. As a result of his enterprise, the University itself acquired premises and equipment, so that the printer was more in the position of a manager; and the Curators of the Press (later the Syndicate) became the continuing body which owned the University's premises and material, employed the Printer, and wielded the imprint of the University as publisher. The strange result of the recommendation of the Commissioners in 1852 was in part a retrogression rather than a forward evolution, for the partnership placed the Clays on a more nearly equal footing with the University than previous printers had been. The changes between 1854 and 1916 steadily eroded the Clays' position, as if it were realised that while the arrangement worked well in practice, it was constitutionally anomalous. It was an odd feature of these changes that Charles John Clay began his career as University Printer, and ended it contemplating the rise to power of a new kind of executive – the Secretary of the Syndicate. For a few years he exercised both functions himself, and was therefore the point at which the new system evolved from the old one.

The rise of the Secretary, from Wright's appointment in 1891, marked the determination of the University, through the Syndicate, to have its own executive. Once the idea had crystallised, it was bound to lead to the final dissolution of the partnership in

1916. Almost sixty years later the whole constitutional process since 1891 was completed by the appointment of Geoffrey Cass as Chief Executive, his executive reorganisation of the Press, the recognition of the charitable nature of the whole enterprise, and the new Statute. During the twentieth century the Press has acquired its own professional officers, and this executive organisation now runs the two Divisions. At a certain moment in the late nineteenth century one can imagine a potential, perhaps an actual, tension between the old professional 'bookmen', the Clays, and the new University men who were supplanting them. Now that the transition is completed, the staff of the Press can feel an essential solidarity with all their predecessors, right back to the three stationers and printers or sellers of books whom the University was empowered to license in 1534. The solidarity is to be found in their common dedication to the same enterprise – the publication of the books which the University chooses to issue under its imprint.

Obviously, Thomas Thomas would be amazed to see the product of four hundred years of growth: in terms of the Press's size, the technology available to it, the worldwide diffusion of its products. That kind of change is natural enough, and is produced by successful survival, and the application of science: it is the way of the world. He might be as interested in the development of the concept of the University Press itself: something which as scholar-printer he helped to initiate, and something which has grown in the mind, is implicit in actions and attitudes, and cannot be pointed to in machines and buildings.

Considered in that way, the nature of the Cambridge University Press can be stated. It is not a limited company, or a company of any sort: nor is it incorporated overseas. It is the printing and publishing arm of the University of Cambridge, recognised by Statute, and committed in the Statute defining it to the same general aims as the University itself. The University pursues these aims by teaching and research in its Colleges, institutes and departments, by conservation in its libraries and museums, by publication through its Press. As part of the University and pursuing its aims, and by pursuing its own aims, which are by definition charitable, the Press has charitable status.

It receives no regular outside subsidy as of right, either from the University or from the State. It is therefore one of those charities which has to support itself by its own activities, which may to the outside world look indistinguishable from the trading activities of other academic publishers. The Press differs however in that unlike other publishers it can neither acquire outside capital on the open market, nor vary its activities fundamentally in order to secure its viability – still less in order to make a profit. Its primary purpose is to publish learned books, and if it does not do that in ways and on a scale which satisfy the academic community, it does not fulfil its function. It is accepted that a certain proportion of the books which are published each year will by commercial standards lose money; and a further category can never generate a surplus which would interest an ordinary firm or satisfy a shareholder as a reasonable line to go on producing. These books are among the more important publications of the Press, judged academically, and it is essential that it should be in a position to go on publishing them. During the years of recession, other publishers have tended to withdraw from these difficult areas, which in England leaves Cambridge and Oxford carrying the main responsibility for the highest levels of scholarly publishing, and for virtually all scholarly publishing in some academic subjects.

A publisher may, for various reasons including prestige, decide to publish some 'loss-leaders' and carry this loss by means of publishing more profitable books. This is a public-spirited thing to do, but is usually pursued as an option – the amount is variable, and such publishing can always be jettisoned in an emergency. The Press is constitutionally able neither to treat scholarly publishing as an option, nor just to publish any best-selling book that takes its fancy for the sake of generating a surplus which can be spent on the other thing. There are no roundabouts and swings here; the Press only has roundabouts, though it is reasonable to say that some go round faster than others, or that they find more customers. But that, though important, is not the primary consideration. The schoolbook market in Britain and elsewhere is large, and has been rewarding; but the Press publishes school books because the University itself has a necessary interest in educational standards, and has in various ways shown its practical concern with what goes on in schools. No less rewarding, if one is thinking in those terms, is the market for English Language Teaching. But the Press could not cultivate it if it did not also present an intellectual challenge (the application of linguistics, for instance) and a cultural benefit (the status of English as a world language is the condition of most of the Press's other activity).

The art has been to analyse the various kinds of educational and academic publishing which are consistent with the constitutional requirement, and then in an enterprising way to develop those kinds of book which complement and assist the slower sellers. In doing this the Press is greatly helped by the status of the English language as a vehicle of science and learning throughout the world, and by its own constitution and history. It is a truism now that English has taken the place that Latin had in Thomas Thomas's time; equally a truism that, at their highest level, science in particular and scholarship generally are international. During the course of this century the Press has acquired considerable strength first as a marketing organisation and then as an editorial service. With a large Branch in the USA closely coordinated with the editorial and marketing activities in Cambridge, with a Branch in Australia, with representatives regularly visiting Europe, the Middle East, Japan and the other major markets, the Press has since the Second World War found more buyers for its books outside Britain than inside. It therefore offers writers of scholarly or scientific books access to a world market, not just a national market. That being so, it is in a position to attract books from wherever they are written in English. These are related to a coherent editorial programme, assessed by a common (but not parochial) standard, and presented to the Syndicate at its meetings in the Pitt Building on alternate Fridays in termtime, starting at 2.15 p.m. – a historic formula going back a hundred years. The Syndicate, as the body representing the University's interest in publishing, formally considers every book published by the Press, whether it is secured by an editor in New York, or one in Cambridge, or through the Branch in Australia, or one of the agencies or representatives.

This coherence, combined with a genuinely international operation, is still relatively rare in academic publishing; and access to the whole world market by a single organisation is inevitably much prized by any author who has a book which needs that kind of diffusion. Nor is the fundamentally idealistic nature of the enterprise a disadvantage in the academic world. The non-profit-making nature of the Press is actually inconsistent with inefficiency or amateurishness. The notional handicap of publishing very scholarly books requires strength and effectiveness all round. To have survived the recession, to have increased output dramatically and in the same period to have financed the Edinburgh Building – to have done all this through publishing academic books without external subsidy, is a proof of that effectiveness.

The two great English university presses are therefore a distinctive feature of English cultural life, much envied – for instance in Europe, where no exact parallel exists, and where for lack of such a parallel there is now a tendency for French, German and Italian scholars to make their way towards Cambridge in particular. The university presses serve this national and in-creasingly international function without making any call on the taxpayer's purse.

On social occasions friendly people often say, 'Ah, you're at the Press. What are you publishing at the moment?' If you know the questioner's interests, an answer may be possible; but it is getting increasingly difficult to give a short one. 'About nine hundred books and sixty journals; and many editions of the Bible and the Book of Common Prayer' is a possible reply, but would sound either boastful or a put-down. One can produce one's favourite title, and of course a good editor is likely to be very full of his latest authors and their books, and can go on about these until (and after) the listener's eyes begin to glaze. But there is now no short and easy way of characterising the output of a major press which has the momentum of four hundred years of commitment to scholarly publishing and a current output which is expanding yearly.

Also the enterprise of scholarly publishing over the long term acquires a kind of impersonality – or so it appears to this observer. The specialist can be told what is happening in the subject of interest, and historically-minded specialists will know and respect Cambridge books of previous generations. In the humanities especially, these are the books which go on appearing in bibliographies and footnotes, and would be read to pieces in the libraries if Cambridge books were not so physically durable. To the non-specialist the whole large human endeavour looks like some kind of city that is being eternally rebuilt. There are cathedrals and palaces (from Newton's *Principia* to Needham's *Science and Civilisation*) but a large part of the endeavour consists partly of clearing the ground and starting again, partly of building higher and higher in small units on old but firm constructions, partly of extending the city limits. It is one of the world's great activities, and characteristically human. The writer who has built a new level in one of these old structures seems to recede ultimately into a sort of anonymity, like a medieval mason – except that in the great library catalogues the authors' names and the titles of the books remain; and the intellectual historians eventually retrieve these people as lives and personalities for the interested reader. For me, in writing this account, many of the books printed in Cambridge in previous centuries started as a mere surname, title and date; and yet with a little research many of the authors became more real, as men with an intellectual cause, or men with an important part in the history of the Cambridge or the England of their time. Some of course retain their over-life-sized personalities in posterity as they did in life: Bentley, Newton, Porson, Bishop Watson, Whewell, Doughty ...one could go on; but my point is that most of them were engaged in the more impersonal activity of a precise contribution to a subject, adding their cell to a structure which is always ramifying and always renewing itself.

That is my sense also of what is going on today. It is always heartening for a publisher to be able to point to 'his' book in this week's national reviews, enjoying its moment of reception. But the learned journals are, every quarter, reviewing the books which the daily or weekly papers never notice. Fifty years from now, the mention of a title or an author's name will cause some scholar to say, 'Ah yes, that's a good book', or even to add some phrase like '...laid the foundations of the subject', or 'provided an entirely new point of departure'. That is the kind of reputation which a scholarly publisher wants.

These are books very often published in series, called, perhaps 'Cambridge Studies in [the name of the subject]'. There are now very many such series, and their purpose is to publish each year the best contributions to that subject – often by young scholars, and often their first substantial piece of research. With entry to the academic profession now governed largely by professional qualifications, many of these books also started life as doctoral dissertations. Good academic publishers and their series editors are now skilled at choosing the best among these – and those who scoff at the Ph.D. would be startled to discover how many books which they respect once passed through that mill.

These books provide one basic constituent of scholarly publishing. Another is the mature study by the more senior scholar who has passed beyond the doctoral phase and settled down to the fundamental treatment of a self-chosen topic: I think again of Knowles on the religious orders or Runciman on the Crusades, but also of the Taylors on Anglo-Saxon Architecture, Dodd on the Fourth Gospel, Elton on the Tudor Revolution in Government, Robertson on Greek Art, Taylor on Hegel, Guthrie's history of Greek philosophy – but the list is too long.

Then there is that other kind of book which represents the conservation of the literary heritage. The publication of major editions is a typical university press enterprise, and the Cambridge contribution has been specially directed towards Shakespeare and the early dramatists (Dekker, Beaumont and Fletcher, and Marlowe, all edited by Fredson Bowers; other editions in preparation) and to the careful recension of classic modern authors (Lawrence and Conrad are now in progress). There are also other kinds of publication or analysis: H. C. Darby's great series *The Domesday Geography of England* takes a crucial archival source and patiently derives a modern survey from it. To leap into another science, the Clapham–Tutin–Warburg *Flora*, its popular derivatives, and the great *Flora Europaea* itself, present the standard modern taxonomic analyses of British and

European plants. An analogy with the texts of literature is provided by the important texts in the history of science. The complete Correspondence of Newton, sponsored by the Royal Society, and the careful re-editing of the mathematical papers and the *Principia* itself, have produced over the last quarter of a century another range of impressive volumes. The Newton Letters were one of the last and finest monuments of the Monotype era. The other Cambridge scientist who ranks with Newton is Darwin, and the Press is now committed to the publication of his correspondence, a great venture of Anglo-American scholarship which gives the computer a central place in the preparation of edited text.

These large enterprises, carefully planned and pursued over many years to eventual completion, are not confined to Cambridge or to British intellectual concerns – though of course the University and the nation have a natural first call on the Press's services. Centred in Cambridge, the Press publishes for the scholarly world as a whole, and its initiatives are meant to reflect an international spirit (perhaps it is only in the intellectual world that such a notion can be more than a pious wish). The *Cambridge History of China*, in its eventual sixteen volumes, will be the first such history on such a scale, has stimulated the fundamental research required if it was to be written at all, and will take a number of years to complete. The *History of Africa*, also written without the sponsorship or support of international cultural bodies, is also the only one on that scale. One can imagine such things being done again, for they need to be replaced in time; but this kind of large endeavour can be faced only once in a century or so, and it is only the university presses which are likely to be still in existence when the time comes round again. It is a matter of some cultural importance that they should continue to exist, and continue to be strong and active.

In the last four hundred years Cambridge University Press has grown to be a large publishing house of the kind suggested above, with strengths and skills devoted entirely to the promotion of 'education, religion, learning and research'. It has associated with it a historic printing house with a tradition of scholarly printing – that is to say, with skills derived from the analysis of the specific problems of printing learned and scientific books, and discovering the best solutions provided by the current technology. Here the Monotype keyboard has been largely replaced by computer-aided photo-composition. It is already obvious that the new technology of word-processing facilities interfacing with computer type-setting may, skilfully developed, counterbalance the present economic effects of recession, and be exploited in any future period of growth. Indeed in the very near future the technology of book production may become radically different in ways inconceivable to the printers of earlier times.

The Press is in a good position to look forward to its next hundred years, even its next four hundred years. If the processes of growth and change go on as rapidly as in the last few years, the future historian will of course look back on us as representing a stage which is past. There are however some things which cannot change because they are fundamental: like our predecessors and our successors we shall be seen as serving the same cause.

# THE LETTERS PATENT OF 1534

Henricus Dei Gratiâ Angliae et Franciae Rex, Fidei Defensor et Dominus Hiberniae, Omnibus ad quos praesentes Litterae pervenerint Salutem. Sciatis quod nos de Gratiâ nostra speciali, ac ex certa Scientia et mero Motu nostris concessimus et Licentiam damus pro nobis et Heredibus nostris dilectis nobis in Christo Cancellario Magistris et Scholaribus Universitatis nostrae Cantebrigiae, Quod ipsi et Successores sui in perpetuum per eorum Scripta sub Sigillo Cancellarii dictae Universitatis sigillata, de tempore in tempus, assignent, eligant, et pro perpetuo habeant inter se et infra Universitatem nostram praedictam perpetuo manentes et inhabitantes tres Stationarios et Librorum Impressores seu Venditores tam alienigenos et natos extra Obedientiam nostram, quam Indigenos nostros et natos infra Obedientiam nostram, tam conductitias quam proprias Domus habentes et tenentes. Qui quidem Stationarii sive Impressores Librorum in Forma praedictâ assignati, et eorum quilibet, omnimodos Libros, per dictum Cancellarium vel eius Vices gerentem, et tres Doctores ibidem approbatos seu in posterum approbandos, ibidem imprimere, et tam Libros illos, quam alios Libros ubicunque, tam extra quam infra Regnum nostrum impressos sic, ut praedicitur, per praedictum Cancellarium seu eius Vicem gerentem et tres Doctores ibidem approbatos seu approbandos tam in eadem Universitate quam alibi infra Regnum nostrum ubicunque placuerint, Venditioni exponere licitè valeant seu valeat et impunè. Et quod iidem Stationarii sive Impressores etiam extra Obedientiam nostram oriundi, ut praedicitur, et eorum quilibet, quamdiu infra Universitatem praedictam Moram traxerint, et Negotio praedicto intendant, in omnibus et per omnia tanquam fideles Subditi et Legei nostri reputentur habeantur et pertractentur, et quilibet eorum reputetur, habeatur, et pertractetur; ac omnibus et singulis Libertatibus, Consuetudinibus, Legibus et Privilegiis gaudere, et uti valeant, et quilibet eorum valeat liberè et quietè prout aliquis fidelis Subditus et Legeus noster quoquo Modo uti et gaudere possit, ac Lottum, Scottum, Taxam, Tallagium, et alias Consuetudines et Impositiones quascunque non alitèr nec alio Modo quam ceteri fideles Subditi et Legei nostri solvunt et contribuunt, solvant et contribuant: aliquo Statuto, Actu, Ordinatione sive Provisione inde in contrarium facto, edito, sive proviso in aliquo non obstante. Proviso sempèr quòd dicti Stationarii sive

Impressores extra Obedientiam nostram sic, ut praemittitur, oriundi, omnia et omnimoda Custumias, Subsidia, et alios Denarios pro Rebus et Merchandizis suis extra vel infra Regnum nostrum educendis vel inducendis, nobis debita, de tempore in tempus solvent, prout Alienigenae nobis solvunt et non alitèr. In Cuius Rei testimonium has Literas nostras fieri fecimus patentes. Teste meipso apud Westm. 20° Die Iulii, An. Reg. 26°.

# STATUTE J OF THE UNIVERSITY: THE UNIVERSITY PRESS*

**1.** There shall be in the University a University Press which shall be devoted to printing and publishing in the furtherance of the acquisition, advancement, conservation, and dissemination of knowledge in all subjects; to the advancement of education, religion, learning, and research; and to the advancement of literature and good letters.

**2.** There shall be in the University a Press Syndicate. The management of the finance, property, and affairs generally of the University Press shall be the responsibility of the Press Syndicate which shall exercise in relation thereto all the powers of the University except in so far as the Statutes and Ordinances expressly or by necessary implication provide otherwise. The Press Syndicate shall consist of the Vice-Chancellor (or his deputy) as Chairman, the Treasurer, and such number of members of the Senate appointed in such manner as shall be determined from time to time by Ordinance.

**3.** The Press Syndicate shall have power in the name of the University and for the purposes of the University Press to purchase, lease, retain, sell, or transfer property real or personal and to purchase, retain, sell, or transfer securities (which term shall include stocks, funds, and shares) of any description whether or not authorized by law for the investment of trust funds, and this power shall extend to the investment (including the variation of the investment) of all endowments or other funds of the University Press.

**4.** All income accruing to the University Press shall be credited to the accounts of the Press Syndicate and all University Press capital and income shall be controlled by the Press Syndicate and applied by them at their sole discretion for the purposes of the University Press.

**5.** The Press Syndicate shall have power to borrow money for the purposes of the University Press and to make the property or income of the University Press security for any loan, provided that

    (*a*) the Council shall have authority to impose limitations on the power of the Press Syndicate to borrow money under this section, and

* as amended to 1999.

(*b*) the terms of any loan so secured on the property or income of the University Press shall be in accordance with the Universities and College Estates Acts 1925 and 1964, and shall be approved by the Treasurer on behalf of the Council.

**6.** The Press Syndicate shall have power in the name of the University to engage persons for employment in the service of the University Press, determine their salaries and pensions, and prescribe the conditions of their service.

**7.** Persons holding certain posts in the University Press which have been specially designated under this section by the Council of the Senate on the recommendation of the Press Syndicate shall be treated as University officers for the purposes of Statute A, III, 7(*b*), Statute B, I, 1, Statute B, III, 6 and Statute K, 3(*h*).[1]

**8.** The accounts of the University Press shall be audited annually by one or more qualified accountants appointed by the Council. The Council shall in every year appoint one or more persons from among the members of the Finance Committee, who shall examine these accounts, confer with the auditor or auditors, and report to the Council.

**9.** There shall be a Press Seal, as a seal of the University to be used on the directions of the Press Syndicate in matters relating to the affairs of the University Press; but the existence of the Press Seal shall not invalidate the use in connexion with such matters of any other seal of the University. The University shall have power to make Ordinances concerning the custody and affixing of the Press Seal.

**10.** The Press Syndicate shall have power to delegate any of their powers under this Statute subject to any limitations imposed by Ordinance.

**11.** The term property of the University Press here and elsewhere in Statutes and Ordinances shall refer to property of the University held or used for the purposes of the University Press. In favour of any person having dealings with the University Press a certificate signed by the Treasurer that any particular property is the property of the University Press, or that any limitations on borrowing have been complied with, shall be conclusive.

**12.** The Press Syndicate shall make an Annual Report to the Council, which shall be published to the University either as a whole or in summary.

**13.** Notwithstanding the provisions of the foregoing sections, the Council of the Senate shall have power in circumstances which the Council deems to be exceptional, on the advice of its Finance Committee, to discharge the Press Syndicate, and to assume full responsibility itself for the management of the Press for the time being. If the Council has occasion to exercise the power available under this section, the Council shall make a full report to the University on the circumstances necessitating such action.

---

[1] The following have been specially designated under this section: the Secretary of the Press Syndicate, Directors, Associate Directors, Senior Editors, and Senior Managers of the Press.

# UNIVERSITY PRINTERS 1583–1984

| | | | |
|---|---|---|---|
| 1583 | Thomas Thomas, M.A. | 1730 | Mary Fenner |
| 1588 | John Legate | | Thomas James |
| ? | John Porter (before 1593) | | John James |
| 1606 | Cantrell Legge | 1740 | Joseph Bentham |
| ? | Thomas Brooke, M.A. (before 1608) | 1758 | John Baskerville |
| | | 1766 | John Archdeacon |
| 1622 | Leonard Greene | 1793 | John Burges |
| 1625 | Thomas Buck, M.A. | 1802 | John Deighton |
| | John Buck, M.A. | 1802 | Richard Watts |
| 1630 | Francis Buck | 1804 | Andrew Wilson |
| 1632 | Roger Daniel | 1809 | John Smith |
| 1650 | John Legate the younger | 1836 | John William Parker |
| 1655 | John Field | 1854 | George Seeley |
| 1669 | Matthew Whinn | 1854 | Charles John Clay, M.A. |
| 1669 | John Hayes | 1882 | John Clay, M.A. |
| 1680 | John Peck, M.A. | 1886 | Charles Felix Clay, M.A. |
| 1682 | Hugh Martin, M.A. | 1916 | James Bennet Peace, M.A. |
| 1683 | James Jackson, M.D. | 1923 | Walter Lewis, M.A. |
| 1686 | Jonathan Pindar | 1945 | Brooke Crutchley, M.A. |
| 1693 | H. Jenkes | 1974 | Euan Phillips, M.A. |
| 1697 | Jonathan Pindar | 1976 | Harris Myers, M.A. |
| 1705 | Cornelius Crownfield | 1982 | Geoffrey Cass, M.A. |
| 1730 | William Fenner | 1983 | Philip Allin, M.A. |

# INDEX

Acton, Lord, 182–3
Albert, Prince, as Chancellor, 290
Allin, Philip
  joins Press, 260–1
  heads Publishing Division, 262
  and Edinburgh Building, 289–92
Almanac Duty Act, 105, 117, 118,
    275–6; *see also* Government
    Annuity
almanacs
  in 17th c., 71–3, 84, 207
  in 18th c., 101, 155
  Carnan's Case, 116–18
American Branch of the Press
  founded, 226
  importance, 230, 310
  growth, 286, 289
  as part of a unitary organisation,
    288
Archdeacon, John, 115, 118
Assistant Secretaries
  appointed, 185, 186, 194, 196, 206
  rise to two, 205
  as editors, 208
  other duties, 208, 224, 234
assizes of bread and ale, 85, 303
Australian Branch of the Press
  founded, 235
  as Branch, 288, 302–3, 310
Aylmer, John, Bishop of London, 38–9

Barker, Christopher, Queen's Printer,
    32, 50, 52, 53, 62
Barker, Robert, prints 'wicked Bible',
    62
Barnes, J.
  *History of Edward III*, 80

edition of Euripides, 80; of
    Anacreon, 102; of Homer, 102
Barrow, Isaac, 145, 150
  Euclid, 76
Bartlett, Sir Frederick, 203
Baskerville, John, 111–15
Baskett, John, as monopolist, 106–8
Bathurst, Charles, 108
Bentham, Joseph, 108, 111, 115
Bentley House, *see* London office
Bentley, Richard, 86, 87, 89–90, 108
  given power of attorney, 90
  'design of ye Press', 93–4
  his Horace, 95, 98
  sponsors Newton's *Principia*, 95–6
  as controversialist, 102–3
Bible, English versions
  Tyndale, 13, 23
  Coverdale, 28
  Bishops', 31, 32
  Geneva, 32, 50
  Authorized Version (King James),
    61–2
  Revised Version, 157, 158, 164–5
  New English Bible, 227–8
Bibles, printed
  as staple sellers, 30, 73
  as a monopoly, 31–2, 50, 64, 73,
    137, 157
  poorly printed in 17th c., 62, 73
  printed by Canstein, 73, 107, 126
  stereotyped, 73, 127–8
  in Scotland, 106, 137, 140
  total annual output, 137, 144–5,
    147, 155
  Revised Version statistics, 165
  relative importance declines, 205

Bibles, *cont.*
  Cambridge editions: in 1590–1, 50;
    by the Bucks, 61, 73, 78, 111; by
    Buck and Daniel, 64, 67, 69,
    73, 111, 158; by Field, 78;
    by Bentham, 108, 111, 115; by
    Baskerville, 111–13; edited by
    Parris, 111, 158; Cambridge
    Stereotype Bible, 127–8; Cam-
    bridge Paragraph Bible, 158,
    164
Black, M. H.
  appointed, 224
  becomes Chief Editor, 234
  becomes University Publisher, 262
Blackstone, William, 108
Blore, Edward, 132
Book of Common Prayer, 59, 84, 110
  folio printed by Buck and Daniel, 74
  printed by Baskerville, 111
  as part of Press output, 129
Boys, John, 55, 62
British and Foreign Bible Society,
  125–8, 135
Browne, E. G., 177, 183, 201
Browne, George Forrest, 156–7
  edits *Reporter*, 156
  instigates Pitt Press Series, 159
Brownrigg, Ralph, 54
Buck, Francis, 66
Buck, John
  co-prints Bible, 61
  Printer in 1668, 79
Buck, Thomas, 17, 57, 79
  prints Bible of 1629, 61, 73
  co-prints Bible of 1638, 63–4, 73
  his printing house, 64–5
  agreement with Legate, 75
Buckingham, Duke of, as Chancellor,
  60, 67, 68
Bullock, Henry, 15
  *Oratio*, 19
Burbidge, P. G., 235
Burges, John, 118
Burghley, William Cecil, Lord, 35–41,
  47, 52, 82
Butler, President, 276

Cambridge Bible Commentary, 228
Cambridge Bible for Schools, 162, 166,
  184, 201

Cambridge Bibliography of English
    Literature, 204
Cambridge Histories, 198
  Modern History, 182–3
  History of English Literature, 187
  Medieval History, 195–6
  History of British Foreign Policy,
    196
  Ancient History, 196
  History of Africa, 229, 314
  New Modern History, 230
  History of China, 314
Cambridge University
  as licensing authority, 2, 7, 8, 22,
    23, 26, 30, 33, 69, 81–2, 104,
    109–10
  as independent corporation, 6, 81,
    109
  as sponsoring education, religion,
    learning, and research, 3, 109,
    268, 273–8, 302, 318
  medieval curriculum, 9–10
  in the Reformation, 13
  after Newton, 119
  Royal Commission, 124, 146–50,
    151
  Royal Commission of 1922, 278
  represented by Press Syndicate, 170,
    176, 251, 269, 287
  as charitable organisation, 271
  relationship with the Press, 271,
    304
  *see also* Council of the Senate,
    Financial Board, Press Syndicate,
    Statute J, Vice-Chancellor
Camden, Lord, 132–3, 150, 276
Canstein Society, as Bible printers, 73,
  107, 126
Carey, G. V.
  Assistant Secretary, 196
  Education Secretary, 200
Carnan, Thomas, 116
Carrington, C. E., 207
Cartmell, James, 152–3, 155, 158, 161
Cartwright, Thomas, 41
Cass, (Sir) Geoffrey
  joins the Press, 244–5
  as Managing Director, 246–56
  on financial Sub-Committee, 247
  views on the nature of the Press, 251
  becomes Chief Executive, 256

Cass, *cont.*
becomes Secretary, 257
policy for inflation, 263
analyses charitable status of the Press, 265–83
and review committee of Press Statute, 296
completes constitutional process, 308
Catalogue of Press books: 1875, 155, 164; 1900, 205; 1921, 205; 1945, 205
charitable organisations, trading of, 266, 268, 300
Charles I, 60, 67, 68, 74
Charter, *see* Letters Patent
Clay, Charles Felix
enters partnership, 169
co-partner in 1894, 180
as London Manager, 191
retires, 192
Clay, Charles John
becomes partner, 152–3
University Printer, 153
founds Warehouse, 160
becomes Secretary, 161, 174
to sign agreements, 167
resigns, 175, 180
achievement, 192
venerated by Mason, 219
continuity with stationers, 307
Clay, John
enters partnership, 169
co-partner in 1894, 180
dies, 192
and Keetch, 223
Clay, Richard, I, 152
Cockerell, Sir Sydney, 210
Codex Bezae, edition of 1793, 123
Colbatch, John, 102–3
Collins, William, and English Bible trade, 137, 157
Combination Papers, 85
Convocation of Oxford, 1408, 6–7, 81
copyright, 7, 27
conferred by registration, 29; by deposit, 67, 77, 105
Whitford Committee, 266
corporation (income) tax
in 1940, 225–6

Cass's analysis, 265–83
1940 assessment challenged, 267
case of 1940 examined, 267–8
case for exemption, 268–81
exemption granted, 282
Corrie, G., *Homilies*, 145
Cotes, Roger, edits *Principia*, 96–8
Council of the Senate, 296, 297, 299
Notice of 10 March 1980, 300–1
under Statute J, 319
Cowell, John, *The Interpreter*, 54
Crashaw, Richard, *Epigrammatum Sacrorum Liber*, 69
Croke, Richard, 14–15
Cromwell, Oliver, 68, 75, 77
Crownfield (Cronefelt), Cornelius, 90
appointed Printer, 91
as manager, 100
as printer, 103
Crutchley, Brooke, 217
appointed Printer, 224
and new Printing House, 231
and subediting, 234
head of Printing Division, 256–7
retires, 261
Curators of the Press, 307
appointed 1698, 93, 100
first meeting, 94

Daniel, Roger, 64, 66, 69, 73
appointment cancelled, 75
Darby, H. C., *Domesday Geography*, 313
David, R. W., 197, 208, 216, 231
Secretary, 234–8
University Publisher, 239
aids transition, 244
head of Publishing Division, 256–7
retires, 262
Dawes, R., *Miscellanea Critica*, 120
Deighton, John, 129, 149
Dillingham, William ('W.D.'), 77–8, 109
quoted by Cass, 275
Donn, James, 140–1
Donne, John, Sermons, 69
Doughty, C. H., *Travels in Arabia Deserta*, 167–9
Dover Wilson, John, 197, 233
'draw-back' on paper, 105, 146
Dreyfus, John, 217

Duport, James, 76
Eachard, John, 89
Eddington, A. S., 202
Edinburgh Building, 289–94
Edinburgh, HRH The Prince Philip, Duke of, 290, 293
Eldon, Lord, 276
Eliates, Papyrius Geminus, *Hermathena*, 20
Elizabeth II, HM Queen, 293
*Encyclopaedia Britannica*, 193, 200
English Dictionary declined, 162–4
Erasmus, Desiderius, 12, 14–15
  *De conscribendis epistolis*, 19

Farish, William, 119
Fenner, Mary, 108
Field, John
  acquires Bible monopoly, 76
  University Printer, 76–7, 78
  composition with Stationers, 78
  his printing house, 78–9
Finance Committee of the Press, 246, 255, 256, 257, 298
Financial Board
  reports, 239, 241, 242, 246, 247, 249, 251, 253, 254, 256, 261, 264
  its role, 258, 298, 301
  under Statute J, 319
Fisher, Cardinal John, 14, 20, 23
*Flora Europaea*, 231
*Flora of the British Isles*, 231, 313
Froschauer, Christoph, II, meets Guidon, 27
Fuller, Thomas, 2, 27, 56
  *The Historie of the Holie Warre*, 69
Furnivall, F. J., 162–4

Galen, *De temperamentis*, 19
Gardner, T. C.
  Secretary of the Press Syndicate, 239, 247–8
  and Lord Todd, 243
  and Cass's appointment, 244
  and tax exemption, 266
Glasgow warehouse, 164
Godfrey, Garret, 8, 12, 16, 22, 26
Government Annuity, 118, 146, 189, 190, 225; *see also* Almanac Duty Act
Gray, Thomas, 123

Greene, Leonard, 56, 65
Guidon, Remigius, 27–8
Hadley, John, *Plan of a Course of Chemical Lectures*, 119
Hagger, 'Buck', 221–2
Hardy, G. H., 188, 201
Hardy, John, 8
Hare, Julius, 139, 140, 141
Harris, Brian, 302
Harris, Kim, 302
Hayes, John
  appointed Printer, 79
  his printing house, 90–1
  active to 1705, 101
Henslow, J. S., 139, 140
Herbert, George, *The Temple*, 69, 72
Hills, Henry, 76
Hodgson, Peter, 261
Holdsworth, Richard, Vice-Chancellor, 69
Holland, Henry, Earl of, 67, 74
Housman, A. E.
  work on Propertius declined, 172
  publishes at the Press, 204
  on Cambridge printing, 218
How, James Massett, traveller, 161
Hullier, John, burnt, 21
Hunt, Thomas, 22

income tax, *see* corporation tax
Incorporated Council of Law Reporting, 279–80

James I
  *A Prince's Looking Glasse*, 53
  *A Remonstrance for the Right of Kings*, 53
James, Henry, 89, 91
James, Thomas, and Company,

Jeans, Sir James, 201–2
Jebb, John, *Remarks on Education*, 120
Jones, Professor Gareth, 296, 299

Keetch, Mr, 206, 221–2
Kendon, F. H., 200, 208, 216, 231
Kidson, Frank, *The Beggar's Opera*, 213

Kingsford, R. J. L., 197
London Manager, 206
designs bindings, 208, 216
proposes American Branch, 226
as Secretary, 226ff
as publisher, 230–1
retires, 231
Kingston, John, 36
Knight, David 260
Knight, S., *Life of Erasmus*, 102, 142
Knowles, Dom David, 203–4, 313

Laud, Archbishop, 84
Leathes, Sir Stanley, 183
Lee, Sir Frank, 242–3
Legate, John, 50, 53
his publications, 53–4
Legate, John (the younger), 75
Legge, Cantrell, 56, 57
legislation on printing and publishing
Act of 1484, 22, 24; of 1523, 23; of 1529, 23; of 1534, 23, 82
Star Chamber, 1586, 44, 67, 82
Star Chamber, 1637, 67
Star Chamber, abolished, 76
regulations of 1649, 76
Licensing Act, 1662, 77; lapsed, 1695, 104
Act of Uniformity, 1662, 84, 110
Almanac Duty Act: 1711, 105; 1781, 117
Letters Patent
of 1534, 5, 267, 302; granted, 23; English text, 24–5; Latin text, 316–17; reproduced, 25; preceded Stationers' charter, 30; and Barker's patent, 33; invoked in 1538–4, 37ff, 45, 82; in 1591, 52–3; in 1620–1, 57–9; in 1755, 109; still implemented in 1886, 175; and the Press as Bible publisher, 267; relation to the modern Press Syndicate, 270; quoted by Cass, 274; Lord Eldon's comment, 276
of 1628: granted, 60–1; invoked in 1755, 109; cited by Cass, 275
*see also* legislation on printing and publishing, licensing of printing and publication, monopolies,

Royal Printers, Stationers' Company
Lewis, Walter, 215, 216, 233
appointed, 213
retires, 224
licensing of printing and publication
by the University, 2, 7, 8, 22, 23, 26, 45, 82ff, 104
through the Stationers' Register, 29, 83
by Star Chamber, 44, 45, 67
Lily, William, on the parts of speech, 19, 30, 57, 61, 116, 207
Local Examinations Syndicate, 157, 159, 229
London Manager
C. F. Clay, 191
R. J. L. Kingsford, 206
R. W. David, 231
and the Secretary, 191, 233
London office (Warehouse)
founded, 160–1
to Ave Maria Lane, 164
to Fetter Lane, 187
function in 1904, 191
functions develop, 194–5
size of staff, 205
to Bentley House, 206
office closed, 292
Loney, S. L., 170, 177, 208
Long, Roger, 119
Lucian, *Dipsades*, 19
Luther, Martin, books burnt in Cambridge, 13, 20
Lyons, I., Hebrew Grammar, 102

McKenzie, D. F., xi, 78, 86, 88, 99
Macmillan Company, as agents, 182, 205, 226
Macmillan, Daniel and Alexander, 141–2, 149, 154
Macnaghten, Lord, in Pemsel's Case, 273
Maison des Sciences de l'Homme, 285–6
Maitland, F. W., 170, 177, 182–3, 201
Mansbridge, F. Ronald, 205, 286
becomes Manager, American Branch, 226

Martyn, Thomas, 123, 140
Mason, Alfred, 219
Maurice, F. D., 139, 141
Middleton, Conyers
  criticises Bentley, 102
  publishes at the Press, 103
Milner, Isaac, 125, 129
Milton, John, *Lycidas*, 69
monopolies, printing, 31, 34, 36, 45,
  47, 104
  of Bible-printing, 32–3, 50, 73, 76,
    106–8, 126, 129, 137, 157–8,
    228
  of prayer books, 59
  of Acts of Parliament, 108–9
  of almanacs, 116–18
  *see also* legislation on printing and
    publishing, Letters Patent, licens-
    ing of printing and publication,
    Royal Printers, Stationers' Com-
    pany
Monotype system, 209, 231
  introduced at Cambridge, 210
  its heyday, 215–18
Moore, G. E., *Principia Ethica*, 187
Morison, Stanley, 213–14
Morris, William, 209
Myers, Harris, 284

Needham, Joseph, *Science and Civili-
  sation in China*, 231, 312
Nessfylde, William de, 8
New Shakespeare, 197, 211
Newton, Isaac
  editor of Varenius, 79
  *Principia*, 1st edn, 90; 2nd edn,
    95–8; modern edn, 314
  on Bentley, 96
  on Cotes, 98
  and Whiston, 101
  Correspondence, 314
Nicholson, R. A., 183, 201
Niebuhr, *History of Rome* translated,
  140
Nobbs, F. G., 211, 215, 220
Nycolson, Segar, 12–13, 21, 22, 23,
  26

Owen, David, *Herod and Pilate
  Reconciled*, 54

Oxford University, as licensing authority, 33, 82
Oxford University Press, x, 3, 44, 48,
  84, 91, 106, 108, 109, 117–18,
  137, 158, 163, 228, 283

Parker, John William, 118, 129, 135–6
  as publisher, 138, 142–3, 145
  introduces machine-printing, 136
  advises on partnership, 151
  resigns, 152
Parker, Archbishop Matthew, 32, 35
Parris, F. S., 111
Partnership, the
  recommended by Royal Commis-
    sion, 148; by Sub-Syndicate, 151
  first deed of, 153
  bank accounts, 154, 170
  second deed of, 155
  renewed 1866, 156
  renewed 1876, 161
  John Clay enters, 169
  Charles Felix Clay enters, 169
  renewed 1886, 169
  becoming anomalous, 175–6
  reviewed 1894, 179
  revised, 180, 185
  analysed 1901, 188–90
  revised 1905, 190–1
  commented on, 191–2
  terminated, 192, 225
Peace, J. B., University Printer, 192,
  195, 198, 211, 213, 223
Pemsel's Case, 273
Pergamentarius, William, 8
Perkins, William, 55–6
Perowne, J. J. S., 162, 177
Phillips, Euan
  appointed University Printer, 260–1
  becomes Director, American Branch,
    284
Pindar, Jonathan, 107
Pitt Building, 130–4, 236
Pitt Press Series,
  founded, 159
  status in 1875, 165
  profitability, 166
  in 1898, 184
Pitt Professorship, 225

Pitt, William, 131
Porson, Richard, 120, 138, 176
Powell, W. S., *Observations on Annual Examinations*, 120
Power, Eileen, 203
Press Syndicate
of 1733, 99
of 1737, 99, 101, 105
of the 1850s, 143, 145, 146, 149–50
reconstructed, 155
Secretary appointed, 161, 174
Syndics' term of office increased, 169
nature and functions, 170, 186, 269
represents University, 170, 176, 251, 269, 287
reorganised 1904, 191
since 1972, 258
approves all publications, 269, 300, 310
centre of unitary organisation, 287–8, 303
in 1981, 299
under Statute J, 319
*see also* Curators of the Press
privilege, *see* monopolies
Prothero, Sir G. W., 183
Pufendorf, *Jurisprudence*, 79–80

Quiller-Couch, Sir Arthur, 196

Raleigh, Sir Walter, 81–2
Ramée, Pierre de la (Ramus), 46, 79
Ray, John, 140
*Catalogus plantarum*, 76
reserve fund (endowment), 189, 190, 225, 252–3, 282
Rivington, John
as agent, 115, 135
in 1861, 156
founds *Reporter*, 156
agency ends, 160
Roberts, S. C., x–xi, 186
appointed Assistant Secretary, 194
as designer, 197, 213, 216
portrait, 199
appointed Secretary, 200
as publisher, 201–2, 208
sets up US agency, 205
appoints Lewis, 213
and Morison, 213

retires, 224
and Pitt Professorship, 225
Robertson Smith, William, 168, 172
Rogers, Bruce, 114, 197, 210, 211–13
Romilly, Joseph, 132–3, 134, 150
Rood, Theodoric, 10
Royal Commission, *see* Cambridge University
Royal Printers
office established, 31
Barker's patent, 32–3
rights in the Bible, 50, 62, 73, 157–8, 228
abolished under Commonwealth, 76
Baskett as monopolist, 106–8
in Scotland, 106, 137, 157
*see also* legislation on printing and publishing, Letters Patent, licensing of printing and publication, monopolies, Stationers' Company
Runciman, Sir Steven, 203–4, 313
Russell, Bertrand (Earl Russell), 183
Rutherford, Lord, 188

St Albans, early printer of, 23
St Paul's Churchyard, 14, 86
Sawbridge, George, 80
School Mathematics Project, 228
Schulman, Jack
Manager, American Branch, 226
retires, 284
as Director of American Branch, 286, 289
Scrivener, F. H., 64
Cambridge Paragraph Bible, 158, 164
Seatonian Prize, 122–3
Secretary of the Press Syndicate
C. J. Clay appointed, 161, 174
R. T. Wright appointed, 175
as head of publishing business, 184, 233, 238
duties defined, 174, 185–6, 307
relationship with London Manager, 119, 233
A. R. Waller appointed, 194
S. C. Roberts appointed, 200
R. J. L. Kingsford appointed, 226
R. W. David, 234
T. C. Gardner, 239
Geoffrey Cass appointed, 257

Sedgwick, Adam, 139–40, 165
Seeley, George, 151, 152, 153, 154, 155
Seward, A. C., 193
Sherrington, Sir Charles, 203
Siberch, John (Johann Lair), 10, 12, 14, 22
  early life, 14
  works in Cambridge, 15–17
  returns to Germany, 18, 21
  books printed, 18–20
Siddons, A. W., 187, 201, 208
Skeat, W. W., 163
  Anglo-Saxon Gospels, 156, 157
Smart, Christopher, and the Seatonian Prize, 122–3
Smith, John, 129, 132, 134, 135, 136
Somerset, Charles Seymour, Duke of, 87–8, 118
Sparke, Michael, *Scintilla*, 73
Sperynge (Spierinck), Nycholas, 12, 16, 22, 26
Stanhope, Charles, Earl, 126, 128
Star Chamber, Court of, 26, 44, 67
  abolished 1641, 76
stationers, University
  defined, 1
  in medieval Cambridge, 6–9, 22, 82
  guild of, 22
  continuity of function over centuries, 191, 306–7
  *see also* Godfrey, Garret; Nycolson, Segar; Sperynge, Nicholas
Stationers' Company of London
  incorporated, 28
  nature and powers, 28–30
  as benevolent society, 34
  its Stocks, 32, 34, 71, 76, 80, 106
  seizes Thomas's press, 38–40
  monopolising tendencies, 45, 47
  dispute with Cambridge, in 1591, 52–3; in 1620, 57–9; in 1629, 61; in 1662, 76
  agreement with Cambridge, 71, 75
  invades Bible monopoly, 76
  ignored by Licensing Act, 76
  composition with Hayes, 79–80
  composition with Crownfield, 91, 106
  and right to print almanacs, 116–17
  *see also* legislation on printing and

publishing, Letters Patent, licensing of printing and publication, monopolies, Royal Printers
Statute J
  drafted, 294–6
  objects clause, 297, 302
  discussed, 298–300
  approved, 301
  text, 318–19
stereotyping
  by Ged, Fenner and James, 107–8
  by Stanhope and Wilson, 126–8, 134–5
  under Watts, 152
Stourbridge Fair, 52, 86
Sturt, George, 200
Sub-Syndicates
  in the 19th c., 143–5, 146, 151, 165–6, 167, 169, 172, 176, 179
  1900–72, 185, 239, 254, 256
Sugden, Sir Morris, 284
Suidas Lexicon, 98–9, 101
Swinnerton-Dyer, Professor Sir Peter, 293, 296

Talbot, James, 88, 95
Taylor, Sir Robert, 239, 247
Thirlwall, Connop, 139, 140
Thomas, Thomas, 306–7
  appointed Printer, 37–8
  reappointed, 41
  his publications, 46–8
  Dictionary, 46, 48, 53
Thompson, D'Arcy, 203
Todd, Lord
  becomes Chairman, 242–4
  on financial Sub-Committee, 247
  reports to Financial Board, 254
  paper on organisation of the Press, 255
  resigns, 284
Tonson, Jacob, 86
  his editions, 95, 101
Torr, Cecil, 198
Travers, Walter, 36, 41
Tripos verses, 85, 303

University printing house
  under Buck, 64–5; Field, 78–9; Hayes, 90; Bentley, 91; Crownfield, 91–2, 130

University printing house, *cont.*
  Pitt Building, 130–4
  expenditure on buildings, 147
  moves to Shaftesbury Road, 231, 235
University Printing Services, 303
*University Reporter*, 156

Verity, A. W., 171, 177, 201, 208
Vice-Chancellor, and the Press Syndicate, 93, 100, 133, 134, 143, 150, 154, 155
Vice-Chancellor's deputy, as Chairman, 146, 155, 176, 225
  Cartmell as Chairman, 153, 155

Waller, A. R.
  appointed Assistant Secretary, 186
  edits *History of English Literature*, 187, 195
  succeeds Wright, 192, 194
  as Secretary, 195
  initiates New Shakespeare, 197
  dies, 200, 213
Ward, Sir Adolphus
  edits *Modern History*, 183
  introduces Waller, 187
  edits *History of English Literature*, 187
  edits *History of British Foreign Policy*, 196
  on the Press's activities, 277
Watson, Bishop Richard, 120–2
Watts, Richard, 118, 129–30, 152

Whewell, William, 133, 139
  *Of a Liberal Education*, 139
  edits Sanderson, 145
  offers to edit Grotius, 145, 165; Barrow, 156
Whibley, Leonard, 186, 193
Whinn, Matthew, as Printer, 79
Whiston, William, 101–2, 104
Whitaker, William, 40–1, 46
Whitehead, A. N., 183, 202
Whitford Committee on Copyright, 266–7
Whitgift, John, 41, 44, 45
Willers, George, 220
Wilson, Sir Alan, 202, 239, 247
Wilson, Andrew, 126, 134
Wilson, Anthony
  joins Press, 253
  Operations Director, 259
  and review committee of Press Statute, 296
Wright, R. T.
  joins Syndicate, 169–70
  re-elected, 172
  portrait, 173
  appointed Secretary, 175
  present at Syndicate meeting, 177
  initiates Cambridge Histories, 182–3, 198
  eliminates loss on publishing, 184
  his powers, 186
  analysis of 1901, 190
  achievement summarised, 192–3
  retires, 194